ISBN 978-1-5277-6740-9
PIBN 10889229

THE HISTORY

OF

ANCIENT EUROPE.

WITH A

VIEW OF THE REVOLUTIONS

IN

ASIA AND AFRICA.

OF

ANCIENT EUROPE.

WITH A

VIEW OF THE REVOLUTIONS

IN

ASIA AND AFRICA.

IN A SERIES OF LETTERS

TO A YOUNG NOBLEMAN.

BY WILLIAM RUSSELL, LL. D.

AUTHOR OF THE HISTORY OF MODERN EUROPE.

VOL. I.

PHILADELPHIA:

PRINTED BY H. MAXWELL, COLUMBIA-HOUSE,

FOR WILLIAM YOUNG BIRCH AND ABRAHAM SMALL

....

1801.

TO THE MOST NOBLE

CHARLES-WILLIAM HENRY,

EARL OF DALKIETH,

THIS

HISTORY OF ANCIENT EUROPE

IS

RESPECTFULLY INSCRIBED,

BY HIS LORDSHIP'S MOST HUMBLE,

AND MOST OBEDIENT SERVANT,

WILLIAM RUSSELL.

ADVERTISEMENT.

THE favourable reception which the History of *Modern Europe* has met with, and the public wish, expressed through the author's friends, encouraged him to undertake the History of *Ancient Europe*, on a similar plan. In the composition of this work, he has been peculiarly studious to found his facts on original authorities, and to clear his narration from unimportant events. By comprehending the Revolutions in Asia and Africa, it becomes, in some measure, a concise history of the WORLD, from the most early ages.

For these two introductory volumes, which contain the establishment of religion and government in all the *three divisions* of the *ancient globe*, and carry down the *History of Greece* to the beginning of the PELOPON-NESIAN WAR, the author must beg the indulgence of the learned. And he doubts not to obtain it, from those he has most to fear —the truly learned. They will see the difficulty of accurately investigating so many intricate subjects; and of combining, within a moderate compass, so much historical matter.

THE HISTORY

OF

ANCIENT EUROPE.

PART I.

FROM THE FOUNDATION OF THE GRECIAN STATES, TO
THE DESTRUCTION OF CARTHAGE, AND THE FINAL
CONQUEST OF GREECE BY THE ROMANS.

LETTER I.

INTRODUCTION.

CONTAINING A VIEW OF THE NATURAL PROGRESS OF HU-
MAN SOCIETY, WITH A SKETCH OF THE EARLY PART OF
THE HISTORY OF THE ASSYRIANS, EGYPTIANS, PHOE-
NICIANS, AND HEBREWS.

I EMBRACE, my lord, the most early oppor- LETTER
tunity of fulfilling that pleasing command, which you   I.
imposed upon me at your departure from England;—
"to recal to your mind occasionally, by letters, the
"*more important events* in the *history of ancient nations;*

     B   "but

PART I. "but especially of such nations as formerly inhabited "this section of the globe." Those events will acquire new interest, while you travel through the countries in which many of them happened, and compare their ancient with their modern state. And the remains of ancient statuary and architecture, in conjunction with your knowledge of the ancient classics, will illustrate the history of ancient arts, and also of ancient. manners.

Unless we have recourse to that divine revelation communicated to the Hebrews, emphatically styled *the people of God,* we shall forever remain ignorant of the creation of the world, and of the primitive state of man; subjects which, among all other nations, are lost in the chaos of fable. Yet have we, setting aside reverence for such revelation, a strong desire to trace as high as historical records reach, or as heathen tradition furnishes a chain of probable facts, the rude story of the human race. To gratify, without abusing, this curiosity, is the business of the historian.

One circumstance strongly strikes the inquisitive and discerning mind, in entering on the History of Ancient Europe. We find all its various nations and tribes, before the introduction of foreign improvements, in a similar state of barbarism[1]. The course of civilization seems, therefore, to point out to us the line we ought to pursue, in studying their history.

1. The Greeks bear testimony to their own barbarity, and also to that of the Romans; (see Herodotus, Thucydides, Polybius, Diodorus Siculus, and Dionisius Halicarnassensis, passim). And the Romans, while they own their obligations to Greece, attest the barbarity of all the other European nations, when they first became acquainted with them, in the course of their conquests. See Tit. Livy, Cæsar, and Tacitus, passim.

Let

Let antiquarians bewilder themselves in attempting
to discover the origin of the first European nations: for
our purpose it will be sufficient, having found them
barbarous, to follow them in their progress toward
civility, military prowess, and political power; and to
investigate the causes which retarded or accelerated
that progress, together with those that afterward produced a relaxation of manners, a decline of the martial
spirit, and the downfal of empire.

In making this grand historical tour, which will bring
within our view the growth and decay of the wisest and
bravest nations that ever appeared upon the face of
the earth, we shall have occasion to contemplate MAN in
all the different conditions of his being, and under every
form of government. Consequently we shall be enabled
to collect, in our range, all the instruction that history
(which has been defined *philosophy teaching by examples*)
can furnish for the conduct of human affairs.

With Greece, whence science and civility were
conveyed, through various channels, over the western
world, we are naturally led to begin our survey. It
will,. however, be necessary, my lord, for the better understanding of the Grecian history, and the whole
run of European transactions, at the same time that it is
truly liberal, to take an introductory view of the most
ancient state of the nations to whom the Greeks were
indebted for their knowledge of arts and of letters.
For history may be compared to a river: we must
ascend to the fountain, to be able distinctly to trace its
course.

Independent of the testimony of the *sacred books*, all
things conspire to prove, that the human race must
have had a beginning; nor has scepticism dared to
deny

PART I. deny, That the earth, during early ages, was but thinly peopled, and imperfectly cultivated. And ancient historians, with one accord, inform us, That the inhabitants of Asia, and those of the contiguous part of Africa, were more early civilized and enlightened than the European nations.

Before the date of any remaining records, before the birth of Moses, the illustrious Hebrew legislator, and the father of sacred history, population, policy, and arts, had made considerable progress among the Assyrians, Egyptians, and Phœnicians[2]. But whether this so early population, and consequent civility, were the natural effects of climates more favoured than any in Europe, and greater fertility of soil, or of the more early planting of the human race in the heart of Asia, is a question not yet settled among divines and philosophers; and which is, on each side, attended with many difficulties.

If we receive, in a literal sense, the Mosaic history of the creation, of the antediluvian world, and the dispersion of mankind, after the flood, at Babel, or Babylon, we shall find little difficulty in assigning a reason, why the banks of the Euphrates and Tigris were crowned with great cities, crowded with inhabitants, skilled in all the useful and ingenious arts, before a single city was erected on the banks of the Danube or the Rhine. Yet shall we still be at a loss how to account for the no less early population and improvement of Egypt, India, and China; for the two latter countries were very distant from the scene of dispersion, and the former separated from it by almost impassable deserts.

2. This appears evident from many passages in the writings of *Moses*, and also in the books of *Joshua*, *Judges* and *Kings*. And similar testimony is borne by Herodotus, the father of civil history, lib. i. ii. passim.

But

But if, with a liberal antiquarian, we consider that that mysterious narrative of the Hebrew legislator, as a *mythical* and *political apologue*, composed for the *introduction* and *support* of the *Jewish theocracy*[3]; or if, conformable to the opinion of many learned writers, we suppose that, in consequence of the confusion of tongues and the dispersion of mankind, the great body of the human species degenerated, during their emigration, into a state of savage barbarity; and, in that state, spread themselves widely over the face of the earth, the causes of such population and improvement may be deduced in a satisfactory manner. For this purpose we must carry our inquiries to what has been called, *the state of Nature.*

Various have been the descriptions of poets and historians, and the opinions of philosophers, both ancient and modern, concerning the *natural condition* of MAN; or that rude state in which he is supposed to have

---

3. See a *Treatise on the Study of Antiquities, as the Commentary to Historical Learning*, by T. Pownall, esq. Several of the christian fathers were partly of Mr. Pownall's opinion; and the late learned and celebrated Dr. T. Burnet is very explicit on the subject. " I " have avoided," says he, " to mention Moses's *Cosmopæia*, because, " I think, it is delivered by him rather as a *lawgiver*, than a *philo-* " *sopher*," &c.

"Almost all the *christian interpreters*," adds Dr. Burnet, " agree with " us, that the Mosaic *tohu bohu* is the same thing as the *chaos* of the " ancients; that the *darkness*, described by Moses, is their *tartarus*, and " *erebus*, and *night*; that his *incubation of the Spirit*, or *breath of God*, " is collusive with the *birth of Phanes*, *Eros*, or *Love*." (Burnet's *The-* " *ory of the Earth*, first edit.) " So far," observes he, " Moses and " the old philosophers agree; but here he breaks off his *philosophic* " *strain*, and takes up a *human*, or a *theological strain*; in which he has " *framed a popular relation* of the *rise of things*, in the manner we all " know." (Id. ibid.) To the same purport writes Mr. Whiston, concerning the creation of the celestial bodies. " Moses, indeed," says he, " mentions the *making* of the sun, &c. in order to *accommodate* " his *narrative* to *vulgar apprehension*; but chiefly to *secure the Jews* " from the *worship* of the *host of Heaven*." Whiston, *Disc. of the Mosaic Creation*, p. 4.

existed

existed before the establishment of government, the framing of laws, or the invention of arts.   In order to induce mankind to set an higher value upon the benefits of civil society, or for the purpose of debasing the human character, some have represented the state of nature as a state of warfare and wretchedness; in which force was the only law, and where man was on a level with the brutes: while others, of a more benevolent temper, or enemies to refinement, have described the natural state as the happiest of human conditions; a state, wherein men, having few wants, if they had few accommodations, and few interfering interests, had little temptation to violence or fraud, and lived in the most perfect harmony. Hence the fables of the golden age.   The former represent the state of nature as the reign of force, cruelty, and misery; the latter of justice, humanity, and felicity.

But a more perfect acquaintance with rude nations, and consequently with undisguised human nature, has proved both those representations to be, in a great measure, false.   For as we find no room to believe, that there ever was an age, or a country, in which the human race were not raised above the level of the brute creation, we find none where the presence of one human creature was to others a signal of hostility[4].

.Man is a complex being.   He has found, in every age, country, and condition, the sources of variance and dissension, as well as of concert and union.   Nature seems to have sown in his mind the seeds of animosity with those of affection.   He embraces with

4. See *Hist. Gen. des Voyages*, passim.   If, in some islands of the southern ocean, all *strangers* are regarded as *enemies*, we may seriously question, Whether this hostile *antipathy* had not its *origin* in the *injuries committed* by *foreign invaders?*

alacrity

alacrity occasions of personal opposition, and he flies with ardour to the relief of a fellow-creature in distress; without any motive but the impulse of the heart, or any command but that of sympathetic feeling.

The shouts of joy are to man yet more attractive than the shrieks of woe. Prompted, by a taste for society, to mingle with the herd of his species, he longs to share their happiness, to become acquainted with their sentiments, and to communicate his own[5]. He delights to act in conjunction with them, is ambitious of distinction under their eye, and proud of their approbation[6]. Hence emulation and competition, the two great sources of illustrious actions. Man is equally disposed to friendship and enmity; to return benefits, and resent injuries; to retain a sense of favours con-

5. " A *state of nature*," says the most sagacious of all philosophers, " is a *state of society to man*. He is by *nature* a *social animal;* and " although a *sense* of *mutual wants*, and *mutual aid*, did not *dictate* the " *necessity* of *civil union* and *cohabitation*, yet would *mankind herd*, and " *live together*." (Aristot. *Polit*. lib. iii. cap. iv.) To the same effect writes the great geographer : " Man," says he, " is born with " this *inclination* to *associate*." It is an *appetite* common to the human " species." (Strabo, *Geog*. lib. xvi.) I have had recourse to these authorities, in order to overthrow an opinion, which has been propagated, not only by the followers of Hobbes, but by many other respectable writers, on the foundation of society, That men were originally induced to unite in society *merely* to avoid the injuries to which they were exposed from each other in a state of nature. (See the *Divine Legation of Moses*, book i. sect. ii. et seq.) Whereas the truth is, That men associated from instinct, or natural affection ; and laws were invented, and religion instituted, to bind them more closely together; to curb their irregular passions, and render them more happy in the social state. Hence the general mistake, into which even Warburton has partly fallen : the *effect* was substituted for the *cause*.

6. This sentiment is mutual. " The man who, in defence of " others," observes Polybius, " is seen to throw himself foremost " into every danger, and even to sustain the fury of the fiercest ani- " mals, never fails to obtain the loudest expressions of applause " from all present." Polyb. lib. vi. Excerpt. i.

ferred,

ferred, when he wants ability to repay; and a remembrance of wrongs, when he is unable to retaliate[7]: whence gratitude and revenge.

· The seeds of all the virtues as well as vices, and whatever is generous in human nature, may be found in the heart of the savage. In his pride of independency, and his consciousness that no man has a right to injure another in his person or property; because no man is *naturally* indebted to another for those things, we discover the foundation of *justice* and *natural* freedom. And although savage man is commonly more sullen in disposition than the citizen, by reason of his mode of life, he is no stranger to the influence of the social principle. He chuses his dwelling in the neighbourhood of other savages, instead of shunning their sight, or lodging in the solitary cave ; he goes in company with them in quest of food; and when he returns from the chace, and has satisfied his hunger, and that of his family, with his prey, he joins his companions in the song and the dance[8].

As man is possessed of the social principle in every stage of his being, he has also, at all times, and in all places, been possessed of reason and imagination, the

---

7. "Man, who alone, of all animals, is endowed with the faculty " of reason, cannot," remarks the same deep discerner of human nature, " overlook such actions with indifference." Polyb. ubi sup.

8. *Hist. Gen. des Voyages*, passim. If savage man any where appears in a state of degradation, it is in the extreme regions of the · north, or toward the south pole; where the rigour of the climate checks the principle of animal life in the human species, and with it all the nobler springs of action, the more generous sentiments, and finer feelings of the soul. Yet, even there, in those regions of darkness and of frost, the social character of man is not utterly destroyed; his intellectual faculty, or his power of dominion over the brute creation. Ibid. art. *Iceland, Lapland, Greenland, Kamchatka, Terra del Fuego*, &c.

two grand sources of invention. *Art is natural to*
man. He can find his happiness and accommodation
in any condition. But they who have contemplated him
in every point of view, will be at no loss to determine,
in what state he attaineth the perfection of his character. That state which affords the fullest exercise to
his intellectual faculties, without injury to his corporeal
powers, must be found in cultivated society; in a com-

9. This was the general maxim of all the ancient philosophers, except those of the sect of Epicurus; but more especially of the Pla-
tonists. And an enlightened modern philosopher (lord Shaftesbury)
who wrote as early as the beginning of the present century, when
savage life was less perfectly known than at present, has admirably
refuted and ridiculed the idea, " That *mankind* ever *lived* in a *state,*
" *where they were unacquainted with the use of speech,* the more ne-
" *cessary arts, or strangers to social affection.*" ' Without belying
' *nature,*' observes he, ' and contradicting what is evident from *na-*
' *tural history, fact,* and the *natural course of things,* it is impossible
' to admit this *ill-natured* proposition. For if *Providence,* not *chance,*
' gave MAN his being, he must have been *at first,* nearly what we
' *now* find him. But let us suppose him to have sprung, as the old
' poets feigned, from a *bigbellied oak;* and, at first, to have had little
' *form,* and no more *life* than the *sensitive plant;* that, by degrees,
' the *members* of *this fortuitous birth* were *displayed,* and the *organs*
' of *sense* began to *unfold themselves;* that here *sprang* an *ear,* there
' *peeped* an *eye!* Belike, a *tail* too came in company ! for what *super-*
' *fluities* Nature may have been charged with, *at first,* is difficult to
' determine! They *dropt off,* however, *it seems,* in time; and happily
' have left things, *at last,* in a *good posture;* and, to a wonder ! *just*
' *as they should be.*

' This is surely the *lowest view* of *the origin of humankind!*' adds
he. ' But granting it to have been such as I have described it, and as
' a certain philosopher would needs have it, yet will our conclusion
' be the same. In a word, if *generation* be *natural;* if *affection* to,
' and the *care* of, *offspring,* be *natural,* it follows,' " That *society*
" must also be *natural to mankind;* and that *out of society* and com-
" munity, MAN never *did,* nor ever *can* subsist." ' And can we allow
' this *social* part to man, and go no farther? Is it possible he should
' *pair,* and *live* in *fellowship* with his *partner* and *offspring,* and re-
' main still wholly *speechless,* and without those ARTS of *storing,*
' *building,* and other *economy,* as *natural* surely, *to him,* as to the
' *beaver,* the *ant,* or the *bee.*' Shaftesbury's *Characteristics,* vol ii.
Moralists, part. ii. sect. iv.

munity

munity polished but not corrupted, and pressing forward in the career of military fame, policy, and arts.
Hence the sage remark of Aristotle *// "* We are to *judge*
"* of man in his state of *advancement*, not in that of *ig-*
"* norance or barbarity; a progress in knowledge* and
"* civility* being *natural* to him[10]." *//*

Such, according to the accounts of the most judicious travellers, and the observations of the most profound philosophers, is the natural or rude state of man
in all countries, and such his advances toward refinement. But these advances are very different in different regions of the earth.

In northern countries, where the soil is rugged, the
climate severe, and the spontaneous productions of the
earth, fit for the support of human life, few, and of
small value, the progress of society is slow. Hunting
is there long the sole employment of man, and his
principal means of subsistence. He feeds upon the
flesh, and clothes himself with the skins of wild animals[11].

But in southern latitudes, where the earth is more
bountiful, the soil more susceptible of culture, and the
use of animal food less necessary, the savage state is
of shorter continuance. Little inclined, in such climates, to active exertions, mankind soon relinquish the
pursuit of wild beasts, or cease to consider the chace
as their chief occupation. They early acquire the art
of taming and rearing the more docile and useful animals, and of cultivating the most nutritive vegetable
productions[12].

In

10. Aristot. *Polit.* lib. i. cap. ii.
11. *Hist. Gen. des Voyages*, passim, et auct. cit.
12. I am not ignorant, that the passion for hunting has been represented as so strong in the human species, that men never betake
themselves to the taming or rearing of animals, until the wild breed
becomes

In proportion as food becomes more plentiful men
are enabled to indulge more freely the appetite for
society. They live together in larger bodies. Towns
and cities are built. Private property in land is ascertained, and placed under the guardianship of laws[1].
Agriculture is prosecuted; metals are discovered, and
mines worked. Genius is called forth by emulation,
and arts and sciences are invented. The political union
among the members of the same community, is ren-

becomes too scarce to furnish them with food; and their aversion
against labour so great, that they do not apply themselves to agriculture, while they can find sufficient room to pasture their herds and
flocks. (See lord Kaims's *Sketches of the History of Man*, book i.
passim.) But this reasoning, founded on the practice of the North-
American savages and Asiatic Tartars, though plausible in theory,
is contradicted by facts; and, therefore, cannot be of universal application; because unsupported by general observation or experience,
in the history of ancient or modern nations, inhabiting the milder
climates of the earth. Such of the ancient Scythian tribes as had
seized upon fertile districts, cultivated the ground; and several of
them had attained, by these means, to a considerable degree of civility; while those tribes, less fortunately situated, were utterly
rude and barbarous. (Herodot. lib. iv. passim.) The same observation may be extended to some North-American tribes, on the banks
of the Ohio, Missisippi, &c. and to every people inhabiting such
districts, over the face of the globe. See *Hist. Gen. des Voyages*,
passim.

13. This may be considered as the first great stage in the progress
of civil society: the advance from *hunting* to *herding*, or even from
herding to *rude agriculture*, such as is found among pasturing nations,
being comparatively small. For while men pasture their cattle, or
cultivate the ground *in common*, their industry is languid, and the
product of their flocks and fields scanty. *Personal property*, in *land*,
and the prospect of reaping *exclusively*, the fruits of his labour, can
alone give activity and perseverance to the labours of the husbandman, or fertility to the earth. Hence the attention of ancient legislators to the preservation of *land-marks*; and the vengeance, both
human and divine, that was denounced against such as should remove them. They considered the *division* of *lands*, which gave birth
to *jurisprudence*, as the *parent* of *civil order*; in making each man the
guardian of his own possessions, and the magistrate the guardian
of all, by the *regulations* which it made necessary. See *Mem. de l'Acad.
des Inscript.* tom. i. et auct. cit. (Edit. Paris, 1736), p. 50, et seq.

dered

PART. I. dered more close, by an apprehension of danger from abroad; and the intercourse between them more general, from a sense of mutual conveniency. Hence patriotism and internal traffic, the two great sources of national happiness and prosperity.

Men acquire a strong affection for their native country, and for their fellow-citizens, soon after the division of lands; in consequence of their common struggles to defend their cultivated possessions against the ravages of barbarous and hostile neighbours. An unlimited exchange of commodities, originating in a desire of mutual accommodation, takes place between the people of the same state; and that exchange quickens industry, gives birth to new arts, and calls forth all the ingenuity of man, in order to improve the fashion or fabric of the articles of barter. A general instrument of exchange, under the name of *money*, is invented : and commercial transactions being thus rendered more easy and expeditious, trade is extended from the members of a particular community to those of other states. Nations, like individuals, mutually supply each other's wants, and the social system is gradually perfected.

Conformable to this view of the natural progress of society, we find Assyria and Egypt, countries abounding in spontaneous productions proper for the food of man, and of easy culture, more early populous and civilized than any other regions intimately known to the ancient inhabitants of our division of the earth. India and China, favoured with similar advantages, boast as old an acquaintance with the arts of civil life. And the kingdoms of Mexico and Peru, in the *new world*, owed their superiority in population and improvement over the other American districts, at the time of their discovery, also to soil and climate. But America, perhaps, had not emerged from the ocean at

the

the period of which I speak. India had little, and China no connection with the affairs of ancient Europe. The case was very different with respect to Assyria and Egypt.

The Assyrians, who possessed the fertile banks of the Euphrates and Tigris, and the fat and extensive plain between these two rivers, anciently known by the name of Mesopotamia, had many inducements to indulge the social principle, independent of all ideas of mutual safety and support. If nature denied them the olive, the fig, and the vine, she had bountifully bestowed on them the palm-tree[14]; which includes most of the virtues of those choice fruits, beside many others peculiar to itself[15]. And to that precious gift was added a soft and rich soil[16], that rewarded the labours of the husbandman with abundant crops of wheat, barley, and other kinds of grain—with the incredible increase of two, and even of three hundred fold[17].

The

14. Herodot. lib. i. cap. cxciii. Strabo, lib. xvi. p. 742, Edit. Lutet. Paris, typis Regiis, 1620. Pliny, *Hist. Nat.* lib. xiii. cap. iv.

15. Id. ibid. et Kæmpfer, *Amænitat. Exoticæ,* fascicul. iv. The inhabitants of Assyria celebrated, in songs, the three hundred and sixty virtues of the palm-tree. Strabo, lib. xvi. p. 742.

16. Strabo, lib. xvi. p. 740.

17. Herodot. lib. i. cap. cxciii. Theophrast. *Hist. Plantar.* lib. viii. cap. vii. Strabo, lib. xvi. p. 742, For that extraordinary fertility, Assyria was partly indebted, in its most cultivated state, to artificial canals, that conveyed the waters of the Euphrates into the channel of the Tigris ; and which, intersecting the plain of Mesopotamia, in various directions, by means of cross-cuts, afforded a constant supply of moisture to the fields, during the absence of rain. (Herodot. et Strabo, ubi sup.) Nor was this the only purpose these canals served : they prevented the lands from being deluged by the overflowing of the Euphrates ; which was annually swelled, in the beginning of summer, by the melting of snows on the mountains of Armenia. (Strabo, lib. xvi. p. 740.) They served also to facilitate commercial intercourse, some of them being navigable. (Id. Ibid.) The confining of rivers within their banks, and draining off stagnating

The inhabitants of such a country must have multiplied fast; and when united under one government,
they must soon have become powerful. The Assyrians.
are accordingly represented, by all ancient historians,
as the first people who exercised extensive dominion
among men. And the cities of Nineveh and Babylon,
which might be considered as their two state an-
chors, afforded an early display of oriental magnificence[18].

The great temple at Babylon, erected to Belus, Bel,
or Baal, the *lord of heaven*, in eastern language, peculiarly attracted admiration in old times. It was a square
building, measuring two stadia[19], or about twelve hundred feet, on each side; and out of the middle of it
rose a solid tower, or pyramid, also of a square figure,
six hundred feet high[20], and of an equal width at the
base[21]. On the top of that tower was formed a spa-

ing waters, seem to have been the first efforts made by man, for rendering comfortable his terrestrial habitation.

18. Herodot. lib. i. cap. clxxviii—clxxxiii. Diod. Sicul. lib. ii.
p. 91—98, edit. Hanovæ, typis Wechelianis, 1604. Strabo, lib. xvi.
p. 737, 738, edit. sup. cit. The building of the former of those cities is, by Diodorous and Strabo, ascribed to Ninus, the first Assyrian emperor; and that of the latter to his widow, Semiramis.
(Diod. Sicul. et Strabo, ubi sup.) But we have the authority of *sacred writ* to affirm, that Nineveh and Babylon were founded in more
early times; (*Genesis*, chap. x. ver. 9, 10.) though they probably owed to Ninus and Semiramis, that strength and grandeur which made
them the wonder of succeeding ages. This opinion, so far as it regards Babylon, is supported by Herodotus, (lib. i. cap. clxxxiv.) and
countenanced by another passage in the same venerable author; (lib.
iii. cap. clv.) where we are told, That one of the gates of Babylon
bore the name of *Ninus*, and another that of *Semiramis*. And the
testimony of scripture is corroborated by Berosus, (ap. Joseph *cont.
Apian*, lib. i.) who blames the Greeks for ascribing the foundation of
Babylon to Semiramis, queen of Assyria. Babylon, which I shall
afterward have occasion to describe, stood on the banks of the Euphrates. Herodot. lib. i. cap. clxxx.

19. Herodotus, lib. i. cap. clxxxi.   20. Strabo, lib. xvi. p. 738.
21. Id. ibid. et Herodot. ubi sup.

cious

tious dome[22], which served as an observatory to the ancient Chaldean astronomers[23]. In this dome was a table of gold, and a pompous bed, but no statue[24]. The lower part, or body of the temple, which surrounded the tower, was adorned with sacred furniture in the same precious metal; a golden altar and table, and a magnificent statue of the God, seated on a throne of solid gold[25].

The description of this superb temple cannot fail to awaken your lordship's curiosity, to become, acquainted with the religion and learning of the Assyrians of Babylon. And I shall endeavour to gratify it in some degree; as I may not, perhaps, afterward find an opportunity of so doing; and because the utter destruction of Nineveh, the chief city in Assyria Proper, and the capital of the Assyrian empire, before it had been visited by any European traveller, has left us totally ignorant of the state of knowledge among the inhabitants of that ancient metropolis; which stood on

---

22. Herodot. lib. i. cap. clxxxi.   23. Diod. Sicul. lib. ii. p. 98.
24. Herodot. ubi sup. Diodorous places in this dome, or aerial temple, three statues of prodigious weight and size. But he could only speak by report; for the great temple at Babylon, as he himself informs us, (lib. ii. p. 98.) had been pillaged by the sacrilegious rapacity of the Persian monarchs, long before his time. And if we believe Arrian, (*Expedit. Alex.* lib. vii. p. 480, edit. Amst. 1668.) it was destroyed, or utterly dismantled, by Xerxes, on his *return from Greece;* and consequently, Herodotus can hardly be supposed to have seen it, as he was then very young. But the honest testimony of this original historian, who may be trusted in regard to what fell under his own observation, and when he speaks in his own person, beyond almost any ancient writer, leaves us no room to doubt that he viewed the temple of Belus before it was much despoiled. He relates distinctly what *he saw* in that temple; and he also mentions what *he was told,* by the Chaldean priests (lib. i. cap. clxxxiii.) concerning a gigantic statue of gold, that *formerly* stood in the *lower part* of it, and which was *seized* by Xerxes, (Id. ibid.) who slew the priest that attempted to oppose him.
25. Herodotus, lib. i. cap. clxxxiii.

the

the banks of the Tigris[26], as Babylon did on those of the Euphrates[27].

All ancient authors agree in representing the Babylonians as very early skilled in astronomy[28]. Herodotus ascribes to them the invention of the gnomon, or sun-dial, with the knowledge of the pole, and division of the day into twelve equal parts[29]: and he gives us reason to believe, that the Egyptians, as well as the Greeks, were indebted to them for these discoveries in the astronomical science[30]. This science, and every other part of philosophy, was chiefly cultivated among the Babylonians, by a body of men called *Chaldeans ;* who were set apart for the superintendence of religious worship, and invested with great authority[31]. They maintained that the universe was eternal, the work of an eternal God; whose will gave it birth, and whose providence continues to govern it[32].

The Chaldeans are supposed to have owed their early proficiency in astronomy, partly to the early civi-

26. Herodotus, lib. i. cap. cxciii. lib. ii. cap. cl.   Plin. *Hist. Nat.* lib. vi. cap. xv.   27. Strabo, lib. xvi. p. 738.

28. The testimony of philosophers on this subject is uniform, from Plato and Aristotle downwards ; and with them concur all ancient historians, who have treated of Assyrian affairs.

29. Herodot. lib. ii. cap. cix.   30. Id. ibid.   31. Diod. Sic. lib. ii. p. 115.   They were, says he, the *most ancient Babylonians.*

32. Ibid. lib. ii. p. 116.   The learned Cudworth questions the accuracy of Diodorus on this subject; and conjectures, that if the Chaldeans held such an opinion as the *eternity of the world,* in the time of that historian, they had received it from the disciples of Aristotle; because Berosus, a more ancient writer than Diodorus, declares they maintained a cosmogonia, or *creation of the world,* in the manner of the Egyptians and Greeks. (*Intellectual System,* book i. chap. iv.) But I am disposed to think, that the doctrine of the eternity of the world, so consistent with an astronomical priesthood, was the most ancient tenet of the Chaldeans ; and if they entertained, at any time, another opinion in regard to it, that such opinion was imbibed after the intercourse between Egypt and Assyria was opened, in consequence of the conquest of both countries by the Persians.   lization

.lization of Assyria, and partly to the nature of the
country; where, in the midst of extensive plains, under a clear and serene sky, they had opportunity of
observing, during the greater part of the year, the
course of the heavenly bodies, and the whole chorus
of the firmament, without the intervention of rain or
clouds[33]. And the vast height of the tower, in the
middle of the temple of Belus, must farther have
contributed to perfect their astronomical observations.

Various have been the opinions of antiquarians
concerning the building, and design of this stupendous
edifice, which greatly exceeded in altitude the highest
of the Egyptian pyramids. It has been supposed to
be the tower erected by the sons of Noah[34], in order
to serve as a signal, and centre of union, to the growing families of the human race, after the flood[35]: and
it has been represented as a sepulchral monument[36].
But its immensity and durability prove it to have been
the work of a great people, skilled in the mechanical
arts; and the contemplation of the heavenly bodies,
by a priesthood devoted to the study of those bodies,
appears evidently to have been the purpose for which
it was built, and raised to such a mysterious height.
That it was made subservient to that end, we have the
authority of Diodorus[37].

· This intelligent historian also informs us, to what
pitch the Chaldeans had carried their discoveries in
astronomy. They had found out, and taught, as fixed prin-

33. Plato *Epinom.* Aristot. *de Cælo*, lib. ii. cap. xii. Cicero, *de
Divinat.* lib. i. ·   34. *Gen.* chap. xi. ver. 4.
35. Perizon. *Orig. Babylon.* cap. x. xi. xii. Bochart, *Phaleg*, part
i. lib. i. cap. ix. Prideaux, *Connect. of the Hist. of the Old and New
Testament*, part i. book ii.
· 36. Strabo, lib. xvi p. 738.   37. Diod. Sicul. lib. ii. p. 98.

ciples,

ciples, That each of the planets moved in an orbit, or
course peculiar to itself; that they were impelled with
different degrees of velocity, and performed their revolutions in unequal portions of time; that the moon is
nearer to the earth, and performs her revolution in less
time than any of the solar planets; not because of the
velocity of her motion, but by reason of the smallness
of her orbit; that her light is borrowed, and her
eclipses produced by the intervention of the shadow of
the earth[38].

But the Chaldean priests, in contemplating the
beauty and harmony of the *solar system*, seem soon
to have lost sight of the *Great Author of order and
excellence;* or to have held the people in ignorance of
that *Supreme Mover* of the stupendous machine of the
universe, and to have represented the heavenly bodies
as the gods who governed the world[39]; while they pretended to fortel the fates of men, and of kingdoms,
by reading the aspects of those luminaries[40]. Hence,
from the unhappy conjunction of the astronomical
science with priest-craft, *solar* or *star-worship*, and
judicial astrology, were propagated over the east in
very ancient times, and paved the way for idolatry
and blind superstition.

This subject I shall afterwards have occasion to investigate, in tracing the progress of *polytheism*. At
present, we must take a view of the rise and progress
of the Assyrian empire.

Ninus, the reputed founder of that empire, and king
of Assyria Proper, is said to have extended his sway
from the Persian gulf to the banks of the Tanais, and
from the Indus to the Nile[41]. He began his ambi-

38. Ibid. lib. ii. p. 117.   39. Diod. Sicul. lib. ii. p. 116, 117.
40. Id. ibid.   41. Ctesias, ap. Diod. Sicul. lib. ii.

tious

tious career with the invasion of Chaldea, or the ancient kingdom of Babylon, which he subdued. Media
and Amenia next submitted to his arms[42]. He appears
to have been the first prince, who united the spirit of
conquest with the science of politics: for to him may
reasonably be ascribed the division of the Assyrian
empire into provinces, and also the institution of the
three councils, and three tribunals, by which government was administered, and justice distributed, in
subordination to the will of the sovereign[43].

Semiramis, the widow of Ninus, a woman of
masculine abilities, who assumed the supreme power
during the minority of her son Ninyas, and swayed
the sceptre forty-two years, is reported to have shed
new lustre over that monarchy which her husband
had founded[44]. She visited in person every part of
her extensive dominions; built cities in various
districts of the Assyrian empire; cut roads through
mountains, in order to facilitate intercourse between
contiguous provinces; traversed Egypt, and conquered
Ethiopia, if we may credit her historian[45]. And
having overawed the tributary princes, by the number
and valour of her troops, as well as by the vigour of
her administration, she was encouraged, we are told,
to undertake the conquest of India; but failed in that
grand enterprize, and with difficulty made her escape
into Bactria, with the remains of her immense army[46].
The

42. Id. ibid.   43. Strabo, lib. xvi. p. 745, et seq.
44. Ctesias, ap. Diod. Sicul. lib. ii. Diodorous informs us, that,
according to some historians, Semiramis usurped the Assyrian sceptre during the life of her husband, whom she threw into prison.
Bib. lib. ii. p. 107, 108.   45. Ctesias, ap. Diod. Sicul. ubi sup.
46. Id. ibid. I have forebore to relate the particulars of this expedition, because the detail is too extravagant to entitle it to historical
credibility. Yet ought we not to consider the exploits of Semiramis,
or those of Ninus, as mere fables; for we are assured that the Assyrians kept *chronicles*, or records of public transactions. (Diod. Sicut.
lib. ii. Joseph. *cont. Apian.* lib. i.) And these records Ctesias, who
was

PART I. The kingdom of Bactria, which lay to the east of the Caspian sea, and on the confines of Asiatic Scythia, is said to have been the last and mo st arduous conquest of Ninus[47].

To Semiramis is ascribed the building of the walls of Babylon, the temple of Belus, and other magnificent works; which were ranked among the wonders of the ancient world[48]. She is believed to be the first woman that ever swayed a sceptre; and the ability with which she reigned, has induced Plato to maintain, " That " women, as well as men, ought to be intrusted with " the government of states, and the conduct of mili- " tary operations[49]." But admitting this position to be just, so far as it respects talents, the example of the Assyrian queen seems also to prove, what subsequent experience has seldom contradicted ; " That women, in " exercising sovereignty, lose the virtues of their own

was physician to the younger Cyrus, and resided long in high favour at the Persian court, seems to have examined ; though he has surely exaggerated many circumstances, in order to excite the wonder of his readers, and give them lofty ideas of the power and grandeur of the Assyrian monarchs. Among such exaggerations, may be ranked the three million of infantry, five hundred thousand cavalry, and one hundred thousand chariots of war, with which Semiramis is said to have invaded India. (Ctesias, ubi sup.) But the tradition of her Indian expedition is preserved by all ancient historians and geographers, and therefore could not be omitted here.

47. Diod. Sicul. lib. ii. p. 93, 94.

48. Diod. Sicul. lib. ii. et Strabo, lib. xvi. passim.

49. Plato *de Repub.* lib. v. To this opinion of Plato the honest Rollin opposes the reasoning of Aristotle and Xenophon; who assert " That the Author of Nature, in giving different qualities of mind and " body to the two sexes, has marked out their different destinations:" (Aristot. *de' Cura Rei Famil.* lib. i. et Xenoph. *de Administ. Domest.*) and justly concludes, " That woman is destined for the conduct of do- " mestic affairs;" in the superintendance of which, far from being de- graded, she finds her most honourable station, and exercises her proper empire; her brightest talents appearing to most advantage, under the veil of modesty and obedience. *Hist. Ancienne,* tom. ii. chap. i.

" sex,

"sex, without acquiring those of ours." For unbridled
ambition, and inordinate lust, are the strongest traits
in the character of Semiramis; who sunk the mother
in the usurping and aspiring empress, and the matron
in the vainglorious and insatiable prostitute; and who,
in gratifying her passion for dominion, and her appetite for sensual pleasure, paid no regard to justice or
humanity[50].

Ninyas, who succeeded to the Assyrian sceptre on
the death of his imperious mother, being a prince of a
mild disposition, employed himself in framing regulations for the security of his throne, and the conservation of those dominions which his parents had
acquired. Having no turn for war or conquest, he
did not command his troops in person, agreeable to the
custom of ancient kings; but, confining himself chiefly
to his palace, committed the conduct of his armies to
his most approved officers[51].

50. As her wars were undertaken without provocation, (Diod.
Sicul. lib. ii. passim.) they seem to have been prosecuted with a sanguinary spirit. Her amours were yet more atrocious. Her custom
was, to single out one of the handsomest men in her army; and when
she became tired of him, to order him to be put to death, and choose
another to supply his place. (Ibid. lib. ii. p. 101.) A modern Semiramis, in the North of Europe, is known to have made love and war
in a manner so similar, as to give some degree of credibility to the
story of the Assyrian queen, setting aside other marks of resemblance.—If, with the learned and ingenious Mr. Bryant, we were to
substitute the NINEVITES for NINUS, and the SAMARIM for Semiramis; two branches of the family of CHUS, as he conjectures (New System of Ancient Mythol. vol. ii. p. 106, and seq.), this reasoning would
be altogether impertinent. But as I am determined to follow the testimony of the most respectable Greek and Roman historians, without
regard to his system of hero-annihilation, I have considered Ninus and
Semiramis as real persons; and as such, have reasoned on their actions.
Some regard will, however, be due, in the course of this history, to
Mr. Bryant's inquiries concerning SOLAR WORSHIP.

51. Diod. Sicul. lib. ii. p. 108.

On

On this account, Ninyas has been accused of indolence and effeminacy, though seemingly without reason. By seldom appearing in public, he inspired his people with more awe of his presence[12]; and by devolving the executive government upon others, he had more leisure to attend to the affairs of the cabinet, and provide for the general interests of his empire. He accordingly framed, and carried into operation, a system of jealous policy, admirably calculated for preserving peace and tranquillity in a great monarchy. He ordered the governor of every province to raise annually a certain number of men, for the support of his military establishment; and the whole army when completed, to be mustered in the neighbourhood of his capital, where he appointed a commander in chief over the troops of each nation[13]. At the close of the year, the army was dissolved; and a new one, levied in the same manner, supplied its place; the soldiers of the former being absolved from their military oath, and permitted to return home[14].

No system of martial policy could be better adapted than this to the ends proposed by Ninyas. A numerous body of disciplined men always under arms, and ready to march to the most distant part of his dominions, enabled him effectually to repel invasion, as well as keep,

52. The Greeks, a restless and warlike people, who could esteem no prince that was not distinguished by martial exploits, concluded Ninyas shut himself up in his palace only to conceal his vices. (Diod. Sicul. lib. ii. p. 108.) But this is a very unfair inference. If the secluded life of Ninyas can be ascribed to any cause beside despotic policy, it may perhaps be imputed to the domestic habits which he had contracted during the reign of his mother Semiramis; whose love of power made her retain the sceptre after her son had attained the age of manhood, and decline second nuptials, lest she should give herself a master in taking a husband. Diod. Sicul. lib. ii. p. 101.

53. Diod. Sicul. lib. ii. p. 108.   54. Id. ibid.

his

his subjects in obedience; while the annual change of the troops, which composed that body, prevented the officers and soldiers from leaguing together[55]; and, consequently, from forming ambitious attempts against the Imperial authority.

Nor was the attention of Ninyas confined solely to military regulations. He duly appointed able judges, and civil governors, for the several provinces of his empire[56]; and each governor was obliged to repair, once a year, to Nineveh, and give an account of his administration, in person[57].

The same plan of government was invariably pursued by the successors of Ninyas[58]. And so firmly was the Assyrian empire established, by this jealous policy, that it subsisted longer, without being dismembered, than any great monarchy in the ancient world[59], notwith-standing the indolent and lascivious lives its sovereigns are said to have led[60]. At length, however, the

Medes,

---

55. Diod. Sicul, *ubi sup.*   56. Id. ibid.

57. Nicol. Damasc. ap. Vales. *Excerpt.* 58. Diod. Sic. lib. ii. p. 108.

59. Herodotus affirms, that the Assyrian empire had subsisted five hundred and twenty years, before any of the subject nations recovered their independency. (Herodot. lib. i. chap. xcv.) This chronology I have chosen to follow, as more consistent with probability than that of any other ancient historian. Diodorus and Justin assign a much longer duration to the Assyrian empire before the revolt of the Medes; and the want of the Assyrian history of Herodotus, to which he frequent-ly alludes, has made these copiers of Ctesias be generally followed.

60. Diod. Sicul. lib. ii. p. 108. Justin, lib. i. cap. ii. It is impossible to believe that Ninyas and his successors were so dissolute as they have been represented. For, as the president Goguet very judiciously re-marks, the Assyrian monarchy could not have subsisted unbroken by revolutions for so great a length of time, if the princes who governed it had been abandoned to debauchery, and sunk in effeminacy. (*Orig. des Loix*, &c. par. ii. liv. i. chap. i.) We may therefore, presume, that the contempt with which the successors of Ninyas have been treated by the Greek and Roman historians, who have scarcely conde-

scended

Medes, strenuously contending for liberty, threw off the Assyrian yoke[61].   Other nations followed their example[62].   The Babylonians revolted[63].   And the city of Babylon became the capital of an independent kingdom, under Nabonassar[64]; the beginning of whose reign forms the first æra in Ptolemy's *Astronomical Canon*; and, therefore, is supposed to be the first we can fix with certainty, in tracing the line of oriental history.

The Medes, after they had recovered their independency, lived under the controul of their own laws, during a period of about forty years, in a state of freedom[65].   But that freedom having degenerated into anarchy, the Median chiefs, in order to remove the miseries under which the nation groaned, chose a king named Dejoces[66]; who repressed the public disorders, and founded the city of Ecbatana, which became the seat of a new and powerful monarchy.

In this revolution, we have a striking instance of the slender partitions between licentious liberty and despotism; but by no means a proof of the necessity of regal authority, to give stability to government.   Dejoces during the anarchy of the Medes, was distinguished among his countrymen, by his sagacity and regularity

cended to preserve their names, ought to be ascribed to the tranquillity with which they reigned ; and that they owed this tranquillity to the political maxims of Ninyas ; who, by confining himself to his palace, where he secretly moved all the wheels of government, was revered by his people as a god. (Diod. Sicul. lib. ii. p. 108.) Mysterious obscurity seems essential to the support of despotism ; and *despotism*, with *religious veneration* for the *sovereign*, to the *secure ruling* of *a great empire ;* which is consequently *a great evil* in the system of human affairs, however mild the administration.

61. Herodotus, lib. i. cap. xcv.   62. Id ibid.

63. Diod. Sicul. lib. ii. p. 111.   64. Ptolem. *Canon. Astronom.*

65. Herodot. lib. i. cap. xcvi.   66. Ibid. cap. xcviii.

of manners. Having cast his eye upon the throne, he applied himself diligently to the redress of grievances; and being appointed judge of the district to which he belonged, he approved himself worthy of that high office, alike by the rectitude of his decisions and the unwearied discharge of the duties of his function[67].

The people of other districts, and at last the whole body of the Medes, except such as lived by acts of violence, looked up to Dejoces for justice, and resorted to his tribunal. Now secure of his object, he withdrew himself from the seat of judicature; oppressed, as he pretended, with the weight of business, and under the necessity of attending to his private affairs[68]. An universal alarm was spread. The public calamities increased, when licentiousness had no longer any curb; and a national assembly of the Medes, secretly influenced by the friends of Dejoces, invested that arch-politician with regal power, as the only effectual remedy for the disorders of anarchy[69].

Ant. Ch.
710.
Nabonass.
æra 37.

The first act of sovereignty that the new king exercised, was to command his subjects, to build him a palace, and the second to found a strong city; in the centre of which his palace stood, and where he reigned, encompassed with battlements, and protected by guards[70]. Having thus provided for the security of his person, and the perpetuity of his power, this jealous prince, aiming at despotic rule, became in a manner invisible and inaccessible to his people[71]. In order to inspire them with more respect for his authority, none but his confidential ministers were permitted to appear in his presence[72]. It was solely from the heart of Ecbatana, from the innermost circle of his seven-walled capital, that Dejoces, by

---

67. Herodot. lib. i. cap. xcvi.   68. Ibid. cap. cvii.
69. Herodotus, lib. i. cap. xcviii.   70. Id. ibid. et seq.
71. Herodot. lib. i. cap. xcix.   72. Id. ibid.

means of emissaries, surveyed his dominions[73]. He continued, however, to preserve the esteem of the Medes, by the impartial administration of justice ; and after maintaining his sway, with a steady hand, during a reign of fifty-three years, he transmitted the Median sceptre to his son, Phraortes.

Meanwhile the Assyrian empire, though broken, was not subverted. Nineveh was still the metropolis of a powerful monarchy[74]. With many proofs of this power we are furnished both in sacred and civil history, and with strong presumptions, that the seat of dominion was not affected by the revolt of the Medes and Babylonians, or the grandeur of the Assyrians thereby much obscured, notwithstanding what we are told by Diodorus and Justin, on the authority of Ctesias.

Herodotus, the father of civil history, confidently tells us, That Phraortes, king of the Medes, " not " satisfied with the absolute sovereignty of. Media, " which he *assumed* on the death of his father, Dejoces,

---

73. Herodot. lib. i. cap. c. The description of no city in the ancient world has afforded so much room for exaggeration as that of Ecbatana. Herodotus, who appears to have seen it, says, it was about the size of the city of Athens; that it was seated on the declivity of a hill, and encompassed with seven walls of unequal height, and of a circular form, within *the innermost circle of which* the king's palace and treasury stood. (Herodot. lib. i. cap. xcviii.) Polybius, who had certainly seen the Median capital, but who lived full three hundred years later than Herodotus, and when the outer walls of Ecbatana seem to have been fallen to decay or thrown down, thus describes it. " This city stands," says he, " on the north side of Media. It was, *from the most ancient times,* the *seat of the royal residence,* and seems in *splendour and magnificence* to have *exceeded all other cities.* It is *built on the declivity of the mountain* Orontes, and *not enclosed with walls.* But there is *a citadel in it,* the *fortifications of which are of wonderful strength.*" (Polyb. lib. x. Excerpt. iv.) This citadel was probably the original palace of Dejoces, or the innermost circle of the ancient city.

74. ii. Kings, chap. xix. ver. 35, 36. Herodot. lib. i. cap. cii.

" made

" made war upon the Persians," and "*first reduced*
" *them* under the Median sway[75];" that with " *the*
" *united forces of these two nations*, he subdued all the
" neighbouring countries, attacking one people after
" another[76];" that, at length, "he turned his arms
" against the Assyrians;" and on " *those Assyrians*
" *who inhabited the city of Nineveh*[77]; *formerly the go-*
" *verning people in Asia*, and *still formidable*, though
" *deserted by their confederates*;" so that in this expedition " Phraortes *perished* with *the greater part* of
" his army[78]." And to say nothing of the wars of the
Assyrians *to the west of the Euphrates*, immediately
after the revolt of the Medes and Babylonians[79] (the
particulars of which I shall afterward have occasion to
relate from the Hebrew records), it appears from *the
agreement of sacred history* with Ptolemy's *Astronomical
Canon*, that Esarhaddon, or Assaradon, the son and successor of Senacherib, sovereign of Assyria, had reunited the kingdom of Babylon to that ancient monarchy in
the sixty-seventh year of the Nabonassarean æra[80].

The glory of the Assyrian empire, however, after
this reunion, was of short duration, notwithstanding
the defeat of the Medes. Cyaxares I. the son of Phraortes, a brave and warlike prince, having resolved to
take vengeance upon the Assyrians for the death of
his father, assembled his numerous and disciplined
forces, and marched into the heart of their country[81];
defeated

---

75. Herodot. lib. i. cap. cii.   76. Id. ib.   77. Herodot. ubi sup.

78. Herodotus, lib. i. cap. cii. This event happened in the twenty-
second year of the reign of Phraortes. Id. ibid.

79. See ii. Kings, chap. xvi.—xix. and ii. *Chron.* chap. xxxii. xxxiii.

80. Compare ii. *Kings*, chap. xix. ver. 35, 36. and ii. *Chron.* chap.
xxxii. ver. 11. with Ptolemy's *Canon. Astronom.*

81. Herodotus, lib. i. cap. ciii. This venerable historian says that
Cyaxares had united under his standard, when he invaded Assyria,
all the nations of Upper Asia as far as the river Halys; and that he had
greatly

defeated the army that attempted to obstruct his progress, and invested Nineveh[82]. But before he could make any impression upon the fortifications[83], he was obliged to raise the siege, in order to defend his own dominions against an irruption of the European Scythians[84]; who had entered Asia under their king Madyes, after having driven before them the Cimmerians, from the Chersonesus Taurica[85], now known by the name of the *Crimea*.

Ant. Chr.
633.
Nabonass.
rae 114.

This is the first occasion on which history makes mention of the Scythians; whose mode of life, and manner of making war, appeared to have been nearly the same in all ages[86]. Those fierce barbarians broke, in a great battle, the power of the victorious Medes, and over-ran all the countries between the Caspian sea and coast of Syria[87]. Of Upper Asia they remained masters twenty-eight years[88]; and so long did they continue

greatly improved their military discipline, by forming them into distinct bodies of spearmen, cavalry, and archers; (Herodot. ubi sup.) they having been accustomed, before his reign, to join battle in a confused manner. (Id. ibid.) These circumstances sufficiently account for his victory over the Assyrians; and for the future success of his arms, which I shall afterwards have occasion to relate.   82. Id. ibid.

83. The fortifications of Nineveh, according to Diodorus Siculus, the only author who describes them, were of amazing strength; the walls being one hundred feet high, and so thick that three carriages might drive abreast upon them; and the towers, with which they were flanked, two hundred feet in height. (Diod. Sicul. lib. ii. p. 92.) Whence Diodorus had his information, he has not told us.

84. Herodotus, lib. i. cap. ciii.

85. Id. ibid. et seq. The Cimmerians, an enemy scarcely less terrible than the Scythian horde that had expelled them, directed their course to the west, along the coast of the Euxine sea; over-ran Asia-Minor, and pillaged the kingdom of Lydia. (Herodotus, lib. i. cap. vi. xv.) The citadel of Sardis alone withstood their fury. Herodot. lib. i. cap. xv.

86. See Gibbon's *Hist. of the Decline and Fall of the Roman Empire.* chap. xxvi. xxxiv.

87. Herodotus, lib. i. cap. civ.—cvi.   88, Ibid. lib. i. cap cvi.

tinue

tinue to ravage with their inroads the most fertile provinces of Lower Asia[89].

During this period of violence and calamity, in
which barbarian force reigned triumphant, and when
strong cities only can be supposed to have resisted
the shock of the ferocious invaders, Nabopollassar,
viceroy of Babylon, revolted from Chyniladan, emperor of Assyria, and assumed independent sovereignty[90]. He had been encouraged in his rebellion
by the hostile Cyaxares, who still meditated the destruction of Nineveh[91]. And no sooner did the king
of the Medes find himself freed from the domination
of the Scythians, whose chieftains he had invited to a
feast, and slain while drunk[92]; and from a war, in which
some Scythian fugitives involved him, with Alyattes,
king of Lydia, that lasted five years[93], than he renewed
hostilities against Assyria[94].

Cyaxares again entered that rich country, in conjunction with Nabocolassar, or Nebuchadnezzar, king
of Babylon, the son and successor of Nabopollassar;
and these two powerful monarchs, who were knit in
close alliance, finally subverted the empire of the first

Ant. Chr.
625.
Nabonass.
æra 122.

Ant. Chr.
605.
Nabonass.
æra 142.

---

89. Id. ibid.   90. Alex. Polyhist. ap. Cyncel. *Chronograph* p 110.
91. Id. ibid.   92. Herodotus, lib. i. cap. cvi.
93. Herodot. lib. i. cap. lxxiv. That war was terminated in consequence of a solar eclipse, which had been predicted by Thales the Mi-
lesian; (Id. ibid.) who to his own natural sagacity had added the learning of Egypt. When the Medes and Lydians had joined battle, in
the sixth campaign, says Herodotus, the day was suddenly changed
into night; an appearance which so affected them, that they desisted
from action. (Herodot. ubi sup.) A suspension of hostilities took place;
and peace was concluded between the contending monarchs, through
the mediation of the kings of Babylon and Cilicia. (Id. ibid.) This
peace was ratified with the oath of the contracting parties; and, as a
farther tie, Alyattes gave his daughter Aryenis, in marriage to Asty-
ages, the son of Cyaxares. Herodot. lib. i. cap. lxxiv.
94. Ibid. lib. i. chap. cvi.

Assyrians,

Assyrians[95]. Nineveh, the famous capital of this ancient people, was utterly destroyed[96]: and the remaining provinces of their monarchy (as I shall afterward
have occasion to relate) were divided between the kings
of Media and Babylon.

The taking of Nineveh, my lord, is one of the
greatest events in the history of ancient nations; but
we are left totally in the dark by historians, both civil
and sacred, in regard to the circumstances with which
it was attended. The prophet Nahum is the only
writer that has entered into particulars on the subject;
and as he is supposed to have been divinely inspired, if
he had not the advantage of historical information (for
ecclesiastical writers have not been able to fix the time
when he lived), I shall copy the most marking strokes
in his sublime description; which gives us a very high
idea of the grandeur of the old Assyrians, and of the
power of the Medes.

" Woe to the bloody city!"—exclaims the prophet;
—" because of the multitude of the whoredoms of the
" well-favoured harlot, the mistress of witchcrafts;
" that selleth nations through her whoredoms, and
" royal families through her witchcrafts. Keep watch!
" make thy loins strong, fortify thy power mightily;
" for he that dasheth in pieces is come up before thy
" face. The shield of his warriors is made red, the

95. Compare Herodotus, lib. i. cap. cvi. with Alex. Polyhist. ap.
Syncel. Chronograph. p. 110. et ap. Euseb. Chronicon. p. 46. Herodotus
declines entering into the particulars of this expedition, saying he shall
have occasion to relate them in another place; (Herodot. ubi. sup.)
alluding, no doubt, to the history of Assyria, which he proposed to
write. But he observes, that the Medes conquered all the Assyrian
territories, except what belonged to the king of Babylon. (Id. ibid.)
We have, therefore, great reason to believe, independent of the authority of Polyhistor, that Cyaxares and Nabocolassar were joint adventurers in this enterprize, and that Nineveh was taken immediately
after the close of the Lydian war.   96. Strabo, lib. xvi. init.

. " valiant

" valiant are in scarlet. Behold, thy people in the
" midst of thee are women!—the gates of thy land
" shall be set wide open unto thine enemies; the fire
" shall devour thy bars. I hear the noise of a whip;
" and the noise of the rattling of the wheels, of the
" prancing of horses; and of the jumping of chariots:
" they rage like a tempest, in the streets; they blaze
" like torches; they run like lightnings! The horse-
" man lifteth up both the bright sword and the glittering
" spear; there is a multitude slain, yet no end of the
" slaughter; they stumble upon the corpses, because
" of their great number!—The victors take the spoil
" of silver, they take the spoil of gold; the store is
" beyond computation; and above all, the spoil of
" splendid and rich furniture. Nineveh is empty, de-
" solate, and waste!—Where is the dwelling of the
" lions, and the feeding-place of the young lions?—
" There the lion, even the old lion walked, and the
" lion's whelp, and none made them afraid. The lion
" did tear in pieces enough for his whelps, and
" strangled for his lionesses; and filled his holes with
" prey, and his dens with ravin. Nineveh, which was
" established of old, is like a pool of water. Her
" princes were as the locusts, and her captains as the
" great grasshoppers, which encamp in the hedges
" during the cool of the morning; but, when the sun
" ariseth, they fly away, and their place is not known.
" Thy shepherds slumber, O king of Assyria! thy no-
" bles dwell in the dust: thy people are scattered upon
" the mountains, and no man gathereth them[97].

SKETCH OF THE HISTORY OF EGYPT TO THE REIGN OF
PSAMMITICHUS.

BEFORE the foundation of the Assyrian empire,
Egypt was a populous and powerful kingdom, under

—————————
97. Nahum, chap. ii.—iii. passim.

a regular

PART I.   a regular government and police[98]. This early population and improvement Egypt owed, like Assyria to
the fertility of its soil[99].   Fattened by the annual overflowing of the waters of the Nile (which prepares the
land for the reception of the seed with little assistance
of tillage), the immense vale of Egypt, extending from
the mountains of Ethiopia to the Mediterranean sea,
and from the deserts of Arabia to those of Libya,
furnished food for man in profusion.   There the
tropical plants thrive, with many of those more commonly found in colder climates; and there all kinds of
grain, wheat and barley as well as rice, yielded large
increase[100].

In a territory so highly favoured by nature, the
social principle must quickly have ripened; and the
mutual wants of men assembled in society, and their
mutual desire of multiplying the accommodations of
life, and of guarding against the evils inseparable
from mortality, would soon give birth to all the useful,
and even to many of the ornamental arts.   The sciences, intimately connected with the arts, it may be
expected, would also rear their head: so, we find, they

98. *Genesis*, chap. xxxvii. xl. xli. et seq. *Exod.* chap. i.—xiv. Herodot. lib. ii. et Diod. Sicul. lib. i. passim. See also Dr. Warburton's
Divine Legation of Moses, book iv. sect. i.—iv. et auct. cit.

99. " The *countries on the Tigris and the Nile*," says Sir Isaac Newton," being *exceeding fertile*, were *first frequented by mankind*, and *first
" grew into kingdoms*." (*Chron. of Ancient Kingdoms amended*, p. 160.)
In proof of this great natural fertility, see Herodotus and Diodorus,
ubi sup. and Pliny, lib. xxi. cap. xv.

100. Idem. ibid. This fine country, about six hundred miles in length,
and near three hundred at its greatest breadth, is divided by geographers
into Higher, Lower, and Middle Egypt. Of these divisions, I shall
afterward have occasion to speak. I shall therefore only here remark,
that Higher Egypt, in ancient times, was generally known by the name
of *Thebais*, and that the whole three divisions lie between the twenty-
second and thirty-third degrees of northern latitude.

                                                        did.

did. But the sciences most successfully cultivated in Egypt, were those of government and legislation. And fortunate is it for us, in treating of the affairs of this venerable country, that, although left in a great measure ignorant of the history of the old Egyptian monarchs, we are amply furnished with information relative to the laws and constitution of the kingdom over which they ruled.

Menes, the first sole monarch of Egypt[101], and the first legislator who regulated religious worship, and gave written laws to the Egyptians[102], appears to have been an adept in the science of human nature. In order to procure implicit submission to his laws, he pretended they were delivered to him, for the good of the people, by the god Hermes[103]; and on purpose to restrain the wanderings of carnal appetite, and give stability to the amorous passion, he instituted the *law of marriage*, and placed the nuptial union under the sanction of the altar[104].

That law, my lord, suggests to us a curious subject of disquisition; the *original connexion between the sexes* : and I cannot dismiss it without hazarding a few remarks.

---

101. Menes, according to Herodotus (lib. ii. cap. iv.), was the first mortal that reigned in Egypt; for the Egyptians vainly exhibited a genealogy of *immortal* princes, supposed originally to have ruled over them, and whom they afterward worshipped as gods (Herodot. lib. ii. cap. cxliv. Diod. Sicul. lib. i. init.) ; and all ancient chronologers agree, that Menes, or Menas, was the first sovereign that exercised dominion over the whole land of Egypt. Nor were his territories very extensive; for if we may believe the report of the Egyptian priests, all Lower Egypt was then a morass (Herodot. lib. ii. cap. iv.), and the greater part of it entirely covered by the waters of the sea. Id. ibid.

102. Diod. Sicul. lib. i. p. 84. edit. ubi cit.   103. Id. ibid.

104. Palæph. ap. Clem. Alex. p. 45. Suidas, voc. Ἥφαιστος.

The respect paid by all ancient nations to the memory of the institutors of the law of marriage, and the solemn rites, with which the nuptial ceremony is accompanied, have led to a popular opinion, that the intercourse between the sexes in the human species, was originally promiscuous, like that of grazing cattle. Hence the well known comparison of Horace, *ut in grege taurus*[105]; which may be thus paraphrased :

   " With women men, like bulls among the herd,
   " Roving at large, indulged venereal acts,
   " As lust incited."

But this representation, which makes the state of nature, a state of prostitution, is equally, contradicted by reason and experience. As man is by nature a *herding*, he is also a *paring* animal. He singles out *one* woman from a multitude of others, where such an opportunity of choice is offered : he endeavours to win her regard by courtship and kind offices ; and he has little satisfaction in her arms, unless when convinced that he gives, as well as receives pleasure, in the conjugal embrace[106]. Nor is he disposed to abandon her during her pregnancy, or in the time of child-birth ; but is happy in propagating his species, and prides himself in multiplying his own likeness, and that of the partner of his affections. In a word, as the *assistance* of *both parents* is *necessary* to the *rearing* of the *human offspring*, condemned to a long and helpless infancy, Nature, in order to accomplish her purpose, has endowed *both* with that *sympathic attachment* called LOVE,

---

105. *Satirar.* lib. i. sat. iii. ver. 110.

106. "Were this *belief* to be taken away," observes the philosophic Shaftesbury, "there would be hardly any, *even of the grosser sort of mankind*, who would not perceive *their remaining pleasure* to be of *small estimation.*" *Characteristics*, vol. ii. book ii. part ii. sect. i.

                                              without

without which the *race* must have become *extinct.*
We accordingly find *the union of the sexes,* and *nuptial
ceremonies,* universal among savages[107].

But although the union of the sexes is *formed* by
instinct in the savage state, the sacred matrimonial tie
is nevertheless necessary, for the preservation of order
in society. As civil and criminal laws, respecting property and personal safety, are required, to restrain the
excesses of the selfish and irascible passions; *to fortify,*
not to *create,* the *sense* of *justice,* or the *sentiment* of
humanity; in like manner, the laws concerning marriage, and the connexion between the sexes, are requisite to curb the irregularities of libidinous desire, and
the intemperance of the sexual passion; which, in proportion to the increase of luxury, become prurient and
variable. Hence the wisdom of the Egyptian legislator, in confining *one* man to *one* woman, agreeable to
the intention of nature[108].

Having thus discovered the origin of marriage, and
the policy of such an institution, let us inquire after
the rise of civil government.

As the first *social connexion* is that of *husband* and
wife, the first *civil superiority* is that of a *father*
over

107. *Hist. Gen des Voyages* et Picart's *Relig. Ceremon.* passim, with
the authors there cited. If the narration of any traveller, or navigator,
seems to contradict this opinion, it will generally be found supported
by some other more worthy of credit. The subject is set in a just
light by Dr. Robertson. *Hist. of America,* book iv.

108. Herodotus pointedly asserts (lib. ii. cap. xciv.), that the
Egyptians, *like the Greeks,* had only *one* wife. Now the law of marriage, as we shall have occasion to see, was brought from Egypt into
Greece; where it was universally established upon Egyptian principles, and according to the practice of an Egyptian colony. Yet Diodorus Siculus tells us (lib. i. p. 72.), that the Egyptian *priests only* were
confined

over his *family*. Nature, therefore, points us to *patriarchal rule*, as the *original government* among men. For although a father has no natural right to govern his sons, after they have attained the years of manhood, they will find it necessary to recur to some person for the arbitration of their common differences. And who is so likely to be chosen for that purpose, as their common parent?—They have been habituated in infancy, to submit to his authority: he has settled their boyish disputes; and they have wondered at the strength of *his* understanding, while their own was weak. Early impressions are not easily eradicated. His counsel is sought; and to him they are led to appeal, not only from a persuasion of his superior wisdom, but from a conviction that his decisions will be just, because he is equally concerned in the welfare of all. To him, as their common head, his offspring look up; and he exercises, during life, the joint office of governor and judge.

The farther progress of government, it is not more difficult to trace. Families naturally grew into *tribes;* held together by common consanguinity; and of which the head of the eldest family, in each tribe, was revered as *chief*. When exposed to danger from foreign enemies, or induced by considerations of mutual advantage, two or more tribes united into

confined to *one* wife, and that the laity might take as many wives as they pleased. But if such a custom prevailed in Egypt, in the days of Diodorus, it must have been introduced after the final conquest of that kingdom by the Persians, among whom a plurality of wives was tolerated. For Herodotus was too well acquainted with the manners of the Egyptians, among whom he had long resided, to be mistaken in such a material circumstance; consequently, men of all orders, in Egypt, had only *one* within his time. Nor could the Egyptians, in more early times, have communicated to the Greeks a law or custom, which was not in general use among them, and then held sacred.

one

one body, and composed a *nation* or *state*. In the new community, which generally formed a kind of *rude republic*, some man of superior sagacity in council, or superior prowess in war, never failed to acquire the ascendant; and when those qualities happened to be combined in the same person, he was not only intrusted with the command of the forces of the state, but took the lead in all public deliberations. With or without the forms of election, he was constituted chief magistrate and captain-general, for life. A portion of the respect for the father was necessarily transferred to the son. He usually possessed the same elevated station[109]. With office, wealth and influence accumulated, and chief magistracy became hereditary[110]. Thus was one family raised above others, and *monarchy* gradually founded.

When monarchy was established in Egypt, or by what means Menes acquired the sovereignty of that ancient kingdom, history has not informed us: nor do we know, with any degree of certainty, the age in which he reigned[111]. We are only told, that beside imposing upon the Egyptians the restraints of law, and the offices of religion[112], he diverted the course of the Nile, which had hitherto washed the foot of the sandy mountains

109. Vid. Polyb. lib. vi. Excerpt. i. " The people," says this profound politician, "not only confirmed these leaders in the possession of " the powers to which they have been exalted, but preserve it to their " children; being persuaded that those, who have received their birth " and education from illustrious parents will resemble them." Id. ibid.

110. Polyb. ubi sup.   111. The reign of Menes is commonly placed by modern chronologers about 2200 years before the christian æra. But the Egyptian chronology, until the reign of Psammitichus, is a mere chaos; and all attempts to elucidate it have hitherto proved fruitless.

112. It was reserved for modern scepticism to call in question the necessary connection between *religion* and *government,* and the salutary influence of the former upon moral conduct. All ancient legislators interwove religion with their civil and political institutions: and the
philosophers

mountains on the frontiers of Lybia[113]; founded Memphis, within the former bed of the river; and built the magnificent temple of Vulcan, in that city[114].

The history of Egypt, from the reign of Menes to that of Sesostris, is involved in impenetrable obscurity. During this long and dark period, is supposed to have happened the irruption of the eastern, or Arabian herdsmen, UKSOUS, or *king-pastors;* an event which has afforded modern antiquarians and chronologers

philosophers recommended it, as the true basis of legislation. Even such as believed it to be of human invention, yet admitted its utility. Of this we have a remarkable instance, in the famous fragment of the atheistical Critias. " When the laws had restrained an open viola-
" tion of right," says he, " men set upon contriving how *secretly* to in-
" jure others. And then it was, as I suppose, some cunning politician,
" well versed in the knowledge of mankind, counterworked this de-
" sign, by the *invention* of a *principle that would hold wicked men in awe;*
" even when about to say, or think, or act *ill* in *private.*   And this
" was to bring in the *belief of a God;* whom he taught to be immortal,
" of infinite knowledge, and of a nature transcendantly excellent.
" This God, he told them, could *bear* and *see* every thing said and
" done by mortals here below; nor could the *first conception* of the
" *most secret wickedness* be *concealed from Him,* of whose nature *know-*
" *ledge* was the very *essence.*
" In order to add *terror* to *reverence* for the gods," proceeds Critias,
" our politician said they inhabited that place, where swift corrusca-
" tions of enkindled meteors, accompanied with horrid bursts of thun-
" der, run through the starry vaults of heaven, the beautiful fret-work
" of that wise old architect, Time!—where the consociated troop of
" shining orbs perform their regular and benignant revolution, and
" whence refreshing showers descend to saturate the thirsty earth.
" Such was the habitation he assigned to the gods; a place most proper
" for the discharge of their function!—and such the *terrors* he *employ-*
" *ed* to repress secret mischief, stifle disorder in the seeds, give laws
" fair play, and *introduce religion, so necessary to the magistrate.*"
Frag. Critias, ap. Sext. Emperic, *Advers. Phys.* cap. ix. sect. liv.
113. Herodotus, lib. ii. chap. xc.   114. Id. ibid. This temple,
adorned with porticos and statues, by the piety and munificence of
succeeding monarchs, as we shall have occasion to see, was the most
superb monument of superstition in Egypt (Herodot. lib. ii. passim.);
but antiquity has left us no description of it.
                                                        great

!!! great field for speculation and conjecture. These
rude invaders are said to have conquered all Lower
and Middle Egypt, to have established their dominion at Memphis, and to have maintained it with an
iron sceptre for two hundred and fifty-nine years [116];
after which, their power being broken by a king of
Thebais, or Higher Egypt, they retired according to
treaty, with their families and goods, and settled in
the country afterwards known by the name of Palestine, where they built the city of Jerusalem [117].

But this singular invasion, upon which so much
learning has been wasted, I shall forbear to rank
among the revolutions of ancient Egypt; not merely
because no notice is taken of it by Herodotus or Diodorus, but because the passage in which it is related
(said to be extracted from Manetho), bears strong
marks of forgery. That passage is professedly quoted
by Josephus, to shew the antiquity of his own nation,
and obviously to induce a belief, that the king-pastors
were the Israelites. He declares he transcribed it faithfully from the Egyptian historian: but it is impossible
to give him credit for his assertion. For the pretended
Manetho not only says, that the king-pastors, after
their departure from Egypt, took possession of Palestine; but, in order to render the story more applicable to the ancient countrymen of the Jewish historian,
he observes, that in books of great authority he finds
these people distinguished by the name of *captive pas-
tors*[118]. Admitting the extract, however, to be genuine, notwithstanding these indications of its being
spurious, it can but be considered, at best, as a fabulous account of the *descent, sojourning* and *exodus* of

115. Sir John Marsham, Perizonius, sir Isaac Newton, Greaves,
Bryant, &c.   116. Maneth ap. Joseph. *Cont. Apian.* lib. i.
117. Id. ibid.   118. Maneth. ap. Joseph. ubi sup.

PART I.   the Israelites; which your lordship will find very differently related in the book of Moses[119].

In the obscure period, between Menes and Sesostris, are placed the reigns of five kings, whose names were famous in antiquity; Busiris II. Osymandes, Uchoreus, Egyptus, and Mœris.

Busiris II. the eighth in descent from the *first* of that *name* (commonly represented as a cruel tyrant), is said to have built, or much enlarged, the celebrated Egyptian Thebes[120], the chief city in Higher Egypt, and the seat of the first Egyptian monarchs, which was one hundred and forty stadia, or seventeen miles

---

119. See *Genesis*, chap. xl. et seq. *Exodous*, passim. Conformable to the writings of the sacred historian, Diodorus affirms, That Egypt had never been conquered, unless by the Ethiopians, before it submitted to the Persian power (*Biblioth.* lib. i. p. 41. edit. ubi cit.); and his testimony is corroborated by the narrative of Herodotus, (lib. ii. iii. passim). I am sensible Mr. Bryant (*Analysis of Ancient Mythology*, vol. iii.) endeavours to throw new light upon this subject; and that, in consequence of his theory of deriving all learning and civility from the *Cuthites*, he places the *invasion* of the *king-pastors* before the foundation of the Egyptian monarchy; makes them the builders of the pyramids, the raisers of the obelisks, and of all the other magnificent works in ancient Egypt. But this theory is as romantic as that of Gale (*Court of the Gentiles*, vol. i. ii. passim.): who attempts to prove, that the Egyptians borrowed all their arts, learning, and even their religion, from the *Israelites!*

120. Diod. Sicul. lib. i. p. 42. The same historian had before said, that the founding of this city was ascribed to Osiris, the tutelary god, and one of the fabulous monarchs of the Egyptians: but that, on this subject, not only Grecian authors, but the Egyptian priests themselves were divided (Diod. Sicul. lib. i. p. 14.). In a word, the founder of Thebes was so utterly unknown, that his name had not been distinctly preserved even by tradition. Diodorus afterwards insinuates (p. 79.), that the Egyptians never had any king named *Busiris*. Such is the uncertainty of this portion of history!—Yet he tells us, in a subsequent book (lib. iv. p. 225.), that Hercules, after he had killed Antæus, went into Egypt, and slew the tyrant Busiris.

and

and a half in circuit[121]. That ancient capital, called
latterly *Diospolis*, or "the city of Jupiter," was distinguished in early times, for wealth and power, beyond
all others known to the Greeks[122]. And its ruins,
and hieroglyphical inscriptions, continued long to attest its former greatness[123]. In Thebes stood four
temples of singular beauty, and astonishing magnitude[124]; one of them being above a mile and an half
in circumference[125].

But of all the structures at Thebes, or in its neighbourhood, where the ruins of many grand buildings
are still to be seen, the most superb was the mauso-
leum of Osymandes[126]. This king is reported to have
been a mighty warrior[127]. To his exploits, however,
as embellished by Egyptian vanity, no credit can be
given: nor can we admit the description of his monument, as transcribed by Diodorous from Hecatæus,
among the number of historical facts[128]. We might
as well ingraft into the page of history, what is copied by the same historian from Ctesias, concerning
the wonderful works of Semiramis[129]; to which
those ascribed to Osymandes bear a striking resemblance[130].

Uchoreus,

121. Id. ibid. In speaking of *miles*, I wish it to be understood, that
I always mean *English miles;* and, in like manner, of all long measures common to modern nations, unless when particularly expressed.
122. Homer's *Ilias*, lib. ix. ver. 381. 123. Strabo, *Geog.* lib.
xvii. p. 815, 816. Tacit. *Annal.* lib. ii. cap. lx. 124. Diod.
Sicul. lib. i. p. 43. 125. Id. ib. 126. Diod. Sic. lib. i.
p. 44. 127. Id. ibid. 128. Hecatæus, ap. Diod. Sic.
lib. í. p. 44, 45, 46. 129. Ctesias, ap. Diod. Sicul. lib. ii. p. 97,
98, 99. et seq. 130. Compare Hecatæus and Ctesias, ubi supra.
The circle of gold, one cubit thick, and sixty-five cubits in circumference, with which the tomb of Osymandes is said to have been
surrounded, is surely as little credible as the smoothing of the
rocky side of mount Bagistan, two miles in height, on which was re-

presented·

PART I.
Uchoreus, the eighth descendant from Osymandes, is said, by Diodorus, to have built Memphis[131]; which, as I have related on the credit of Herodotus, was founded by Menes. That Uchoreus gave to this city the form in which it afterward appeared, and the magnificence that made it thenceforth become the seat of the Egyptian monarchy[132], for which its situation was favourable, may be well believed; and that circumstance occasioned the gradual decline of Thebes[133].

·Memphis was seated on the western side of the Nile[134], twenty-two miles[135] above the place, where that river divides itself into two great branches which form the *Delta*[136]; so called from its triangular figure, or resemblance to the fourth letter in the Greek alphabet, and which comprehended the most fertile part of Lower Egypt[137]. This city, one hundred and fifty stadia[138], or about nineteen miles in circumference, was secured on the south side by a strong rampart[139], which served both for a dyke against the inundations of the Nile, and a bulwark to defend it, in case of the approach of an enemy[140]. On all other sides, it was fortified, not only with walls but by a large and deep moat[141]; which being, at all times, filled with water from the river, rendered the city in a manner impregnable[142]. Memphis was accordingly considered as the

presented the figure of Semiramis, attended by two hundred of her guards; (id. ibid) to say nothing of the sculptured and painted galleries, by a people yet ignorant of the arts of design, that exhibited the fabulous conquest of Bactria by Osymandes, and the library formed before any books had been written.

131. Diod. Sicul. lib. i. p. 46.   132. Id. lib. i. p. 47.
133. Id. ibid.   134. Herodotus, lib. ii. cap. xcix.   135. Strabo, lib. xvii. p. 807.   136. Id. ibid. et Diod. Sicul. lib. i. p. 46.
137. Diod. Sicul. lib. i. p. 29, 30.   138. Ibid. lib. i. p. 46.
139. Id. ibid.   140. Diod. Sicul. lib. i. p. 46.   141. Id. lib. i. p. 47. Herod. lib. ii. cap. xcix.   142. Id. ibid.

key

key of the Nile, and the capital of Egypt, till the
founding of Alexandria[143].

Five miles north-west of Memphis[144], stood the
three famous pyramids, or quadrangular towers, that
filled the ancient world with astonishment, and which
continue to excite the wonder of modern travellers[145].
These immense masses, which appear to have been intended for sepulchral monuments, are built with stones
of an enormous size, piled upon one another in regular
rows[146]; and so hard, and firmly compacted[147], that
they have withstood the ravages of time, the revolutions of empires, and the force of the elements, for
almost three thousand years[148]. The reputed founders
of those pyramids, I shall afterwards have occasion to
mention.

The reign of Egyptus is rendered memorable by
the flight of his brother Danaus[149]; whose voyage
into Greece with his daughters[150], forms a memorable

143. Diod. Sicul. ubi sup. et Strabo, lib. xvii. p. 807.

144. Strabo, lib. xvii. p. 808.

145. The first, and largest pyramid, is near five hundred feet in
perpendicular height; six hundred and sixty feet square at the base,
and sixteen at the top. (Gogut, *des Orig. des Arts*, &c. et auct. cit.)
The second pyramid, according to Greaves, is of the same dimensions with the first; but he did not measure it, and all other travellers agree that it is smaller. The third pyramid is three hundred
feet square at the base, and proportionally high with the two former.
Greaves *Pyramidographia*, passim.

146. Herodot. lib. ii. cap. cxxiv. cxxv. Maillet, *Descript. de l'Egypte*,
p. 224—253. Edit. Paris, 1735.　　　147. Herodot. ubi sup. Strabo,
lib. xvii. p. 808.

148. When the Egyptian pyramids were built, is not certainly
known; but, from the relations of modern travellers, they seem to
be nearly in the same state as when they were viewed by Herodotus,
above two thousand two hundred years ago.

149. Apollodorus, lib. ii. p. 62. Diod. Sicul. lib. v. p. 329.

150. Herodotus, lib. ii. cap. clxxxii.

æra

æra in the history of Peloponnesus, as I shall have occasion to notice[151]. Egyptus, renowned for his justice and beneficence, had the honour of giving to the venerable country over which he ruled, the appellation of *Egypt*[152], by which it is still known.

Twelve reigns after that of Egyptus, Mœris; or Myris, was raised to the throne[153]. He built the grand portico on the north-side of Vulcan's temple at Memphis[154]; and is said to have formed the vast lake that bore his name[155]. This lake is commonly ranked among the extraordinary works of the ancient Egyptians. And if artificial, it must have been hollowed at an amazing expence, and by the most astonishing efforts of labour; as we are told, that it was fifty fathoms in depth, and four hundred and fifty miles in circumference[156]. It appears, however, to have been partly

151. Strabo, lib. v. p. 221. lib. vii. p. 321. et lib. viii. p. 371.

152. Diod. Sicul. lib. i. p. 47.

153. Id. ibid. In early times, as Diodorus informs us, the Egyptians paid less regard to hereditary right than to the virtues of their sovereigns (*Biblioth.* lib. i. p. 41.); the body of the people being vested with the power of raising to the throne, the person they esteemed most worthy to reign over them (Id. ibid.). But after the offices of state came to be confined (as I shall have occasion to observe), to the ecclesiastical and military orders, the crown seems to have been strictly hereditary; and when the royal line failed, the sovereign was chosen out of one of those two orders, and by the members of those orders exclusively. Hence we may draw these important conclusions, that in this ancient kingdom, as in all other states, the people originally possessed the privilege of chusing their own chief magistrate; but that *priests* and *soldiers* under the name of *nobles*, gradually wrested the rights of the people from them: a progress which I shall have frequent opportunity to exemplify; and to shew, that in proportion to the share which the people have in public affairs, the administration of government is, every where, mild or oppressive, and that venerated hereditary succession naturally leads to despotism.

154. Herodot. lib. ii. cap. ci. Diod. Sicul. lib. i. p. 47.   155. Id ib.

156. Herodotus, lib. ii. cap. cxlix. Diod. Sicul. lib. i. p. 48. Herodotus,

partly the work of nature, partly of art[157]; to have
been hollowed by the Nile, before the course of that
river was diverted by Menes, or by the sea, when its
waters covered all Lower Egypt[158].

. But in whatever manner the lake Mœris was originally formed, it contributed greatly to the fertility.
of the surrounding country, and to the conveniency
of the people. Being capable of containing a prodigious
quantity of water, by reason of its vast compass and
depth, it served to receive the superflux of the inundations of the Nile, when that river rose to too great
an height[159]; and thereby prevented the lands from
being choaked with mud, or the houses in low situations,
from *being* overflowed[160]; while it furnished, during the
season of ebb, moisture to the surrounding fields[161].
For these purposes a wide sluice, which was opened
and shut as occasion required, admitted the waters of
the Nile into the lake[162]; and various canals conveyed them out of it, when necessary, in different directions[163].

dotus, not satisfied with calculating the *circumference* of this lake at full
three thousand six hundred stadia, in which Diodorus agrees with him,
(Id. ibid.) adds, by way of explanation, that its *circumference* was *sixty
schene;* and *equal* to the *length* of the *whole sea-coast of Egypt.* (Herodot. ubi supra). Strabo does not calculate the circumference of the
lake Mœris; but he says, it was *like a sea for magnitude*, and that *its
banks resembled the shores of the ocean. Geog.* lib. xvii p. 809. .

157. Strabo, lib. xvii. p. 809—811.

158. This last conjecture seems most probable, as the lake Mœris
extended far into the Libyan desert, in a western direction, between
the mountains of Memphis, and the Mediterranean sea. Herodot.
lib. ii. cap. cl.   159. Diod. Sicul. lib. i. p. 48. Strabo, lib. xvii.
p. 810.   160. Id. ibid.   161. Strabo, lib. xvii. p. 810, 811.

162. Diod. Sicul. et Strabo, ubi sup.

163. Id. ibid. According to the accounts of modern travellers, this
lake is now much diminished in size, as might have been expected.
But the canals still remain; and certain fens, in its neighbourhood,
seem to indicate that it was formerly much larger.

Sesostris

PART I.   Sesostris, or Sesoosis, the seventh Egyptian king after Mœris, surpassed all his predecessors in great achievements[164]. He is supposed, by sir John Marsham, and other chronologers, to be the Shishak, or Sesac, who plundered the temple of Jerusalem in the fifth year of the reign of Rehoboam[165]. And their conjecture seems well founded[166].

                                            This

164. Diod. Sicul. lib. i. p. 49.   165, i Kings, ch. xiv. ver. 25, 26.

. 166. This chronology is perfectly conformable to the succession of eight Egyptian kings, given by Herodotus, from Sesostris to Psammitichus; the beginning of whose reign is generally placed by chronologers in the six hundred and seventieth year before the christian æra. Nor does it interfere with the subsequent narration of that venerable historian, unless in one particular; and, in that, he is obviously inconsistent with himself; he says (and Diodorus agrees with him), that Proteus, the second successor of Sesostris, reigned in the time of the Trojan war. (Herodot. lib. ii. cap. cxii. et seq.) But in this he must have been misinformed, or mistaken one way or other; for the six kings, whose reigns, in his history, merely complete the period between Proteus and Psammitichus, could not possibly make the reign of that prince ascend so high as the siege of Troy. And other circumstances conspire to fix the reign of Sesostris to the æra here assigned it. The daughters of Danaus, we are told, fled from the sons of Egypt. (Herodot. lib. ii. cap. clxxxii.) Now Egypt, according to Diodorus, lived twelve reigns before Mœris (Biblioth. lib. i. p. 47.); and Sesostris was the seventh king after Mœris. (Ibid. 49.) These nineteen successions cannot be computed at less than five hundred years. Danaus and his daughters arrived in Greece about three hundred years before the Trojan war, (Marm. Oxon. Ep. 18.) consequently the reign of Sesostris must have been two hundred years later than that war, and not above a thousand years before the christian æra.

If farther argument should be deemed necessary, to prove that the great Sesostris was the Shishak, who pillaged the temple of Jerusalem, and "took away the treasures of the king's house," (i. Kings, chap. xiv. ver. 26.) they are ready. Herodotus informs us, that, in passing through the Syrian Palestine, he saw a pillar set up by Sesostris, indicating that the inhabitants had tamely submitted to his arms (Herodot. lib. ii. cap. cvi.) and Josephus owns, that Rehoboam permitted his capital to be entered by Shishak, without striking a blow in its defence; (Joseph. cont. Apian. lib. i.) To crown the whole collected evidence, sacred history acquaints us, that "in the fifth year of king "Rehoboam,

This politic and warlike monarch, whose reign forms the æra of the military power and glory of the ancient Egyptians, is said to have proposed no less an object for his ambition, than the conquest of the world[167]. And an army of six hundred thousand infantry, twenty-four thousand cavalry, and seven and twenty thousand armed chariots[168], corresponded with the grandeur of such an undertaking.

Having put that vast body, or whatever might be his force, in motion, Sesostris first invaded Ethiopia, which he conquered; imposing upon the inhabitants a tribute of gold, ebony, and ivory[169]. He next built,

"*Rehoboam*, Shishak, king of Egypt, came up against Jerusalem, " and took the fenced cities of Judah. And *the people were without* " *number that came with him;* the Lubims, the Sukkiims, and the " *Ethiopians.*" (ii. Chron. chap. xii. ver. 2, 3, 4.) Now Herodotus assures us, (lib. ii. c. cx.) that "*Sesostris* was *the only Egyptian mo-* " *narch,*" who ever *conquered Ethiopia:* therefore, he only could have a body of *Ethiopians* in his army. The Lubims and Sukkiims were probably some of those African nations, whom Sesostris is said to have conquered during his father's life-time (Diod. Sicul. lib. i. p. 49.) And the scope of the sacred narrative shews, that they were *vanquished nations,* swelling the host of a mighty conqueror, whose troops and attendants were without number (ii. *Chron.* ubi sup.); and in the sweep of whose operations the kingdom of Judah was subdued, and rendered tributary to Egypt. ii. Chron. chap. xii. ver. 8, 9.

167. Diod. Sicul. lib. i. p. 49.

168. Id. p. 50. The number of *cavalry,* here mentioned, seems to bear an *unequal proportion* to the *infantry.* But it ought to be observed, before we accuse Diodorus of inconsistency, that *chariots* were used in war before *horsemen;* (Goguet. *Orig. des Arts,* &c. part. i. liv. v. passim.) and that it was long before *cavalry* bore a *due proportion* to *infantry.* (Ibid. part ii. liv. v. chap. i. iii. et part iii. liv. v. chap. ii.) Sacred history, however, assigns to Shishak *threescore thousand horsemen,* and only *twelve hundred* chariots. (ii. *Chron.* chap. xii. ver. 3.) Herodotus is silent as to the number, or quality of the forces of Sesostris; but, like all other historians, says (lib. ii. cap. cii.) his army was *immense.*

169. Id. ibid. Herodot. (lib. ii. cap. cx.) and Strabo (lib. xvi. p. 769.) also mention the conquest of Ethiopia by Sesostris, though only in general terms.

on

on the Arabian, gulf, a fleet of four hundred sail;
which circum-navigated the Arabian peninsula, while
he enterd Asia with his mighty host[170]. Every nation
he attacked, in that vast continent, submitted to his
power[171]. We must not, however, believe, that he
passed not only the Euphrates and Tigris, but also the
Indus and Ganges, and subdued all the intermediate
countries; extending his sway from the Mediterranean
sea to the Eastern ocean, and from the Nile and the
Ganges to the Tanais and Danube[172]. Credibility is
startled at such a sweep of conquest; and the narra-
tive.of the venerable Herodotus, whose authority, in
regard to the affairs.of.ancient Egypt, ought to be
highly respected[173], leads us ·to more moderation.
He seems to confine the Asiatic conquests of Sesostris to Arabia, Syria, and Asia Minor[174]. And all

                         ancient

170. Diod. Sicul. lib. i. p. 50. Herodot. lib. ii. cap. cli.

171. Herodotus, ubi supra.

172. Diod. Sicul. lib. i. p. 50. Diodorus seems to have been here mis-
led by the vain traditions of the Egyptian priests; who, in his time,
appear to have confounded the exploits of Sesostris with the mystical
adventures of their tutelary god, Osiris. This similarity imposed upon
the great sir Isaac Newton, and made him conclude, that Osiris and
Sesostris were the same; (Newt. *Chron.* p. 191.) an opinion which has
been fully refuted by Dr. Warburton. (*Divine Legation of Moses,* book
iv. sect. v.) Mr. Bryant considers Sesostris as a personage as ideal
as Osiris. *New System of Ancient Mythol.* vol. ii.

173. Herodotus, like Diodorus, received his information from the
Egyptian priests (*Hist.* lib. ii. passim); but the Egyptian records, in
his time, were less corrupted. For the Egyptians, after their country had been subjected not only to the Persian, but to the Macedonian
and Roman sway, endeavoured to console themselves for the loss of
their former power and independency, by many fabulous relations of
their former greatness, both in arts and arms. (*Divine Legation,* lib.
iv. sect. v.) Hence the inextricable obscurity in which their history
is involved.

174. Herodotus, lib. ii. cap. cii. ciii. He indeed conjectures that
Sesostris had penetrated to the river Phasis, at the. east end of the
                                  Euxine

ancient historians assign Scythia and Thrace[175], as the boundaries of the arms of the Egyptian conqueror in Europe.

But whatever might be the extent of the conquests of Sesostris, it does not appear that he took effectual measures to preserve them, or that they descended to his posterity. His conduct was very different with respect to his hereditary dominions. Laying aside all thoughts of war, after his return to Egypt, he employed that leisure which peace afforded him, in securing it against invasion from Arabia and Syria, by a wall extending across the desert, its most exposed side, from the city of Pelusium, seated near the eastern mouth of the Nile, to Heliopolis, or the *city of the sun*[176]; which stood a little below the present Grand Cairo, and where the majestic river begins to divide itself into those channels, through which it enters the Mediterranean sea[177].

Euxine sea, and there left a colony, which gave beginning to the kingdom of Colchis (*Herodot.* lib. ii. cap. iv.) because the Colchians had dark complexions, frizzled hair, and used the rite of circumcision, in the manner of the Egyptians (Id. ibid.) But on this subject, he speaks with diffidence. And although Colchis appears to have been an Egyptian colony, history has left uncertain when that colony was planted. It seems, however, to have been prior to the Argonautic expedition; and, consequently, long before the reign of Sesostris, according to the chronology which I have followed, and about the time of the Egyptian emigrations into Greece under Cecrops and Danaus.

175. Thus far and no farther, says Herodotus (lib. ii. cap. ciii.), the Egyptian army seems to have advanced; and Diodorus (lib. i. p. 51.) corroborates his testimony.

176. Diod. Sicul. lib. i. p. 52.

177. The seven channels, or mouths of the Nile, are celebrated both in ancient history and poetry; but Herodotus (lib. ii. cap. xvii.) mentions only *five*, two of which were artificial, and no more than navigable canals; (Id. ibid.) an account that agrees perfectly with the relations of modern travellers.

. Nor was this the only care of Sesostris. Beside
many works of piety and ostentation; temples[178],
obelisks[179], and colossal statues[180], on which he had
the glory to say *no native laboured*, they being all erected by the captives he had led in triumph[181], he made
Egypt be intersected by an additional number of canals, communicating with the stream of the Nile, and
widely distributing its healthful and fructifying waters[182]; while he removed to higher situations such
towns as were liable to injury from the annual flux of
that river[183].

These illustrious labours, and the wealth acquired
by conquest, with which this magnificent monarch
had enriched his native kingdom[184], rendered the
name of Sesostris long dear to the Egyptians; who
considered him as the greatest king that had ever
reigned, even after they were subjected to the Persian
sway[185]. Nor had he neglected to perpetuate his fame
among foreign nations. Wherever, in the course of

178. He is said to have built in each of the chief cities of Egypt,
a temple to the god that was peculiarly adored there. Diod. Sicul.
lib. i. p. 51.

179. Sesostris erected two obelisks, each one hundred and twenty
cubits high (Diod. Sicul. lib. i. p. 53.), with hieroglyphical inscriptions, exhibiting the extent of his conquests, the amount of his reve-
nues, and the number of the nations he had vanquished. (Id. ibid.)
The Egyptian obelisks, the most extraordinary monuments of antiquity, were square pillars, composed of one stone, terminating in a
point. The granite of which they were formed was found in the
mountains of Syene, in Higher Egypt, (Pliny, lib. xxxvi. cap. viii.)
whence the immense blocks were conveyed by water, to the places
where they were to be erected. Calixenus, ap. Plin. lib. xxxvi. c. ix.

180. Before the temple of Vulcan, Sesostris erected six of those
statues; two of thirty-six cubits in height, representing himself and
his wife; and four, twenty cubits high each, representing his four
sons. Herodot. lib. ii. cap. cx. Diod. Sicul. lib. i. p. 53.

181. Diod. Sicul. lib. i. p. 52.   Herodot. lib. ii. cap. viii.

182. Herodotus, ubi supra.   183. Diod. Sicul. lib. i. p. 52.

184. Id. lib. i. p. 51.   185. Herodotus, lib. ii. cap. ex.
Diod. Sicul. lib. i. p. 54.

his

his conquests, he found a people, who strenuously defended their liberties, he had ordered a pillar to be
erected, with an inscription, declaring his name and
country, and that he had subdued them by his forces[186]..
And on the pillars set up in those districts, he ordered
also, says Diodorus, the sculptured figure of the male
parts of generation to be added, in testimony of the
courage of the inhabitants[187]. But where a nation
had meanly submitted to him, without hazarding a
battle, he commanded to be carved, along with the
usual inscription, the genital parts of a woman, on
such pillar, as a memorial of their cowardice[188].

In some countries, Sesostris likewise ordered his
own statue, in stone, to be erected; holding a bow in
the left hand, a javelin in the right, and otherwise
armed after the Egyptian and Ethiopian manner, with
a belt drawn across the breast from shoulder to shoulder[189]; on which was engraved, in the *sacred letters*
of Egypt[190], an inscription purporting, that he had
obtained,

186. Herodot. lib. ii. cap. cii. Diodorus has preserved a more
pompous inscription, to the following purport:—" Sesostris, king of
" kings, and lord of lords, conquered this region by his arms." Diod.
Sicul. lib. i. p. 51.

187. Diod. Sicul. lib. i. p. 51. 188. Herodot. et Diod. Sicul.
ubi sup. 189. Herodotus, lib. ii. cap. cvi.

190. Idem. ibid. These *sacred letters*, according to Dr. Warburton, were the most perfect kind of *hieroglyphics;* formed in the progress from *picture-writing* to the invention of *alphabetic characters;*
(*Divine Legation of Moses*, book iv. sect. iv.) and *afterward* used by the
priests as a *veil* for their *mystical learning*, as they had *formerly* been
employed, by all orders of men, in recording general transactions,
for want of a more intelligible mode of writing. (Id. ibid.) They
continued also to be used, after the invention of alphabetic characters,
on all public monuments of stone; (Warburton, ubi sup.) so that the
hieroglyphical inscriptions on the statues and obelisks of Sesostris prove
nothing in favour of the high antiquity of that monarch.

These observations, while they illustrate our subject, will serve to
rectify a common mistake among the learned; " that *hieroglyphics*
" were *invented* by the *Egyptian priests*, in order to *conceal* their *occult*
" *science*,

PART I. . obtained, by his personal prowess, the territory in which
the statues stood[191]. Herodotus saw two of these
statues in Asia-Minor; one between Ephesus and
Phocæa, and another between Sardis and Smyrna[192];
each six feet and three inches in height[193].

In consequence of the public works of Sesostris,
Egypt attained an higher degree of prosperity and population, than it had known in any former period[194]. For
he not only fertilized the country, and supplied the inhabitants with drink for themselves and their cattle, by
conveying the waters of the Nile at all times, to the parts
most distant from it[195], but cut navigable canals from

" science, after the art of alphabetic-writing was known and practised;"
where they were only a stage, as already observed, in the progress
toward that art, and afterward used for particular purposes. For
this discovery, the world is indebted to the late Dr. William Warburton, latterly bishop of Gloucester ; who united the most profound
erudition to a penetrating genius.

191. Herodotus, lib. ii. cap. cvi.   192. Id. ibid.

193. Herodot. ubi sup. Diodorus says these statues were exact representations of the *natural* statues of Sesostris, and seven feet high.
(*Biblioth.* lib. i. p. 51.) But he does not tell us whence he had his
information. Herodotus saw the statues, and probably measured them.

194. Egypt, in its highest prosperity, is said to have contained
eighteen thousand cities and considerable villages, and seven millions
of inhabitants; (Diod. Sicul. lib. i. p. 27.) a number by no means
incredible, considering the high cultivation, and fertility of the country.

Many reasons may be assigned, why Egypt is now less fertile than
in ancient times. The Nile no longer brings down from Ethiopia that
rich black mud and slime, which formerly fattened the lands; (Herodot. lib. ii. cap. xii. et seq. Diod. Sicul. lib. i. p. 30. Strabo, lib. xv.
p. 695. Plin. *Hist. Nat.* lib. xviii. cap. xvii. xviii.) and only a small
quantity of red earth, of an inferior quality, such as composes its
banks. (Granger, *Voyage en Egypt*, p. 20. Shaw's *Travels*, vol. ii.
p. 188.) Nor is the country any where so perfectly cultivated, or to
such an extent as under its ancient monarchs. (Maillet, *Descript de
l'Egypte*, let. i. ix.) Yet, even under Turkish despotism, Maillet com-
putes, that Egypt may contain four millions of people. (*Descript.* let.
i.) This gentleman resided long at Grand Cairo, as French consul.

195. Herodotus, lib. ii. cap. cviii.

the

the river to the chief cities below Memphis, for the benefit of inland commerce, and banked those cities
against the annual inundations[199]; so that Lower
Egypt, during the high flow of the Nile, to use a
simile of Herodotus, resembles the Egean sea, crowned
with its castled islands[197]. And during the season of
ebb, it presented, and still offers the most delightful,
spectacle that human imagination can conceive; rich
fields of corn, all kinds of fruit and flowers, and herds
and flocks feeding in luxuriant pastures[198]; while ships
of burden in the river, and barges on the canals, convey, in various directions, the produce of industry, and
the means of plenty, under a serene and cloudless sky,
genially warmed with the beams of the sun[199].

From

196. Diod. Sicul. lib. i. p. 52.

197. Herodot. lib. ii. cap. xcvii. Diodorus, who makes use of the
same comparison, was not ignorant that the Nile has its source in the
mountains of Ethiopia, and that its annual inundations are occasioned by the tropical rains. (*Biblioth.* lib. i. p. 39. edit. Rhodoman. ubi
cit. Hanov. 1604.) The Nile begins to rise about the end of April;
but the swell is not considerable till after the summer-solstice. (Herodot. lib. ii. cap. xix. Diod. Sicul. lib. i. p. 32. Plin. *Hist. Nat.* lib. v.
cap. ix. lib. xviii. cap. xviii.) According to ancient authors, it continued to increase till the autumnal equinox; (id. ibid.) but the most
accurate modern observers declare, that it usually attains its greatest
height by the middle of August. (Pococke, *Descript. of the East*, vol.
i. p. 200. Shaw's *Travels*, p. 383. Maillet, *Descript. de l'Egypte*, let.
ix.) By the first of November the inundation has subsided; the husbandmen then prepare the land for the reception of the seed; (auct.
cit. ubi. sup.) and reap their harvest in March and April. Id. ibid.

198. Diod. Sicul. lib. i. p. 32. Maillet, *Descript. de l'Egypte*, let. ix.
Egypt is by no means intensely hot during our winter season. Hence
it produces many fruits seldom found in such a southern latitude;
olives, grapes, peaches, &c. (Id. ibid. et Strabo, lib. xvii. p. 809.)
And during the summer months, it is refreshed by the inundation of
the Nile; the great source of its subsequent fertility, and the cause of
that deep verdure for which it is distinguished beyond all the neighbouring countries.

199. Diod. Sicul. lib. i. p. 52. Maillet, *Descript. de l'Egypte*, let. ii.
The Nile is at all times navigable as high as the cataracts, on the frontiers

PART I.   From the reign of Sesostris, to the interregnum
that preceded the elevation of Psammitichus, we have
a regular succession of Egyptian kings[200]; but their
reigns afford few important events.

Pheron, the son and successor of Sesostris, undertook no military enterprise; nor was he the author of
any civil institution. But having been afflicted with
the loss of his sight, which was restored in a miraculous manner, he dedicated many offerings in all the temples of Egypt, in gratitude to the gods for his recovery[201]; and, to perpetuate the memory of that event,
he erected, in the *temple of the sun* at Heliopolis, two
obelisks, each one hundred cubits high, and eight cubits square at the base[202].

tiers of Ethiopia, and about six hundred miles from the sea; where, says
Diodorus, (lib. i. p. 28.) the water runs with the rapidity of an arrow
shot from a bow; and being dashed against rocks, and forced back,
whirls, rages, and foams, in a manner terrible to behold. Id. ibid.

200. This succession is furnished by Herodotus; who, as I have
already had occasion to observe, possessed better means of information
than any subsequent writer. To the reasons formerly offered, in support of this opinion, I may add, that soon after the Persian conquest,
Herodotus travelled through Egypt, and held long discourses with
the priests; who were entrusted with the keeping of the archives of
the kingdom, and seem to have disclosed to him their most important
secrets; (Herodot. lib. ii. passim.) and that if the Egyptian records
had suffered injury from the rage of Cambyses against the temples
where they were kept, memory might then supply the defect. But
after those records had been seized, and carried off by order of Darius
Ochus, or Artaxerxes III. (Diod. Sicul. lib. xvi. p. 448, 449. vol. ii.
edit. Rhodoman. ubi cit.) the Egyptians themselves must have become
in a great measure ignorant of the history of their own country; as I
shall afterward have occasion to shew, when I treat of the seizure of
the records. False records were forged by priestcraft and vanity;
and from these it appears, the fabulous dynasties of Manetho were
composed. Nor could the judicious Diodorus, with the utmost zeal
for truth, always detect the delusion.

201. Herodotus, lib. ii. cap. cxi.   202. Id. ibid.

                                             Pheron

Pheron was succeeded in the Egyptian throne by Cetes, to whom the Greeks gave the name of *Proteus*[203]; because he was said to transform himself into a variety of shapes. This fable seems to have had its origin in a singular custom, which afterwards became common to the Egyptian monarchs. They wore upon their heads, as a sign of their royalty, and in order to inspire their people with superstitious veneration, the figure of a lion, a bull, or a dragon[204]. Cetes, the author of this custom, is reported to have been deeply skilled in the arts and sciences[205]; and divine honours were paid him, after his death, in an elegant temple, erected to the south of that of Vulcan, at Memphis[206].

Rhampsinitus, the successor of Cetes or Proteus, added a magnificent portico to the western side of the temple of Vulcan, and set up two statues before the front of the building, each twenty-five cubits high[207]. He was a wise and just prince; so that Egypt, during his reign, greatly flourished in plenty, and enjoyed, as hitherto, the equitable administration of her wholesome laws[208]. He is said to have descended, while alive, to the habitations of the dead; where, playing at dice with Ceres, he sometimes won, and sometimes lost[209]; by

203. Herodotus, lib. ii. cap. cxii. Diod. Sicul. lib. i. p. 56.
204. Diod. Sicul. lib. i. p. 56.   205. Id. ibid.
206. Herodotus, lib. ii. cap. cxii. I formerly said, that this venerable historian must have been misinformed in respect to the reign of Proteus, otherwise he would not have placed it so high as the Trojan war; and the account which he gives of that war, (lib. ii. cap. cxiii—cxx.) on the credit of the Egyptian priests, shews the whole was a fable, devised by those sacred sages, in order to exalt the character of their own nation; to maintain its claims to superior antiquity, and to recriminate upon the Greeks, who accused the Egyptians of offering human sacrifices.

207. Id. lib. ii. cap. cxxi.   208. Herodotus, lib. ii. cap. cxxiv.   209. Id. lib. ii. cap. cxxii.

which

which we ought perhaps to understand, that good and evil are *blended* in *all human conditions*, and that even the *just* and *wise* cannot expect, in this world, an *uninterrupted run* of *success*. And Ceres at his departure, we are told, presented him with a golden mantle[210]; as a mark of her favour, no doubt, because of his attention to agriculture, by which only plenty can be procured, and the blessings of civil life preserved.

The Egyptians annually held a solemn festival, from the day of the descent of Rhampsinitus, to that of his re-ascension[211]. Here Herodotus takes occasion to inform us, that the Egyptians believed the sovereign power in the state of the dead, was exercised by Ceres and Bacchus[212], or Isis and Osiris[213]; and that they were the first people, who taught the *immortality* of the *human soul*[214]. This tenet was more especially inculcated, as I shall often have occasion to shew, in the mysteries of Isis, or Ceres[215]; where the veil of heathen superstition being pulled aside, the true nature of God and the soul was *revealed* to the *initiated*, and the doctrine of a *future state* of *rewards* and *punishments* enforced[216].

Herodotus

210. Herodot. lib. ii. cap. cxxii.   211. Id. lib. ii. cap. cxxii.

212. Herodot. lib. ii. cap. cxxiii.

213. Herodotus takes great pains to prove, that Isis was the same deity with *Demeter* or Ceres, (lib. ii. cap. lix. clvi.) and Osiris with *Dionusos* or Bacchus: (lib. ii. cap. cxliv.) And he has at least proved, that the worship of both was nearly the same, in Egypt and in Greece; (ubi sup.) and given us good reason to believe, that the Greeks borrowed that worship from the Egyptians, (ibid.) not the Egyptians from the Greeks.

214. Herodot. lib. ii. cap. cxxiii.

215. The mysteries of Ceres were celebrated in various countries, beside Egypt; but the most famous were those solemnized at Eleusis, in the territory of Attica, commonly known by the name of the *Eleusinian mysteries*.

216. That these were the objects of the *Eleusinian mysteries*, and that
they

Herodotus also tells us, that the Greeks accounted *Bacchus, Hercules* and *Pan,* the *youngest of all the gods*[217]; but that the Egyptians considered PAN as " the *most ancient,* even of the *eight primary deities*[218]." This is a curious article of information, and

. . . .

they were of Egyptian origin, Dr. Warburton has proved, with great strength of reasoning, supported by many learned quotations. (*Divine Legation of Moses,* book ii. sect. iv.) He has also endeavoured to prove, that the same doctrines were inculcated in all the heathen mysteries; in those of Bacchus, and even in those of Venus; (id. ibid.) a position that cannot be so readily admitted. I shall, therefore, confine myself to the mysteries of Ceres, as celebrated at Eleusis. In those mysteries, an *hymn* to the following purport, was sung:—" I will " *disclose* a *secret* to the *initiated;* but let the doors be *shut* against the " *prophane.* Look on the *Divine Nature;* incessantly *contemplate it,* and " *govern well* the *mind* and *heart.* Go on in the *right way,* and see the " *sole Governor of the world.* HE is ONE, and *of Himself alone;* and to " that ONE all *things owe their being!*—HE *operates through all;* was " *never seen* by *mortal eyes,* but doth Himself *see every thing.*" (*Orphic Hymn,* ap. Clem. Alexand. *Admonit. ad Gentes,* and Euseb. *Prep. Evangel.* lib. xiii.) " Ceres," says Isocrates, " has made the Athenians " *two gifts* of the highest importance: the CULTURE *of* CORN, which " *brought us out of a* STATE *of* BARBARITY, and the MYSTERIES, " which *fortify* the *soul* against the *fear of death,* and *inspire* the *initi-* " *ated* with the *pleasing hope of an happy* IMMORTALITY." (Isocrat. *Paneg. Athen.*) " The thing" adds he, " which *human nature chiefly* " *stands in need of.*" (ibid.) And Cicero declares, " That those MYS- " TERIES, *by which we are drawn from an irrational and savage life,* " *and cultured in humanity,* are justly called INITIA ; because *they are* " *the beginning of a true life; a life of virtue and of reason!* Hence we " *not only* enjoy *happiness in this world, but die with tranquillity, in* " *hopes of becoming yet more happy in a future state of existence.*" Cicero *de Legib.* lib. ii. cap. xiv.

217. Herodotus, lib. ii. cap. cxlv.

218. Id. ibid. Herodotus had before made the same observation; (lib. ii. cap. xlvi.) but confined that belief to the *Mendesians,* or the inhabitants of the district of Mendes, in Lower Egypt. (Ibid.) Pan was the tutelary deity of the Mendesians. (Herodot. ubi sup. et Strabo, lib. xvii. p. 802.) " The Mendesian painters and sculptors, " like those of Greece," adds Herodotus, (lib. ii. cap. xlvi.) " repre-

and of the utmost importance for the explication of the whole system of heathen theology; which, as I shall have occasion to shew, passed from Egypt and Syria, into Greece.

These *eight primary deities*, were God and the *heavenly bodies; or the sun, moon*, and *five* solar planets, *Jupiter, Venus, Mars, Mercury* and *Saturn*, under the controul of the First Cause : for the ancients, at least in the first ages, were not sufficiently skilled in astronomy to know, that the earth is one of the solar planets. And the *four* additional deities, that completed the number of the *twelve* great gods, were, the *four elements* : by whatever names, or under whatever symbols, they might be worshipped[219]. Consequently PAN, or the *whole* of *nature* (as his name imports), the *eldest* of those *great gods*, was symbolical of the Creator and Governor *of the* universe, as *pourtrayed* in his *works*[220].

" sent Pan with the *face* and *legs* of a *goat :* Not that they believe *this* " to be his *real form*," remarks the venerable historian, " for *they* " *think him like other gods !*" (Ibid.) The natural interpretation of which words is, that they thought him an *incorporeal being ;* and, therefore, only capable of *symbolical representation.*

219. This subject I shall afterward have occasion to discuss. I shall therefore, only here remark, that the ancients, in adoring the *celestial bodies,* and the *elements,* did not worship them as *mere masses* of *matter,* but paid their adorations originally to the *Spirit,* by which they were supposed to be actuated or governed ; and that this worship, at first ejaculatory, came afterward to be offered through the intervention of *symbols,* and terminated in gross *idolatry.* See Pococke, *Specim. Hist. Arab.* passim, et Maimonid. *Moreh Nevoch.*

220. Servis, in Virgil, *Eclog.* ii. The *shaggy figure* of PAN was a symbolical delineation of *Nature* in her *rude state :* his *spotted robe,* of leopard's skin, represented the *spangled sky ;* and his person, made up of various parts, *rational* and *irrational,* a *man* and a *goat,* expressed the WORLD, composed of jarring elements, *fire, water, earth,* and *air,* under the direction of an *all-governing* MIND. Id. ibid.

The

The orphic hymn to PAN[221], while it justifies the
high character here assigned him, (as will appear from
the following extract) sublimely expresses the ideas of
the Egyptian priests, concerning that divinity ; for the
first Grecian sages are allowed to have drawn their
theology, and philosophy, immediately from Egyptian
sources[222].

" Thee I invoke, O mighty PAN!—the univer-
" sal Nature! the *heavens*, the *sea*, the *all-nourish-
" ing earth*, and the element *fire;* for these are thy
" *members, omnipotent* deity[223].—Come, thou source
" *of ever-wheeling motion! revolving* with the *circling
" seasons*[224]; parent of generation, divine *enthusiasm,
" and soul-warming transport!*—Thou *livest* among
" *the stars*, and *leadest* in the *symphony of the planets,*
" by thy *all-cheering music*[225]. Thou *scatterest visions,*
and

221. That the hymns ascribed to Orpheus, commonly called the
Orphic Hymns, are of great antiquity, we have the authority of Pausanias, (lib. ix. p. 305. edit. Xyland. Frankfort, 1588.) to affirm.
He tells us, that although inferior in elegance to those of Homer,
they were more reverenced in the religious ceremonies of Greece:
(Ibid.) and that those which have come down to us are genuine, we
know from ancient quotations.

222. They who have any doubts on this subject, may consult the
Divine Legation of Moses, vol. i. and Bryant's *Analysis of Ancient Mythol.* vol. ii. passim.

223. Or, as the same sentiment is more concisely expressed by our
philosophic poet:
" *All* are but *parts* of ONE stupendous *whole ;*
" Whose *body* NATURE *is*, and GOD the *soul.*"

224. This fine idea did not escape the poetic eye of Milton, whose
learning was equal to his genius : and who has wrought it into one
of the most beautiful images, in his description of Paradise.
————" Airs, vernal airs
" Breathing the smell of fields and grove, *attune*
" The trembling leaves; while *universal* PAN,
" *Knit with the graces and the hours in dance,*
" *Led on th' eternal spring.*"

225. Hence Pan was said *continually to play* upon a *mysterious* PIPE,
composed of SEVEN *unequal reeds*, but so fitted as to produce *together*
the

" and *sudden terrors, among mortals; delightest* in the
" *towering goat-browsed rock; in the springs also, and*
" *pastured vallies of the earth.* Of *sight all-pervading;*
" searcher *of hidden things;* lover *of the* echo of thine
" own *eternal* harmony[226]! *all-begetting* and *unbegot-*
" *ten* god!—*Supreme governor of the* world! invok-
" ed under a thousand *names*[227]."

Cheops,

the most perfect *melody.* (Servius in Virgil *Eclog.* ii.) This *pipe* was
symbolical of that *celestial harmony,* (metaphorically called the *music
of the spheres*) which results from the sublime and wonderful order of
the SEVEN great luminaries; (Id. ibid.) moving in *orbits of unequal
dimensions,* and performing their *revolutions* with*different degrees of velocity, but all* with *unerring concord.* Forever *singing, to the ear of the
philosophic mind,* " as they shine,".

The hand that made us is divine!

226. That is, *lover* of the *beauty* arising from the *harmony of the
universe.*

227. That the *enlightened part* of the ancient heathens believed in
ONE *eternal* GOD, under whatever name he might be worshipped; and
that the *created* deities, held up to the *adoration* of the *vulgar,* were
only the *attributes* of the *supreme self-existent Being;* the *celestial bodies,*
or the *elementary principles* of nature, mythologically represented as
his *ministers,* has been proved at great length by the learned Cudworth,
(*Intellectual System,* chap. iv.) and by the reverend Mr. Spence, (*Po-
lymetis,* Dialogue vi.) from the writings of the heathen poets and
philosophers.

This subject I shall afterward have occasion to investigate, and
illustrate, in tracing the *progress of idolatry;* so that it will be sufficient here to quote, from the hymn of Cleanthes to Jupiter, (Ap.
Poes. Philosoph. Grec. a H. Steph.) a passage in point.

" O! worshipp'd *under various sacred names,*
" DIVINITY SUPREME! *all-powerful God!*
" *Author of nature!* whose *unbounded reign,*
" And *legislative will* all things obey:
" The *heavenly orbs,* that *round this earthly sphere*
" *Incessant wheel,* thy *sovereign law* admit,
" And *roll spontaneous,* where THOU point'st the way,
" *Through all the realms of space;* obedient still!—
" Exalted above *all,* by *all* ador'd,
" *Strength, wisdom, goodness,* JUPITER! are *thine.*"

To this extract I shall add a fragment of Valerius Soranus, preserved by St. Augustine, (Ap. *Civitat. Dei.* lib. iv. cap. xi.)

" *Almighty*

Cheops, the successor of Rhampsinitus, was an impious and unfeeling tyrant, who trampled upon every thing sacred and civil. Having ordered all the temples of Egypt to be shut, and prohibited public sacrifices to the gods, he oppressed his people with hard labour; with digging and hewing stones, and building, beside other stupendous works, the first and largest of the three great pyramids in the neighbourhood of Memphis[228]. One hundred thousand men were employed, for twenty years, in rearing this ponderous mass[229]; and an inscription upon it declares, that a sum, equivalent to sixteen hundred talents of silver, had been expended in purchasing radishes, onions, and garlic, for the builders[230]. Cheops reigned fifty years[231].

" *Almighty* JUPITER! of men and gods
" *Father* and *mother* both :—ONE *Divinity!*"

228. Herodotus, lib. ii. cap. cxxiv. This pyramid I have already had occasion to describe (note 145.); but in order to revive the idea of its magnitude, I shall here observe, that its base, each side of which is exactly equal to its sloping height, forms a square of six hundred and sixty feet ; (auct. cit. ubi sup.) consequently it covers exactly ten English acres of ground. It appears to have been originally coated with marble; but now presents only a rugged surface, in which is discovered the layers of stone that compose the body of the building. Mallet, *Descript. de l'Egypte*, p. 224—253.

229. Id. ibid. These men were relieved every three months, by the same number of fresh hands; (Herodot. lib ii. cap. cxxiv.) so that the whole number of men called out by Cheops every nine months, to what may be called *statue-labour*, amounted to three hundred thousand.

230. Herodotus, lib. ii. cap. cxxv. This inscription is also mentioned by Diodorus Sicul. (lib. i. p. 58.) These vegetables probably composed the greater part of the food of the labourers, and perhaps all that was furnished them by the king; yet, admitting the workmen to have received no wages, the other parts of the expence, as Herodotus justly observes, (lib. ii. cap. cxxv.) for digging, squaring, and conveying the stones; the tools and apparatus for building, must have been immense. Ten years were spent in constructing the subterraneous chambers, or vaults, on which this wonderful fabric rests, and ten in erecting bridges, and making roads, for transporting the stones from the quarries in the Arabian mountains to the Nile, and from the Nile to the hill on which the pyramids were built. Id. ibid.

231. Herodotus, lib. ii. cap. cxxvii.

Chephrenes,

PART I. Chephrenes, the brother of Cheops, who succeeded to the Egyptian throne, on the death of that prince, imitated him in his impiety, as well as in his tyrannical oppressions[232]. He built the second great pyramid near Memphis[233]; equal to the first in height, but *without any subterraneous chambers*, and of inferior dimensions at the base[234].

All intelligent travellers, both ancient and modern, have considered these pyramids as sepulchral monuments, or mausoleums, for the kings by whom they were built[235]. But the learned antiquarian, Mr. Jacob Bryant, supposes them to have been temples; and conjectures, that from the *top* of the pyramids the Egyptians observed the heavens, marked the constellations; and *there* also "offered up vows and oblations[236]." This conjecture is ingenious, and consistent with Mr. Bryant's system of *solar worship*, but utterly void of probability; whether we consider the structure of the pyramids (without any door, by which they could be readily entered, or any stair-case, either within or without, by which they could be ascended) or consult ancient testimony concerning them. Herodotus, who early visited Egypt, and when the Egyptians were perfectly acquainted with the purpose of their public

---

232. Id. ib.   233. Herodot. ubi supra.

234. Id. ibid. et Diod. Sicul. lib. i. p. 57. I have already observed, that the first Memphian pyramid appears to have been coated with marble; and I have the authority of eminent travellers (Greaves, Thevenot, Lucas,) to say, that several Egyptian pyramids still are so coated.

235. Herodotus, Diodorus, Strabo, Pliny, Greaves, Pococke, Lucas, Thevenot, Maillet, &c.

236. *Analysis of Ancient Mythology*, vol. iii. p. 531. Mr. Bryant includes the *subterraneous apartments* among his arguments, to prove, that the Egyptian pyramids were *solar temples*. (Id. ibid.) The second pyramid, however, we find, had no such apartments, (Herodot. lib. ii. cap. cxxvii.) according to the information of the venerable father of history. Nor have modern travellers been able to discover any.

buildings,

buildings, never hints at such an opinion. He mentions
many Egyptian temples, and describes the sacred ceremonies, but not once insinuates that the pyramids had
any relation to religious worship. And the numbers of
pyramids, both in Higher and Lower Egypt, and in
the neighbourhood of each other, seem to prove, that
they were sepulchral monuments of the kings who
reigned at Thebes and Memphis[237].

Various conjectures, however, have been offered,
concerning the motives that could induce the Egyptian monarchs to raise such enormous fabrics, for their
place of burial. Ostentatious vanity, and tyrannic
policy, have been imputed to them[238]; and these
might have their share in swelling the size of the pyramids. But as those monuments were erected by
good, as well as bad princes, we must seek for other
inducements; and these we find in the theological tenets of the ancient Egyptians. They believed, that the
soul remained with the body after death, as long as
the body continued entire[239]. Hence the care which
persons of all ranks took in embalming the bodies of
their dead relations, and in depositing them in places
of strength and security[240]. For they considered their
habitations,

237. I have formerly had occasion to notice, that Thebes was originally the seat of the Egyptian monarchs, and afterward Memphis. And I shall here remark, that Egypt seems *hitherto* to have
been under *one* king, notwithstanding the various co-ordinate and
cotemporary dynasties invented by chronologers, in order to reconcile *sacred* and *prophane* history. *Moses, Herodotus* and *Diodorus*, knew
only ONE *Egyptian monarchy.*

238. Aristot. *de Repub.* lib. v. cap. xi. Plin. *Nat. Hist.* lib. xxxvi.
cap. xii.

239. Servius, ad Virgil. *Eneid.* lib. iii. ver. 67.

240. The Egyptians had three methods of embalming the dead,
which are particularly described by Herodotus; (lib. ii. cap. lxxxvi.
—lxxxviii) one for persons of superior rank, one for the middling class,
and one for people of low condition (Id. ibid). The first, and most
perfect method, I shall relate:

The

habitations, in this life, only as *transitory abodes*, while they gave to the intombs, by a bold mode of expression, the name of *perpetual mansions*[41].

In a country where such opinions prevailed, we cannot wonder that kings were desirous of giving to themselves a kind of eternity in the tomb. For this end, it was necessary to erect cemeteries, which could long resist natural decay, and preserve their bodies from ex-

The men, who made embalming their employment in Egypt, and who were publicly appointed to that profession, proceeded in this manner. They drew out the brains, through the nostrils, with an iron hook; cut open the belly with a sharp Ethiopian stone, and took out the intestines. These they replaced, after having cleansed them, steeped them in palm-wine, and cured them with odoriferous drugs. Then they filled the belly with pounded myrrh, cassia, and all kinds of aromatics, except frankincense, and sewed up the incision they had made. They next buried the body in nitre for seventy days; and, after they had taken it out, and washed it, they swathed it in fine linen, and anointed it with gums. Herodot. lib. ii. cap. lxxxvi.

Diodorus, who gives a similar description of the process of embalming, remarks, that when the body thus prepared, was restored to the relations of the deceased, the symmetry of form was perfectly preserved, and the likeness of features, even to the hair of the eye-brows, and eye-lids. (Diod. Sicul. lib. i. p. 82.) He also tells us, that many of the Egyptian grandees deposited the bodies of the dead in *magnificent* sepulchral *monuments*, and there delighted in contemplating the features of their ancestors, for centuries back; (Id ibid.) and that such Egyptians (of the middling class, it may be presumed) as had no family-sepulchre, formed a tomb in their own houses; placing the embalmed bodies of their relations in a cell of the *strongest wall*. (Id. lib. i. p. 83.) And we learn, from the observations of modern travellers, that the public sepulchres of the ancient Egyptians were dry and deep pits, or caverns, generally toward the Libyan mountains or desert, where the bodies, though embalmed in the cheapest manner, as being those of the inferior classes, still remain entire; and whence they have been carried to various countries, under the name of *mummies*.

241. Diod. Sicul. lib. i. p. 47. They accordingly paid little regard to the structure of their houses, but spared no expence in augmenting the magnificence of their sepulchres. (Id. ibid.) Nor was the care of the Egyptians to prolong the continuance of the soul with the body, inconsistent with their belief of the *immortality* of the *soul*, which was connected with the doctrine of the *metempsychosis*; (Herodot. lib. ii. cap. cxxiii.) a purgation that must have filled them with much horror.

ternal

ternal violence, and all moral contingencies. The pyramidal form was accordingly chosen, as better calculated for durability than any other. And strength and magnitude appear to have been added to the pyramids, in proportion to the fears of the Egyptian monarchs, of molestation after death[242]; to the ambition with which they were actuated, of perpetuating their name, by such stupendous monuments; and to the desire of bending, with heavy task, to the controul of regal sway, the proud and licentious spirit of their people, nursed in bigotry, and fattening in peace.

Mycerinus, the son of Cheops, who became king of Egypt on the death of Chephrenes, detesting the conduct of his father and uncle, ordered the temples to be opened[243]; the sacrifices to be renewed, and the people to apply themselves to their private affairs; releasing them from public tasks, and studiously attending to their happiness and prosperity [244]. He built, however, the third Memphian pyramid[245]; which some Grecian writers have vainly ascribed to the famous courtezan Rhodopis, who acquired great riches in Egypt by the sale of her favours[246].

Asychis, who ascended the Egyptian throne on the death of Mycerinus, built the grand portico of the

242. That the Egyptian monarchs, who governed oppressively, were in danger of such molestation, we have the authority of Diodorus to affirm (Diod. Sicul. lib. i. p. 66). And Herodotus tells us (lib. ii. cap cxxviii.), that the memory of Cheops and Chephrenes were held in such execration, that their very names were condemned to oblivion.

243. Herodotus, lib. ii. cap. cxxix.   244. Id. ibid. et Diod. Sicul. lib. i. p. 58.   245. Herodotus, lib. ii. cap. cxxxiv.

246. Id. ibid. Herodotus not only ridicules this idea (ubi supra), but shews that Rhodopis lived in a later age; that she was fellow-servant with Esop, the author of the Fables, and contemporary with Sappho, the poetess. And she contrived, he tells us (lib. ii. cap. cxxxv.), such a memorial of herself as had never been before imagined; sending to Delphos an offering of strong iron spits; which, adds he (ibid.), still stand in the temple, behind the altar bequeathed by the Chians.

PART I.

temple of Vulcan, fronting the east[247]. He also erected a pyramid of brick, with an inscription to the following puport :—" Degrade not me by a compa-"rison with the pyramids of stone, which I excel as "much as Jupiter the other gods[248]!"—And, in order to enlarge the credit of the Egyptians, among whom he found wealth imperfectly to circulate, he enacted a law, by which they were enabled to borrow money on the embalmed bodies of their fathers[249]; but with this restriction, that unless the debtor should redeem the sacred pledge before his death, neither he nor any of his descendants should be allowed funeral honours[250].

During the reign of Anysis, the successor of Asychis, Egypt was invaded by Sabaco, king of Ethiopia, at the head of a powerful army[251]. Sabaco obliged

247. Herodotus, lib. ii. cap. cxxxvi.   248. Id. ibid.

249. Herodot. ubi supra.   250. Id. ibid.

251. Herodotus, lib. ii. c. cxxxvii. Ethiopia was bounded on the north by Egypt, and on the north-east by the Arabian gulph; but with its other boundaries, the ancients were utterly unacquainted. (Strabo, lib. xvii. sub fin.) The Greeks gave the name of *Ethiopians* to all people of a *black colour*. Hence they had *oriental*, as well as *African* Ethiopians; but Herodotus (lib. vii. cap. lxix.) discriminates the one from the other, by marks which continue to distinguish them. " The *oriental* Ethiopians," observes he, " have *flowing hair*; but those " of *Africa*, the most *frizzled hair* of any race of men." (Id. ibid.) He also tells us (lib. ii. cap. civ.), that the Ethiopians were *circumcised*, like the Egyptians; but declares he could not pretend to determine which of the two nations first used the rite, though he was strongly persuaded, it had its origin in Egypt (ibid.). The Ethiopians, however, asserted, that they were the most ancient people in the world (Diod. Sicul. lib. iii. p. 143.); and as they believed, like many other nations, that men originally sprung from the earth, they not irrationally concluded, that those countries which lie nearest the sun, animated by his genial influence, must first have produced all kinds of animals (Id. ibid.). That they were a very ancient and powerful people is not to be questioned; but those on the frontiers of Egypt excepted (who seem to have profited by intercourse with their more polished neighbours, and to have been of the same stock), they

appear

liged the Egyptian monarch, who is said to have been blind, to seek refuge in the fens on the sea-coast, and took possession of the kingdom[252]. But he, instead of exercising the rigour of conquest, set an example of humanity to succeeding princes. No Egyptian was put to death for any transgression, during the reign of Sabaco[253]. He wisely issued an edict, when he seized the government, ordering persons convicted of capital crimes to be chained together, and employed in public works, instead of being led to execution[254].

The labour of these criminals consisted chiefly in cutting *canals*, and raising *mounds* with the earth dug out of them, in order to secure the cities of Lower Egypt from the inundations of the Nile[255]. Those mounds, which had been raised to a considerable height by the great Sesostris, were carried still higher by the mild policy of Sabaco[256]; who, uniting justice with mercy, and punishment with lenity, made the forfeited lives of his offending subjects contribute to the advantage of the honest and industrious citizen.

The benefits resulting from the canals must have been general; and several cities were, no doubt, more perfectly secured against any extraordinary flow of the river, by the mounds; which at once protected the former buildings, and afforded the new streets and squares more elevated situations[257]. But the city of

appear always to have remained in a rude, and most of them in a savage state (Herod. lib. iii. cap. xxii. xxiii. Diod. Sicul. lib. iii. passim. Strabo. lib. xvii. sub *Ethiop.*). Diodorus (ubi sup.) accurately distinguishes the proper Ethiopians from the Negroes, whose flat faces, woolly hair, brutal manners, and cruel disposition, he traces in strong lines.

252. Id. ibid. Sicul. lib. i. p. 59. Diod. Sicul. ubi sup. 257. Id. ibid.

253. Herodotus, lib. ii. cap. cxxxvii. Diod. 254. Id. ibid. 255. Herodot. et 256. Herodotus, lib. ii. cap. cxxxvii.

Bubastis

Bubástis was particularly indebted for its future prosperity and grandeur, to the labours of the malefactors
preserved from death by the humane edict of Sabaco[258].

In that city stood a temple dedicated to Diana,
whom the Egyptians called *Bubastis*, and the Greeks
Artemis, well worthy of notice. For, as Herodotus
(to whom we are indebted for the description of it)
ingeniously remarks, although some Egyptian temples
were larger, some more sumptuous, none gave more
pleasure to the spectator[259].

This beautiful fabric was erected on a peninsular
eminence, surrounded on all sides by the water of the
Nile, except at the avenue from the city to the portico
of the temple. The two canals by which it was
flanked (and which, without meeting, conveyed the
water from the river to both sides of the avenue),
were each one hundred feet wide, and overhung with
umbrageous trees. The portico was forty cubits in
height, and adorned with well-wrought statues six
cubits high. The temple itself stood in the middle
of the city, whence it every where attracted the eye.
And this distinction it had eminently maintained in
more ancient times; for when the ground which the
city of Bubastis afterwards covered, was raised by
the accumulation of earth dug out of the canals, the
temple of Diana remained on its original foundations,
unaltered, yet still conspicuous to the view. It was
encompassed with walls, on which were engraved
symbolic figures. Within the walls grew a huge
grove of venerable trees, out of the heart of which
rose the nave of the temple, containing the *sanctum
sanctorum*, or most sacred place, with the image, or

---

258. Herodotus, lib. ii. cap. cxxxviii.   259. Id. ibid.

symbol,

symbol, of the goddess. The whole temple was a furlong in length, and of the same extent in breadth. To the entrance under the portico, which fronted the east, ran a street, from the temple of Mercury through the market-place, near half a mile long, and four hundred feet wide, paved with marble, and planted, on each side, with trees that seemed to reach the clouds[260].

After Sabaco, or his sons as viceroys, had ruled the Egyptian monarchy for fifty years, he relinquished his conquest, and finally returned to Ethiopia[261], leaving the Egyptians in possession of their ancient independency. The causes of this singular event merit investigation.

The sacred sages told Herodotus, that Sabaco fled from Egypt in consequence of a dream[262], that a certain form stood conspicuous to his view in sleep, and admonished him to assemble all the Egyptian priests, and sever them by the middle; and that he, alarmed at the idea of such a crime, and considering the vision as a trial sent him by the gods, voluntarily abdicated the throne[263].

The most natural interpretation of that pretended dream is, that Sabaco found the members of the sacerdotal body, or sacred order in Egypt, become so powerful and factious, that he could no longer hold the reins of government, unless he had employed his military force to massacre them; and that being a prince of a religious turn of mind, as well as of a humane

260. Herodotus, lib ii. cap. cxxxviii. 261. Id. lib. ii. cap.
cxxxix. Diod. Sicul. lib. i. p. 59. 262. Herodotus, lib. ii. cap.
cxxxix. 263. Id. ibid.

disposition,

disposition, he chose rather to abandon the kingdom, than be guilty of such cruelty and impiety[264].

On the departure of the Ethiopian conqueror, Anysis quitted his retreat in the fens, and resumed the government of Egypt[265]. But as he must then have been old, his future reign could not be long. And after his death, the kingdom was governed by Sethon, high-priest of Vulcan[266]; who, depending upon the awe inspired by his sacred character, and the influence of the sacerdotal body, disregarded the military order, and seized the lands appropriated for the maintenance of the army[267]. The consequence of this unkingly policy (dictated by a contempt for the mass of the people, hoodwinked by superstition, and a jealousy of the soldiery) was such as might have been expected. When Sennacherib, emperor of Assyria, afterward invaded Egypt, no military man would stand forth in defence of Sethon[268]. But the Assyrian monarch, who was probably bribed to with-

264. This interpretation is countenanced by the narrative of the judicious and penetrating Diodorus (lib. ii. p. 59). It makes the tutelary god of Thebes appear to Sabaco in a dream, and inform him, that the massacre of the priests, by his guards, only could secure the future prosperity and happiness of his reign over Egypt. (Id. ibid.) Hence his resolution of returning to Ethiopia.

265. Herodotus, lib. ii. cap. cxl.   266. Id. lib. ii. cap. cxli.
267. Id. ibid.

268. Herodotus. lib. ii. cap. cxli. This venerable historian calls Sennacherib, or *Sanacharib*, as he writes the name, " king of *Arabia* and *Assyria*." (Ibid.) And we are informed by the sacred records (2. Kings, chap. xviii. xix.), that Sennacherib had subdued, in his march, the greater part of Lower Syria ; which was often comprehended, by the early Greek writers, under the general name of *Arabia*, and seems always to have been considered as an Arabian district by the Egyptians. The tributary princes of this country, as we shall have occasion to see, were perpetually revolting from the Assyrian emperors, and leaguing themselves with the kings of Egypt.

draw

draw his forces, is said to have been obliged to retire by a miracle[269].

The story was thus told by the Egyptian priests to Herodotus. Sethon finding himself destitute of human support, had recourse to divine aid. He betook him, in his distress, to the temple of Vulcan; and prostrating himself before the altar of the god, deprecated the calamities he was in danger of suffering. Amid his devotions he fell asleep, and was exhorted by the presiding deity, who appeared to him in a dream, to take courage, and face the invaders: for, if he so did, auxiliaries should be sent him[270]. Animated by the propitious vision, Sethon assembled the artificers, traders, retainers upon the courts of law, and people of all classes that would follow him, and marched into the Pelusian district. But he had no occasion to hazard a battle; for field-mice, actuated with rage against the enemy, had entered the Assyrian camp in the night, and gnawed the quivers, bows, and thongs of the shields, of the hostile army:

269. Id. ibid. Josephus tells us (lib. x. cap. i.), That Sennacherib had undertaken the siege of Pelusium; and that he abandoned his enterprize when ready to give the grand assault, and returned back, on hearing that Tharsikes, king of Ethiopia, called *Tirhakah* in sacred history, was marching with a numerous army to the assistance of the Egyptians; and meant to cut off his retreat, by taking the route of the desert (Id. ibid.). But we learn from higher, and cotemporary authority, that Egypt was ravaged, and Tirhakah defeated by Sennacherib: "The king of Assyria," says the prophet Isaiah (chap. xx. ver. 4, 5.), "shall lead away the Egyptian prisoners, and "the Ethiopian captives, and *they* (i. e. the Jews) shall be *ashamed* of "*Ethiopia*, their *expectation*, and of *Egypt*, their *glory*." (Id. ibid. et 2. Kings, chap. xviii. xix.) The conjectural cause, which I have assigned for the retreat of the Assyrian conqueror, therefore, seems as probable as any. For if Sennacherib had finally retired, at the intelligence of the arrival of Tirhakah, to the assistance of the Egyptians, an event which actually took place, Sethon could have found no pretext for ascribing his deliverance to a miracle.

270. Herodotus, lib. ii. cap. cxli.

so that Sennacherib, naked and defenceless at morning, was obliged to fly in confusion, and *lost many men* in his retreat[271].

In commemoration of this miraculous event, a marble statue of Sethon, holding a *mouse* in his right hand, was erected in the temple of Vulcan; with these words, on a label, proceeding from his mouth: —" Let every one that beholds me, learn to be pious[272]!" —

After the reign of Sethon, Egypt experienced a shock of anarchy, which was followed by a kind of aristocratical interregnum; the government of the kingdom being divided among twelve chiefs, seemingly the heads of the military order; each of whom presided over his particular district, and among whom a community of interests was established[273]. These twelve kings, or governors, ruled for a time with great harmony[274]; and erected, at their common expence, the famous Egyptian LABYRINTH[275], which Herodotus esteemed the most superb monument of architecture.

" Although I confess," says he, " that the temples " of Ephesus and Samos merit particular attention, "this is evidently a work of *greater labour* and *expence.* " The Egyptian pyramids are beyond expression " magnificent, and singly equal in magnitude to many " of the largest structures in Greece; yet is the

271. Id. ibid. The sacred records, however, give a very different account of the loss which the army of Sennacherib suffered in its return from Egypt (2. *Kings*, chap. xix. ver. 7.), as I shall afterward have occasion to relate.

272. Herodotus, lib. ii. cap. cxii.   273. Id. lib. ii. cap. cxlvii. Diod. Sicul. lib. i. p. 59.   274. Id. ibid.   275. Herodotus, lib. ii. cap. cxlviii.

labyrinth

" labyrinth more worthy of admiration than the pyra-
" mids[276]." It contained twelve spacious halls, mysteriously communicating with each other, and with
fifteen hundred apartments of various dimensions, all
encompassed by one wall, and closely roofed with
stone[277].

Below ground were an equal number of apartments[278]; but, those being appropriated to sacred
uses, travellers were not permitted to see them[279];
therefore, we have no description of them. The roofs
and walls of the apartments above ground, were en-
crusted with white marble, and adorned with figures
in sculpture. The halls were surrounded within with pillars of the same marble, finely polished[280].
And at the angle, where the labyrinth ended, was
erected a pyramid two hundred and forty feet high;
on which were sculptured colossal figures of animals,
and into which there was a subterraneous passage[281].

The Egyptian labyrinth stood near Crocodeilon, or
the *city of Crocodiles*, afterward known by the name of
Arsinoe; which was situated on the western side of the
Nile, a little above the lake Mœris, in Libya[282]. But
that harmony among the twelve chiefs, which gave
birth to so wonderful a structure, was not permanent,
notwithstanding this stupendous memorial of it. The
prosperity of Psammitichus, whose jurisdiction lay on
the sea-coast, excited the jealousy of his colleagues[283].

276. Id. ibid.
277. Herodot. ubi sup. This building is also described by Diodorus and Strabo ; but I have confined myself to the description of the
venerable father of history, who saw it in its more perfect state ; and
who, as it afforded him great cause of admiration and wonder, seems
to have examined it with peculiar attention.
278. Id. ibid.   279. Herodotus, lib. ii. cap. cxlviii.
280. Id. ibid.   281. Herodotus, ubi sup.   282. Id.
Ibid. et Diod. Sicul. lib. i. p. 60.   283. Diod. Sicul. ubi sup.

PART I.

Ant. Ch.
670.
Nabonas-
sarean
æra, 77.

They excluded him from any share in the general government of the kingdom, and confined him to his own district[284]; yet he, by the help of foreign troops, made himself master of all Egypt[285]; and gave to the Egyptian name a lustre which it had not known since the days of Sesostris.

The particulars of this revolution, which opened a ready intercourse between Egypt and Greece, I shall afterward have occasion to relate[286]. At present, I must offer to your lordship an account

OF THE GOVERNMENT, LAWS, RELIGION, LEARNING, MANNERS, AND ARTS, OF THE ANCIENT EGYPTIANS.

THE Egyptian government was monarchical, and the king was revered as a god; but his authority was subordinate to the laws[287]. By the laws he was obliged

284. Id. ibid. et Herodot. lib. ii. cap. cli.

285. Herodotus, lib. ii. cap. clii. Diod. Sicul. lib i. p. 60.

286. It was accomplished six hundred and seventy years before the Christian æra, and in the seventy-seventh year of the Nabonassarean æra. The date is thus ascertained. Diodorus Siculus informs us (lib. i. p. 62. edit. Rhodoman.), that Cambyses, king of Persia, conquered Egypt in the third year of the sixty-third Olympiad, when Parmenides of Camarina was victor in the stadion; and Herodotus gives us a regular succession of Egyptian kings, the *years* of whose *reigns* he has distinctly marked, from the elevation of Psammitichus to the Persian conquest (Herodot. lib. ii. cap. clvii.—clxxii. et lib. iii. cap. x.—xiv.). The sum of the years of the reigns of those kings fix the beginning of the reign of Psammitichus; which may be called the *true* EGYPTIAN ÆRA.

If Herodotus had marked the *years* of the *reigns* of *all* the *Egyptian kings, of whom he has given a regular succession,* from Sesostris downward, we might have carried the chronology of this ancient kingdom as high as the accession of that victorious monarch. But as the father of history has not so done, the Egyptian chronology, before the reign of Psammitichus, is, in a great measure, *conjectural*.

187. Diod. Sicul. lib. i. p. 63. " The *first kings of Egypt*," observes Diodorus (ibid.), " *did not govern, like other monarchs, according to their*

" own

liged to rule, and even to regulate his private conduct
more exactly than the meanest subject; certain hours
being set apart in the night, as well as in the day,
wherein he was enjoined to do something prescribed
by the constitution[288]. Hence stated times were appointed not only for the dispatch of public business,
but for the king's taking the air, bathing, sleeping
with the queen, and almost every function in life[289].
The very quality of his food was fixed, and his wine
dealt out by measure[290].

The Egyptian monarchs rose by break of day, and
read in the morning the dispatches from all quarters,
that they might be enabled to give the necessary instructions to their ministers[291]. They then washed
themselves, and having put on their robes, with the
ensigns of royalty, they went to the temple, attended
by their courtiers, in order to sacrifice to the deity[292].
The manner of so doing is sufficiently curious to require description; especially as it furnishes us with an
account of the public worship of the ancient Egyptians.

When the victims were brought to the altar, the
high-priest prayed, with a loud voice, for the health

"*own arbitrary will*, without being subject to censure or controul."—
Here I must remark, that by these *first kings*, we are to understand the
native monarchs of Egypt, before the conquest of that country by the
Persians; and consequently, those of whom I am at present speaking.
  288. Id. ibid.   289. Diod. Sicul. ubi sup.
  290. Idem. lib. i. p. 64. " It was indeed strange," remarks Diodorus, " that *the king should not be left at liberty* in regard to his *daily food;*
" but it was still more extraordinary, that *he could not punish any man*
" *to gratify his humour or passion*" (*Biblioth.* ubi sup); a striking instance of the high idea the ancients had of monarchical power!—And,
by a necessary chain of reasoning, of the *tyrannical manner* in which
it was *generally exercised*. Hence, no doubt, the detestation in which
it was held by the Greeks and Romans.
  291. Diod. Sicul. lib. i. p. 63.   292. Idem. lib. i. p. 64.
                                                            and

and prosperity of the king, recounting his virtues;
his piety towards the gods; his kindness to his people,
his temperance, justice, magnanimity, and good faith;
his lenity in punishing offenders, and his liberality in
rewarding merit[293]. He next denounced a curse upon such crimes and miscarriages as the monarch might
have ignorantly committed; charging the guilt and
blame upon his ministers and counsellors[294]. After
the king had examined the entrails of the victims, and
offered the sacrifice of atonement, a priest or scribe
read, out of the *sacred books*, the edicts, laws, and
meritorious actions of those Egyptian monarchs, who
had reigned most illustriously in their several ages,
that the prince upon the throne might profit by their
example, adhere to their maxims of government, and
respect the principles of the constitution[295].

The Egyptian monarchy was divided into thirty-
six *nomi*, or provinces, each of which had its proper
governor; who levied the royal revenue, and was invested with the administration of public affairs within
his district[296]. Ten of these provinces lay in Higher
Egypt, sixteen in Middle Egypt, and ten in Lower
Egypt[297].

Beside this political division, the territorial property of all the lands of Egypt, was divided into three

293. Id. ibid.   294. Diod. Sicul. lib. i. p. 64.
295. Id. ibid. This I conceive to be the sense, though not the literal meaning of the words of Diodorus.
296. Diod. Sicul. lib. i. p. 50.
297. Strabo, *Geog.* lib. xvii. p. 787. To make us sensible these divisions were not made by the Persian emperors, or Macedonian monarchs, the same geographer observes, that the Egyptian monarchy
was thus divided *from the beginning* (Id. ibid.); that is to say, from
the most ancient times of which he had any information. And it
seems highly probable, that Egypt was divided into provinces by
Menes, its first king; but the division here mentioned, into thirty jurisdictions, Diodorus affirms was made by Sesostris. *Biblioth.* lib. i. p. 50.

portions;

portions; the first being allotted to the priesthood, for
their maintenance, and the furnishing of public sacrifices; the second to the king for the support of his
houshold, the exigences of war, and the expence of
the civil establishment; the third to the national milita
or soldiery, instead of pay[298]. The king, and the
members of those two bodies, let their lands to the
husbandmen, at a fixed rent[299]; so that no subject
in Egypt, unless such as belonged to the ecclesiastical
or military order, had any property in land. And as
power naturally follows property, the bad effects of such
arrangement may be easily conceived.

298. Diod. Sicul. lib. i. p. 66, 67. The reasons offered by Diodorus, why so large a portion of land was assigned to the soldiery, are
very satisfactory. "Attached to their country," says he, "by that
"plentiful share, they more cheerfully undergo the hazards of war.
"For it would have been absurd to have intrusted the safety and pre-
"servation of the kingdom, to men who had nothing in their coun-
"try that was dear or valuable to them. And a weightier reason,"
adds he, "why so large a share was allotted to them, is this; that
"they might be induced to marry, and rear children; so that
"there might be no need of foreign troops" (*Biblioth.* lib. i. p. 67.).
This last argument has peculiar force, as applied to the kingdom of
Egypt, where all professions were hereditary; and where consequently, the army could only be recruited with the sons of soldiers.
But that those would be more brave and expert than volunteers,
or such as from natural inclination chose a military life, can by no
means be admitted. The son of the most valiant warrior, unallured
by his father's exploits, may have no turn for war: his genius may
incline him to the offices of civil government; but from these he
was excluded in Egypt. He may be fitter to attend a flock of sheep,
or a herd of cattle, than to command a battalion, or to lead an army
to battle. But the Egyptians thought differently. Diodorus has attempted to vindicate their policy; not only in this instance, but in
their whole scheme of hereditary professions; as contributing at once
to public quiet, and to the advancement of professional excellence.
And modern writers have generally subscribed to his opinion.

299. Diod. Sicul. lib. i. p. 67. They must also have let their lands
to the graziers, or feeders of sheep and other cattle, as these formed
a distinct class in Egypt, and had no land-property.

In

PART I.   In consequence of that territorial appropriation, the members of these two orders only had any share in the government; the members of every other order being confined to their proper calling, and prohibited from interfering in public affairs[300]. This we may consider as an usurpation of the two higher orders in league with the crown; for we are told there was a time, when the whole body of the Egyptians voted at the election of a king[301], in case of an interregnum, or where the lineal·successor was judged unworthy of swaying the sceptre; and that, in such election, they paid no regard to rank[302]. But from the æra of this new state of property and policy, the election, on these occasions, must have been made by the ecclesiastical and military orders exclusively.

From one or other of these two orders, the king could only be elected; and as the power of the priesthood or soldiery predominated, the prince appears to have been either a bigot or a warrior[303]. The Egyp-

---

300. Id. ibid. Struck with the turbulence of ancient republics, and the corruption into which democratic government was fallen, Diodorus applauds the Egyptian policy in confining every citizen to his particular profession, and prohibiting the people from intermeddling in public affairs. (ibid.). But the citizens of Great-britain have too high a sense of their own dignity, to be enslaved by such maxims; and I should be unworthy of the character of a British citizen, to inculcate them.

301. Diod. Sicul. lib. i. p. 41.   302. Id. ibid.

303. When this martial spirit was not exerted in foreign enterprise, it sometimes became the instrument of domestic tyranny (Herodot. lib. ii. cap. cxxiv—cxxx.); notwithstanding the barriers of the Egyptian constitution, which were those of limited monarchy. For no checks upon prerogative, unless imposed by the collective body · of a nation, will ever be found effectual. Nor can the guardianship of public privileges and immunities ever be placed in worse hands than those of priests and soldiers. Warped by the prejudices of their particular professions, whatever share they may have in the territorial property, or in the government of the kingdom, the characteristic features of each will still be prominent. Experience has proved this in all ages, and in all countries.

tian

tian monarchs, however, were generally under the dominion of the priesthood[304]; hence the unwarlike, and superstitious character of the nation[305]. Nor could it be otherwise ; for the ecclesiastical order seems to have filled all civil offices in Egypt[306]; from the ministers of state, down to the collectors of the public revenue[307]. That civil authority, with the possession of one-third of the lands of the kingdom exempt from taxes[308], must have given the priesthood great influence, independent of the awe inspired by their sacred function, and their privilege of interpreting the will of the gods. But this subject I shall have farther occasion to consider, in treating of the Egyptian religion.

Justice was regularly administered in Egypt by a president and thirty judges, whose salaries were paid by the king[309]. No advocates were allowed to plead

304. An effort to throw off this ecclesiastical dominion, seems to have driven Cheops to shut up the Egyptian temples (Herodot. lib. ii. cap. cxxiv.) ; and a desire of bending the body of his people to royal authority, and civil obedience, without the aid of superstition, might perhaps induce him to impose upon them those tasks, which have been *represented* as so grievous (Id. ibid. et Diod. Sicul. lib. i. p. 58.). I say *represented;* for the account of those oppressions, and the whole history of Egypt, was delivered to Herodotus and Diodorus by the priests; who would naturally delineate, in the darkest colours, every defect in the character of the princes that were inimical to their order.

305. That this was the general character of the Egyptians, is sufficiently attested by facts, both in the early and later periods of their monarchy. Their military men were never able to repel any invader; and the conquests they are said to have made were transitory.

306. Diod. Sicul. lib. i. p. 66. Strabo, lib. xvii. p. 787. Elian. *Var. Hist.* lib. xiv. cap. xxxiv.

307. Clem. Alexand. *Strom.* lib. vi.

308. The lands of the soldiery, we are told, were also exempted from taxes (Herodot. lib. ii. cap. clxviii.) ; so that the whole weight of the land-tax, in Egypt, must have fallen upon the husbandmen and graziers.   309. Diod. Sicul. lib. i. p. 68.

before

before them: nor were the persons prosecuted permitted to speak in their own defence, or plaintiffs or accusers in support of their own cause, that eloquence or sympathy might not bias the judgment of the court[310]. The whole process was carried on in writing[311]; and, in order to prevent the protracting of suits, an answer on the part of the defendant, and one reply only was indulged on each side[312]. The judges consulted together, after both parties had been heard, before they proceeded to judgment; and the president turned an emblematical picture of *Truth*, which he wore upon his breast, toward the party in whose favour the decision was given[313].

The spirit of the laws of Egypt was worthy of that solemnity with which they were administered. Respecting the natural liberty of man, they allowed a creditor to seize the property, but not the person of a debtor[314]. In order, however, to temper the mildness of this law, every Egyptian was commanded to give in annually, to the governor of the province in which he resided, an attestation of his name, profession, and the means of his subsistence; and whoever

---

310. Idem. p. 69.　　　311. Id. ibid.　　　312. Diod. Sieul. lib. i. p. 69.

313. Id. ibid. This picture, encircled with precious stones, was suspended by a gold chain, that hung round the president's neck (Id. p. 68.). The image of *Truth* was represented with *closed eyes* (Diod. Sicul. lib. i. p. 45.); thereby signifying, that judges, in the discharge of their office, ought impartially to weigh the merits of the cause before them; blind to every circumstance but truth, and every object but justice.

314. Diod. Sicul. lib. i. p. 71. Whatever doubts may be stated, in regard to the policy of this law, its humanity cannot be called in question. The humane spirit of the Egyptian laws is also conspicuous in another instance, which has served as an example to all civilized nations: women convicted of capital crimes were not permitted to be executed, until they had been delivered. Diod. Sicul. lib. i. p. 70.

forged

forged such certificate, or could not make it appear that he lived by an honest calling, was punished with death[315]. The punishment of death was also decreed against perjury; which the Egyptians considered as a most atrocious crime, as injurious at once to the gods and to men; to the gods, for impiously bringing their divinity into question; and to men, by destroying the strongest bands of human society, veracity and good faith[316]. On a similar principle, false accusers were condemned to suffer the punishment that would have been inflicted on the persons against whom the accusation was brought, if they had been convicted[317].

Adultery was severely punished in Egypt: with a thousand stripes in the man; and in the woman, with the loss of her nose[318]. They who revealed to a public enemy, the secrets of the state, had their tongues cut out; and those that counterfeited the current coin of the realm, the king's seal, the signatures of private persons, or forged deeds, with such as diminished the weight of money, were condemned to lose both their hands[319]. Wilful homicide was punished with death,

315. Id. p. 69, 70. 316. Diod. Sicul. lib. i. p. 69.
317. Id. ibid.

318. Diod. Sicul. lib. i. p. 71. If this, and some other Egyptian laws, should be thought cruel, they were at least calculated to obtain the great end of all penal laws, the prevention of crimes. For, as Diodorus well observes (ubi supra), on the present case, " it was fit " that the adultress, who attired herself in order to allure men to wan- " tonness, should be punished in that part where her charms chiefly " lay." Nor will the influence of such punishment upon manners, be disputed by the most devoted admirer of beauty; nor by the licen- tious libertine, who prides himself in disturbing the peace of fami- lies; and who, for the sake of his lawless pleasurse, would perhaps hazard a thousand lashes at the cart's tail.

319. Id. ibid. " That every one might be punished," says Diodo- rus (ubi sup.), " in those members with which he had offended." Upon the same principle, he that was convicted of having committed a rape upon a free-woman, had his privy parts cut off. Id. ibid.

whether

whether the person killed happened to have been in a state of freedom, or of slavery[320].

From this statute it appears, that as no man in Egypt, however elevated in his condition, had the power of vengeance in his own hands, so none was below the protection of the laws[321]. The prince and the peasant were equally amenable to justice; the minister of state, and his most abject bond-servant. And what is yet more memorable and praise-worthy (as it must have proved a strong incentive to virtue, as well as a restraint upon vice), neither the sovereign, nor his meanest subject, could enjoy a reputation after death, that had not been justly merited while in life. For the operation of the laws of Egypt was not confined to the period of existence.

To be deprived of funeral honours, so highly valued by all ancient nations, the Egyptians considered as the greatest possible disgrace; yet could none of them expect to enjoy those honours, unless by a public and solemn decree[322]. This decree was pronounced by a court of inquest; consisting of forty judges, of high reputation for probity; who listened to all accusations against the person deceased, and denied him public burial, if it appeared that he had been a bad member of society[323]. But if no stain was fixed upon his memory, his relations were permitted to bury

320. Diod. Sicul. lib. i. p. 70.

321. Of this we have an early and striking instance, in the adventure of Joseph with Potiphar's wife (*Gen.* chap. xxxix. ver. 7—20.). Potiphar, one of the great officers of the court of Egypt, though convinced that Joseph, his bought slave, had made an attempt upon his wife's virtue, at which "his wrath was kindled," did not offer violence to his person; but sent him to prison, that he might be punished according to law. Id. ibid.

322. Diod. Sicul. lib. i. p. 82.　　　　323. Id. lib. i. p. 83.

him

him with as much funeral pomp as they thought proper[324].

Nor were the Egyptian monarchs, as already observed, exempted from that awful jury. On the day appointed for the royal funeral, a court of inquest, according to law, was held. There all complaints and accusations against the deceased monarch, were re-

[324]. Id. ibid. Diodorus tells us, on the authority of the Egyptians, that from this custom of giving sentence upon the actions of the dead, and the ceremonies with which the Egyptian funerals were accompanied, the Greeks borrowed their doctrine of a future state of rewards and punishments (*Biblioth*. lib. i. p. 82—84.). And all modern writers have considered his report as infallible evidence. But if we reflect, that the belief of the immortality of the soul was universal in the heathen world, as it is at this day among savage nations, we shall find no reason for subscribing to such an opinion. The belief of a future state is necessarily involved in that of the immortality of the soul; and as soon as society was established, moral distinctions formed, and civil and criminal laws instituted, the notion of rewards and punishments, in an after-state, would naturally become, as we find it, part of the popular creed in every country.

They who question what I have affirmed, that the belief of the immortality of the soul, and of a future state, is now held by the most savage nations, may consult *Hist. Gen. des Voyages*, passim; but especially tom. xv. init. Robertson's *Hist. of America*, book iv. Hutchinson's *Hist. of Massachusett's-Bay*, chap. vi. and the authors there cited. That it was universally taught among ancient nations, and consequently believed by the body of the people, I shall afterwards have occasion to prove. I shall, therefore, only here remark, that Diodorus, seemingly disgusted with the popular creed of Greece, and desirous to give a mortal origin to all the heathen gods, upon the plan of Euhemerus, takes every opportunity of assigning a frivolous origin to religious opinions.

In apology for this otherwise judicious historian it may be urged, and with great justice, that he lived near the beginning of the Christian æra, when heathen worship was greatly corrupted;—to such a degree, that Divine Wisdom then saw fit to promulgate a NEW RELIGION; in which the *doctrine* of the *immortality of the soul*, and that of a *future state of rewards and punishments*, are *more clearly* set forth, and *connected*, not only with *moral conduct*, and *civil obligations*, but with the *purity* of the *heart*.

ceived.

ceived. And if it was found that he had been a good
prince, the whole multitude of his subjects, assembled
on the occasion, accompanied with loud acclamations
the priest who pronounced his panegyric; but if it appeared that his administration had been cruel or oppressive, an universal clamour, or murmur of disap-
probation, ensued[325]. Hence many Egyptian kings were
deprived of funeral honours by the voice of the nation,
and their bodies exposed to public insult[326].

These laws and institutions command our veneration,
whether we consider them in a moral or political view;
and give us a very high idea of the sagacity of the ancient Egyptians. But the system of Egyptian government had, as formerly noticed, some radical de-
fects. It did not sufficiently restrain the power of the
priesthood. Egypt groaned under a debasing superstition.

This remark leads us, my lord, to investigate the
natural origin of RELIGION; and the moral causes that
have contributed to its establishment, among all civilized nations.

The adoration of ONE GOD, the *Creator of the universe*, and the *supreme Disposer of all events*, requires
a compass of thought and a sublimity of sentiment,
little suited to the gross ideas and narrow conceptions
of savages. Chiefly occupied in supplying their physical wants, or in gratifying their animal appetites,
they are incapable of *contemplating* the Deity *in his
works*. But the worship of *superior* and *invisible
powers*, the *supposed* CAUSES of *extraordinary events*,
and the AUTHORS of *good* and *evil*, is natural to man

325. Diod. Sicul. lib. i. p. 66.   326. Id. ibid.

in

in his rudest condition[326]; and necessarily proceeds
from *hope* and *fear*, the two main springs of the human
soul[328].

Ancient legislators wisely took advantage of this
propensity, in order to subdue the ferocity, and restrain
the licentiousness of mankind[329]. They gave a regular
establishment to religion, and made it a chief engine

---

327. In order to establish this position, I might collect the united
testimony of the most intelligent travellers, both ancient and modern.
It is even admitted by the most sceptical philosophers. " All human
" life," observes Mr. Hume, " especially *before the establishment of order*
" *and good government*, being subject to *fortuitous accidents*, it is *natural*
" *superstition should prevail every where* in *barbarous ages*; and *put man*
" on the *most earnest inquiry* concerning the INVISIBLE POWERS, who
" *dispose of happiness* or *misery*" (*Nat. Hist. of Religion*, sect. iii.).
A similar observation had been made by Plutarch, who lived late in
the heathen world, and whose historical knowledge was extensive.
" Examine the face of the globe," says he (*advers. Coltes.*), " and you
" may find cities unfortified, without the use of letters, a regular
" magistracy, or distinct habitations; without possessions, property,
" or the use of money, and unskilled in the arts; but a *people without*
" *the knowledge of a* GOD *or* RELIGION; without the *use of vows, oaths,*
" *oracles*, and *sacrifices*, to procure good, or *deprecatory rites*; to avert
" *evil*, no man can, or ever will find."
328. " I suppose," says Dr. Warburton, " it was neither *one* nor
" *other* of these passions *alone*, but *both together*, that *opened to these*
" early mortals (whose *uncultivated reason* had not *yet gained* the *know-*
" *ledge*, or whose *degenerate manners* had *lost* the *tradition of the true*
" God), the *first idea* of SUPERIOR BEINGS."—(*Divine Legation of
Moses*, book iii. sect. vi.) If it should be objected, from the early
practice of ancient nations, that *barbarians worship only visible powers*,
the example of the savages of North-America will furnish an answer.
They pay little regard to the *heavenly bodies*, but worship the GREAT
SPIRIT, an *invisible power* (See *Hist. of America*, book iv. chap. i.
and the authorities there cited). Thunder and lightning, heat and
cold, storms and fair weather, naturally suggests to the least cultivated mind, the existence of some intelligence superior to itself.
329. " Tying them thereby," says venerable Austin, " more closely
to civil society, that they might be more easily governed," *De Civitate
Dei*, lib. iv. cap. xxxii.

of

of government[330]; blending sacred rites with certain civil forms of high importance to society—the nuptial union, the inauguration of magistrates, and the ratification of treaties[331]. They also took advantage of that *belief* of a *future state of existence*, which has prevailed in all ages, and among all nations[332]; by strongly picturing it, as a *state of rewards and punishments*[333];—a state where the souls of men shall be for-

ever

330. Menes, Theseus, Romulus, Numa, and all early legislators, as I shall have occasion to shew, called in religion to the aid of their civil and political institutions. The practice of Menes I have already had occasion to mention. Dr. Warburton has, therefore, belied universal experience, perverted truth, and contradicted reason, in affirming that the MAGISTRATE was *called in* to the *aid* of RELIGION (*Divine Legation of Moses*, book i. sect. ii.). For, in that case, *kings* or *chief magistrates* must have been *originally constituted* by *priests*, and not *priests* by *kings*; a dogma better suited to the dark ages of papal tyranny, than to the enlightened period in which this learned ecclesiastic lived.

In a word, there is no historical fact better attested than this; that the first royal legislators instituted the ceremonies of religion, and regulated divine worship within their several jurisdictions. And, in order to strengthen *regal* by *sacerdotal authority*, as well as to keep the ministers of religion in due obedience, early kings generally retained the *pontificate* in their own hands (Herodot. lib. vi. cap. lvi. Dion. Halicarnass. lib. ii. cap. xiv. Tit. Liv. lib. ii. cap. ii. Cicero, *de Divinat.* lib. i. cap. xl. Servius, *ad Virgil En.* lib. iii. ver. 80). In so doing, they proved its subserviency to the *supreme civil power*; and held it, as they did the *chief command of the army*, as part of their *prerogative* (Id. ibid.). Among the ancient Romans, ecclesiastical dignities were conferred in the same manner as civil offices: by the people, assembled in their several *curiæ*. Dion. Halicarnassensis, lib. ii. cap. xxi.

331. The rites with which these were accompanied, among nations in different degrees of civilization, I shall have occasion to describe in the course of this work.

332. " From the *consent of all nations*," says Cicero (*Tusc. Disp.* lib. i. cap. xvi.), " we conclude, that the *soul survives* the *body*." And Seneca remarks (*Epist.* cxvii.), that the *consent of all mankind*, in the *fears* and *hopes of a future state*, is of no small weight in determining the question of the *immortality* of the *soul*.

333. " All the religions in the world," says Mons. Bayle, " the " *false* as well as the *true*, turn upon this *great hinge*, that there is an " INVISIBLE JUDGE, who *punishes* and *rewards*, after the *present life*,

" actions

ever *happy* or *miserable*, according to the *merit or de-* merit of their actions in this world[334].

Thus, by more clearly displaying to mankind, beyond the grave, an impartial tribunal, whose decrees admit of no reversal, and whose justice it is impossible to elude; toward which criminals are taught to look for final punishment, and to which witnesses are made to appeal in attestation of the truth of their evidence, did some enlightened heathens *fortify* the *moral principle* in the *human breast*, and lay a *solid foundation* for *juris-prudence*, as well as for *public faith*[335].

Considered

" *actions of men*, both *open* and *secret.*" (Art. SPINOZA, ap. *Dict. Crit. et Hist.* tom. iv.). But this *belief* he ascribes to the *invention* of the *magistrate* (ibid.). whereas I have only said, that the *magistrate* took *advantage* of it. And Plutarch (*Consolat. ad. Apollon.*) declares it was *so ancient*, that he could neither *discover* the *author*, nor the *origin of it.*

334. In the most ancient Greek poets, Homer and Hesiod, who have given systems of theology according to the popular belief of their country, we find the *doctrine of a future state of rewards and punishments* always a *fundamental article.* Æschylus, Sophocles, and Euripides, whose business it was to represent the manners and opinions of nations both barbarous and civilized, bear also testimony to the universality of this tenet. But no ancient author has expressed himself more distinctly on the subject than Pindar.

" In the *sad regions of infernal night,*"
Says he, " beyond the verge of life and light,
" The *cruel* and *inexorable mind*
" *Avenging gods and penal woes shall find.*
" There *strict inquiring justice shall bewray*
" The *crimes committed in the realms of day;*
" Th' *impartial judge the rigid law declare,*
" No more to be revers'd by penitence or pray'r.
" But in *the happy fields of light,*
" Where Phœbus with an equal ray,
" Illuminates the balmy night,
" And gilds the cloudless day;
" In *peaceful, unmolested joy,*
" The *good* their *smiling hours employ.*" PIND. Olymp. ii.
335. " Who can deny," says Cicero, " that *these opinions* are *use-*
" *ful,* when he considers what *internal stability* the *state derives* from
" the

   Considered in this point of view, *religion, whether true* or *false*, is highly beneficial to society; consequently, any *attempt* to *weaken* its *influence*, is at once *immoral* and *impolitic.* We accordingly find, that the most wise and virtuous of the ancient historians and philosophers, whatever might be their private opinions, always respected *public religion*, and bore testimony in its favour. Timæus the Locrian, therefore, in discoursing of the *remedies of moral evil*, after he had treated of the *use of philosophy* to lead men of well-formed minds to happiness, by *teaching* the *measures* of *just* and *unjust*, declares, that the *coercions* of *law* and *religion* are necessary to keep men of perverse and intractable dispositions in awe; both *those punishments* which *penal laws inflict*, and those *torments* that *religion denounces* against the wicked[336].

With this venerable sage, well practised in human affairs, agrees the profound historian Polybius; whose knowledge of mankind and civil society was equally deep and comprehensive. " If a state," says he, " could be composed solely of wise men, perhaps *a* " *public religion* might be *unnecessary.* But as this is " not practicable, there is no possibility of keeping in " order the mass of the people, ever capricious and " agitated by irregular passions, without the *terrors of* " *superstition.* The learned ancients, therefore, acted " *wisely*," adds he, " in *propagating* the *belief of the* " *gods*; and those of the present age *absurdly* in *discre-*

" the *religion* of an *oath*, and what *security without* from the *holy rites*
" that *accompany national compacts?*—How *efficacious* the *fear* of *di-*
" *vine punishment* is to *deter* men from *wickedness;* and what *purity of*
" *manners* must *reign* in that *community*, where the *immortal gods* them-
" *selves* are supposed to *interpose*, both as *judges* and *witnesses!*"—
Cic. *de Legib.* lib. i. cap. vii.

336. *Peripsuchas Chosma.*

                 " *diting*

" diting such opinions, and thereby *encouraging the popu-*
" lace to *contemn religious restraints*[337]." For, as the
great geographer remarks, *" it is impossible to govern*
" women, and the common people, and to keep them *pi-*
" ous and *virtuous,* by the *precepts* of *philosophy*[338]." .

But religion, to produce these effects upon the
body of a people, must be free from licentious doctrines and obscene ceremonies : it must ascribe to the
deity no acts or attributes unworthy of human imitation. And, in order to render the hierarchy politically beneficial to a state, farther provision must be
made ; that the *ecclesiastical order,* though interwoven
with, be *subordinate* to the *supreme civil power.* It was
not sufficiently so in Egypt.

Judges of the nation[339], and masters of all state
affairs[340], the Egyptian priests added enormous temporal authority to spiritual influence. To their custody was committed the records and archives of the
kingdom[341]; and they directed the levying of taxes[342].
The monarch himself was, in some measure, subordinate to them, as his conduct was daily subjected to
their controul[343]. And they, as the heads of the public administration, and also the interpreters of the will
of the gods[344], had the power of swaying his councils.
They were the first order in the kingdom[345]; the de-
positaries of the sciences, as well as of the laws[346]; and

337. Polyb. lib. vi. cap. liv.   338. Strabo, lib. i. p. 19, edit. ubi.
cit.   339. Elian. *Var. Hist.* lib. xiv. cap. xxxiv.   340. Diod.
Sicul. lib. i. p. 66.   Strabo, lib. xvii. p. 787.   341. Id. ibid.

342. Clem. Alex. Strom. lib. vi.   343. Diod. Sicul. lib. i.
p. 63.,   344. Elian. ubi sup. et Diod. Sicul. lib. i. p. 66.

345. Id. ibid. As a proof of this superiority, the new king, in
case of a failure of the royal race, if elected from the military order,
was obliged to procure admission into the sacerdotal body, before
he could ascend the throne. Plut. *Is. & Osir.*

346. Diod. Sicul. lib. i. p. 66. Strabo et Elian. ubi sup.

by them must have been moved the whole machine of government, as they only were acquainted with its secret springs. One third of the lands of Egypt, as formerly observed, belonged to the priesthood, who, in consequence of their civil offices and sacred functions, generally maintained dominion over both the king and the people.

The Egyptians, as might be expected in a nation under the government of priests, and priest-rid kings, were slavishly superstitious. They worshipped a multitude of gods. Of the chief of these I shall extract an account from Herodotus and Diodorus, as the least suspicious authorities.

The deities most highly and generally adored in Egypt were Osiris and Isis[347], in early times understood to be the *sun* and *moon;* whom the Egyptians, in one stage of their idolatrous progress, believed to govern and preserve the world, and whom they regarded as the chief causes of nutrition and generation[348]. Both seem also, in later ages, to have been *titles*, under which the Creator and Governor of the universe was worshipped. For Isis was sometimes *symbolically represented* by a ship *and* pilot; and the Egyptian *symbol* for the Governor *of the* universe was a *ship and pilot*[349]. Hence the memorable speech of Isis in Apuleius;—
" I am the *parent of nature*, and *queen of all the elements;*
" *every where present;* one supreme deity, *worshipped*
" *over the whole world*, under *a variety of names*, and
" with *various rites*[350]."

Osiris

347. Herodotus, lib. ii. cap. xlii.   348. Diod. Sicul. lib. i. p. 10, 11. edit. ubi cit.   349. Jamblicus, *de Myst. Egypt.*
350. Apul. *Metamorph.* lib. xi. And Lucius, in his prayer to Isis, addresses her as the *mover of the celestial bodies, and queen of heaven,*

earth,

Osiris, in like manner, was regarded as the *Governor of the universe*, and the *Author of nature;* and worshipped under a *variety of names or titles*[351]. He was not only considered as *Dionusos* or *Bacchus*, but as *Pluto*, and as Ammon or Hammon, the Egyptian name for the *supreme God;* and frequently as Pan[352]. And we have seen that *Pan* was worshipped by the Egyptians as the *Governor of the universe*, the *Author of nature*, and the *Parent of generation.*

In the first rank of Egyptian deities was also placed mind, or *spirit;* the animating principle in the universe, and equivalent to the Grecian Zeus, and the Latin Jupiter; Vulcan, or *fire;* Pallas, or *air;* Ceres, or

earth and hell; the CREATRIX and PRESERVER of all things (Id, ibid.). That she was considered as *Demeter* or *Ceres*, I have formerly had occasion to observe, on the authority of Herodotus (lib. ii. cap lix.), and the same is affirmed by Diodorus (*Biblioth.* lib. i. p. 13.). If I might here indulge a conjecture, I should say, that the Egyptians, as early as the time of Herodotus, seem not only to have known, that the MOON is a *planet attendant upon the* EARTH, but that the EARTH is one of the *six* SOLAR PLANETS. And this leads me to observe, that the *different names* of the HEATHEN GODS, in *different countries*, and the coincidence of their *names* as *planets, elements*, and *spiritual substances*, has introduced great *confusion* into *gentile theology;* but nothing so much as the *various names* for the SUPREME GOD; and the *necessary distinction*, not always clearly marked, between JUPITER as a *planet*, and as the *spiritual governor of the universe.*

351. Auson. *Epig.* xxx.

352. Diod. Sicul. *Biblioth.* lib. i. p. 22. Dr. Warburton asserts (*Divine Legation*, book iv. sect. iv.), that this mode of *allegorising* the Egyptian gods, and including different deities under the *name* and *attributes* of the SUPREME BEING, was a *late invention.* We have undisputed evidence, however, beside the *Orphic* hymn to Pan, before quoted, that it was *very ancient.* The goddess *Neith* or *Pallas*, worshipped as the *air* in the time of Diodorus (as we shall see), was not only worshipped as *divine wisdom* in the time of Plutarch (*Is. et Osir.*), but in the *earliest ages*, at Sais; whence her worship in *that character* was introduced into Greece (Plato, *in Timeo.*). And seemingly by Cecrops and his Egyptian colony.

earth;

PART I.   *earth;* Oceanus, or the element of *water*[353]. " These
gods," adds Diodorus, " the Egyptians say, *travel*
" *through the world; representing themselves* sometimes
" to men in the *shape of sacred living creatures*, some-
" times in the *human* or *other form*. And this,"
remarks he, " is not a *fable*, but *strictly true*, if it be
" admitted, that *those gods generate all things*[354]." Hence
it plainly appears, that the theology of the Egyptians,
properly understood, was *allegorical*, and their public
worship *symbolical*.

The Egyptian gods of the *second class* consisted,
according to Diodorus, of *illustrious men exalted*, after
death, to *divine honours*[355]. His words are to the following purport. " This is the account given by the
" Egyptians of the *heavenly* and *immortal gods*. And
" beside those, they say, there are terrestrial dei-
" ties, *sprung from the former*, and who were origi-
" nally *mortal men;* but who, *by reason of their bene-*
" *ficence*, have obtained the rank of gods[356]." Here
we have an irrefragable proof, that the GREATER

                                              GODS

353. Id. p. 11, 12. *Water* or *moisture*, says Diodorus, the ancient
Greeks called *oceanus;* but the Egyptians account their *Nile* to be
oceanus (*Biblioth*. lib. i. p. 12.). This, if any more than a complimentary *title*, could only be the opinion of the vulgar.

354. *Biblioth*. lib. i. p. 12.

355. Diod. Sicul. ubi supra. The deeply learned and candid Shuckford, therefore, very justly concludes, that the *worship* of *men* and
women was the *last step* of *Egypti.m* IDOLATRY. *Sacred and Profane
Hist. of the World connected*, vol. ii. p. 320.

356. *Biblioth*. lib. i. p. 12. Among the *latter*, adds Diodorus, are
numbered certain Egyptian monarchs; *some of whom* have, if *interpretation* be used, got the *same names* with the CELESTIAL GODS
(Id. ibid.). This remark is obviously offered to reconcile his readers to
the account which he afterward gives of the reign and adventures of
Osiris and *Isis*. But it requires only a sound understanding, and unprejudiced mind, in reading his narration (all previous information
apart), to discover, that Isis and Osiris are *mythical personages*. Osiris
travelled over the whole world, dispensing benefits to mankind; and both he
and Isis claimed *celestial birth* (Diod. Sicul. lib. i. p. 13—23.). Nor

                                              need

GODS of Egypt were *not dead men deified*, as Dr. Warburton and other learned men have asserted. For Diodorus was a professed disciple of Euhemerus, on whose authority, chiefly, they build their arguments[357].

Yet, even on the testimony of Diodorus, I am able to maintain what I formerly advanced, "That the " *twelve gods, the dii majorum gentium*, of the hea- " then world, by whatever names worshipped, were the

need this excite our wonder; for the historian had before to Idus, that they were the sun and moon (*Biblioth*. lib. i. p. 10.). Yet have the reign and adventures of Isis and Osiris been seriously related by many grave authors; and systems have been written on the supposition, that they, and other *mythological sovereigns*, were *mortal kings and queens*, who had been placed among the *celestial gods* by the *gratitude* of *ancient superstition*, for their *beneficence*, while on earth. I am far, however, from denying the deification of kings and heroes; but they always held a subordinate rank among the heathen gods.

357. And he has industriously collected every fabulous tradition concerning the *birth, nursing, reign*, and *death*, of the *gods*, both Egyptian and Grecian (*Biblioth*. lib. i. iii. v. passim.). But these *tales*, as Mr. Bryant has demonstrated, in his *Analysis of Ancient Mythology* (vol. i. ii.), had all their origin in the *rise, propagation, prevalence*, and *decay* of HEATHEN SUPERSTITION in *different places*, as *connected* with the *worship* of any *particular god*; or of the *same god*, under *different names*.

Mr. Bryant indeed conjectures, that all the heathen gods were only so many *titles* of the sun. But this whim, not the most singular in his system, does not destroy the force of his reasoning; nor invalidate the authorities by which his arguments are supported, in regard to the point in question. One prime authority, however, seems to have escaped his notice. Herodotus dates the *reputed birth* of *certain Grecian heroes* (real or imaginary), who *afterwards bore* the *same names* with *certain Egyptian deities*, from the *time* that the *worship* of *those deities* was *introduced* into *Greece* (Herodot. lib. ii. cap. cxlv. cxlvi.). He therefore declares, after *questioning* the *mortal existence* of DIONUSOS or BACCHUS, the *reputed* son of Semele, and *acknowledging* that of HERCULES, the son of Alcmena, " who *lived famous*, and *grew old* in *Greece*;" that he thinks those Greeks act most wisely, who *build temples* to *both* the *Egyptian* and *Grecian* HERCULES, *sacrificing* to the *former* as an *immortal being*, under the *name* of OLYMPIAN; and *honouring* the *latter* as a *hero* of *mortal birth*. Herodot. lib. ii. cap. xliv. cxlv.

" *heavenly*

PART I.   "*heavenly bodies*, and *four elements*, under the direc-
"tion of a *spiritual Governor;*" for if we add the *five*
primary planets to the *seven* gods mentioned, on the
report of this historian, we shall complete the number.   And that these *five* planets, *Saturn, Jupiter,
Mars, Venus,* and *Mercury,* included among the
CELESTIAL GODS, and consequently of the *first order*
of heathen deities, has never been disputed.

In these particulars, the public religion of the Egyptians resembled that of other ancient polytheists; but
in one it differed widely from every other form of
superstition. The *Egyptians worshipped all their*
GREATER GODS *under the form of brutes,* or in *brute*
and *human forms conjoined*[358]; a farther proof that
their *worship* was *symbolical.* Various, however, have
been the conjectures, and laborious the inquiries of
the learned, concerning the *origin* of *brute-worship.*

An account of the *rise* and *early progress* of IDO-
LATRY, will form a necessary prelude to the investigation of this subject.

I have laid down as a fundamental principle, that
"*religion* is *natural* to *man.*" And although it is

358. This practice, which appears to have been as old as the days of
Moses (See Warburton's *Divine Legation*, book iv. sect. iv.), was universal in later times (Diod. Sicul. lib. i. Strabo, lib. xvii. passim).
Dr. Warburton rests his proof of the antiquity of that mode of worship, chiefly on the *golden calf*, worshipped by the Israelites in the Arabian desert (*Divine Legation*, ubi sup.). This he considers as an *imitation* of the Egyptian *sacred bull*, the *symbol* under which OSIRIS was
worshipped. And he thinks the Israelites did not pay their adorations
to the *brutal form*, but the TRUE GOD, under that *form* (Id. ibid.). He
also conjectures, and seemingly with great truth, that the *worship* of
OSIRIS, in the *living bull*, had not then been introduced into Egypt.
For otherwise the Israelites would have been satisfied with a *real
calf* or *bull*, instead of being at the expence of a *golden image* of one.

                                     found

found that mankind, in the *savage state*, are generally
too much occupied in supplying their physical wants,
and in gratifying their animal appetites, to be able to
contemplate the Deity in his works; yet they no sooner
emerge from that condition, and apply themselves to
the pasturing of cattle, and the cultivation of the earth,
than, having occasion more accurately to observe the
regularity of the *seasons*, with the *appearing* and *disappearing* of the *celestial bodies*, they begin to discover
a *first cause*, or *prime mover* of the *stupendous machine
of the universe*. Conscious of their dependence upon
that *great being*, and desirous *of conciliating* his *favour*,
or *averting* his *displeasure*, they offer to him, *under the
wide expanse of heaven*, and usually on *eminences*[359],
the *most valuable produce* of their *fields* and *flocks*[360].

This

359. That mankind *originally sacrificed* in the *open air*, is too well
attested by writers, both sacred and prophane, to be disputed; and that
they also *sacrificed*, in *early times*, upon *high places*, on hills and mountains, we have sufficient evidence, both in the worship of the *false* and
the *true* God. When Balak, king of Moab, wanted to obtain an answer in his favour, he took Balaam the prophet " up to the *high places*
" of BAAL (*Numbers*, chap. xxii. ver. 41.); and when Abraham, in a
still earlier period, was commanded to *sacrifice* his son Isaac, as a
burnt offering to the Lord, he carried him to the top of " one of the
" *mountains* in the land of Moriah" (*Gen.* chap. xxii. ver. 2—13.); and
there actually *sacrificed* a *ram* (Id. ibid). They imagined, it appears,
that they thereby obtained a nearer communication with the Deity.

360. That the first men *sacrificed* to the Deity the *produce* of their
fields, and the *offspring* of their *flocks*, we have the authority of the father of sacred history to affirm. For we are told, that " Cain *brought*
" of the *fruits of the ground*, an *offering* unto the Lord (*Gen.* chap. iv.
ver. 3.). and that Abel also *brought* of the *firstlings* of his *flock* ;" (Id.
ver. 4.). Nor are we left in doubt that the *pious offered* what they thought
most valuable; for it is not only said, that " Abel *brought* of the *firstlings*
" of his flock;" but " of the *fat* thereof" (*Gen.* ubi sup.). In a word, it
appears, that mankind have always offered to the Deity whatever was
most *acceptable* to *themselves* as *food* or *drink*. Hence we may *trace* the
progress

This pure worship, paid to one almighty God, without the intervention of *images*, prevailed over Arabia and Syria in the time of Abraham; when the head of every family, or the chief of the tribe, officiated as priest[361]: and we find it also in Arabia, among Job and his friends, in a still later age[362]. Into Arabia, however, *solar* or *star-worship* had found its way in the days of Job. Hence the expostulation of that venerable patriarch, in vindication of his innocence. "If I beheld the sun, when it shined," says he, "or the "moon *walking* in *brightness;* and my *heart hath been* "*secretly enticed;* or my *mouth* hath *kissed my hand,* I "should have *denied* the God *that is above*[363]." Here we discover an allusion to the worship of the *heavenly bodies.* And that seductive worship, which is supposed to have had its origin in Chaldea, soon spread over the east, under the name of *zabiism*[364].

progress of *nations* in *civil improvement,* but more especially in *agriculture* and *grazing;* in their *libations* and *sacrifices;* from a *head of barley,* and a *simple cake,* to *kids, goats, lambs, rams, bullocks,* and *heifers;* and from *water* to *milk, oil* and *wine* (See Prophyr. *de Abstin.* lib. ii. and Euseb. *Prep. Evangel.* lib. i. cap. ix.). The Arabians were become so profuse in their sacrifices, as early as the days of Job, that his three offending friends offered to the Lord, "*seven bullocks* and *seven rams,* as a burnt-offering." *Job,* chap. xlii. ver. 8, 9.

361. *Gen.* chap. xiv. ver. 18—20. Chap. xx. ver. 4—6, and chap. xxii. ver. 13.

362. When Job lived is uncertain; but it is generally agreed, that the *dramatic history,* which bears his name, was composed after the time of Abraham, and not later than that of Moses. One thing, however, is incontrovertible, that Job and his friends, though obviously strangers to the Mosaic institutions, and to the history of the creation, as delivered by the Hebrew legislator, all zealously *maintained* the tenet of *one* God, the *Maker* of *heaven* and *earth;* and they, in *acknowledging* the *justice* and *goodness* of *his moral government,* also *maintained* the doctrine of an *all-knowing, all-wise,* and *merciful* Providence. See *Job,* chap. iv. v. ix. xii. xiii. xxxiii. xxxiv. xxxv. xxxvi. xxxvii.

363. *Job,* chap. xxxi. ver. 26—28.

364. See Maimonid. *Moreh Nevoch.* et Pocock. *Specim. Hist. Arabice.*

La

In the *rise* of ŻABIISM we discover the *root* of PO-
LYTHEISM and IDOLATRY. For all the *various forms*
of *heathen superstition*, were only so many *shoots* from
it; adapted by artful politicians to the *state* of *barbarism* or *civility* in different nations, and *modified* according to *climates*, and *incidental circumstances*. To attempt, therefore, to *account systematically* for *these va-
rieties*, would be to expect to find order in chaos, and
uniformity in the brain-sick visions of fanatics; or in
the tricks, which princes and priests have devised, to
take advantage of human weakness.

I shall have occasion, however, in unfolding the
history of distinguished nations, to treat of their *religious* as well as *civil instiutions*. There it will farther
appear, that the *great objects of worship*, in *all Gentile
nations* were the *same*. Here I shall offer to your lordship a short account of the early *progress* of ZABIISM;
necessary, not only for the better understanding of the
superstition of the *Egyptians*, but of *heathen superstition* in general.

The Chaldeans, or Zabians, added to the *original*
worship of ONE almighty GOD, the Creator and Governor
of the universe, a *secondary* worship of the *heavenly
bodies*; which they regarded as his ministers[365], and
adored as mediators between HIM and sinful men[366].
They considered these glorious orbs as the habitations
of

---

365. Diod. Sicul. lib. ii. p. 116.

366. Maimonid. *Moreb Nevoch.* et Pocock. *Specim. Hist. Arabica.*
" The *necessity* of a *mediator* between *God* and *man*," says the pious
and learned Prideaux, " was a general notion, which obtained among
" all mankind from the beginning. For being conscious of their own
" meanness, vileness and impurity, they could not conceive how it was
" possible for them of themselves, to have any access to the all holy, all
" glorious, and supreme Governor of all things. They considered him
" as too *high*, and too *pure*, and themselves too *low* and *polluted*, for
" such

of *genii*, or vehicles of pure *spiritual intelligences*, by whom they were moved; who animated them, as the soul does the human body; and through whose agency, they supposed, the supreme Being governed the world; that holding a *middle nature* between the most High and man, they were best fitted to become mediators between God and offending mortals[367].

The Zabians were at first satisfied with merely lifting up their souls in prayer to these ministers of the *divine will;* but they afterward proceeded to burn incense to them, and to make such oblations as they thought most agreeable to their several natures. They accurately observed their appearing and disappearing, their conjunctions and aspects; dividing the superintendence of the world among them, and assigning this or that species of being to each particular planet's administration[368]. And according to the number, and rank of the *celestial bodies* in their estimation, they

" such a converse. And therefore concluded, that there must be a
" *mediator*, by whose means only they could make any address unto
" the *most High;* and through whose intercession alone any of their
" petitions could be accepted. But no clear revelation being then
" made of the mediator, whom God had appointed, because as yet
" he had not been manifested unto the world, *they took upon them to*
" *address unto* Him, by *mediators* of *their own chusing*. And their notions
" of the sun, moon, and stars," &c. *Connect. of the Old and New*
Testament, part. i. book. iii.

  367. Id. ibid. A doctrine similar to the Zabian appears to have been
held by Socrates, from what his scholar makes him deliver in the character of Diotima. " Through this *middle species of being*," says he,
" *prophecy* in all its *different shapes*, and all *forms* of *divination* are con-
" *veyed* to *men;* for the *divine Nature* never *immediately mixes*, or com-
" *municates* with the *human*. But, through the *intervention* of GENII,
" all *communion* and *intercourse* between the *Deity* and *mankind* is car-
" ried on" (Plato, *Sympos.*). Hence the *belief* in the visitation of ANGELS, and in *celestial visions;* whether presented to mortals, while *waking* or *asleep*.

  368. Maimonid. et. Pocock. ubi sup.

                                              marked

marked a *successive revolution of time* in *seven* DAYS,
which we *call* a week; and consecrated each DAY to
its *guardian* orb[369].

The rites of the Zabians, however, gradually multiplied; and their *worship* grew more *sensual,* Their
mediatory and *guardian* planet, they observed, frequently *withdrew from their sight;* while they stood in
constant need of his *intercession* or *protection.* They,
therefore, formed to themselves *symbolical figures;*
allegorically *representing* the *powers* and *properties,*
not only of each *celestial orb*, but of the supreme BEING
and his *chief attributes*[370]. These they put into shrines,
to which they paid divine worship; placing above
every other shrine that of the FIRST CAUSE, as worthy
of the highest adoration[371].

From the worship paid to those shrines, and to the
symbolical figures they contained, intelligible only to
the learned, it was natural for the superstitious vulgar
to go one step farther; to desire an *image* of the
genius supposed to inhabit each planet, in place of a
mystical symbol. Such images, or fancied likenesses,
were accordingly devised by the Zabian priests and
made of the metal imagined to be most consonant to
the nature of the several celestial orbs; of *gold*, to the
SUN; of *silver*, to the MOON; of *iron*, to MARS; of
quicksilver, to MERCURY; of *tin*, to JUPITER; of *copper*, to VENUS; and of *lead*, to SATURN[372]; thereby
fixing

369. *Specimen Hist. Arabicæ*, ap. Pocock. This custom, which has
prevailed in most nations, seems to favour the assertion of the Zabians, that their religion, as it is among the oldest in the world, has
spread over the whole earth; or to prove, that mankind, in all countries, are *disposed* to the *worship* of the *celestial bodies*, and *capable of observing* their *motions, distances*, and degrees of *magnitude.* Here also we
discover the *origin* of the opinion of the *guardianship* of ANGELS.

370. Id. ibid.   371. *Specim. Hist. Arabicæ*, ap. Pocock.

372. Id. ibid. If Mr. Bryant had attended to this *application* of the
several metals to the *formation* of the *images* of the *celestial bodies*, he
might

PART I. fixing the application to the *names* given by the *chy-mists* to the *different metals*, as universally received over the world as the number and order of the days of the week.

To those *images*, after their consecration, the Zabians burnt the richest perfumes, and made the most costly sacrifices : believing that their prayers and oblations to the *genius* thought to inhabit each planet, the minister of the MOST HIGH and *mediator* with HIM, were as acceptable when offered to the image, as to the real orb, when splendent in the heavens[373]. We may therefore conclude, with learned Owen, that *idolatry* had its origin in zabiism, or the worship of the celestial bodies[374]. And I shall add, that its cause was the need of a *visible object* of worship ; which human nature, unless aided by philosophy or illuminated by revelation, seems to require to assist its devotions.

But zabiism, even in its corrupted state, was not inconsistent, we find, with the doctrine of a FIRST CAUSE : nor (as we have seen in treating of the Chal-

might have saved himself the trouble of attempting to prove, that *chrusos,* the Greek word for *gold*, was a corruption of *chusos* or *chus:* nor would he have said that *gold* had no *relation* to the *worship* of the SUN. Far less would he or Selden, if they had attended to the *early worship* of the *celestial bodies*, have asserted, that *all* the *gods* of *gentile antiquity* are *resolvable* into the SUN (Selden, *de Diis Syris*, Syntag. ii. Bryant, *New System of Ancient Mythology*, vol. i. passim.). The sun indeed, as might naturally have been expected, was universally worshipped over the heathen world. The *most glorious* heavenly body, the *visible ruler of the day*, and the *immediate cause* of *light* and *heat*, could not fail to receive *adoration*, from *nations* who *blended* the *worship* of the CREATOR with *that* of his *works*. But that the SUN was ever *worshipped* as the SUPREME DEITY, unless by *rude barbarians*, we have no reason to believe : for all *civilized* heathen nations acknowledged a HIGHER POWER than the *celestial bodies ;* and the SUN was *one* of those *bodies*.

373. Maimonid. *Moreh Nevoch.* et Pocock. *Specimen Hist. Arabicæ.*
374. Owen, *de Ortu Idol.* lib. iii. cap. iv.

deans

deans of Babylon) with the belief of a supreme governor[375]; who assigned the sun its station, and, according to whose eternal laws the planets, with unerring concord perform their revolutions[376].

Whether celestial worship passed from Chaldea
into Egypt, or took its rise in the latter country, as in
the former, from the perpetual visibility, and alluring
beauty of the heavenly bodies, I shall not pretend to
determine. But that the adoration of those bodies, in
subordination to a divine intellect, was the most ancient
public worship of the Egyptians, is universally allowed[377];

375. Diod. Sicul. lib. ii. p. 116.

376. Id. ibid. "The Chaldeans believe," says Diodorus, "That the
" *order* and *beauty* of the *universe* are the *effects* of a certain DIVINE
" PROVIDENCE; and that the *heavenly bodies* are not *moved of them-*
" *selves*, or *fortuitously*, but according to the *determinate* and *firmly ratified*
" *decree* of the DEITY" (*Bibliotb.* lib. ii. p. 116.). But the Chaldeans
believed in the *eternity* of the *world* or *universe* (Id. ibid.). How then,
it may be said, could they believe it to be the *work* of a *Deity* ?—The
difficulty is thus solved by the Grecian commentators upon Plato and
Aristotle, who held nearly the same opinion. " MIND or GOD was
" before the *world;* not as if the *one existed* before the *other* in TIME,
" but because the *world proceeded* from MIND ; which was in *order of*
" *nature,* FIRST; as the *cause* thereof, and its *archetype*" (Plotinus,
En. iii. lib. ii. cap. i.). "Whence it follows," says the same philosopher,
" That the *world*, which *proceeds* from the DEITY by way of *efful-*
" *gence*, must have been *coeval* with God; as *light* was *coeval* with the
" *sun*" (Id. *En.* v. lib. viii. cap. xii.). To the same purport Simpli-
cius (*in* Aristot. *Phys.* lib. viii) : " Aristotle, though he considers GOD
" to be the *cause* of the *existence*, and of the *motions* of the *celestial*
" *bodies*, yet concludes the *universe* to have been *eternal*, and *unmade;*
" but to have *proceeded* from the DEITY," &c.

377. This Dr. Warburton *admits*, and even takes pains to *prove*
(*Divine Legation*, book iii. sect. vi. and book iv. sect iv.) : though he
makes a very singular use of it. He thinks, however, it is not only
possible, but *highly probable*, that the *worship* of the FIRST CAUSE was
prior to the *worship* of the *celestial bodies*, or *any form* of *idolatry* (*Divine Legation*, book iii. sect. vi.) : a position which I have endeavoured
to establish ; as equally necessary, for the vindication of God's *moral
government* and the *sagacity* of the human mind. I may even venture to
go a step farther ; and conclude with the deeply learned and impartial
Cudworth,

ed; · and that their greater gods were the *sun*, *moon*, and *five* primary planets, in conjunction with the *four* elements, under the government of an all-ruling and all-pervading SPIRIT, I have already proved.

These gods were represented by allegorical symbols, expressive of their supposed qualities. And as the meaning of those symbols was only known to the learn-ed, the ignorant multitude, we may believe, often wor-shipped the mere symbol of each God, as the ultimate object of their adoration. Here we discover the true origin of what has been called brute-worship.

Dr. Warburton was, therefore, wise in rejecting all former theories of brute-worship[378]; and in ascribing it to allegorical symbols[379]. But I can by no means agree with him in thinking, that the symbols, which led to this worship, among the Egyptian vulgar were merely those employed in hieroglyphic writing[380];

Cudworth, "That all that *multiplicity* of *pagan gods*, which makes so " great a shew and noise, was really nothing but *several names* and no- " tions of ONE *supreme Deity*, according to its *different manifestations*, " *gifts*, and *effects* in the world: so that ONE *unmade*, *self-existent* " DEITY, and no more was *acknowledged* by the *more intelligent* of the " *ancient pagans*; for of the opinions of the *sottish vulgar* no man can " pretend to give an account, in *any religion*" (*Intellectual System*, chap. iv. sect. xiii.). That the Egyptian vulgar were truly *sottish* I shall afterward have occasion to shew.

378. Three of these deserve particular regard: 1. That the Egyp-tian invention of *distinguishing the constellations*, and *marking each of them* with the *name* of *some animal* gave rise to *brute-worship* (Lucian *de Astrologia*); 2. That it had its *origin* in the *doctrine* of *God's pervading all things* (Porphyr. *de Abstinentia*, lib. iv.); 3. That *brutes* were made the *objects* of *worship* only as the *symbols* of the FIRST CAUSE, consi-dered in his various *attributes* and *relations* (Jamblic. *de Myst Egypt.*). But these three *supposed causes* of *brute-worship*, if combined, account rather for the *use* of *brutal forms* in *allegorical symbols*, than for the *worship* of *brutes*; whether in the *image* or *living* animal.

379. *Divine Legation*, book iv. sect. iv. ·   380. Id. ibid.

though

though I can readily admit, that it had its rise in the symbolical figures sculptured on the porticoes of the Egyptian temples.

For we know that those symbolical figures were more striking than hieroglyphical inscriptions[381] : they consequently would make a greater impression upon the minds of the superstitious Egyptians. And when explained, they probably contained more meaning. Nor have we any reason to believe, that the body of the people in Egypt ever paid much regard to hieroglyphic writing, or revered its feigned divine origin[382]. Though chiefly, if not solely confined to the two higher orders in the kingdom, it was sufficiently familiar to prevent adoration.

Yet if the profound doctor had liberally interpreted the allegorical symbols employed in hieroglyphic writing, great merit must have been ascribed to him. But he had no such liberal views. The champion of a paradoxical system, in the prosecution of which the whole vigour of his genius was exerted, he pushed aside every authority, and trampled upon every opi-

381. Herodot. lib. ii. passim.

382. See the *Divine Legation of Moses*, book iv. sect. iv. where this position is maintained. I have already had occasion to make some remarks on the nature of hieroglyphic writing, in order to rectify a general mistake; " that it was *invented* for *secrecy*, not for *public use.*" And I shall here hazard an opinion, accompanied with a corroborating testimony, that *symbolic writing*, which arose out of *picture-writing*, common to all rude nations, in a certain stage of their progress (to the Mexicans and Japanese, as well as the Ethiopians and Egyptians), is no proof of the antiquity of a nation; though its early or happy invention, may be considered as a mark of the ingenuity of a people. " The Egyptians," says Tacitus (*Annal.* lib. xi.), in *tracing* the *rise* of *alphabetic writing*, *originally expressed* the *conceptions* of their *minds* by " the *figures* of *animals.*" This respectable authority seems to have escaped the notice of Warburton; or perhaps it did not, in all respects suit his purpose ; though a strong testimony in support of his theory (which I have adopted), that hieroglyphic writing was *not* invented for secrecy.

nion

PART I. nion, that stood in the way of his favourite hypothesis.
Instead of explaining the Egyptian symbols with the
liberality of a philosopher, a character which he sometimes affects, we discover only in his inquiries the
narrow mind of a candidate for a bishopric. "The
"brute-worship of the Egyptians," says he, "was at
"first altogether objective of their hero-gods[383]."

But the venerable father of history affirms, on his
own knowledge and observation, that the Egyptians,
worshipped no heroes[384]. And he supports his assertion by the testimony of the Egyptian priests; who,
after having given him, in a chronological series, an
account of the long succession of their kings, declared
that none of those kings had been either reputed a god,
or deified as a hero[385]. They also declared, that, in
Egypt, *no god* had taken the *form* of a man; nor had
they ever heard of such a thing, either during the
reigns of their more ancient or later monarchs[386].

383. Warburton's *Divine Legation of Moses*, book iv. sect. iv. Yet
he had before told us, that the *first* gods of the Egyptians, after the
establishment of polytheism, were the *sun* and *moon*. Must not their
allegorical symbols, therefore, have been *at first objective* of *those gods?*
as we find such symbols were among the ancient Chaldeans, and all
oriental worshippers of the celestial bodies. And the "first natural
"gods of the Egyptians," Dr. Warburton afterward allows to have
"been the host of heaven." See *Divine Legation*, book iv. sect. iv.

384. Herodotus, lib. ii. cap. l.　　385. Id. lib. ii. cap. cxlii. cxliii.

386. Herodotus, lib. ii. cap. cxliii. The Egyptians, therefore,
could not, in the most early times, worship their gods in the human
form : nor could the allegorical symbols, engraved on the porticoes
of their temples, or otherwise employed for religious purposes, be
objective of their dead kings or heroes ; for they did not deify them.
Yet Dr. Warburton had the boldness to maintain both these positions,
and arrogantly asks, when asserting, that the symbolic worship of
brutes brought human images into disrepute, whether any one
can believe, that the *hero-god* OSIRIS was not worshipped in his own
figure, before that of an ox ?—(*Divine Legation of Moses*, book iv.
sect. iv.) But that *Osiris* was no mortal king, I have already endeavoured to prove ; and shall now call in aid of my opinion, the suffrage
of the Egyptian priests.

The

The sacred sages added, however, that before the
time of those mortal kings, the *gods* had been sovereigns of Egypt, but had no intercourse with men;
and that the last of their celestial monarchs was *Orus*,
the son of *Osiris*, who dethroned *Typhon*[387]. Here we
have a new proof, that Osiris was a mythical personage,
and the reputed history of the reign of the gods in
Egypt, a mythical legend; for Herodotus tells us,
that *Orus*, the last celestial sovereign, was the same
with the Grecian *Heliot* or *Apollo*[388].

Nor does it require much learned sapience to discover, that by the dethroning of TYPHON by ORUS, is
mythically to be understood, the expulsion of the
principle of natural evil, by the emanation of LIGHT,
or the benignant influence of the sun upon our world.
Hence Orus is called the son of Osiris; one of the names
or titles of the sun, as well as of the Creator and Governor of the universe[389].

The manner in which these names or titles were
originally confounded, and the literal meaning of the
reign of the gods in Egypt, may thus perhaps be accounted for, and explained. While the Egyptians remained in a state of barbarism, they, like many other
barbarians, considered the sun and moon as the gods,
who jointly governed the world[390]; and when, become
civilized and enlightened, they obtained the knowledge
of a SUPREME BEING, the same names, which had

---

387. Id. ibid.   388. *Historiar.* lib. ii. cap. cxlii.
389. This I have already had occasion to prove.
390. Diod. Sicul. lib. i. p. 10, 11. edit. sup. cit. His words are to
the following purport. " The most ancient Egyptians, looking up to
" the world above them, and filled with astonishment and admira-
" tion at the structure of the universe, concluded there were *two* chief
" gods; namely, the *sun* and *moon*. And to the *sun* they gave the ap-
" pellation of *Osiris*, or *many-eyed*; and to the MOON that of *Isis*, or
" *ancient.*" Id. ibid.

formerly been applied to the two most glorious visible orbs, were also applied by them indifferently to the DEITY, or FIRST CAUSE of all things.

‘ This *moral revolution*, and the introduction of *physiological* or *mythical theology*, may be conjectured to have taken place about the time that Menes founded the Egyptian monarchy; promulgated written laws, and gave a regular form to religious ceremonies. But before the introduction of physiological theology, the Egyptians seem not only to have worshipped the sun and moon, but the whole host of heaven, or all the planets in the solar system; as appears by the number of their *greater gods*[391]. And as monarchy had not been regularly constituted, if it had ever been instituted in Egypt, before the reign of Menes, the Egyptians, in after times, looked back to that period of ignorance and barbarous freedom, when they knew no kings, but the heavenly bodies, as the reign of the gods.

They did not, however, describe it as the Greeks did their golden age, or the Romans their Saturnian reign; but represented it as a period during which they were emerging from barbarity, and gradually acquiring, under their celestial sovereigns, the use of the more necessary arts[392]; surely great cause of con-

391. The *greater gods* of the Egyptians, *originally* two, as I have just had occasion to notice, were afterward multiplied to *eight* (Herodot. lib. ii. cap. xlvi.), when they became better acquainted with astronomy; and were at last increased to *twelve* (Id. ibid.) on the introduction of *physiological* theology; which, together with the worship of the celestial bodies, under the direction of a *divine intellect,* added the adoration of the *four elements.*

The number of the greater gods among the Greeks and Romans was also *twelve,* as I shall have occasion to shew; and even among the more northern nations of Europe. EDDA, *Mythol.* xix.

392. Diod. Sicul. *Biblioth.* lib. i. p. 13—19.

solation

solation to them, and worthy of grateful remembrance.

Small wonder, therefore, that the Egyptians ascribed to Osiris or the sun, and to Isis his queen and
sister; who seemed to divide with him the empire of
the heavens, and was regarded both as the moon and
all-nourishing earth; on which the moon attends, and
throws, during the absence of the sun, a refulgent
light: small wonder that they ascribed to those first
gods, and other celestial divinities, the invention of
whatever contributes to the accommodation and enjoyment of life; that they made Osiris be attended by
the *muses;* or that they ascribed to Isis, under the
character of DAMATER, or mother earth; and as the
patroness of *agriculture,* the institution of laws[393];
which necessarily flow from that primary art.

This mode of allegorizing the early periods of history, and throwing a mystical veil over the *operations*
of *nature,* the *rise of religion,* and the *invention of arts,*
passed from the Egyptians to the Greeks; who,
mistaking the meaning of the Egyptian allegories,
blended real with imaginary personages. And modern
historians and chronologers, not distinguishing the
false from the true, have built systems upon the reigns
of *kings* that never existed, and confounded the order
of events in attempting to reconcile them. In a word,
building their reasonings upon fabulous æras, as when
Osiris reigned in Egypt, or Jupiter in Crete; and en-
deavouring to ascertain by these the date of transactions
well authenticated, they have hurt the credibility of
ANCIENT HISTORY, and afforded scepticism a triumph,
in decrying great part of it as fable.

These reflections, I hope, will be sufficient to satisfy
your lordship on a subject into which I do not wish

393. Id. ibid.

you

you to dive, but which it is necessary you should view without prejudice ;—" That the *Egyptian theology* was " mythical or physiological, and that the allegorical " symbols it employed in public worship, were *not* ob- " jective of the virtues or qualities of hero-*gods*." Con- sequently those symbols could not be intended to con- ceal from the vulgar, as has been asserted, the mortal origin of such gods[394].

No man, however, was better qualified than Dr. Warburton, to have given a just account of the Eyp- tian theology. But his system, like Olympus, stood in his way; and threw a shade over every object, unless such as served to adorn its heavenly brow. Yet truth sometimes broke from him by surprise. " One of the " chief maxims of Egyptian wisdom, as applied to re- " ligious matters, was," says he, " that the govern- " ment of the world was committed, by the supreme " Rector of the universe, into the hands of subordinate, " local, tutelary deities; that these were the proper " objects of public and popular religion; and that the " knowledge of the only one God, the Creator of all " things, was highly dangerous to be communicated to " the people; but was to be secreted and shut up in " their mysteries, and there only to be communicated " to a few; and those only the wise, and learned, and " ruling part of mankind[395].

This is a just account of the political object, not only of the Egyptian religion, but also of that of the Greeks and Romans. They all endeavoured to conceal from the people, the simple doctrine of one God, the Creator and Preserver of the universe, as dangerous to the state ; and wrapped up the principles of their theo-

394. See Dr. Warburton's *Divine Legation of Moses;* book iv, sect. iv. where a contrary doctrine is maintained.
395. *Divine Legation*, book iv. sect. vi.

logy

logy in *symbols, allegories,* or *fabulous legends,* fitted to
amuse and overawe the vulgar[396], and inscrutable by
them.

But the theology of the Egyptians, suited to the
gloomy character of the nation, was more especially
involved in darkness. The Egyptian priests, jealous
of their temporal authority, as well as of their spiritual dominion, took advantage of the proneness of the
people to superstition, to plunge them into the grossest
idolatry. Learned themselves, they imposed upon
the ignorant and credulous vulgar; and made them
worship *every thing in nature* but its great AUTHOR,
the only true and proper object of human adoration.
Brutes, reptiles; the deadly asp, and all the serpent-
breed; the amphibious and devouring crocodile; all
the fowls that wing the air, and all the fish that swim
the deep; whatever could inspire *hope,* excite *fear,* or
be considered as the cause of *good* or *evil,* was transform-
ed into a god in Egypt, and held up to the idolatry of the
people; the images of all these being used in the symbolical figures, and hieroglyphical inscriptions, on the
walls and porticoes of the Egyptian temples[397].

But of all the sacred symbols of the Egyptians, the
most general was that of the serpent. It seems to
have been employed as an attendant emblem, in the
worship of all the greater gods; but was more peculiarly appropriated to that of the sun, by whatever
appellation adored, and before whatever image[398];
whether under the name of *Apis, Osiris,* or *Vulcan;* in
the form of a BULL, to indicate the return of summer-

396. Vide Strabo, lib. i. p. 19, 20. edit. Lutet. Paris. 1620.
397. See *Divine Legation of Moses,* book iv. sect. iv. vi. and the
authors there cited.
398. *New System of Ancient Mythol.* art. OPHIOLATREIA, et auct. cit.

heat,

heat, while the sun is in that sign of the zodiac[399];
the beginning of the rains in Ethiopia, which occasion
the overflowing of the Nile, and the consequent fertility of Egypt; or without any symbol but itself, beside
the perpetual fire, and before the great fountain of
light and heat, the most sublime natural emblem of
the eternal and invisible NUMEN[400]; who pervades,
generates, and nourishes all things, and whose intellectual brightness can only be displayed by similitude.

This general use of the *serpent* as a sacred symbol
will not, however, appear wonderful, when we are informed, that it was considered as an emblem of time
and eternity[401], as well as of the *principle* of *darkness*,
the *angel* of the *bottomless pit*[402]. Nor is it strange,
that the symbol of time should be constantly associated
with that of the sun, by whose apparent motion time is
measured; or that the principle of darkness should
be worshipped along with that of light, as darkness is
only the privation of light[403]. The shadow must follow the sun.   The

399. I am not unacquainted with the causes that have been assigned by
ancient or modern writers, why the Egyptians worshipped their tutelary *god* in the shape of a BULL; but having rejected the mortal origin
of *Osiris*, whose soul is said to have passed into such an animal (Diod.
Sicul. lib. i. p. 76.), the influence of the SUN in *taurus* appeared to me
the most rational way of accounting for this predominant symbol. In
saying the soul of Osiris passed into a BULL; the Egyptian priests
might mean allegorically to intimate, that genial and vivifying spirit
which animates all nature, when the SUN enters that constellation, and
diffuses through the animal and vegetable world the principle of generation.

400. Cicero, *de Nat. Deor.* lib. iii. Elian. *Hist. Animal.* lib. x. xvii.
Euseb. *Preparat, Evangil.* lib. i. The impression made by the *sun* upon
the human mind is so strong, that minkind have in all ages been led,
in speaking of the *Creator* and *Governor* of the universe, to illustrate
their meaning by metaphorical allusions to that glorious orb. The examples of this mode of expression are numerous in our sacred scrip-
tures; and some of these misinterpreted, and applied to the support of a
system, would furnish a proof, that the *god* of the *Hebrews* was the SUN.

401. *Divine Legat.* b. iv. s. iv.   402. Heinsius, *Aristarch.* init.

403. If this explication be admitted, all attempts to deduce from

The obvious conclusion to be drawn from this reasoning is, That *light* and *darkness*, *day* and *night*, being the prime objects of human attention, the former was naturally associated, by rude mankind, with the *good*, the latter with the *evil* principle in the universe. Hence most ancient nations, actuated in their devotions by the human passions, have worshipped not only the *celestial*, but also the *infernal* powers; the sun, chiefly from *love* and *gratitude*, as the emblem of divine beneficence, under the figure of a countenance *illuminated* with *rays*, in a lofty temple; and the SERPENT, or some such horrid form, in a deep cavern, as the symbol of the evil one, from motives of fear.

Human reason cannot easily comprehend, how both *good* and *evil* should proceed from the same being: an analogy, drawn from human turpitude only, could conduct it to such an idea. And unless revelation had taught us, that the BEING of whom the serpent has been made symbolical was the cause of such turpitude, we should still have been at a loss to account for the introduction of natural and moral evil into our world. A malignant spirit, operating upon human frailty, is the best solution of the difficulty, and the happiest vindication of divine justice[404].

Thus we find the symbol of the *serpent* alike applicable to the purposes of religion, whether we consider it in a natural, moral, or theological point of view. And hence it was introduced in the celebration of all the heathen mysteries[405].

But

NOAH's ARK the symbols expressive of *light* and *darkness*, employed by ancient nations in celebrating the mysteries of their religion, must be considered as absurd. See Bryant's *New System of Ancient Mythol.* vol. ii. iii. passim.

404. Compare *Genesis*, chap. iii. ver. 1—15. with *Revelations*, chap. ix. ver. 1—11.

405. Elian. *Hist. Animal.* lib. xvii. cap. v. Augustin. de *Civitat. Dei.* lib.

But the great body of the people of Egypt, as already observed, being utterly unacquainted with the meaning of their sacred symbols, they looked no farther than the mere image, or the creature which it naturally represented. Hence their besotted attachment to such creatures as blind superstition, under the direction of priestcraft, led them more particularly to regard.

Herodotus and Strabo hint at the most abominable intercourse between the women of the Mendesian district, where the he-goat was worshipped, and that animal[406]. And Diodorus, though an admirer of the Egyptians, cannot help expressing his astonishment at the gross familiarity in which they lived with their sacred animals; the care they took in procuring them delicate food, and voluptuous accommodation, while alive; their lamentations at the death of any of them; and the incredible sums expended on their funerals[407]. Nor does he conceal from us an obscene ceremony, that attended the deification of the sacred BULL; when, after the death of his predecessor, he was placed in the temple of Vulcan at Memphis[408]. During the first forty days, none were permitted to see him but women; who, standing before him, with their petticoats pulled up, shewed him their privy parts[409].

But the superstition of the Egyptians was productive of other bad effects, beside debasing their manners. It precluded them from all liberal intercourse with other nations, whom they considered as impure[410]; and consequently obstructed the sources of knowledge, and the

lib. iii. cap. xii. et lib. xvii. cap. xv. Arnob. *Cont. Gen.* lib. v. Justin Martyr, *Apol.* i. ii. Clemens. Alex. *Cobort.* init.

406. Herodot. *Historiar.* lib. ii. Strabo, *Geog.* lib. xvii. p. 802.

407. Diod. Sicul. *Biblioth.* lib. i. p. 74—76. edit. sup. cit.

408. *Biblioth.* lib. i. p. 76.   409. Diod. Sicul. sup. cit.

410. Herodot. lib. ii. cap. xli. See also *Genesis,* chap. xliii. ver. 32.

means of civil improvement. It sanctioned the marriage of brothers and sisters[411]. And this unnatural
union of the sexes, in conjunction with the political
regulation of hereditary professions, narrowed still farther the social system; prevented the diffusion of
wealth, or the revolution of property, and served to
nurse hereditary hate, and professional contempt.

I have formerly, my lord, had occasion to observe,
that professions were hereditary among the Egyptians;
and that no subject in Egypt, unless he belonged to
one of the two higher classes, to the sacerdotal or military order, could enjoy any property in land, or have
any share in the government of the kingdom. The
three inferior classes consisted of husbandmen, graziers or feeders and rearers of cattle, and artificers in
various branches[412]; each of whom was confined by
law to his particular calling; in which he had succeeded his father, and which his son was bound to
follow, however strongly the bent of his genius might
be turned to another employment[413].

This regulation has been much praised by historians both ancient and modern, as contributing to the
perfection of the arts, by adding successively the attainments of the son to those of the father; and for
being calculated to curb aspiring ambition, by confining every one to his own profession, whatever might
be the strength or extent of his talents. But the benefit resulting from the experience of ancestry, would
be more than balanced by the disadvantages connected
with it; in dooming many to professions, which they
had neither inclination to prosecute, nor ability to
improve. And although the institution of hereditary

411. Diod. Sicul. lib. i. p. 23.   412. Id. *Bibliath.* lib. i. p. 67.
413. Id. ibid.

employments might, in bridling ambition, sèrve the purposes of an usurping priesthood by depressing the spirit of the people, it must at the same time have depressed genius, by imposing a restraint upon its versatility, and extinguished the ardour of emulation, without which the liberal arts can never attain superior excellence. These can only be cultivated with success among a people in a state of professional freedom; where genius is left unfettered, and talents have their full range; and where a possibility is left to men of all classes of rising to public honours and offices.

Depression of genius, however, in consequence of the restraints imposed upon it, is not the greatest evil attending the institution of hereditary professions, considered in a political light. It has a tendency to destroy that social concord, which should subsist among the members of the same community. A set of men confined to a particular calling, from generation to generation, view those of every other with envy or disdain. Hence a division of the members of a state into professional classes, between which a perpetual bar is fixed, very different from the distinction of ranks, originating in different degrees of merit, engenders animosity, and obstructs the most necessary and salutary effects, which men ought naturally to derive from living under the guardianship of the same laws. Each class forms a separate body in the state, and all national union is lost, and all sense of a common interest.

Brute-worship fostered new animosities among the Egyptians. As the animal adored by the inhabitants of one district, was often held in detestation by those of another, intestine feuds thence arose among their votaries, and never-ceasing religious antipathy[414]. Yet this diversity of worship is said to have been esta-

414. Diod. Sicul. *Biblioth.* lib. i. p. 81. edit. sup. cit.

blished,

blished, in order to preserve the kingdom from greater shocks[415]; a wretched artifice of sacerdotal power, combining with regal authority, to maintain its dominion over the people at the expence of private happiness.

Notwithstanding so many causes of dissention, Egypt was a powerful, and even a peaceful kingdom[416]. Watered by one great river, to which it owed its fertility, and which served as a centre of civil union; bounded on the the north by the sea, and there secured by impracticable harbours, and impassable fens; and, on all other quarters, by mountains or burning deserts of billowing sand, it was strongly fortified against invasion by nature, as well as by art. And nature, in assigning it such boundaries, and such a common source of plenty, seems to have marked it out as the seat of one monarchy. Early divided into provinces, under a regular government and police, every licentious motion was repressed by the vigilance of the magistrate; and the military body, a perpetual militia, stationed in different districts[417], were always ready to quell any popular tumult, bred by intestine discord. From peace flowed public prosperity; population, industry, arts and manufactures; the accumulation of wealth, and the conveniences of life.

415. Id. ibid.

416. For the uninterrupted enjoyment of peace, Egypt seems to have been long celebrated; for when the miserable remains of the kingdom of Judah, after the taking of Jerusalem by Nebuchadnezzar, were promised indulgence if they would stay in their own land, they said, "No! but we will go into Egypt, where we shall see no war, "nor hear the sound of the trumpet" (*Jeremiah*, chap. xlii. ver. 14.). It was also plentiful, notwithstanding its full population. Hence the fugitive Jews added, in proposing to retire into Egypt, "Nor shall "we there *know hunger*" (Id. ibid). And in a more early period, the Israelites, under Moses, often looked anxiously back from the frontiers of the *promised land*, to the luxurious plenty which they had enjoyed in Egypt. See particularly *Numbers*, chap. xi. ver. 5—20.

417. Herodotus, lib. ii. cap. clxiv.—clxviii.

Proud

PART I.

Proud of these acquisitions and accommodations, and restrained by their religion from a free intercourse with foreigners, as well as by the boundaries of their country, and the maxims of their policy, the Egyptians held all other nations in contempt. Yet, viewed with a philosophic eye, their character as a people is less entitled to respect, than that of any other ancient nation, that had attained the same degree of civilization. The blind idolaters of that debasing system of superstition by which they were enslaved, they possessed few of the nobler virtues. Their manners were polished[418], and the severe prohibitions of law, with the rigid administration of justice, had subdued in them the excesses of the natural passions. But bigotry had kindled in their bosoms other passions, as violent as those of the rudest barbarian; and as little under the controul of reason, or the government of political prudence[419].

418. Herodotus, *Historiar.* lib. ii. cap. lxxx. Diod. Sicul. *Biblioth.* lib. i. p. 81.

419. I here allude to their extravagant sorrow on the death of their *sacred animals*, and the fanatical fury with which they were transported against those that killed any of them; but especially against such as killed an ibis, a hawk, or a cat, whether by design or accident (See Herodotus, lib. ii. cap. lxv. lxvi. et Diod. Sicul. lib. i. p. 75.). Diodorus has furnished us with a famous instance to this purpose, in the killing of a cat. When the Romans were negociating an alliance with Ptolemy Auletes, whose right to the throne of Egypt they haughtily condescended to acknowledge, the Egyptians, conscious they were at the mercy of that conquering people, loaded the Roman deputies and their attendants with caresses, and took every possible care to avoid any cause of disgust or quarrel; yet, during that season of anxious solicitude and apprehension, a cat being killed by a Roman, the Egyptian populace tumultuously ran to his lodging; and neither the officers sent by the king to command forbearance, nor the fear of the Romans, could deliver the man from the fury of the enraged multitude, though he had not intentionally killed the cat (Diod. Sicul. lib. i. p. 75.). " Of this," adds the historian (*Biblioth.* ubi cit.), " I was an eye-witness, at the time of my travels in Egypt."

Genius

Genius the Egyptians certainly possessed; though that genius was more acute and steady, than liberal or elevated. They prosecuted works of expence and ingenuity with singular perseverance, and upon principles perfectly mathematical[420]; but being totally destitute of taste, they have failed to acquire a distinguished rank among the cultivators of the finer arts[421]. Their architecture attempted to supply greatness of design, by immensity of fabric; substituting altitude for sublimity, and ponderous solidity for stability[422]; Their statuary, like their architecture, delighted in huge masses of stone[423]. These they nicely chiseled into human or brute-forms, or a compound between the two; but displayed neither elegance of figure, animation of expression, nor grace in attitude[424].

Their

420. Diod. Sicul. lib. i. p. 88, 89.

421. Winkelmann, *Hist. de l'Art de l'Antiquité*, liv. ii, chap. i. '

422. Strabo. lib. xvii. p. 806. et seq. edit. Lutet. Paris, Typ. Reg. 1620. As the Egyptians were ignorant of the art of constructing an arch, they could not give stability to their buildings without great waste of labour and materials; nor do they, after all, convey to us the idea of stability (See the plates in Pococke's and Norden's *Travels into Egypt*, &c.). A straight stone laid over a door, however thick or strongly supported by columns, has not the firmness of an arch. Hence the Egyptians, from want of skill to cast an arch, were obliged to make their doors very narrow. The inconvenience and inelegance of which may be easily conceived.

423. Many of these I have already had occasion to describe, on the authority of Herodotus; who saw the stupendous works of Egyptian art before they had been much defaced, and when they had suffered no admixture from the ingenuity of other nations. His testimony, therefore, is superior to that of every other ancient author. Diodorus Siculus, also highly deserving of credit, and next in point of time, mentions a statue in a sitting posture, the work of Memnon Syenesis, larger than any noticed by that venerable historian. The measure of the foot was seven cubits in length (Diod. Sicul. *Biblioth.* lib. i. p. 44.). And the head of the wonderful Sphinx is still to be seen, which measures fifteen feet from the ear to the chin. Maillet, *Descript. de l'Egypt*, p. 221.

424. Winkelmann, ubi sup. The human figures in Egyptian sculpture have, with a few exceptions, their hands hanging down by their sides,

Their painting, if we except brilliancy and durability of colours, was void of every excellence belonging to that captivating art[425]. The magical effects of light and shade, figures detached from their base, and seeming to aspire after immortality; that beauty more than human, yet copied from human forms, familiar in the paintings of Grecian artists, never animated an Egyptian tablature. Poetry they seem never to have cultivated; and music, as an art, their gloomy minds proscribed[426]. But music was employed, in celebrating the festivals and mysteries of their religion; and poetry had produced one hymn, which was chanted on such occasions[427].

The learning of the Egyptians early attracted the curiosity of the Greeks. Their first sages travelled into Egypt[428], and their most enlightened philosophers continued to consider the Egyptian priests as their masters in science, and resorted to them for instruction[429]. But in what the learning of the Egyptians consisted, we are left in some measure to conjecture, as none of their ancient books have come down to us. That they were deeply skilled in the principles of mechanics, appears from the machinery requisite to erect their wonderful obelisks, and amazing pyramids. Geometry was necessary to enable them to conduct the numerous canals with which Egypt was intersected, as well as to enable them to divide their lands anew, after

sides, and their feet close, or nearly so (Id. ibid.). This learned, and enlightened antiquarian, has taken great care to distinguish the ancient Egyptian style, from that which was introduced into Egypt under the Macedonian monarchs, or Roman emperors.

425. Winkelmann, *Hist. de l'Art. de l'Antiquité*, liv. ii. chap. iii. *Relat. du Sayd.* ap Thevenot, tom. ii. Paul Lucas, *Voyage to the Levant*, vol. i. and all modern travellers of taste in the arts.

426. Diod. Sicul. lib. i. p. 73.

427. Herodotus, lib. ii. cap. lxxix.

428. Diod. Sicul. lib. i. p. 86.

429. Id. ibid.

the

the annual inundations of the Nile[430]. In this necessity geometry is said to have had its origin[431].

That the Egyptians had carried their astronomical observations to a high degree of perfection, is put beyond dispute by the exact computation of their year[432]; by their calculation of eclipses, both lunar and solar[433]; and also by their conjectures concerning the appearance of comets[434]. Their progress in other sciences cannot be ascertained with any degree of certainty. But whatever might be the learning of the ancient Egyptians, it was confined chiefly to the ecclesiastical body; who involved it in symbols and allegories, which they un-riddled only to those that were initated into their mysteries[435]. And, after all, until it had been refined by flowing through Grecian channels, it seems to have been, like their Nile, but a muddy stream.

What is acquired with difficulty is much prized. The Grecian sages, who travelled into Egypt, were obliged to remain there for many years, and to go through progressive degrees of initiation, before they could obtain access to the arcana of the priests[436]. They, therefore, set great value upon the secrets communicated to them; and kept up the high reputation of Egyptian learning, after their own country was furnished with more precious treasures of science.

430. Herodotus, lib. ii. cap. cviii. cix. Diod. Sicul. lib. i. p. 73. Strabo, lib. xvi. p. 757. edit. sup. cit.

431. Id. ibid.

432. Diod. Sicul. lib. i. p. 46. The Egyptians computed their year at three hundred and sixty-five days, and one fourth (Id. ibid.), or six hours; within twelve minutes of the computation of sir Isaac Newton.

433. Ibid. *Biblioth*. lib. i. p. 73.   434. Id. ibid.

435. Clem. Alexand. *Strom*. lib. v. p. 566. edit. Paris.

436. Strabo, *Geog*. lib. xvii. p. 806. Clemens Alex. sup. cit. et Porphyr. et Jamblic. in *Vit. Pythag.*

Vain

Vain of being able to number among their scholars
the most eminent Grecian philosophers[437], and flattered by the adulation of that haughty and presump-
tuous people, the Egyptian priests arrogated to themselves and their venerable nation, the invention of the
whole circle of the sciences[438]; of *letters* or *alphabetic
characters*[439], by which only science can be readily
communicated; and the ordination of every civil and
sacred institution.   They first erected temples to the
gods, appointed festivals, and practised divination
by oracles and otherwise [440].   They had sent out colonies into all countries, and civilized the human race;
by communicating, along with the elements of the arts
and sciences, their maxims of religion and government[441].

These

437. Strabo, ubi sup.

438. Diod. Sicul. *Bibliotb*. lib. i. p. 63.   439. Id. ibid.

440. Herodotus, *Historiar*. lib. ii. cap. iv. lviii. lxxxiii. Divination
had attained such perfection among the Egyptians, through the ingenuity of priestcraft, that oracular responses were not delivered by any
human being, but *apparently* by the divinity consulted (Id. ibid.).
In what manner this was contrived we are left to conjecture; the venerable historian (who alone could have given us genuine information
on the subject) having only told us, that it was done in different
ways (Herodot. ubi sup.).   Two of those ways we can discover,
with a degree of certainty.   The Egyptians, we know, had *vocal* statues.   That of Memnon has become proverbial.   These statues were
of the colossal kind; and, as they were hollow, could easily admit
priests within them.   Thus the gods might seem to speak.   We have
also reason to believe, that the prophetic answer was often delivered
without any visible representation; by a voice issuing, with awful solemnity, from the profound gloom of the Egyptian temples; while
sacred pomp, and holy symbols, impressed upon the minds of the
people the immediate presence of the Deity.

441. Herodot. lib. ii. et Diod. Sicul. lib. i. passim.   The attachment of
the Egyptians to their own country, and their aversion against intercourse with foreigners, contradict their pretensions to extensive colo-
nization.   Truth will not permit us to rank the Chaldeans or Hebrews
among the number of their emigrants; yet these they claimed (Diod.
Sicul. lib. i. p. 24. 73.).   The Egyptian leaders, who conducted colonies into Greece, seem to have been violently expelled (Herodot.

lib.

These pretensions have been too fully admitted by writers both ancient and modern; but especially by the early and latter Greeks. The wise and learned Strabo allows only to the Egyptians the invention of geometry[442]; while he ascribes to the Phoenicians the invention of arithmetic, the art of keeping accompts, or registers of mercantile transactions, and the discovery of the use of the pole-star in nocturnal navigation[443]. The Phoenicians, or Canaanites, have also a claim to the invention of *letters;* for before the invasion of Canaan by the Israelites or Hebrews, Cadmus had carried the Phoenician alphabet into Greece[444]; and we find in that country a city, which bore the name of Kirjath-sepher, or the *City of Letters,* in more ancient times[445].

The

lib. ii. cap. clxxxii.): and must have been conveyed in Phoenician vessels. For the Egyptians appear to have been utterly unacquainted with navigation till the reign of Sesostris, and to have had no ships on the Mediterranean before the reign of Psammitichus.

442. Strabo, lib. xvi. p. 757.   443. Id. ibid.

444. The Arundelian or Oxford marbles, commonly called the *Parian Chronicle* (Epoch vii.), place the arrival of Cadmus in Greece 1519 years before the Christian æra; and consequently twenty-nine years before the Israelites left Egypt, according to the Hebrew chronology, and sixty-nine years before they passed the river Jordan. That Cadmus brought the Phoenician alphabet into Greece is not disputed; and all ancient chronologers place his arrival nearly as high as the Parian Chronicle.

445. Joshua, chap. xv. ver. 15. It is impossible to fix the æra of the *invention*, or rather *use* of *letters*, as *signs* of *words;* for it appears that *hieroglyphic symbols*, among an ingenious people, naturally and imperceptibly, mould themselves into alphabetic characters (*Divine Legation of Moses,* book iv. sect. iv.). Dr. Warburton conjectures, that after the use of letters became common in Egypt, the Egyptian priests invented a sacred alphabet for secrecy. But from this opinion I must dissent; because symbolical hieroglyphics, soon after they ceased to be of general use (if ever they were so), would become so obscure as to answer the purpose of the most profound secrecy. And Herodotus, in speaking of the sacred and vulgar letters of the Egyptians (lib. ii. cap. xxx.), certainly meant no more than hieroglyphic symbols and alphabetic characters. This sufficiently appears by his telling

PART I.   The strongest argument in favour of the Egyptian claim to the invention of letters is, that Moses, soon after his escape with the Israelites out of Egypt, having broken, in a pet, the two tables of the law delivered to him by the LORD, inscribed the *ten commandments* on other two tables of stone[446]. But Moses might have learned the use of alphabetic characters, (if such he used) during his residence in Arabia with Jethro his father-in-law, the prince and priest of Midian[447]; for the Midianites were merchants, and carried on, in conjunction with the Ishmaelites, in very early times, the trade between Syria and Egypt by land[448], as the Canaanites did by sea.

These reflections, my lord, will prepare your mind for an account of the

---

us (lib. ii. cap. cvi.), that the inscriptions on the pillars erected by Sesostris were in the *sacred letters of Egypt*. For on all such monuments Dr. Warburton allows, and the remains of Egyptian obelisks prove, that *hieroglyphics* only were inscribed.

446. *Exodus*, chap. xxxiv. ver. 27, 28.

447. Sir Isaac Newton did not scruple to ascribe to the Midianites, the honour of instructing Moses in the art of writing (*Chronology of Ancient Kingdoms amended*, p. 210.). But if Moses, during his stay in Arabia, with Jethro his father-in-law, did not acquire the use of alphabetic writing, he was there instructed in matters of higher import. For when he approached Horeb or Oreb, the *mountain of God*, the LORD appeared to him under the symbol of fire (Exodus, chap. iii. ver. 12.); encouraged him to rescue the Hebrews from Egyptian servitude; and gave him a *rod*, which is termed the *Rod of God*, for the performance of *miracles* (Exodus, chap. iv. ver. 17—21.). We also know, that Moses profited by the counsels of Jethro (*Exodus*, chap. xviii. ver. 17—27.); who appears to have been a prince of great wisdom, and experience in human affairs; and, as a priest, was no doubt profoundly skilled in all the mysteries of religion.

448. *Genesis*, chap. xxxvii. ver. 25—28.

EARLY

EARLY STATE OF SYRIA, AND THE CONQUEST OF PALES-
TINE BY THE HEBREWS.

LETTER
I.

UNDER the name of Syria I comprehend all that part of Lower Asia, which is bounded on the east by the Epuhrates and the Arabian desert; on the west by the Mediterranean; and which extends, in a southern direction, from the mountains Amanus and Taurus to Arabia Petrea and the northern frontier of Egypt. This delightful and fertile country, naturally abounding in palm-trees, yielding the choicest dates, and producing, by culture, corn, wine, and oil, is agreeably diversified with hills and vallies, and washed in its whole extent by the sea; which, with refreshing breezes from the mountains Libanus and Antilibanus, whose lofty summits are frequently covered with snow, moderates the heat of the climate. Syria lies between the thirty-second and thirty-seventh degrees of northern latitude.

With the northern part of Syria, or *Syria Proper*, in the first ages, we are utterly unacquainted. It appears to have been subject to the Assyrian monarchs; who, in conjunction with the other eastern potentates, sometimes extended their dominion over the whole inland country, on both sides the river Jordan[449]. Hence Syria and Assyria are frequently confounded by the more ancient Grecian historians and geographers.

But of the state of the central, and southern part of Syria, in early times, we are better informed than of that of any other region on the face of the globe. Here we find men living, as nearly as possible, in a *state of nature;* without any legal institutions, under the fathers

---

449. *Genesis*, chap. xiv. ver. 1—12.

of

PART I. of families and the heads of tribes[450]: yet here we
discover no traces of that unfeeling barbarism, and
brutal licentiousness, which poets have feigned, and
credulous historians and philosophers adopted, concerning the manners of mankind in such a state.
Here we find children obedient to their parents, and
servants to their masters[451]; subjects sharing with
their chief all deliberations respecting general interest[452]; leagues solemnly ratified, and faithfully observed[453]; marriages contracted from love, and from
family connection[454]; the sanctity of matrimonial
engagements held in the highest reverence[455]; the
loss of female virtue thought worthy of death[456];

450. *Genesis*, chap. xiii.—xxxiii. passim.
451. *Genesis*, chap. xxiv. passim.
452. *Genesis*, chap. xxiii. ver. 13—16.
453. *Genesis*, chap. xxi. ver. 22—32.
454. *Genesis*, chap. xxiv. xxix. passim.
455. *Genesis*, chap. xx. ver. 3—16. chap. xxvi. ver. 7—11. It is
remarkable, that in all these transactions, the various Syrian tribes
discovered more confidence, and a higher sense of honour, than the
Hebrews, who dwelt among them; though the Hebrews regarded
themselves as the peculiar people of God, and had received assurances
to that purpose. They wanted faith in man, whatever they might
have in God; and seemed ever willing to prostitute their wives, rather
than suffer in their own persons. The speech of Abimelech to Isaac
is truly memorable. Isaac, like his father Abraham, had said that
his *wife* was his *sister;* " lest the men of the place should kill him for
" *Rebekah*, because she was fair to look upon. And it came to pass, that
" Abimelech, king of the Philistines, looked out at a window, and
" saw Isaac *sporting* with *Rebekah* his wife. And Abimelech called
" Isaac, and said, ' Of a surety she is thy wife: and how saidst thou,
" She is my sister ?'—And Isaac said unto him, ' Lest I die for her.'—
" And Abimelech said, ' What is this thou hast done unto us?—One
" of the people might lightly have lain with thy wife, and thou should-
" est have brought guiltiness upon us.' And Abimelech charged all the
" people, saying, ' He that toucheth this man, or his wife, shall surely
" be put to death" (*Genesis*, chap. xxvi. ver. 7—11.). If disposed to
display the baseness of the Hebrews, I might exhibit their perfidious
cruelty in regard to the Shechemites (*Genesis*, chap. xxxiv. passim);
But it is better to draw a veil over such horrid transactions.
456. *Genesis*, chap. xxxviii. ver. 24.

                                          and

and adultery considered as a crime that called for the vengeance of heaven[457].

In Syria, during those early times, we see religion appearing in its most amiable and simple form : *one* God, the Creator of all things, every where adored, without images, altars, or an established priesthood[458]; equal purity in faith and worship, principle and practice. But in proportion as wealth and luxury increased among the Syrian tribes, their religion grew more sensual. Like all eastern nations, they became addicted to the worship of the heavenly bodies[459]; and priestcraft employed images and the whole apparatus of delusive superstition to attract the devotion of the people[460].

Corruption of manners (as it ever has, and ever will) necessarily followed the corruption of religion ; for corrupt religion can find an apology or an expiation for every crime that does not clash with its own interests. The manners of the Syrians accordingly appear to have been deeply corrupted, when Moses led the Hebrews toward their frontiers[461]; and to have continued so in consequence of the corruptions of religion, for almost two thousand years[462]. Their idolatrous superstition sanctified every licentious vice[463], and drew into its vortex even the Hebrews themselves[464]; though set apart to preserve the worship of

457. *Genesis*, chap. xx. ver. 3—7. 458. *Genesis*, chap. xiv. et seq.
459. *Deuteronomy*, chap. xvii. ver. 3.
460. Selden, *de Diis Syris*, passim. They seem to have had, as early as the days of Moses, moveable tabernacles, vocal statues, and whatever could impose upon the credulity of the vulgar.
461. *Leviticus*, chap. xviii. ver. 6—26. *Numbers*, chap. xxv. ver. 1, 2. *Deuteronomy*, chap. ix. ver. 4.
462. Lucian, *de Syr. Dea*.   463. Id. ibid.
464. *Numbers*, chap. xxv. ver. 2. *Deuteronomy*, chap. xxxii. ver. 16, 17. *Judges*, chap. ii. ver. 13. *Samuel*, chap. vii. ver. 3. See also the two books of *Kings*, and the *Prophets*, passim.

one

PART I. *one* God without the use of idols, and entrenched within multifarious ceremonies.

Milton, whose learning was as great as his genius, has given a striking description of the old Syrian gods; in which poetry is made subservient to historical truth. The geographical delineation is highly beautiful and picturesque; and it is, on the whole, a just and highly-finished picture.

> " First MOLOCH, horrid king! besmear'd with blood
> " Of human sacrifice, and parents' tears;
> " Though for the noise of drums and timbrels loud
> " Their children's cries unheard, that *pass'd through fire*
> " To this grim idol[465].   Him the Ammonite
> " Worshipp'd in Rabba and her watery plain;
> " In Argob, and in Basan, to the stream
> " Of utmost Arnon.

> " Next CHEMOS, th' obscene dread of Moab's sons
> " From Aroar to Nebo, and the wild
> " Of southmost Abtrim; in Hesbon
> " And Horonaim, Sihon's realm, beyond
> " The flow'ry dale of Sibma, clad with vines;
> " And Elealé, to the Asphaltic pool:
> " PEOR his other name[466].

" With

---

465. *Moloch* is thought by the Rabbins to have been *Saturn* (Blackwell's *Mythol.* Letter x.).   And the idol, here alluded to by Milton, seems to be that of the Carthaginian god, to whom Diodorus gives the name of *Kronos*, or *Saturn* (Diod. Sicul. lib. xx. p. 756. edit. sup. cit.). To this god, whose worship was brought from Syria to Carthage, human sacrifices were profusely offered in times of public calamity (Id. ibid. et Justin. lib. xviii. cap. vi.); but especially *male children*, who were offered at all times (Diod. Sicul. ubi sup.).   The idol stood with extended, but declining arms, in the act of receiving; so that, when the human victim was presented to him, it dropt down into a devouring furnace (Id. ibid.).   A similar description of the idol Moloch is given by Selden, *de Diis Syr.* Syntag. i. cap. vi.

466. This god is called *Baal-Peor* by Moses (*Numbers*, chap. xxv. ver. 5.); that is the *lord* PEOR.   For Bel or Baal, which signifies *lord*, was a common title of honour added by the eastern nations to the

proper

" With these came they, who from the bordering flood
" Of old Euphrates, to the brook that parts
" Egypt from Syrian ground, had general names
" Of BAALIM and ASHTAROTH[467]: *those* male,
" *These* feminine.

" ASTORETH, whom the Phoenicians called
" ASTARTE, *queen of heaven!* with crescent horns[468];
" To whose bright image nightly, by the *moon,*

proper names of all the celestial gods; but applied, without any proper name, to the SUN (Servius, *ad Virg. Eniad.* lib. i. ver. 733.); when held up to the idolatry of the people as the supreme Deity, the *Lord,* or *King of heaven;* in the same manner as the MOON was worshipped as the *queen of heaven.*

Peor seems to have been the same with the Egyptian *Bacchus,* or the SUN considered as the *principle of generation.* In Egypt, at the festival of Bacchus, women walked in procession, carrying obscene images; so ingeniously framed, that the very *nerves of the virile member were seen to move,* while the wanton females sung the praise of the genial god (Herodot. lib. ii. cap. xlviii.). And the daughters of Moab appear to have been employed in some such lascivious festival, when they enticed the Israelites, under Moses, to commit whoredom with them, and to worship PEOR (*Numbers,* chap. xxv. ver. 1, 2, 3.). Grotius (*ad Deuteron.* cap. iv. ver. 3.) thinks the name of this god expressive of the sensual part of male nature, as *Aphrodite,* or Venus, was of the motions of female lewdness in the organ of generation.

467. The *Baalim,* or lords, were the host of heaven, or the celestial hierarchy, under the government of BAAL, their supreme lord, or king. To some of those were given male, and to others *female* names, according to the reputed qualities of the spiritual intelligences, by which the several planets were thought to be animated. *Ashtaroth* was the general title for the female planets, as *Baalim* was for the male; and it appears to have been applied individually alike to the planet *Venus* and to the *moon,* both having a real, or imaginary relation, to female nature; to the qualities which lead to enjoyment, and those that are essential to propagation. To the *moon,* however, was paid superior honour, because of her superior influence and effulgence: she reigned as queen, and divided with her lord the empire of the heavens, while both superintended the affairs of the earth. This was the chief article in the popular creed of the Syrian nations.

468. In the form of a *crescent;* to represent the appearance of the *moon* during her increase, the festival of the goddess being at full moon.

" Sidonian

" Sidonian virgins paid their vows and songs :
" In Sion also not unsung, where stood
" Her temple on th' offensive mountain, built
" By that uxorious king[469], whose heart, though large,
" Beguil'd by fair idolatresses, fell·
" To idols foul.

" THAMMUZ, ————
" Whose annual wound in Lebanon allur'd
" The Syrian damsels to lameht his fate
" In amorous ditties all a summer's day ;
" While smooth Adonis from his native rock
" Ran purple to the sea, supposed with blood
" Of Thammuz yearly wounded[470]. The love tale
" Infected

469. The wise Solomon, who built and dedicated the famous temple of Jerusalem to one God, the Creator of the universe.; yet, who
also built in its neighbourhood, temples to most of the Syrian deities ;
and, among others, one to *Ashtaroth* (i. *Kings*, chap. xi. ver. 5—7.).
The worship of this goddess, which early drew aside the chosen people (*Judges*, chap. ii. ver. 13.), was peculiarly attractive to the women.
They considered the *queen of heaven* as the cause of all their felicity,
and obstinately persisted in worshipping her (*Jeremiah*, chap. xliv.
ver. 17, 18, 19.). Living in a land of superstition and sensuality, they
were disgusted at the idea of a *solitary god :* they wanted a female
tutelary deity, a divine patroness, a *wife* for the *lord*.

470. Of this annual mourning for a *wounded god*, which prevailed
in various countries, Vossius has given the most satisfactory explication. He conjectures, that the lamentations for *Thammuz*, or the *sun*
in his beauty, were occasioned by the retiring of that luminary toward
the northern regions after the summer-solstice (when those lamentations were made), and the consequent wound to vegetable and animal
life (*Hist. Idolat.* lib. ii. cap. v.). " Hence," exclaims another learned
antiquarian, " No wonder the loss of this *Adonis* should be loudly la-
" mented in Assyria, in Egypt, in Phoenicia, and in all the countries
" tinctured with their superstitions: or that his return to impregnate
" the world with genial vigour should be welcomed with the highest
" demonstrations of joy. With whom should *Venus*, the susceptive
" power of generation, be in love ?—Whose absence should she mourn,
" when he goes a hunting through the monsters of the *zodiac*, and ap-
" proaches too near the frozen bear, but this mighty source of life and
" love" (Blackwell, *Mythol.* Lett. xvii.) ? The *reddening* of the river
Adonis, or of Thammuz, at the annual mourning for his wound, though
heightened

    " Infected Sion's daughter with like heat ;
    " Whose wanton passions in the sacred porch
    " Ezekiel saw[471] ; when, by the vision led,
    " His eye survey'd the dark idolatries
    " Of alienated Judah.

      " Next came one,
    " DAGON his name ; sea-monster, upward man,
    " And downward fish[472]: yet had his temple high
    " Rear'd in Azotus, *dreaded* through the coast
    " Of Palestine, in Gath, and Ascalon,
    " And Accoron, and Gaza's frontier bounds.
    " Him follow'd RIMMON[473], whose delightful seat
    " Was fair Damascus[474]; on the fertile banks
    " Of Abbana and Pharphar, lucid streams[475]."

The

heightened into a miracle by priestcraft, proceeded from a natural cause (Lucian, *Syr. Dea*, and Maundrel, *Journey from Aleppo to Jerusalem.*).

471. See *Ezekiel*, chap. viii. ver. 13. He afterward describes the idolatries of Judah in language too highly coloured for any page but that of holy writ. I shall, however, transcribe the most chaste passages, for the purposes of illustration. " She (Judah) doted upon the " Assyrians, her neighbours, captains and rulers, clothed most gorge- " ously ; horsemen riding upon horses, all of them desirable young " men ; girded with girdles upon their loins, exceeding in *dyed attire* " *upon their heads*, all of them princes to look to, after the manner of the " Babylonians of Chaldea. And as soon as she saw them with her eyes, " she doted upon them, and sent messengers unto them into Chaldea ; " and the Babylonians came to her into the bed of love, and defiled " her with their whoredom. Yet she multiplied her whoredoms ; in " calling to remembrance the days of her youth, wherein she played " the harlot in the land of Egypt." *Ezek.* chap. xxiii. ver. 12—19.

472. *Dagon*, like his idol, appears to have been a compound deity, allegorically descriptive of the plenty yielded by the land and sea; to which his worshippers were equally indebted for their subsistence. The word *dread* employed by Milton, in speaking of this and other idols, is the natural consequence of his representing the heathen gods as devils.

473. Of *Rimmon*, we know no more than what the poet has expressed.

474. Damascus, like all places where mankind can find plentiful subsistence, appears very early to have been a city; for we find, that the steward of the house of Abraham was " Eliezer of Damascus." *Genesis*, chap. xv. ver. 2.

475. *Paradise Lost*, book i. The Syrians had some gods not des-

cribed

PART I.   The corrupt religion of the Syrian nations, with the
consequent corruption of manners, furnishes the best
apology that can be offered for the violent, and unpro-
voked invasion of their country, by the Hebrews. For
if we admit that the Deity ever miraculously interpo-
ses in human affairs, or sanctions proceedings contrary
to the laws of moral justice, the strongest call for such
interposition must be the extirpation of a bloody and
sensual idolatry; the nurse of every licentious vice,
and the parent of unnatural crimes[476]. Moses, however, makes small use of this argument, as an incentive; but perpetually reiterates to the *chosen people*,
the *promise* made by the LORD to Abraham, their venerable ancestor, and to the patriarchs Isaac and Jacob[477], of all the land on both sides the river Jordan,
and from mount Lebanon to the Egyptian border.
Having found too little zeal in the hearts of that people for the pure religion which he had promulgated
to them, to rest his hopes of success on their zeal for
the destruction of idolatry, though his fears were many
lest they should become infected with it, he held up to
them, along with the *promise* of the LORD, renewed
in their presence, the *beauty* and *fertility* of the destined
country[478]. And he fed them with its spoils.

Mysterious, as it may seem, this desirable country was promised to the seed of Abraham before the

cribed by Milton. The most distinguished of these was *Melicar-
tbus*, by the Greeks called the *Phœnician Hercules*; seemingly one of
the titles of the *sun*, the tutelary god of Tyre (Herodot. lib. ii. cap.
xliv.) and the *patron of bold adventure*. See Selden *de Diis Syr*. Syntag. ii. cap. vii.

476. *Leviticus*, chap. xviii. ver. 2—30. chap. xx. ver. 2, 3. *Deuteronomy*, chap. xii. ver. 31.

477. *Deuteronomy*, chap. i. ver. 8. 21. chap. iv. ver. 37, 38. chap.
vii. ver. 1. 8. chap. ix. ver. 5. chap. xvii. ver. 14. chap. xxxi. ver. 7.

478. *Deuteronomy*, chap. viii. ver. 7, 8, 9. A land of hills and val-
leys, abounding in fountains and brooks; and producing wheat, barley, grapes, olives, figs, and other choice fruit. Id. ibid.

inhabitants

inhabitants had become idolaters[479]; and a prophetic curse had been denounced against them, before they were a people[480]. How wonderful are the councils of Heaven!—but in nothing revealed to man, so wonderful, as in the predilection of the *Most High* for the Hebrew nation[481].

Thus, my lord, am I naturally led to bring under your view this ancient people. The early part of the history of the Hebrews you will find related in the first book of Moses[482], and with a simplicity and mi-

479. *Genesis*, chap. xii. ver. 1—7. That the Canaanites were not then idolaters appears in the subsequent chapters.

480. *Genesis*, chap. ix. ver. 24—27. " And Noah awoke from his " wine, and knew what his younger son had done unto him ; and he " said, *cursed be Canaan!—a servant of servants* shall he be unto his " brethren. And he said, *blessed be the Lord God of Shem!*—and " *Canaan shall be his servant*. God shall enlarge Japheth; and *he shall* " *dwell in the tents of Shem*, and *Canaan shall be his servant*" (Id. ibid). The Hebrews were a branch of the posterity of Shem.

481. Dr. Warburton denies this predilection (*Divine Legation of Moses*, book v. sect. i.); and boldly asserts, that " to pretend *they were* " *chosen as favourites* is both unjust and absurd" (Id. ibid.). But, in so saying he impeaches the veracity of the sacred historian. For Moses expressly tells the Israelites or Hebrews, " because the LORD *loved thy* " *fathers*, therefore, he *chose their seed after them;* and brought thee out " in his sight, with his mighty power, out of Egypt:—to drive out " nations from before thee, greater and mightier than thou; *to bring* " *thee in, to give thee their land* for an inheritance" (*Deuteronomy*, chap. iv. ver. 37, 38.). " The *Lord*," adds he, " did not *set his love upon you,* " nor *choose you*, because ye were more in number than any people; " but *because the* LORD *loved you*, and *because he would keep the oath* " which *he had sworn* unto your fathers" (*Deuteronomy*, chap. vii. ver. 7, 8.). He afterwards tells us, that " when the MOST HIGH *divided* " to the nations their inheritance; when he *separated* the sons of Adam, " he set the bounds of the people according to the number of the chil- " dren of Israel; for *Jacob is the lot of his inheritance*. He kept him " as the apple of his eye," with such affection, " as an eagle flutter- " eth over her young" (Deuteron. chap. xxxii. ver. 8 —11.). Yet the Israelites, we are told (ver. 20.), were " a very froward genera- " tion, children in whom was no faith!"

482. *Genesis*, chap. xii.—xxxviii.

nuteness

nuteness that bear the strongest marks of truth; setting aside all regard to that divine inspiration, which is supposed to have guided the pen of the sacred historian. To the sacred page I must also refer you, for an account of the sojourning in Egypt, and wonderful deliverance of the Israelites or Hebrews from Egyptian servitude, in consequence of a multitude of miracles[483]; for their wanderings in the Arabian desert, where they were supernaturally supplied with food, during the term of forty years[484]; and for the awful manifestation of the *Divine presence*[485] at Mount Sinai or Horeb[486]; where the Lord had first appeared to Moses, under the *symbol of* fire, in the *bush burning* yet *not consumed*[487].

These I leave theological writers to display and investigate. For they partake too much of the marvellous to be submitted to the cool inquiries of the philosophic historian; who is bound to reconcile to the laws of nature and probability every circumstance he relates, or to expose it as falsehood and imposture. It was dangerous to approach too near the Mount[488]: I shall,

483. *Gen.* chap. xxxix —l. *Exod* chap. i.—xiv.

484. *Exod.* chap. xvi. xvii. *Deuteron.* chap. v. ver. 6. 12.

485. The words of the sacred historian only can do justice to the subject. "And it came to pass on the third day in the morning, that " there were thunders and lightnings, and a thick cloud upon the " mount, and the voice of the trumpets exceeding loud; so that all the " people in the camp trembled. And Moses brought out the people " out of the camp to meet with God; and they stood at the nether " part of the mount. And mount Sinai was altogether on a smoke, " because the *Lord* descended upon it in *fire:*—and the smoke thereof " ascended as the smoke of a furnace, and the whole mount quaked " greatly. And when the voice of the trumpet sounded long, and " waxed louder and louder, Moses spake, and *God* answered him by " a *voice*." *Exodus*, chap. xix. ver. 17, 18, 19.

486. Compare *Exod.* chap. xix. ver. 16—19. with *Deuteron.* chap. iv. ver. 10, 11, 12.   487. *Exod.* chap. iii. ver. 1—6.

488. *Exod.* chap. xix. ver. 21. " And the *Lord* said unto Moses, " go down and charge the people, lest they break through unto the " *Lord* to gaze, and many of them perish." Id. ibid.

                                             therefore

therefore, keep at a reverential distance, and maintain a profound silence, in regard to this, and other sacred transactions connected with it. But the institutions of Moses, the illustrious Hebrew legislator, demand my attention as an observer of the progress of human affairs, and of the rise of civil and religious establishments.

In the meantime, I must observe, that Syria continued divided, as formerly, into a number of small kingdoms, when Joshua, the Hebrew general, passed the river Jordan at the head of a mighty host[489].

The conquest of Palestine, by this tremendous warrior, being circumstantially related in the *scriptural book* that *bears his name*[490], I shall here only mention, in general terms, the issue of his enterprize. The heads of the Syrian kingdoms, principalities or townships, having chosen no common leader, nor digested any regular plan of defence, though they knew the Hebrews had been long hovering on their frontier, several of those petty kingdoms, on both sides Jordan, were subdued, and the inhabitants put to the sword, before any league was formed for opposing the cruel invaders[491]. At last, however, threatened with utter extirpation, a general alliance was concerted among the remaining kings between Jordan and the sea[492]; but Joshua, by forced marches, falling twice unexpectedly upon the combined army, routed it with great slaughter[493]. And the victorious Hebrews settled in the southern part of Syria[494], still known by the name of *Palestine.*

489. *Joshua*, chap. iii. iv.
490. See *Joshua*, chap. vi.—xii.
491. *Deuteron.* chap. ii. iii. *Joshua*, chap. vi. vii. viii.
492. *Joshua*, chap. ix. ver. 1, 2. chap. xi. ver. 1—5.
493. *Joshua*, chap. x. ver. 8, 9. chap. xi. ver. 7, 8.
494. *Joshua*, chap. xi ver 16—23.

In

In the centre of the coast of Syria, between the mountains of Libanus and the Mediterranean sea, stood Sidon and Tyre; the two first seats of commerce and naval power. To the narrow territory, belonging to these two famous cities, the Greeks gave the name of *Phoenice*, or Phoenicia, and to the inhabitants that of Phoenicians. But they, and the people of the interior country, were called *Canaanites* by the Hebrews[495]. And we learn from the sacred records, that, when Joshua led the Israelites into the *promised land*, and attempted utterly to destroy the people of the neighbouring districts, he made no attack upon *great Zidon* or *strong Tyre*[496]; yet many respectable writers, both ancient and modern, refer the founding of Tyre to a later age; because no mention is made of it in the poems of Homer. But Herodotus was better informed on this subject[497].

I now return to the institutions of Moses. This extraordinary man having rescued the Hebrew nation from Egyptian servitude, and conducted them into the wilderness of Sinai[498], in Arabia Petræa, there promulgated a body of laws[499]; which, though the most ancient upon record, contain the soundest maxims of legislative wisdom.

495. *Numbers*, chap. xiii. ver. 29. "The *Canaanites* dwell by the "sea, and by the coast of Jordan." Id. ibid.

496. *Joshua*, chap. xix. ver. 28, 29.

497. Herodot. *Historiar*. lib. ii. cap. xliv.

498. *Exodus*, chap. xiii.—xix. There is something very like carnal policy in the reason assigned for the Israelites taking this route. "And "it came to pass, when Pharaoh had let the people go, that *God led* "*them not* through the way of the Philistines, although that was near; "for God said, ' Lest peradventure the people repent when they see "war, and they return to Egypt.' But God led the people about, "through the way of the wilderness." *Exodus*, chap. xiii. ver. 17, 18.

499. *Exodus*, chap. xx.—xxxiv.

Four

Four statutes in the Mosaic code, " Thou shalt not
" *kill;* thou shalt not *steal;* thou shalt not *bear false*
" *witness;* thou shalt not *commit adultery*[500]; comprehend, in few words, the elements of universal jurisprudence. For, although different legislators have
decreed different penalties for the offences they prohi-
bit, they have formed the basis of *criminal law* among
all civilized nations, ancient and modern. Varied in
their application by circumstances, but unaltered in
their object, they are as essential to the good order of
society, as the four elements to the system of nature.

These statutes were closely connected with the
worship of ONE God, whose will imposed them[501],
and who *prohibited* the corrupting *use of images;* with
reverence for the name of that God, to strengthen the
obligation of an oath, and inspire pious awe; with
respect to *parents,* the natural foundation of all civil
submission; with an *admonition* against *covetousness,*
the, contagious root of violence and injustice; and with
the *religious observance* of *one day in the week*[501], set
apart for rest, recollection, and sacred duties.

500. *Exod.* chap. xx. ver. 13—16.

501. In saying that the *will of God* imposed these statutes, so necessary to the welfare of the human race, I mean no arbitrary will, or
will merely imperative; but that constituting will, which regulated
moral fitness, and implanted in the human breast the sense of discerning that fitness. The *will of God,* thus explained, is the same with
moral fitness, which the moral sense was given to recognise. Every
legislator, therefore, who institutes ordinances calculated for the
happiness of mankind, may be said, in philosophic language, to have
a just claim to divine authority. Hence an inquisitive and sagacious
historian (Diod. Sicul. *Biblioth.* lib. i. p. 48.), ranks Moses among the
illustrious ancient legislators, who had asserted their right to such
authority : either, remarks he (ibid.), because they believed their laws
to have something divine in them, for human good; or because they
supposed the people would be more observant of them, from their
veneration for the god, that was thought to have framed them.

502. *Exod.* chap. xx. ver. 3—17.

The

THE HISTORY OF

The Mosaic institutions also contain the most early system of ecclesiastical polity of which history has furnished us with any particulars. There we find a Hebrew tribe constituted into a sacred order, as in Egypt, for the ministration of holy things [503]. But to the worship of God, and to the trespasses connected with that worship and its various ceremonies, the official authority of the Hebrew priests and levites was confined [504]. They had no concern in secular affairs ; in the administration of civil justice, or in public deliberations [505]. These were committed to the *elders* or senators of the several tribes [506]. The levites had not even a share in the division of the promised land [507]; but a certain number of cities, in the territory of each secular tribe, were assigned them, in addition to the emoluments arising from the numerous sacrifices and offerings annually made or devoted to the LORD [508]. Thus dispersed through the whole land, the levites became every where the guardians of that religion by which they subsisted [509]; and the establishment of which, as

I shall

503. *Exod.* chap. xxviii. xxix. throughout ; chap. xl. ver. 12—15. *Leviticus*, chap. viii. ver. 6—26. *Deuteron.* chap. x. ver. 9. chap. xviii. ver. 1.—5.

504. See the book of *Leviticus* throughout.

505. Ibid.

506. *Deuteron.* chap. xxxi. ver. 9. Moses, who had seen the abuses of sacerdotal power in Egypt, wisely separated the ecclesiastical from the civil jurisdiction. He, therefore, delivered one copy of the law to the levites, who had the cognizance of holy things; and one to the elders, who had the superintendence of civil affairs. See also *Deuter.* chap. xvi. ver. 18. " Judges shalt thou make thee, throughout all thy " tribes; and they shall judge the people with just judgment." Id. ibid.

507. *Deuteron.* chap. xviii. ver. 1, 2.

508. *Numbers*, chap. xxxv. ver. 2—8. *Leviticus*, chap. v.—xxvii. *Deuteron.* chap. xviii. ver. 3, 4, 5.

509. The Mosaic religion seems to have had little peculiar to it, but the doctrine of the *unity* of the *Deity* publickly inculcated. Its festivals and ceremonies were chiefly borrowed, with some variation, from the Egyptian worship (*Divine Legation of Moses*, book iv. sect. vi.);
and

I shall shew, was the great object of Moses, the vicegerent of God, in framing his laws.

But what is truly singular, we find not in the Mosaic
institutions, either ecclesiastical or civil, any reference
to a *future state of rewards and punishments*, so zealously inculcated by heathen legislators[510]. This *omission* has been considered by an oracle in learning, and
a dignitary of the church, as an incontestable argument for the *divine origin* of those institutions[511];
though in the eye of impartial reason, it can only be
regarded as a proof of the political sagacity of the
Hebrew legislator. He was leading an obstinate
people through many dangers and difficulties, to the
country promised them by the LORD; and any prospect of 'a happy state, beyond the grave, might have
relaxed their endeavours, for attaining their earthly
Canaan.

In making this remark, I mean not to question the
divine origin of the Mosaic institutions; but to shew
the folly of resting the proof of it on an *omission*, which
naturally leads to a different conclusion. I am even
of opinion, that the Hebrews, both before and after the
Exodus, believed in a future state, though all the promises and threatenings in the Mosaic law are temporal; and that Moses having placed them under the regal
government of God, the mysteriously visible head

and its symbols are evidently Zabian. They have all a reference to
the *seven great celestial bodies*, or to the figures used in the worship of
the heavenly bodies; but especially of the *sun* (Compare *Exod.* chap.
xxv. xxvi. with *Specim. Hist. Arab.* ap.¹ Pocock.). And the *twelve*
tribes of Israel correspond to the *number* of the *greater gods* of Gentile antiquity.

510. See *Divine Legation of Moses*, book ii. sect. iii. and the authorities there cited.

511. This is the fundamental, but paradoxical principle, upon
which Warburton's *Divine Legation of Moses* is declaredly written.
See particularly book vi. sect. i. ii.

of

PART I.   of their theocratic monarchy, did not think it necessary
to propound future rewards and punishments, these
being understood to be ultimately awarded by their
heavenly king[512].   Nor will it derogate from the divinity of Moses's mission, to say that he forebore to
insist on such rewards and punishments for political reasons, suited to the circumstances of the people under

512. The nature of the Hebrew government is little understood.
It was a THEOCRACY, or *mixed monarchy*, under the spiritual and
temporal government of God. Moses was his *minister* or *vicegerent*.
Joshua and the *judges* maintained the same character; and the *kings*
were only his *viceroys*, invested with the ensigns and the functions of
royalty (See *Divine Legation of Moses*, book v. sect. i. ii. iii. and the
passages of scripture there cited.). The manner in which the *Divine
Presence* was to be manifested, after the promulgation of the law, and
the erection of the tabernacle, is thus described by God himself.
" And let them make me a *sanctuary*, that I may dwell among them.
" According to all that I shew thee, after the pattern of the *taberna-*
" *cle*, and the pattern of all the instruments thereof, even so shall ye
" make it. And they shall make an *ark* of Shittim wood : two cubits
" and a half shall be the length thereof, and a cubit and a half the
" breadth thereof. And thou shalt overlay it with pure gold; with-
" in and without shalt thou overlay it, and shalt make upon it a
" *crown* of gold round about. And thou shalt make a *mercy-seat* of
" pure gold; two cubits and a half shall be the length thereof, and
" a cubit and a half the breadth thereof. And thou shalt make two
" *cherubims* of gold ; of beaten gold shalt thou make them, in the
" two ends of the *mercy-seat*. And make one *cherub* on one end, and
" the other *cherub* on the other end. And the *cherubims* shall stretch
" forth their wings on high, covering the *mercy-seat* with their wings;
" and their faces shall look one to another. Towards the *mercy-seat*
" shall the faces of the *cherubims* be. And thou shalt place the
" *mercy-seat* above upon the *ark;* and in the *ark* thou shalt put the
" *testimony*. And there I will meet with thee; and I will commune
" with thee from above the *mercy-seat;* from between the two *cheru-*
" *bims*, which are upon the *ark* of the *testimony;* of all things which
" I will give thee in commandment unto the children of *Israel*"
(See *Exodus*, chap. xxv. ver. 8—22.). " And the *Lord* said unto
" Moses, ' Speak unto Aaron thy brother, that he come not at all
" times into the holy place within the veil before the *mercy-seat*, which
" is upon the *ark*, that he die not; for I will appear in the *cloud* upon
" the *mercy-seat*." *Leviticus*, chap. xvi. ver. 2.

his

his conduct, and calculated to answer the primary end of that mission; the speedy establishment of the worship of ONE God, in a land where idolatrous superstition had given birth to every crime that can disgrace human nature [513].

The author of the *Divine Legation*, however, endeavours to prove, that the Hebrews did not believe in a future state before the Babylonish captivity [514]; and that Moses intentionally concealed from them this important truth [515] But if the Hebrews had been left by God to acquire the knowledge of a future state from other nations, they might surely have learned it from the Egyptians, among whom it had been taught from time immemorial [516]. And as the LORD permitted Moses to borrow from that people many religious solemnities [517], we cannot believe that the doctrine of *immortality;* the hope most congenial to the human soul, and the firmest support of legislation, when regulated by the measures of *just* and *unjust*, could have been forbidden to be inculcated by the Deity.

513. *Deuteron.* chap. ix. ver. 5. chap. xii. ver. 30. This representation of the manners of the Syrian nations, which I have hitherto considered as just, was given, it must be owned, by an historian interested to delineate them in the blackest colours. But the Mosaic history, though calculated to countenance the claim of the Hebrews to the *promised land,* seems to contain a faithful description of the state of government and manners in Syria, from the time of Abraham to that of Moses. I therefore have not scrupled to quote it as sound historical evidence; in whatever regards the state of Syria, and even of Egypt in early times. The vices of the Hebrews are not screened, nor the virtues of other nations concealed by Moses.

514. See Warburton's *Divine Legation of Moses,* book vi. sect. i. ii. iii.

515. *Divine Legation of Moses,* book v. sect. v. "I shall shew," says he, "that this *omission* was not *accidental;* but that, on the contrary, it "was a *designed* omission:—and of a THING *well known by him* (Moses) "to be of *high importance* to *society.*" Id. ibid.

516. *Divine Legation,* book ii. sect. iv.

517. Id. book iv. sect. vi.

To

To maintain, therefore, that Moses *intentionally con-cealed* this doctrine, so worthy of divine goodness, and essential to the happiness of mankind, is to represent him as a mere human politician; the framer of a religious system, which he proposed to establish by violence, in cutting off from the oppressed Hebrews all hopes but those of worldly advantages; stimulating them to acts of blood, in order to desolate the land that he had presumptuously promised them; and there to place a religion, which, though pure in principle, had its origin in imposture, and was founded by the sword.

The Mosaic institutions were distinguished from all others by their *promulgation*, as well as by the *omission* of the doctrine of a *future state*.

Many ancient legislators published their ordinances under the pretended sanction of some God. But Moses is the only ancient legislator, who ever promulgated a body of laws in the name of ONE GOD, the *Creator of the universe*, and introduced them with an account of the beginning of all things[518]; the creation of the Heavens,

518. *Genesis*, chap. i. Dr. Warburton attempts to form a *distinction* between Moses as an *historian* and as a *legislator* (*Divine Legation*, book v. sect. v.); but I can see no reason for such distinction. That portion of his history, which precedes the promulgation of his laws, appears obviously intended to *facilitate* their *reception*. This the doctor is forced, in some instances, to admit. And he pushes the matter even farther than is necessary to establish the point. For he tells us, that Moses, in relating the "*History of the Fall*, mentions only the in-" *strument* of the *agent*, the SERPENT; not the *agent* himself, the DE-" VIL. And the reason is plain;" adds he, " there was a *close connec-*" *tion* between that *agency* and the *doctrine* of a *future state*;" which, according to the doctor's hypothesis, Moses laboured to conceal from the Hebrews. "What but this," asks he, "could be the *cause* of the " *omission?*—When it is so evident, that the *knowledge* of the *grand enemy* " *of our welfare* would have been the *likeliest cure* of IDOLATRY; as " *teaching*

vens and the earth; the formation of animals, both
brute and rational; the *infusion* of the *human soul,*
and the *origin* of *natural* and *moral evil*[519]*:* to say
nothing of the *tremendous signs* of the *divine presence,*
manifested to a whole people[520].

But although the laws of Moses, worthy of their imputed author, discover the deepest wisdom, and abound
with maxims of mild humanity, his instructions to the
Israelites on their approaching the *promised land,*
breathe such a cruel and sanguinary spirit, as fills the
heart with horror. Instead of ordering them to expel,
or make slaves of the vanquished inhabitants, according
to the ungenerous practice of ancient heathen nations,
he commands them, when most lenient, to slay every
man and male child with the edge of the sword, and
every woman who had known man, by lying with
him[521]; but of the people of the land more particularly promised, he orders them to cut off man, woman,
and child, without distinction of age or sex[522].

" *teaching men to esteem it* a mere *diabolical* illusion." *Divine Legation
of Moses,* book v. sect. v.

If Moses could thus have cured mankind, or even the Hebrew nation,
of their rage for idolatry, he acted a part equally weak and wicked in
concealing from them the *cause* of *moral turpitude,* the *agency* of the *de-
vil.* For the propensity of the Hebrews to idolatry vexed him all his
life; and both he and his successors shed torrents of blood, that the
people of God might be preserved from the idolatries of the Syrian nations. Nor were they ever cured of their inordinate passion for idols,
until their return from the Babylonish captivity; when, the learned
prelate allows (*Divine Legation,* book vi. sect. ii.), they had acquired
the *knowledge* of the *author of evil,* and the *doctrine* of a *future state.*

519. *Genesis,* chap. ii. iii.   520. *Exodus,* chap. xix. xx.

521. *Numbers,* chap xxxi. ver. 17, 18. " Now, therefore, kill every
" male among the little ones, and kill every woman that hath known
" man by lying with him; but *all the women children,* that have *not*
" known a man by lying with him, *keep alive for yourselves.*" Id. ibid.

522. *Deuteron.* chap. xx. ver. 16, 17. " That they teach you not to
" do after all the abominations, which they have done unto their
" gods; so should ye sin against the LORD your God." Id. ver. 19.

In

In giving these instructions, Moses appears to have been partly guided by political necessity, partly by the rigid maxims of political prudence. He knew the difficulty of expulsion, and was apprehensive that the conquered countries would not be sufficient for the support of the native inhabitants, and the new comers. He foresaw the probability of a multitude of slaves rebelling against their masters; of women, but especially such as had been connected with the men of the country, aiding rebellion; and also of leading the Israelites into *idolatry*, which his laws had guarded against by the most severe prohibitions. On that hinge his whole system turned.

To preserve a chosen people in the worship of one God; and found their exaltation on their separation from all other nations, by this and other peculiarities in their religious institutions, was the pious purpose of Moses. Hence his exhortation to the Israelites, before they entered the *promised land.*

"Hearken, O Israel! unto the *statutes*, and unto "the *judgments*, which *I teach you;* that ye may live, "and go in and possess the land, which the *Lord God* "*of your fathers* giveth you. Keep, therefore, and do "them; for what nation hath statutes and judgments "so righteous, as all this law, which I set before you? " —Keep thy soul diligently, lest thou forget the things "which thine eyes have seen, especially on the day "thou stoodest before the LORD *thy God* in Horeb; "when the LORD said unto me, 'Gather the people "together, and I will *make them hear my words;* that "they may *learn to fear me* all the days that they shall "live upon the earth, and that they may *teach their* "*children.*' And ye *came near, and stood under the* "*mountain;* and the *mountain burned with fire unto the* "*midst of heaven;* with *darkness, clouds,* and *thick*
darkness

"*darkness.* And the Lord spake unto me out of the
" midst of the fire. Ye heard the voice of the words,
" but saw no similitude : ye only heard a voice. And
" he declared unto you his covenant, which he com-
" manded you to perform, *ten commandments;* and
" wrote them upon two tables of stone. And the Lord
" commanded me, at that time, to teach you statutes
" and judgments, that ye might do them in the land
" ye go over to possess.

" Take ye, therefore, good heed unto yourselves;
" for ye saw no manner of similitude on the day that
" the Lord spake unto you in Horeb, out of the midst
" of the fire :—take heed lest ye corrupt yourselves,
" and make you a graven image : the similitude of
" any figure[123], the likeness of male or of female; the
" likeness of any beast that is on the earth ; the likeness
" of any fowl that flieth in the air ; the likeness of any
" thing that creepeth on the ground ; the likeness of any
" fish that is in the waters :—and lest thou lift up thine
" eyes unto heaven, and when thou seest the sun, and
" the moon, and the stars, all the host of heaven, thou
" shouldest be drawn to worship them, and to serve
" them, which the LORD thy God hath imparted unto
" all the nations under the whole heaven[524]. The Lord
" our God is *one Lord*[525].

Honourable the purpose was ; and the principle, if
adherred to, must have made the Hebrews, to use the

523. The Mosaic worship made use of *figures;* but these were not
exposed to the idolatry of the people. They were confined to the innermost part of the tabernacle or temple; to the *most holy place;*
which the high-priest was not permitted, at all times, to enter (*Leviticus,* chap. xvi. ver. 2): and whence the oracular voice came, from
the mercy-seat *behind the veil.* (Id. ibid). For, as Dr. Warburton
remarks (*Divine Legation,* book v. sect. iv.) " The Mosaic religion,
like the pagan, had a *public part.*"

524. *Deuteron.* chap. iv. ver. 1—19. 525, *Deuteron.* chap. iv. ver. 4.

language

PART I. language of Strabo, worthy of empire[526]. Yet humanity must ever condemn the means employed to attain that empire, and virtue hold them in execration. Cruelty can admit of no vindication in the eye of social man; and any attempt to palliate it, on theologic grounds, must impeach the most amiable attribute of the Deity. The God of Moses seemed to delight in blood. Hence after the arms of the Israelites under Joshua were finally crowned with success, such, of the inhabitants of Palestine and the neighbouring countries, as had escaped the sword, or found themselves unable to maintain their independency, fled to the sea coast, and took refuge in the cities of Tyre and Sidon[527]. And hence those cities, overcrowded with people, were enabled to plant colonies in all the countries to which they traded; on the coast of Africa, in Spain, and in the islands of the Mediterranean, as we shall have occasion to notice. The Phoenician colony, under Cadmus, the Tyrian, had already been settled in Greece[528].

Having thus, my lord, given you an account of the early progress of mankind in government and legislation, and of the ancient state of the nations to which EUROPE was indebted for its science and civility; I shall proceed, according to my plan, to the founding *of the Grecian States,* as a prelude to the history of that celebrated country.

526. *Geog.* lib. xvi. p. 761. edit. sup. cit.
527. *Joshua*, chap. ix. ver. 8.   528. *Parian Chron.* Epoch vii. Herodot. lib. ii. cap. xlix.

LETTER

LETTER II.

THE TRADITIONAL HISTORY OF GREECE TO THE TROJAN
WAR, WITH AN ACCOUNT OF THE FOUNDING OF THE PRIN-
CIPAL GRECIAN STATES.

THE country properly comprehended under LETTER II. the name of GREECE, and included between the thirty-sixth and forty-first degrees of northern latitude, consisted of that eastern promontory of Europe, which fronts Natolia, or Asia Minor; and which, extending from the mountains of Epirus and Macedonia to the Mediterranean sea, is formed into a kind of peninsula by two arms of that sea, anciently called the the *Ægean* and *Ionian* seas. These seas, which are now known by the names of the *Archipelago* and *Hadriatic* open in this promontory many deep gulfs and spacious bays; and, at one place, almost cut it through. The most insulated part, connected with the continent only by a narrow isthmus, was early denominated *Peloponnesus*. And not only that insulated, and southerly part, but the whole Grecian promontory, is marked with strong features by the hand of nature; being intersected, at several places, by stupendous ridges of mountains, whose lofty summits are generally lost in the clouds.

But Greece, though a rugged, is a desirable country. It abounds, on all sides, with excellent harbours. The deep vallies, between the craggy ridges, afford rich pasture for cattle, and yield plentiful crops of corn, when duly cultivated; the more easy declivities produce figs, grapes, and olives; and the mountains, beside being covered with valuable timber, contain beds of marble, and veins of the most useful metals. The climate is alike favourable to health and fertility. For the heat of the Grecian summers, moderated by breezes from the hills and surrounding seas, is sufficient to bring the choicest fruits to maturity, without enervating the human body; and the short Grecian winters are cold enough to brace the fibres, without chilling the constitutions of the people.

Ancient Greece, during the prosperous ages of its liberty, was politically and nominally split, agreeable to the divisions formed by nature, into a number of independent states, or districts of different dimensions, under distinct governments.

Peloponnesus, now called the *Morea*, which has been ingeniously compared to the leaf of the plane-tree, because of its angular recesses or bays, contained seven states of considerable eminence; namely, Corinth, on the isthmus that connects Peloponnesus with the continent; Achaia on the northern, and Elea on the western side; Argolis on the eastern coast; Arcadia in the centre; and Messenia and Laconia toward the points of the peninsula. This peninsula, one hundred and forty miles in length and one hundred and twenty at its greatest breadth, is intersected in many places by mountains; but especially by the two lofty ridges of Zarex and Taygetus, which terminate at its two southermost promontories, Tenarum and Malea.

The territory of Greece without the Corinthian isthmus, was of yet greater extent than Peloponnesus, but less compacted; branching two hundred miles, in a southerly direction, from mount Pindus to the promontory of Sunium; and extending nearly an equal number of miles, in a western line, from mount Olympus,

pus, and the mouth of the Peneus, to the point of the promontory of Leucadia. That territory was divided into a number of independent districts; the most considerable of which were, Ætolia and Acarnania on the Corinthian and Ambracian gulfs; Thessally, including Phthiotis, on the frontiers of Epirus and Macedonia; Doris, Phocis, and Locris, in the neighbourhood of the mountains of Œta and Parnassus; and Bœotia and Attica, diverging in a southern projection, from those mountains to the Ægean sea.

Along the coast of Attica and Bœotia lies the large island of Eubœa (one hundred and twenty miles in length, and from thirty to forty in breadth), which might be considered as a part of *Proper Greece* Its principal districts were those of Chalcis and Eretria. The whole Grecian territory, therefore, would have formed, if combined into one mass, a country three hundred miles square, and consequently as large as *South Britain*.

This celebrated country, which at present makes part of European Turkey, was originally occupied, if we may credit tradition, by various tribes of savage and barbarous men, utterly unacquainted with the arts of civil life, and who fed upon the spontaneous productions of the earth, herbs and wild fruits[1]. The most considerable of those tribes were the Pelasgi, Caucones, Aones, Hyantes, and Leleges[2]. The Pelasgi, however, appear to have been horsemen[3]. They must, therefore, have been above such rude barbarity. But as human learning has not been found equal to the task of reconciling to probability, or reducing to con-

1. Pausan. lib. viii. init.
2. Strabo, *Geog.* lib. viii. ix. x. et Pausan. *Græc. Descript.* passim.
3. Strabo, lib. viii. p. 369, 370. edit. sup. cit.

sistency,

PART I. sistency, the first periods of Grecian history, I shall not
attempt it. I shall only connect the traditional tale,
in order to shew your lordship, what the Greeks believed concerning the founding of their several states,
the exploits of their early heroes, and the introduction
of arts and laws among them; offering such remarks
as may be suggested by circumstances.

  The first civil establishment founded in Greece, by
any person that can be reputed a native, was formed
Ant. Chr. at Lycoria, on mount Parnassus, by a king named Deu-
1574. calion[4]; whose sway extended over Phthiotis and part
of Thessaly[5]. Hellen, the eldest son of Deucalion,
succeeded him in Phthiotis, and also in his Thessalian
dominions[6]. And from this politic and powerful
prince all the people of Greece came finally to bear the
general appellation of HELLENES[7]; while from his
two sons, Dorus and Æolus, and his grandson Ion,
they were gradually discriminated by the names of Dorians, Æolians, and Ionians[8]; the three prime branches

---

  4. *Parian Chron.* Epoch II. Pausan. lib. x. p. 322. edit. Xylander,
Francfort, 1583. Herodotus, lib. i. cap. lvi. Apollod. lib. i. p. 19,
20. edit. Paris. 1599.

  5. Strabo, lib. ix. p. 432.

  6. Herodotus, lib. i. cap. lvi. Strabo, lib. viii. p. 383.

  7. *Parian Chron.* Epoch VI. It does not appear, says Thucydides,
that this general appellation subsisted in Greece before the time of
Hellen, the son of Deucalion; the different tribes formerly taking their
distinguishing names from themselves. And *Pelasgia*, not *Hellas*,
was the *name* of the *largest territory* (Thucyd. *Hist.* lib. i. cap. iii.).
" But when Hellen and his sons had acquired power in Phthiotis,"
adds this accurate historian, " and led out their dependents by way
" of aid to other states, intercourse made the use of this name become
" common among the people of several states; though it was long
" before it became the general appellation of the people of all the
" Grecian states" (Id. ibid.). The Romans gave to *Hellas* the name of
Greece (Plin. *Hist. Nat.* lib. iv. cap. vii.); and from them it passed
to the nations of modern Europe.

  8. Herodotus, lib. i. cap. lvi.—lviii. lib. vii. cap. xciv. Apollod.
lib. i. p. 20. Strabo, lib. viii. p. 333. 383.

of

of the Grecian nation, whose distinct genius and manners gave rise to the three dialects of the Greek
tongue.

The progress of the descendents of Hellen, and
their subjects, in civility, was greater than that of any
other Grecian family[9]. But Greece was not to acquire its civilization, merely through the advances of
its native inhabitants in policy or arts. It was to owe
much to the attainments of foreigners.

A country, in many respects, highly favoured by
nature, and happily situated for commerce; being separated from Asia Minor only by a narrow channel, and
from Syria by a small extent of sea, could not fail to
attract the visits of naval adventurers. Greece was accordingly a prey to invasion in very early ages; and by
naval adventurers were founded the principal Grecian states.

Inachus, stiled the *son of Oceanus and Tethys*[10],
(probably because he was the first person of distinction
that came by sea into Greece), and who is supposed
to have conducted a colony from Egypt or Phœnicia[11],
gave a beginning to the kingdom of Argos[12], long
before the reign of Deucalion. Phoroneus, the eldest
son and successor of Inachus, more firmly established
the settlement his father had made[13]. He induced the
rude natives to submit to his government, and collected them into one city[14].

Ægialus, the second son of Inachus, founded a small
principality or township on the frontiers of Argolis,

9. Herodotus et Strabo, ubi sup.   10. Apollod. lib. ii. init.
11. Bannier, *Explic. des. Feb.* tom. iv. p. 39. edit. Paris, 1748.
12. Apollod. ubi sup.   13. Id. ibid.
14. Pausan. lib. ii. p. 58. edit. sup. cit.

called

called the kingdom of Sicyon[15]. But this kingdom
never rose to any degree of power. And the Inachidæ,
or descendents of Inachus, who seem to have degenerated into barbarism, were supplanted in the kingdom of Argos by the famous Egyptian adventurer,
Danaus[16]; whose arrival in the ship *Pentecontorus*[17],
forms an important æra in the traditional part of the
history of Greece.

To Danaus the Greeks were indebted for many improvements.   He taught the Argives to construct
aqueducts[18], and supplied their city plentifully with
water from four fountains or reservoirs[19].   He built
the citadel of Argos[20]; and he raised the kingdom to
such a pitch of glory and prosperity, by the introduction of arts and laws among the people who owned
his sway, that all the southern Greeks bore, for a time,
the name of DANAI[21].

Nine years prior to the arrival of Danaus in Peloponnesus[22], a Phœnician colony had been planted in
Bœotia, by Cadmus of Tyre[23]. The Hyantes opposed
the settlement of Cadmus and his followers; but being
worsted in battle, they thought fit to evacuate their
country[24]. And the Aones, seeing that resistance
must prove ineffectual, supplicated the clemency of
Cadmus, and were permitted to dwell with the Phœnicians[25]

As soon as Cadmus had established his colony, he

---

15. Apollod. lib. ii. init.   16. Pausan. lib. ii. p. 58.
17. *Parian Chron.* Epoch ix.   18. Strabo, lib. i. p. 23.
19. Strabo, lib. viii. p. 371.   20. Id. ibid.
21. Thucyd. lib. i. cap. iii. Strabo, lib. viii. p. 371.
22. *Parian Chron.* Epoch vii.
23. Herodotus, lib. ii. cap. xlix. Strabo, lib. ix. p. 401.
24. Pausan. lib. ix. p. 285.   25. Id. ibid.

                                              built

built a castle called Cadmea[26]; below which rose the
city of Thebes, the capital of a kingdom of the same
name that, in early times, comprehended the greater
part of Bœotia[27]. That fortress afforded an asylum
to refugees from the neighbouring states; so that
Thebes, of which Cadmea was the citadel, grew soon
a large and populous town, all secured with walls[28].
Cadmus brought into Greece the Phœnician alphabet[29], and the art of working mines[30].

Sixty years before the descent of Cadmus, and fifteen hundred and eighty-two years before the Christian æra, that famous city to which Europe was to owe
its literature and civility, its laws, its arts, and its sciences : Athens, the future seat of learning and politeness,
the theatre of eloquence, and the school of knowledge,
was founded by Cecrops, the leader of a band of emigrants from the district of Sais, in Lower Egypt[31].
Being well received by Acteus, who then reigned over
the territory of Attica, Cecrops obtained his daughter
in marriage[32]; and, on the death of that prince, he
succeeded to his sceptre[33].

No sooner did Cecrops get possession of the government, than he represented to his subjects the necessity
of living amicably together, in order to oppose the ravages and incursions of robbers and pirates; but especially of the Aones from Bœotia, and the Carians of
the Ægean islands, who were perpetually pillaging the

26. Strabo, lib. viii. p. 401.   Pausan. lib. ix. p. 285.

27. Strabo, ibid.   28. Strabo et Pausanias, ubi sup.

29. Herodotus, lib. v. cap. lviii.   Diod. Sicul. lib. iii. p. 200. edit.
sup. cit.   Pliny, *Hist. Nat.* lib. vii. cap. lvi.

30. Strabo, lib. xiv. p. 680.   Clem. Alex. *Strom.* lib. i. p. 363. edit.
Oxon. 1715.

31. African. ap. Euseb. *Præparat. Evangil.* lib. x. cap. x.

32. Apollod. lib. iii. p. 192.   Pausan. lib. i. p. 5.

33. Id. ibid.

PART I.· sea-coast[34]. Having convinced his people, that social
union only could enable them to resist such violences,
he. distributed them·into twelve towns[35]. And he
erected a.castle, called Cecropia[36], afterward known
by the name of Acropolis, around which rose the city
of.Athens[37]; so:denominated·from Athena, or ·Mi-
nerva, its tutelary goddess[38].

Cecrops appears to have been the first prince that
instituted the law of marriage in Greece; or at least,
who ordained, that one man should have only one wife,
as in Egypt[39]; who regulated religious ceremonies[40],
and ordained funeral rites[41].   He erected in every
town a public hall, or Prutaneion, for the settlement of
civil differences among his subjects[42]; and he is supposed to have instituted the venerable criminal tribunal named Areopagus[43], so long and deservedly celebrated for the impartiality of its decrees[44].

From the reign of Cecrops: to that of Theseus, the
traditional and chronological history of Athens is more
consistent, and better authenticated, than that of any
other Grecian state.   I shall, therefore, refer to the

34. Strabo, lib. ix. p. 397.

35. Philacor. ap. Strabo, ubi sup.

36. Apollod. lib. iii. p. 192. Plin. *Hist. Nat.* lib. vii. cap. lvi.

37. Plin. ubi sup. et Potter, *Archæolog. Græc.* chap. ii. viii.

38. Strabo, lib. ix. p. 397. Plut. *Vit. Thes.* et Potter, *Archæolog.
Græc.* chap. viii. Athena, as I have formerly had occasion to observe,
was worshipped by the Saites as *divine wisdom;* hence she was mythologically said by the Greeks to have sprung out of Jupiter's brain.

39. Athenæus, lib. xiii. init. Justin, lib. ii. cap. vi. et Potter, *Archæolog. Græc.* chap. ii.

40. Pausan. lib. viii. p. 237.

41. Cicero, de *Legib.* lib. ii cap. xxv.

42. Thucyd. lib. ii. cap. xv. The *Prutaneion* served also for a senate-
house to the inhabitants of the district in which it stood (Id. ibid.). It
was likewise used as a place of public worship, and as a public gra-
nary. *Etymol. Mag.* et Suidas. in voc. Πρυτανειον.

43. See Potter, *Archæolog. Græc.* chap. xix.   44. Id. ibid.

reigns of some of the successors of Cecrops, in speaking of the establishment of certain civil and religious
institutions, that took place during this period, and
which demand your lordship's attention.

The number of small states into which ancient
Greece was divided, and the various revolutions to
which it had been early subject[45], in consequence of
foreign invasion, made all intelligent men sensible of
the necessity of a general convention, or bond of union
in order to enable the heads of those states to repel the
attempts of new invaders, as well as to preserve peace
between the several communities[46]. A league of mutual friendship and defence was accordingly concerted
by the wisdom of a political prince, named Amphictyon[47], fifteen hundred and twenty-two years before
the Christian æra[48]; and formed among the principal
Grecian states without the Corinthian isthmus[49]. The
deputies from these states met twice a year at Thermopyle (in spring and autumn), vested with full
powers to deliberate and resolve on whatever might
appear to them most beneficial to the common cause[50].

This assembly of the States General of Greece (for
such it became) was called the *Council of Amphictyons.*
But whether it took its name from Amphictyon the second successor of Cecrops, who was king of Athens
when it was established, or from Amphictyon the son
of Deucalion, and brother of Hellen, who at the same
time reigned at Thermopyle[51], is a point in regard to
which modern historians have been much divided.

45. Thucyd. lib. i. cap. ii.   46. Dion. Halicarnass. lib. iv. cap. xxv.
47. Id. ibid. et Pausan. lib. x. p. 323.   48. *Parian Chron.* Epoch v.
49. Dion. Halicarnass. et Pausan. ubi sup.

50. See Strabo, lib. ix. p. 420. and Dr. Leland's *Preliminary Dissertation* on the *Council of Amphictyons,* prefixed to his *History of Philip
of Macedon.*

51. *Parian Chron.* Epoch v.

The

The honour, however, of concerting that illustrious league, which so long preserved the independency of Greece, and made its united states formidable to the greatest monarchies, is certainly due to the king of Thermopyle[52]; in whose hall or chapel the Amphictyons, or Grecian delegates, originally held their deliberations[53].

Nor was the sagacity of the king of Thermopyle less conspicuous in the measures which he took for exciting the vigilance, and perpetuating the power of the Amphictyonic council, than in establishing it. Justly sensible, we may presume, of the force of religion in cementing political confederacies, as well as in awakening their zeal, he charged the diet of Greece with the protection of the oracle of Delphos[54]. And all the Grecian delegates, before their instalment, were required to take a solemn oath, accompanied with many awful imprecations and execrations on such as should violate their engagements[55]; but especially against those that should neglect the protection of the sacred city[56].

52. Prideaux, *Chron. Marm.* p. 122. edit. Oxon. 1676, .

53. Herodot. lib. vii. cap. cc. et Prideaux, ubi sup.

54. No ancient author expressly says, that Amphictyon charged the confederated Greeks with the protection of the Delphic oracle; but Strabo intimates, that they had such charge from the time of their confederation (*Geog.* lib. ix. p. 420.). And it is certain, that the Amphictyonic council was early charged with the protection of the oracle (*Æschin. de Falsa Legat.*); and that the oracle was established before the reign of Deucalion, and in the territory belonging to him and his sons (Vid. Prideaux, *Chron. Marm.* p. 122, 123. et *Premiere Dissert.* sur *l'Oracle de Delph.* par M. Hardion.). Dr. Leland conjectures, that the Amphictyonic council was not invested with the superintendence over the oracle of Delphos, or what he calls the *national religion*, till after it was new modelled by Acrisius, the fugitive king of Argos (*Prelim. Dissert.*). But the whole story of Acrisius founding, or new modelling the Amphictyonic council, seems alike void of truth and probability.

55. Æschines, *de Falsa Legat.*   56. Id. ibid.

                                     Erechtheus,

Erechtheus, the sixth king of Athens, and the third after Amphictyon, was the first Grecian prince who separated the civil from the ecclesiastical power[57]. Before his time, every king had united in his own person the regal and sacerdotal functions, the sovereignty and the pontificate. Satisfied with swaying the sceptre, Erechtheus relinquished the priesthood of Minerva, the tutelary divinity of the Athenians, and also that of Neptune, to his brother Butes[58].

The same prince wisely instituted the Eleusinian mysteries[59], in honour of Ceres, the goddess of the earth, and the patroness of husbandry ; an art that can never be too highly honoured, as it is the grand source of the comforts of civil life, and the parent of jurisprudence. This goddess is figuratively said to have come to Athens, in person, during the reign of Erechtheus, because he was a great promoter of agriculture. Hence we are told, that Triptolemus, who, under the patronage of Erechtheus, first sowed barley with success in the plains of Rharia, near Eleusis, was instructed by Ceres[60].

Of all the religious festivals in the heathen world, the Eleusinian mysteries were celebrated with the greatest solemnity, and the most profound secrecy. They seem to have been calculated to purify the minds of men from the gross tenets of pagan theology, as promulgated to the multitude ; by revealing the *unity* of the DEITY and the *immortality* of the SOUL, divested of superstitious horrors.

57. Apollod. lib. iii. 58. Id. ibid.
59. *Parian Chron.* Epoch XIV. Diod. Sic. lib. v.
60. *Parian Chron.* Epoch XII. XIII. XIV. Diod. Sicul. ubi sup. Justin, lib. ii.

This

This at least was the opinion of some of the most enlightened Greek and Roman writers. " Those sa- " cred mysteries," says Isocrates, " fortify the soul " against the fear of death, and inspire the initiated " with the pleasing hopes of an happy immortality[61]." —And Cicero, in speaking of the same mysteries, con- siders them as the greatest of all the benefits for which Europe was indebted to the city of Athens. " It was she," remarks that philosophical politician, " who taught us not only to live happily, but to die " with tranquillity, in confidence of becoming yet " more happy in a future state of existence[62]."

The affairs of Attica, or those of the more northern states of Greece, afford few memorable events, from the reign of Erechtheus to that of Theseus. The reign of Theseus is highly interesting. It forms the æra of an important change in the Athenian government, and in the manners of all Greece. It may be called *the age of Grecian chivalry.* But before I speak of the trans- actions of that heroic age, or carry farther the history of Athens, I must give your lordship an account of the rise of the kingdom of Lacedæmon, and of the states in its neighbourhood.

The territory of Laconia, in Peloponnesus, was early possessed by the Leleges[63]. And Lelex, the head of that ancient Grecian tribe, and the first king of this illustrious country, is computed by chronologers to have reigned about fifteen hundred years before the

---

61. Isocrat. *Paneg. Athen.*

62. Cicero, de *Legib.* lib. ii. et Orat. vii. ad. *Verrem.* That the doc- trine of the *unity* of the DEITY also was inculcated in the Eleusinian mysteries, I have formerly had occasion to shew.

63. Pausan. *Lacon.* Strabo, lib. x.

Christian

Christian æra[64]. LACEDÆMON, one of the successors of Lelex, gave to the kingdom of Laconia his own name ; and to its capital, that of *Sparta*, in honour of his wife, the daughter of Eurotas, his predecessor[65].

The history of Sparta, from the reign of Lacedæmon to that of Tyndareus, is almost utterly unknown. Tyndareus (whose family affairs will afterward demand our attention) was married to the celebrated Læda, whom Jupiter, in the shape of a swan, is said to have enjoyed[66]. Be this, however, as it may, Læda bore to her husband, or at least fathered upon him, two sons, named Castor and Pollux ; who died in early manhood, and were deified for their exploits ; and two daughters, Helen and Clytemnestra, not less known to fame[67]. Tyndareus was contemporary with Theseus.

The kingdom of Mycenæ, also in the Grecian peninsula, was founded by Perseus, the reputed son of Jupiter, and of Danäe, the daughter of Acrisius, king of Argos[68]. Perseus is the most renowned of the first heroes of Greece ; but his exploits, as embellished by the splendid imagination of his fondly admiring countrymen, are too improbable to be admitted among the number of traditional facts. He is said to have married Andromeda, whom he had delivered from a sea-monster, and to have had by her five sons, Alcæus, Sthenelus, Hilas, Mastor, and Electrion[69].

64. *Parian Chron.* Epoch X. Euseb. *Chron.* Blair, *Chron.* We must not consider *Lelex* as a proper name; but as a title of honour, conferred upon some chief who had acquired high renown among the Leleges, and great sway over them. The same may be said of Pelasgus, and other barbarous chieftains.

65. Pausan. *Lacon.*

66. Apollod. lib. iii.   67. Id. ibid.

68. Pausan. lib. ii.   Apollod lib. iii.

69. Apollod. lib. ii.   Diod. Sicul. lib. iv.

Alcæus

Alcæus left, by his wife Hippomene, a son named Amphytrion, and a daughter called Anaxo. Electrion, the brother of Alcæus, married his niece Anaxo; and had, by her, the famous Alcmena; who became the wife of her uncle Amphytrion, and the mother of Heracles, or Hercules, in consequence of a supposed embrace of the god Jupiter[70].

Electrion governed the kingdom of Mycenæ after the death of Perseus, and Amphytrion should naturally have succeeded him in the throne. He was the husband of Alcmena, Electrion's only daughter, and the son of Alcæus, the eldest son of Perseus, their common progenitor. But Amphytrion having had the misfortune to kill his father-in-law involuntarily, was obliged to abscond for a time[71].

Meanwhile Sthenelus, king of Argos, Amphytrion's uncle, taking advantage of that circumstance, seized upon the inheritance of his fugitive nephew, and gave it to his own son Eurystheus[72]. In consequence of this usurpation, the gallant Hercules, whose generous toils and heroic deeds have so long excited the admiration of mankind, was also excluded the throne of his ancestors. And the kingdom of Mycenæ, on the death of Eurystheus, who was slain in an expedition into Attica, passed from the family of Perseus into that of Pelops[73].

The arrival of Pelops, son of Tantalus king of Phrygia, in the Grecian peninsula, to which he had the honour of giving his name, produced an almost total revolution in the state of PELOPONNESUS. His Asiatic wealth, and numerous family, acquired him

70. Id. ibid. 　　　71. Apollod. lib. ii.
72. Id. ibid. 　　　73. Apollod. lib. ii. Diod. Sicul. lib. iv.

great

great consequence among the inhabitants of that peninsula; so that his daughters were married to the
princes of the country, and he was enabled to procure
sovereignties for most of his sons[74]. He was contemporary with Perseus.

Atreus, one of the sons of Pelops, having married
Ærope, daughter of Eurystheus, king of Argos and
Mycenæ, succeeded to the sovereignty of those two
kingdoms, on the death of his father-in-law[75]. And
Agamemnon, the son of Atreus, who is stiled by Homer, " king of *many isles*, and of *all* Argos[76]," was the
most powerful prince in Greece[77].

Agamemnon married Clytemnestra, daughter of
Tyndareus, king of Lacedæmon or Sparta. And Helen, Clytemnestra's sister, the most celebrated beauty
that had ever appeared in Greece, was given in marriage to Menelaus, Agamemnon's brother, who succeeded to the Spartan throne on the death of Tyndareus, his father-in-law[78].

Corinthus, another son of Pelops, called also the
son of Jupiter, gave his name to the city of Corinth,
formerly named Ephyra[79]. This city, seated at the
narrowest part of the isthmus that unites Peloponnesus to the main land of Greece, and favoured with
two harbours, one on the Ionian, the other on the
Ægean sea, became early distinguished by its wealth
and commerce[80].

74. Diod. Sicul. ubi. Sup.   Thucyd. lib. i.   Plut. *Vit. Thes.*

75. Apollod. lib. ii.   Diod. Sicul. lib. iv.   76. *Iliad*, lib. ii.

77. Thucyd. lib. i. cap. ix. x.

78. Apollod. lib. iii.   Pausan. lib. iii.

79. Pausan. lib. ii. init.   *Ancient Univ. Hist.* vol. v. chap. xviii.
sect. viii. et auct. cit.

80. Thucyd. lib. i. cap. ix.

Pittheus,

Pittheus, a third son of Pelops, built the city, and
founded the small sovereignty, or township, of Troezene[81]. He was a prince of great sagacity and probity, and became the grandfather of Theseus, king of
Attica, in consequence of circumstances sufficiently
memorable to merit a particular detail; especially as
they mark the manners of the age, and will serve as an
introduction to the reign of the illustrious Athenian
monarch, as well as to the rise of Grecian heroism.

· The heroic age in ancient Greece, like that of chivalry in Modern Europe, was preceded by times of un-
speakable violence and calamity; during which all
government might be said to be dissolved, and when
force was the only law. There was then no travelling with safety from one district to another, or even
from place to place, within any particular district.
Every deep cave was the den of some savage plunderer,
who obstructed social intercourse, and preyed without
remorse upon the surrounding country[82].

Strongly awakened to a sense of humanity, by the
contemplation of such atrocious wrongs, which the
civil authority wanted power to prevent or remedy,
some men of generous minds, and of great personal
prowess, stood forth the champions of injured virtue,
of violated beauty, or oppressed worth. Perseus,
Hercules, and Theseus, were the most renowned of
these champions[83]. The exploits of Hercules, as well
as those of Perseus, are justly consigned to the region

81. Pausan. lib. i. Plut. *Vit. Thes.*   82. Plut. *Vit. Thes.*
83. These heroes and their associates, however, in the course of
their adventures, were guilty of many irregularities; but especially
in regard to women. Hence Mr. Bryant calls them "a set of honoura-
"ble banditti, who would suffer nobody to do mischief but them-
"selves!" *New System of Ancient Mythol.* vol. ii.

of fable[84]. Those of Theseus are better authenticated, and intimately connected with the progress of government in Greece.

This hero was the natural son of Ægeus, king of Athens. Ægeus, when past the prime of life, having no legitimate offspring, a faction formed by the sons of his brother Pallas, known by the name of the *Pallantidæ*, gave him perpetual uneasiness. In order to remove that inconveniency, he went to Delphos, and supplicated Apollo for information, how he might obtain the blessing of children. The response of the oracle, little ambiguous, seemed to forbid him the use of any woman before his return to Athens[85].

Not satisfied, however, with that meaning, Ægeus applied for a solution to Pittheus, king of Troezene; who was celebrated over Greece, as a man of the greatest wisdom of his time. What explication Pittheus gave is uncertain: but so much was he enslaved by the popular superstition, or so little sense had he of the merit of female virtue, that he contrived to introduce his own daughter, Æthra, to the bed of his royal visitor[86].

I speak with diffidence, in regard to the motives of Pittheus; as it does not appear from history, whether

84. The Greeks, as I have formerly had occasion to observe, on the authority of Herodotus (*Historiar*, lib. ii. cap. xliii.—xlv.), confounded the worship of an Egyptian deity of the name of Heracles, or Hercules, with their veneration for the son of Alcmena, to whom they gave the name of that god (Id. ibid.). The same may be said of Perseus, whose name was also that of an Egyptian god (Herodotus, lib. ii. cap. xci.); and of *Dionusos*, or Bacchus, whose mortal existence Herodotus seems to question (lib. ii. cap. cxlvi.): Hence the confusion arising from a mixture of Egyptian allegory with Grecian tradition, which renders the fabulous adventures of Perseus and Hercules, to say nothing of those of the reputed son of Semele, utterly inexplicable. Vide Diod. Sicul. *Biblioth*. lib. iii. iv. passim.

85. Plut. *Vit. Thes.*   86. Id. ibid.

he

he was induced to act so indelicate a part, by a persuasion that the response of the oracle contained some latent command, which he was bound to see accomplished, or by a desire of forming a family connexion
with Ægeus. Yet it seems probable, as the wife of
that prince was then alive, that Pittheus was swayed
by the former motive. But let this have been as it
might, it is allowed that Æthra proved with child; and
that Ægeus, before his departure from Troezene, led
her into an adjacent field, and there deposited, under
a great stone, certain tokens, by which the fruit of their
illegitimate commerce, if a son, should be known to
him, and proudly acknowledged; provided he had
sufficient bodily strength, when he arrived at the years
of manhood, to remove that stone[87].

This anecdote, while it shews the importance of
personal vigour in early ages, is highly characteristic
of the manners of those rude times: and that which
follows it is yet more marking. As soon as the pregnancy of Æthra began to grow visible, her father Pittheus, in order to preserve her reputation, circulated a
report, that she had been honoured with an embrace
of the god Neptune, the tutelary deity of the Troezenians[88].

That report was readily received[89]; for, strange as
it may seem, mankind have in all ages believed in the
possible conjunction of the natures divine and human.
" On this subject," says Plutarch, " the Egyptians
" have made a plausible distinction. They think it
" not impossible, that the divine essence of a god may
" be communicated to a woman, and may awaken in her
" some principle of generation; but they hold, that the

---

87. Plut. ubi sup. et Pausan. lib. i.   88. Id. ibid.
89. Plut. *Vit. Thes.*

" nature

" nature of no man can mix with that of a female divi-
" nity, or goddess. In so saying, however," adds he,
" they forget, that there can be no impregnation with-
" out mutual communication of essence[90]."

The more ancient Greeks, in general, had less sublime ideas of the gods, and the Troezenians were incapable of entering into such subtle disquisitions; so
that the reputation of Æthra was perfectly safe. She
was considered as a princess peculiarly favoured by
heaven, and delivered of a son named Theseus;
whose early vigour, both of body and mind, confirmed
all Greece in the belief of his divine origin[91]. And
perhaps the reputed son of Neptune owed his superior
abilities, in some measure, to that belief.

Unwilling, however, that Theseus should remain
ignorant of his mortal father, his mother Æthra took
him to the place where Ægeus had deposited the tokens, as soon as she thought he had acquired sufficient strength to discover them. He removed the
stone with ease; and found in a cavern beneath it, a
sword and a pair of sandals[92].

These tokens, and the story of his birth, which
accompanied the discovery of them, roused every heroic quality in the youthful mind of Theseus. They
seemed to point out to him the course he ought to pursue, independent of the request of his father. He,
therefore, resolved instantly to visit Athens; and, notwithstanding the warm remonstrances of his mother
and grandfather, determined to go thither by land[93].
In vain did the sage Pittheus, who had taken great
care of his education, represent to him the dan-

90. Plut. *Vit. Numa.*   91. Plut. *Vit. Thes.* et Pausan. lib. i. ii.
92. Plut. *Vit. Thes.* et Pausan. lib. i.   93. Plut. ubi sup.

gers to which he must be exposed in such a journey, from the violent attacks of brutal ruffians; and of barbarous chieftains, that pillaged the whole country, and obstructed the roads, while he might safely pass to Athens by water[94]; the fleets of Minos II. king of Crete, having about that time cleared the Grecian seas of pirates[95].

Such remonstrances served only to inflame the courage of Theseus, and to confirm him in his purpose. The dangers held up to be encountered, were to him so many new motives for going to Athens by land. Filled with admiration of the gallant exploits of his kinsman Hercules, he was ambitious of emulating them. He accordingly began his perilous journey; slew many barbarous chieftains, who, subsisting by murder and rapine, infested the Corinthian isthmus and the mountainous coast of the Saronic gulf; arrived safe at Athens; became known to Ægeus, who cordially embraced him, and publicly acknowledged him as his son; quelled a sedition raised by the Pallantidæ, and firmly established his father's throne[96].

Chronology has not fixed the time of the arrival of Theseus at Athens. But it appears to have been before the Argonautic expedition; as some ancient authors include him among the number of the adventurers in that enterprise[97]. And we have the uniform testimony of tradition, that he co-operated with Hercules and other heroes, who were engaged in the Argonautic expedition, in freeing Greece from the depredations of lawless men, as well as from the destructive rage of wild beasts.

94. Id. ibid.
95. Thucyd. lib. i.   Diod. Sicul. lib. iv.   Plut. *Vit. Thes.*
96. Plut. ubi sup.   97. Id. ibid. et Apollod. lib. i.

Of

· Of all the subjects that have excited the curiosity of
antiquarians, on none have they been able to throw so
little light, as on that of the *Argonautic expedition.*
The *golden fleece* of Colchis, we are told, was its declared object; but what we are to understand by that
fleece, whether the fine wool of the flocks of the
country, sheep-skins placed in the beds of rivers to collect gold dust, a rich treasure carried to Colchis in a
vessel with the figure of a gilded ram on her prow, or
some other metaphorical meaning, is a matter not yet
decided among the learned, and in regard to which
scarce two antiquaries are of the same opinion[98]. No
satisfactory account has hitherto been given by any
writer, ancient or modern, of the object of this enterprise.

· All we know with any degree of certainty, in regard to the Argonautic expedition, is, that after having fully explored their own country, cleared its woods
and mountains of robbers and banditti, the early heroes of Greece resolved to embark in a foreign voyage, in order to furnish new exercise for their daring
and restless spirits; that a ship, named Argo, was accordingly built in the port of Iolcus, at the foot of
mount Pelion in Thessaly, and more completely equip-
ped than any former Grecian vessel[99]; that Jason,
the

98. See on this intricate subject Apollod. lib. i.   Diod. Sic. lib. iv.
Bochart, *in Phaleg.* lib. iv. Bannier, *Explic. des Fab.* tom. vii. Pow-
nal, *Stud. Antiq.*

99. The departure of the Argo is finely described by Apollonius
Rhodius:

    " On their allotted posts now rang'd along
    " In seemly order sat the princely throng.
    " Fast by each chief his glitt'ring armour flames:
    " The midmost station bold Ancæus claims;
    " While great Alcides, whose enormous might,
    " Arm'd with a *massy club*, provokes the fight,

                 " Now

the commander of this ship, after encountering many
dangers and difficulties, entered the Euxine sea, either
with or without an attendant fleet, and came to anchor
near the port of Æa, in the river Phasis, at the eastern
extremity of that sea, and then the capital of the kingdom of Colchis, supposed to have been founded by an
Egyptian colony; that the Argonauts carried off with
them from Colchis the princess Medea, the king's
daughter; who, being enamoured of Jason, their leader,
is said to have betrayed to him her father's treasures[100].

In consequence of this expedition, which opened to
Greece the commerce of the Euxine sea, on the coasts
of which the Argonauts are said to have planted colonies[101], the Greeks became henceforth more bold and
skilful navigators; more social in disposition, by having been accustomed to act in concert; and more attentive to civil policy, and to the constitution of foreign
states.

" Now plac'd beside him.   In the yielding flood,
" The keel, deep sinking, feels the demi-god.
   " Their hausers now they loose, and on the brine
" To Neptune pour the consecrated wine;
" While, raising high the Thracian harp, presides
" Melodious Orpheus, and the movement guides.
" On either side the dashing surges broke;
" And hoarse re-murmured to each mighty stroke:
" Thick flash'd the brazen arms with streaming light,
" While the swift barque pursued her rapid flight;
" And ever as the sea-green tide she cleaves,
" Foams the long tract behind, and whitens all the waves.
   " Jove on that day, from his celestial throne,
" And all th' immortal powers of heaven look'd down,
" The godlike chiefs and Argo to survey,
" As through the deep they urg'd their daring way."

Argonaut, lib. I.

100. Bannier, *Explic. des Fab.* tom. vii. et. auct. cit.
101. Diod. Sicul. lib. iv.   Strabo, lib. i. xi.   Eustach. ad Dion.
Periegit. ver. 689.   Plin. *Hist. Nat.* lib. vi. cap. v.

The

The government of none of the neighbouring states was so worthy of attention as that of Crete. In this famous island all the Grecian gods are said to have been born; because they were there first worshipped under Grecian names, and with the ceremonies afterward used by the Greeks. Lying contiguous to Greece and Asia Minor, and seated at no great distance from Egypt and Phœnicia, whence it repeatedly received colonies, Crete exhibited in very early times a constitution planned by the most consummate political wisdom, and a body of laws that long commanded the admiration of mankind. For these advantages the Cretans were indebted to the elder Minos, who reigned about fourteen hundred and thirty years before the Christian æra[102]; and was so renowned for his virtue and sagacity, that the Greeks assigned to him the office of chief judge in the state of the dead.

Ancient historians have left it doubtful whether Minos was a foreigner, or a native of Crete: nor are we informed by what means he acquired supreme authority among the Cretans. He appears, however, to have been a foreigner; to have derived his political knowledge from Egypt; to have conducted into Crete a colony of Egyptians, Phrygians, and Phœnicians, from Rhodes; and to have acquired dominion over the rude natives by his superior sagacity, and his ability of defending them against the barbarous attacks of piratical adventurers[103].

Crete, before the reign of Minos, was exposed to the common calamity of the maritime parts of Greece and the contiguous islands; to invasions, depredations,

102. *Parian Chron.* Epoch XI.
103. See Blackwell's *Life of Homer*, sect. x. and the authors there cited.

and the frequent expulsion of its inhabitants. In order to remedy these evils, Minos framed a system of government, and digested a code of laws; which Plato tells us[104], as they were the most ancient, were deservedly esteemed the most excellent of any European state. He also founded the cities of Cnossus, Cydonia, and Phœstus; into which he collected the great body of his subjects, and taught them to submit to his civil and political institutions[105].

The chief object of the policy of Minos was security against conquest or invasion. For that end he created a navy, and ordered all his subjects to be trained to arms, and inured to hard discipline from their most tender years. And as such discipline, he knew, was by no means flattering to the natural indolence or levity of man, he took every measure that human prudence could suggest in order to inspire the Cretans with respect for the established maxims of government. The young men were not allowed to call in question, even in dispute, the wisdom or utility of any of his regulations[106].

Minos went yet farther. He affirmed that his laws were dictated to him by Jupiter, the supreme divinity of the Cretans, with whom he affected occasionally to hold conversation, and by whom he was ordered, he said, to engrave them on plates of brass[107]. Nor was he less attentive to the enforcing, than to the framing of his laws. The regular administration of justice was committed to his two brothers, Taulus and Rhadamanthus. Taulus, the younger,

104. In *Minoe*.
105. Diod. Sicul. lib. iv. Plato in *Minoe*. Strabo, lib. x.
106. Plato *de Leg*. lib. i.
107. Plato in *Minoe*. Hom. Odyss. xix.

made

made the circuit of the island twice a year, to hear
causes and give judgment; while Rhadamanthus, who
had the cognizance of capital crimes, held his tribunal
in Cnossus, the metropolis[108]. The Cretan monarch
commanded in person his own fleets and armies, and
was very powerful both by land and sea.

A more particular account of the institutions of
Minos would lead me, my lord, to anticipate what I
shall have to say of those of Lycurgus; who made the
Cretan constitution the model of that system of government which he framed for the Lacedæmonians. It
will be proper, however, here to observe, that Minos,
with a view of preserving union, established the most
perfect equality among his subjects; and also obliged
them to eat together in public, their food being furnished at the expense of the state[109]; that he made professions, in Crete, hereditary by law, as in Egypt; and
that the cultivation of the ground, in that island, was
by him committed solely to the care of slaves[110].

This last circumstance seems to prove that the first
Minos[111] must either have been very successful in wars
against his neighbours, or have reduced the greater
part of the inhabitants of Crete to the condition of ser-

108. Plato, ubi sup.

109. Aristot. *Polit.* lib. vii. Strabo, lib. x.

110. Aristot. *Polit.* lib. ii. vii. Athen. lib. vi.

111. Mr. Mitford has laboured to prove, that there was only *one*
Minos (*Hist. of Greece*, chap. i. iv.); because Homer, Thucydides, and
Aristotle, make no mention of a *second*. But this argument appears to
me very inconclusive. For Homer and Aristotle had only occasion to
speak of the great legislator, and Thucydides of the first clearer of
the Grecian seas from pirates. Had the inexorable prince, who so
rigidly demanded (as we shall have occasion to see) the cruel Athenian tribute, and the legislator been the same person, the popular
superstition of Greece would never have dignified *Minos* with the
office of *supreme judge* in the state of the dead, where *mildness* was the
chief feature in his character. PLATO, in *Gorgias.*

vitude

vitude. His grandson, Minos II. was yet more famed for his naval and military exploits. He effectually cleared the Grecian seas from the depredations of Lycian, Carian, and Phœnician pirates[112]: he subdued several of the adjacent islands ; and he humbled some of the maritime. states on the continent[113]. Among others Athens felt the effects of his power and his resentment.

Contemporary with Ægeus king of Attica, and victorious in. war against that prince, the second Minos imposed upon the Athenians a humiliating tribute of seven youths, and an equal number of virgins, as an. atonement for the murder of his son Androgeus[114]; who having acquired distinguished honours in the public games, and associated himself with the Pallantidæ, was thought to have been assassinated by order of the Athenian monarch[115]. How often this tribute was exacted; or for what number of years it was imposed, the Greek historians are by no means agreed; but they all concur in representing the arrival of the Cretan vessel at the stated time, as the cause of great affliction in the city of Athens, and of many murmurs against the government of Ægeus, for continuing to submit to such indignity[116].

That sorrow and dissatisfaction was much heightened by a frightful tale, which seems to have gained universal belief, and was probably first propagated by the Pallantidæ; that the tributary youths and virgins were thrown into an inextricable labyrinth, said to have been built by the famous architect Dedalus, an Athe-

112. Thucydid. lib. i.   Diod. Sic. lib. iv.   Plut. *Vit. Thes.*
113. Diod. Sicul, et. Plut. ubi sup.
114. Diod. Sicul. lib. iv.   Apollod. lib. iii. et Plut. *Vit. Thes.*
115. Diod. Sicul. ubi sup. et Plut. *Vit. Thes.* .   116. Id. ibid.

nian refugee, and there devoured by the fabled Minotaur, a monster represented as half bull and half
man[117].

By this labyrinth we ought perhaps to understand a
strong and magnificent state-prison, abounding with
apartments, in which the tributary captives were confined, until the celebration of certain funeral games,
instituted by Minos in honour of the memory of his
son Androgeus; and at which the Athenian youths and
virgins were the prizes, and became the slaves of the
victors[118]. The idea of the Minotaur was probably
suggested by the ferocious appearance, and brutal disposition, of a man of great bodily strength, named *Taurus*,
who generally carried off the prizes at those games,
and who was also general of the forces of Minos, or
captain of the guards that secured the labyrinth or
state-prison[119].

Let those things, however, have been as they might,
it seems certain, that the payment of the tribute imposed by Minos excited dreadful apprehensions in the
breasts of the Athenian fathers and mothers; and that
Theseus, the third time it was demanded, and the first
time apparently after his arrival at Athens, discovered
a generosity of spirit worthy of his heroic character.
The tributary youths and virgins having hitherto been
drawn by lot, he voluntarily offered himself as one of
the youths; resolved to kill the Minotaur, and free his
country from a cruel tribute, or to perish in the bold
attempt. He accordingly embarked, in a vessel equip-
ped on purpose, along with the other exacted victims[120].

117. Diod. Sicul. lib. iv. Plut. *Vit. Thes.*
118. Philochor. ap. Plut. *Vit. Thes.*
119. Id. ibid.
120. Plut. *Vit. Thes.* Diod. Sicul. lib. iv.

When

When the Athenian prince arrived in Crete, where his gallent exploits had already been announced by fame, the manly beauty of his person attracted the eye of Ariadne, the king's daughter; and his patriotic heroism seems in some measure to have subdued the inexorable heart of Minos, still craving vengeance for the murder of his son. Through the intercession of Ariadne with her father, or by some happy amorous contrivance, Theseus was permitted to combat in the funeral games, instituted in honour of the memory of Androgeus, and vanquished the redoubted champion Taurus[121] ; or, in other words, he was victorious over all competitors ; and, therefore, might be truly said to have *killed* the *Minotaur*, as he thus procured indemnity to the sons and daughters of his father's unhappy subjects, who must otherwise have lingered out their days in foreign slavery. But whether Minos, filled with admiration of the prowess and magnanimity of Theseus, gave him his daughter Ariadne in marriage, and generously remitted the Athenian tribute, as some late writers have affirmed ; or continued to adhere to the austere maxims of rigid policy, ancient historians have not enabled us to decide. All we know, with any degree of certainty, is, that Ariadne accompanied Theseus when he left Crete, and that the Athenians thenceforth paid no tribute to Minos[122].

Were I to hazard an opinion upon this intricate subject, I should say, in conformity with the general tenor of ancient tradition, that Ariadne eloped with Theseus ; and that he chose rather to trust to his own adventurous spirit for the certain possession of that princess, and to his courage and high renown in arms, for an exemption from the odious tribute, than to rest

121. Philochor. ap. Plut. *Vit. Thes.*
122. Plut. *Vit. Thes.* Diod. Sicul. lib. iv.

                                            either

either upon the doubtful generosity of Minos. He therefore embarked in the night, and carried with him his fair preserver[123]; who appears to have been taken ill in the course of the voyage, and to have died[124], or been stolen from him at the isle of Naxos[125].

The glory acquired by Theseus, in having magnanimously freed his country from an ignominious and cruel tribute, raised his already popular character to the height of idolatry. His fortunate voyage to Crete was celebrated at Athens with sacrifices and solemn processions, which were continued down to the latest times of that republic[126]. And the vessel in which he had performed the voyage, supported by constant repairs, was sent annually, for upwards of eight hundred years, to the sacred island of Delos, in order to return thanks to Apollo, for the deliverance the Athenian hero had accomplished[127].

·. But the patriotic voyage of Theseus was followed by other consequences, no less important to Attica than the abolition of the tribute imposed by the Cretan monarch. The Athenian prince, while in Crete, had opportunity to observe the salutary institutions of the elder Minos. These presented to his view a more regular system of policy, and a more rigid civil and military discipline, than was to be found in any Grecian state on the continent.

A plan of government so harmonious, and so firmly combined, could not escape the discerning eye of Theseus. And no sooner did he succeed to the Athenian sceptre, than he endeavoured to profit by his political

123. Diod. Sicul. lib. iv.   124. Hom. Odyss. lib. xi.
125. Diod. Sicul. ubi sup.
126. Plut. *Vit. Thes.*
127. Plato, in *Phædo*, et Plut. ubi sup.

knowledge.

PART I.   knowledge. He saw with concern the little kingdom
of Attica broken into twelve independent jurisdictions;
the inhabitants of one district often hostile to those of
another; and those of each district, enslaved by prejudices against their neighbours, agitated with jealousies
and local antipathies[128].

In order to remedy these evils, and give union and
vigour to the state, Theseus abolished the exclusive jurisdictions; dissolved the separate councils and magistracies; and, establishing in the metropolis one grand
council or national assembly, and one senate-house,
or Prutaneion, which served also for a hall of justice,
made Athens the sole seat of law and government[129].

In consequence of these regulations, every free inhabitant of Attica became in effect an Athenian citizen. The people of no one district having thenceforth
any separate interest, the welfare of the state, its security and grandeur, was made equally the care of all its
members. And yet more perfectly to unite the hearts
and the interests of his subjects, Theseus saw the necessity of one common religion, or a communion of
pious ceremonies. He accordingly instituted, in honour of the goddess Athena, or Minerva, an annual festival for the whole body of the inhabitants of Attica.
To this sacred solemnity he gave the name of *Pana-
thena;* the festival of all the Athenians, or people of
Minerva[130]. And from the time of its institution they
seem all, according to his intention, to have considered
themselves as united under the immediate protection
of that goddess.

128. Thucydid. lib. ii.   Plut. *Vit. Thes.*
129. Id. ibid.   130. Plut. ubi supra.

                                          Aware

Aware, however, that the most perfect civil and religious union is insufficient to preserve order in a populous community, Theseus had recourse to the distinction of ranks, as a farther support to his authority.
He divided the inhabitants of Attica into three classes;
consisting of nobility, husbandmen, and artificers. To
the nobles he assigned the trust of executive justice,
the expounding of the laws, the offices of civil government, the offering of sacrifices, the superintendance of
religious ceremonies, and the interpretation of the will
of the gods. The husbandmen and artificers formed
the body of the state, enjoyed freedom and equality,
and composed the majority of the popular assembly.
To himself he reserved only the military power and
the guardianship of the laws[131].

After the change in the Athenian constitution accomplished by Theseus, which had no small influence
upon the government of the neighbouring states, the
next important transaction in the history of Greece,
was the Theban war. The cause of that war is thus
related by the Grecian historians. Æteocles and Polynices, the two sons of Œdipus king of Thebes (whose
involuntary crimes have furnished so many triumphs
for the tragic muse), agreed to sway by turns the sceptre, each for a year, instead of dividing the kingdom
between them. Æteocles, the elder brother, ascended
the Theban throne first; and found royalty so congenial to his disposition, that he refused to relinquish his
sway at the stipulated term[132].

Enraged at such duplicity, the injured Polynices
sought redress at the court of Adrastus, king of Argos.
Adrastus, warmly embraced his cause, and gave him

131. Aristot. Polit. lib. ii. Plut. Vit. Thes.
132. Diod. Sicul. lib. iv. Apollod. lib. iii.

his

his daughter Argia in marriage. And these two allied princes, assisted by five potent chiefs, collected a large body of forces, or armed followers, and marched toward Thebes[133].

Meanwhile Æteocles, foreseeing his danger, had neglected nothing necessary for his defence. He had negociated alliances, and assembled a numerous army. The hostile princes, and their confederated chieftains, met near the banks of the river Ismenus. The Thebans gave ground on the first shock, and took shelter within the walls of their capital. The victors invested Thebes in seven divisions, under their seven leaders, who took post before its seven gates, and formed the first siege mentioned in Grecian history[134].

The unskilfulness of the assailants, and the valour of the defenders, threatening to make the siege of great length, the rival brothers, Æteocles and Polynices, agreed to decide their dispute by single combat[135]. They accordingly engaged under the walls of Thebes, in sight of both armies; and fought with such ferocity, that they fell by mutual wounds[136]. But although the cause of the war was removed by the bloody termination of this unnatural combat, the Thebans did not suffer the invaders of their country to escape with impunity. Roused to revenge by Creon, the uncle of the two ill-fated princes, they made a vigorous sally; forced the enemy's camp, and put almost every man in it to the sword[137]. Nay, so exasperated were they against the besiegers, that, contrary to all the laws of war and the maxims of ancient piety, they would not permit the Argives to bury their dead[138].

133. Id. ibid. 134. Apollod. lib. iii. Pausan. lib. ix.
135. Apollod. lib. iii. 136. Apollod. ubi sup. Diod. Sicul. lib. iv.
137. Pausan. lib. ix. 138. Apollod. lib. iii.

The

The value, which the early Greeks set upon the privilege of sepulture, made this refusal be regarded with general horror, and considered as a cruel misfortune by the Argives. In the depth of their sorrow for the condition of their deceased countrymen, they applied to Theseus king of Athens, whose humanity and generosity were well known; and that prince, actuated by a sense of religion and natural justice, conducted an army into Bœotia, and compelled the Thebans to grant funeral honours to their slaughtered enemies[139].

About ten years after this mournful tribute had been paid, war was again declared against Thebes. It was besieged by the Epigoni, or sons of the seven chiefs who had formerly invested that capital, and fallen beneath its walls. More fortunate than their fathers, whose insulted manes they undertook to avenge, they made themselves masters of the place; killed many of the inhabitants, dragged more into slavery, and obliged the remainder to acknowledge for their king Thersander, son of the unhappy Polynices, whose injuries had been the occasion of the first Theban war[140].

The sacking of Thebes was soon followed by the siege of Troy; the first great enterprize in which the Greeks acted as one people, having a common interest. But this famous siege, which introduces a new and memorable æra in the annals of ancient Greece, will require a new letter. And before we enter upon the history of the Trojan war, I must turn your eye, my lord, upon the countries against which it was directed, and investigate the causes by which it was produced.

139. Apollod. lib. iii.
140. Diod. Sicul. lib. iv. Apollod. lib. iii. Pausan. lib. ix.

LETTER III.

CONTINUATION OF THE TRADITIONAL HISTORY OF GREECE,
WITH AN ACCOUNT OF THE STATE OF ASIA MINOR, FROM
THE BEGINNING OF THE TROJAN WAR, TO THE RETURN
OF THE HERACLIDÆ.

PART I.   THE large promontory anciently called *Asia
Minor*, and now known by the name of *Natolia;* which
is formed by the Mediterranean and Euxine seas,
and extends toward Greece about seven hundred
miles, from the mountains of Lesser Armenia to the
Hellespont, hath in all ages been considered as one of
the finest regions of the earth.   The oldest inhabitants
of this delightful country (of which history or tradition
make mention) were the Paphlagonians, Phrygians,
Dardanians or Trojans, Meonians or Lydians, the
Carians and Lycians[1].

Compared with the early Greeks, several of those
nations were rich and polished before the Trojan war[2];
and only inferior in arts and civility to the Assyrians,
Egyptians, and Phœnicians.   The Trojans were most
distinguished for wealth and power, at the period of
which I am here treating; when venerable Priam, the
sixth in descent from Jupiter, to use the language of
Homer, filled the throne of Dardanus[3].

The

---

1. Homer, *Iliad.* et Herodotus, *Historiar.* passim. See also Strabo,
Geog. lib. xiii. xiv.   2. Id. ibid.

3. Hom. *Iliad.* lib. **xx.**   When Homer can trace the lineage of a
king or hero no higher traditionally, he generally makes the first of the
race the son of Jupiter; as much as to say, that nothing more was
known concerning the genealogy of the family of which he speaks.

He

The kingdom of Troy, in the reign of Priam, extended from mount Ida over all the eastern coast of the Hellespont, and from the Propontis to the Ægean sea[4]; comprehending also within its jurisdiction the isles of Tenedos and Lesbos[5]. Nor did the Trojans fail to take advantage of so happy a situation for commerce. They had diligently applied themselves to trade and navigation, as well as to arts and manufactures[6]. Hence we find them, at the time of the Grecian invasion, in possession of most of the conveniencies, and even many of the luxuries of life[7].

The city of Ilion or Troy, the capital of the kingdom of Priam, was a large and populous place, with broad streets[8]. It was secured with high walls, and farther

He accordingly calls Dardanus, the founder of the Trojan state, the son of Jupiter (*Iliad.* ubi sup.). All attempts, therefore, to prove that Dardanus was of Grecian descent must be disregarded, as they are built on inferior authority. And the notion, that the Greeks and Trojans spoke the same language, seems equally void of foundation; it being rested chiefly on Homer's *omission* of *interpreters* between the armies of the two nations. If the learned gentlemen, who make use of this argument, had been poets, they would have praised the illustrious bard for his magnanimous neglect of such formality, and eschewed the absurdity into which they have fallen. But in apology for Homer, considered as an *historian*, it may be urged (if such apology should be deemed necessary), that the Greeks might have acquired the language of the Trojans before he opens his scene of action, they having been then almost nine years in the country.

4. Hom. *Iliad.* lib. xxiv. Strabo, *Geog.* lib. xiii.

5. Id. ibid. 6. Hom. *Iliad.* lib. v. xviii. Virgil, *Eneid.* lib. iii. init. Plin. *Hist. Nat.* lib. vii. cap. lvi. The words of Homer, in regard to the Trojan wealth and commerce are too remarkable to be omitted. " The lofty city of Priam," says Hector, " was " rich in gold, and abounding in brass; but now they are perished " from our halls. Our wealth, laid up with care, is fled: our precious " stores are borne from hence to Phrygia, to the pleasing Meonia. " Our *bartered wealth* is fled afar" (*Iliad.* lib. xviii.). From this, and other passages in the Iliad, it appears, that the Trojans paid subsidies to their allies. 7. Hom. *Iliad.* passim. 8. Hom. *Iliad.* lib ix.

defended

PART I. defended with towers[9]. The houses of people of rank consisted of many spacious apartments, well finished, and elegantly furnished[10]. The dress of the women was gay and voluptuous[11], and that of the young men rich and splendid[12].

Paris;

9. Hom. *Iliad.* lib. iii. et lib. xviii.

10. Hom. *Iliad.* lib. vi. xxiv. For the sake of illustration, I shall give the description of Priam's palace, "the beautiful house of the so-" vereign of Troy. Lofty porticoes rose in order *around;* and fifty " halls of polished stone were built near each other *within.* There the " sons of Priam lay in the arms of their lovely wives. The apartments " of the daughters opposite, arose within the spacious court; twelve in " number, with lofty roofs, the walls of polished marble formed. " There lay the sons-in-law of Priam in the arms of their blushing " wives" (*Iliad.* lib. vi.). " To his fragrant chamber, with speed, de-" scended the eager king; with cedar were lined the walls" (*Iliad.* lib. xxiv.). The chambers of the young princes were still more elegant. In that of Paris was " a polished ivory bed" (*Iliad.* lib. iii.). Even in the chambers of Hecuba, his aged mother, was " a fragrant room, " where her high-wrought, varied robes were laid; the work of Sido-" nian dames, and brought from the wealthy Sidon." *Iliad.* lib. vi.

11. The dress of the Trojan ladies was long and flowing, with sweeping trains (Hom. *Iliad.* passim.). And they wore veils of varied dies, with a figure in the middle "bright as a star" (*Iliad.* lib. vi.). For the privacy of their dressing-rooms, and their manner of attiring themselves, we must have recourse to the chamber and toilet of Juno. " Her chamber, which opened with a secret key, she entered, and " closed behind her the glittering door. First she bathes in ambrosial " streams her fair limbs, of proportion divine! then over her beautiful " body she poured rich oil, sweet to the smell. When with this fra-" grant essence she had anointed her lovely form, she combed her long " hair with her hands, she placed in order her shining locks. Her " robe, high laboured with art; wove with many figures to ravish the " eye, she bound beneath her white breast with golden clasps, that " shone afar. She girt her waist with a precious zone, enriched with " tassels of purest gold. The beauteous pendants hung from her " ears: in each three gems beamed bright to view, and shed around " her a heavenly lustre. Her radiant charms she concealed with a " veil." *Iliad.* lib. xiv.

12. Hom. *Iliad.* passim. We have only a description of military dress; which, though sufficiently foppish, Homer lets us understand, was not equal to that of a " youth who moves to the feast, or fits for the spright-" ly dance" (*Iliad.* lib. iii.). Yet were the braided locks of Euphorbus, " renowned at the spear," such as "the graces might wear; bound

" with

Paris, second son of Priam, was reputed the handsomest man in Asia Minor[13]; as Helen, daughter of
Tyndareus, and wife of Menelaus, king of Sparta, was
thought the most beautiful woman in Greece[14]. And,
like Helen, he added to perfect symmetry of form, a
graceful air, a winning manner, and every exterior ac-
complishment[15]. Presuming on these captivating al-
lurements, and his success in employing them, Paris
found a pretence to visit the court of Menelaus; and,
during his stay at Sparta, he engaged the affection of
the lovely Helen, who eloped with him, and took with
her a quantity of treasure[16].

Although the most respectable Grecian writers do
not say, that Helen was carried off by force, they are
unanimous in representing her elopement, or *skape*,

" with silver, and adorned with gold" (*Iliad*. lib. xvii.). The greaves
of Paris were "bound with silver clasps;" and "his sword from his
" shoulders hung, ornamented with silver studs." *Iliad*. lib. iii.

13. Hom. *Iliad*. lib. iii. et seq. The person of Paris, distinguished
by the epithet of *form divine*, was confessedly superior in beauty to that
of every other warrior, among the Trojans or their allies (Id. ibid.).
Hence he is called, *first in form*. Hom. *Iliad*. ubi sup.

14. For so saying, we have the uniform testimony of tradition.
And Homer lets us understand, that the *long-haired* Helen (the epithet he constantly gives her), "in stately steps, in face excelled," all
the beauties of Troy as well as of Greece. *Iliad*. lib. iii. et seq.

15. Hom. *Iliad*. lib. iii. et seq. Paris was so noted for his gallantries,
and so consummately skilled in all the arts of seduction, that he is
repeatedly called "specious deceiver of women" (Id. ibid.). He
seems to have prosecuted his amorous adventures in different countries. For we find he had been in Paphlagonia (*Iliad*. lib. xiii.);
which, as well as Phrygia, is termed a "*peopled land*" (Id. ibid.).
Paris, among his other seductive accomplishments, excelled in playing soft tunes on the harp. Hom. *Iliad*. lib. iii.

16. Hom. *Iliad*. lib. iii. xxii. Of what this treasure consisted, or
what was its value, we are not informed; but it appears to have been
considerable. For it is always mentioned by the Greeks in demand-
ing, and by the Trojans in treating for, or in deliberating on the restitution of the Spartan queen. *Iliad*. passim.

(as

(as usually expressed) as the chief cause of the Trojan war[7]. It is thus they tell the story:

Helen, when only ten years old[18], had been seized because of her enchanting beauty, by Theseus king of Attica, and kept by him for a time in secret[19]. But Castor and Pollux, her two valiant brothers, having recovered her yet untasted charms[20], she became the admiration and wish of every unmarried Grecian prince[21]. Among her declared lovers, who preferred their suit at Sparta, were numbered the most illustrious chiefs and warriors of those heroic times[22].

Apprehensive of danger, if a decided preference was given to any one prince, Tyndareus, the reputed father of Helen, exacted an oath from all her lovers, that they would maintain the choice to be made[23]. Each chieftain flattering himself, that he would be the favoured man, took the oath required[24]; and also bound himself to arm for the recovery of Helen, should she be carried away from her husband[25]. Her hand

17. Homer, in the person of Achilles, represents it as the sole cause. "Why roused Atrides," says he, "whole nations to arms?— "why hither wafted the gathered host?—Was it not for the sake of " Helen?—to recover the long-haired queen" (Hom. *Iliad.* lib. ix.)? And he is so far from representing the carrying away of Helen as an act of violence, that he makes her declare she *chose* Paris (*Iliad.* lib. vi.). To the authority of Homer, I may add that of Herodotus; both in regard to the cause of the Trojan war, and the seduction of Helen (*Historiar.* lib. i. ii.); But it appears that Menelaus did not know of the infidelity of his wife, when he engaged Greece in that war; for " much the king wished to revenge the *rape* of Helen, and her *sighs* " in a foreign land." Hom. *Iliad.* lib. ii. sub. fin.

18. Diod. Sicul. lib. iv.

19. Id. ibid. Apollod. lib. iii. et Plut. *Vit. Thes.*

20. Diod. Sicul. et Plut. ubi sup.   21. Apollod. lib. iii.

22. Id. ibid.   23. Apollod. ubi sup.

24. Id. ibid.   25. Pausan. lib. iii. This oath is also alluded to by Thucydides, lib. i. cap. ix. init.

was

was given to Menelaus[26]; who, in consequence of the violent and immature death of Castor and Pollux, the deified brothers of Helen, became king of Sparta before the Trojan war[27].

Agamemnon, the elder brother of Menelaus, as I have had occasion to observe, was king not only of Argos and Mycenæ, but also of some neighbouring islands[28]. Through the influence of these two powerful princes, and the obligation of the oath taken by the lovers of Helen[29], the assembled states of Greece resolved, that they would compel the restitution of the Spartan queen, or accomplish the destruction of Troy.

In consequence of this resolution, an embassy was sent to Troy, to demand Helen[30].   But no satisfactory answer being given, the Grecian leaders began to assemble their forces, and Agamemnon was chosen commander in chief[31]; a station for which he was well fitted by his character as a king and a warrior[32], and to which he was entitled by his superior sway.

Much time, however, elapsed before the confederated princes were ready to put to sea. They had ships to build, troops to raise, provisions to collect, and precautions to take for the security of their patrimonial dominions during their absence. At length the necessary preparations being made, they sailed from

---

26. Apollod. lib. iii.   27. Hom. *Iliad.* lib. ii. sub. fin.

28. Thucydid. lib. i. cap. ix.   29. Id. ibid.

30. Hom. *Iliad.* lib. ii. Herodot. lib. i. cap. iii.

31. Hom. *Iliad.* lib. ii. iii.

32. Hom. *Iliad.* passim. Helen, in describing the Grecian heroes to Priam, calls him, " the *far-commanding* Agamemnon; a monarch " renowned for justice, a warrior unequalled in arms" (*Iliad.* lib) iii.). " In mien, in stature like Jove, he was conspicuous amid the host." *Iliad.* lib. ii.

the

PART I. the port of Aulis[33], on the coast of Bœotia, in twelve
hundred ships[34]; carrying from an hundred and twenty
to fifty men each[35], and disembarked about one hundred
thousand combatants in the neigbourhood of
Troy[36].

Thucydides conjectures, that Greece could have
furnished a much greater number of men, than embarked
in the Trojan expedition[37]. And the description
of the state of the several countries given by Homer,
in that valuable piece of antiquity, his catalogue of
the Grecian ships and leaders[38], fully justifies the opinion
of this accurate historian. There we find the various
districts of Proper Greece abounding in cattle,
corn or wine, as best suited their different soils ; the
principal maritime and inland towns, distinguished by
the epithets well-built, noble, stately, wealthy, lofty ;
and Eubœa, Crete, Rhodes, and other islands in the
Ægean and Ionian seas, which sent their quotas to the
siege of Troy, filled with populous cities, and flourishing
in opulence and plenty[39].

Having defeated, after an obstinate dispute, the
Trojans that attempted to oppose their landing[40], the
Greeks drew their vessels ashore, and pitched their
camp near their fleet[41]. But many difficulties were
still

---

33. Hom. *Iliad.* lib. ii. Hesiod. *Oper. et Dies*, lib. ii.

34. Hom. *Iliad.* lib. ii. Thucydid. lib. i. cap. x. 35. Id. ibid.

36. The mean between one hundred and twenty, and fifty, is eighty-five;
and twelve hundred, the number of the ships, multiplied by
eighty-five, yields one hundred and two thousand men. But I have
chosen to speak moderately.

37. Thucydid. lib. i. cap. x. xi.

38. *Iliad.* lib. ii. 39. Id. ibid

40. Hom. *Iliad.* lib. ii. Thucydid. lib. i. cap. xi.

41. Id. ibid. et *Iliad.* lib. viii. Thucydides says, that the Greeks
fortified their camp immediately after their landing. (*Hist.* lib. i. cap.
xi.) But Homer, on whose authority he builds, informs us that they
did

still to be surmounted, before they could hope to make themselves masters of the devoted town. The various nature of these difficulties deserves to be particularly considered.

Although perpetually engaged in hostilites, the Greeks seem yet to have been but little skilled in the military art[42], and utterly unacquainted with the manner

did not fortify their camp, until they were hard pressed by the Trojans, in consequence of the quarrel between Achilles and Agamemnon, in the ninth year of the war (*Iliad.* lib. i. vii.). And that Achilles and Telamonian Ajax, confiding in their strength, "dragged their "ships on the strand, at either extreme of the camp." Iliad. lib. viii. . The authority of Homer, as an *Historian* has been so fully establish-ed by some late writers of high reputation, that I need make no apo-logy for quoting him under this character. If he is to be trusted in regard to the remote genealogy of families, and the geography (as Strabo has proved) of every country and district he has occasion to mention, credit may surely be given him for the principal events of the *Trojan war*, which he has wove into an *Historical Poem.* At what distance of time Homer lived from that war, cannot be fixed with certainty. But he flourished near enough it, to collect all the traditions concerning it both in Greece and Asia Minor, while fresh in the minds of the people of the two countries; and to make use of the songs of the military bards (the first historians), who attended the several chiefs; rehearsed their exploits to them in their halls, on their return, or to their surviving kindred; who eagerly listened to the heroic tale, and treasured it in their memory (See Blackwell's *Life of Homer*, et auct. cit.). Homer seems to have written before the conquest of Peloponnesus by the Heraclidæ; for we find in his works no allusion to that great event. And he could not have failed to al-lude to the expulsion of the Atridæ.

42. If we may credit Homer, the Grecian army was not divided into distinct bodies, in battle, till the ninth year of the Trojan war. Then aged Nestor, on a trying occasion, gave the following advice to Agamemnon. "O king! weigh all in thy soul, and listen to my "words. Divide the warriors into tribes: by nations divide the host; "that nation its nation may aid, and tribe its tribe sustain. This "shouldest thou perform, son of Atreus! and should the Greeks in "all obey, to thee will soon be known who of the chiefs from bat-"tle shrinks, and who of the soldiers is brave; for each, distinct in "his place, will engage" (Hom. *Iliad.* lib. li.). It appears, therefore, that the Greeks had hitherto been accustomed to engage in a tumul-tuary manner.

ner of conducting a regular siege.　The city of Troy, beside being strongly fortified, was defended by too numerous and gallant an army to be instantly carried by assault.　The native troops of Priam, independent of foreign aid, were numerous and brave[43].

The place, however, might have been reduced by famine, if all communication with the country had been obstructed.　But the Greeks made no such attempt.　They took no measures for confining the Trojans within their walls; excluding auxiliaries, cutting off convoys, or breaking down those walls by warlike engines.　Having brought with them but a small store of provisions[44], and not being sufficiently expert in navigation to convey regular supplies from home, they could not subsist for any length of time in a body. They were, therefore, under the necessity of dispersing themselves, in order to procure provisions by plunder. They even thought it necessary to cultivate the vallies of the Thracian Chersonesus, lest other means of subsistence should fail[45].

These necessities, the unavoidable consequences of want of political prudence; the ardent temper of

Even after this regulation was established, the ferocious disposition of the Grecian leaders and their followers, perpetually hurried them into disorder in battle (Hom. *Iliad.* passim.); and as they were unacquainted with the use of standards, they had no sure means of restoring their ranks, or recovering their former station.　In the practice of war, when they landed on the Trojan shore, they seem to have differed little from savages.　Their arms and accoutrements, however, were singularly complete.　The chiefs were all cased in armour of brass or steel (Id. ibid).　They carried large shields formed of bull's hides, with a plate of brass in the middle, or behind the boss.　Their principal weapon was a wooden spear, pointed with brass or steel.　With this tremendous instrument they sometimes thrust, but generally threw it (Hom. *Iliad.* passim.).　They also wore a sword; and, when lightly armed, carried a small spear and bow.　Id. ibid.

43. Hom. *Iliad.* passim. but especially lib. viii.
44. Thucydid. lib. i. cap. xi.　　　45. Id. ibid.

the

the Greeks, better adapted to enterprize than persevering efforts; their predatory disposition, and impa-
tience under military command, made them seemingly neglect the great object of their armament for
several years. Having left in the camp (which Agamemnon seems never to have quitted) sufficient force
to protect their ships and tents, or temporary habitations, they desolated the country under different leaders; took many towns, scoured the seas, made themselves masters of the islands belonging to the Trojans,
and pillaged the coasts of Asia Minor[46]. At last, when
booty became scarce, and the country was exhausted
of provisions, they returned, like animals who have
tasted the blood of their prey, to the siege of the Trojan capital; thirsting for spoil and vengeance, and
despising danger[47].

Ant. Chr.
1183.

The Greeks, in a word, though considerably reduced in numbers, were still a formidable enemy.
Inured to toil, trained in peril, and habituated to
subordination, they now seemed capable of acting
with vigour and concert. They had acquired
much military experience, and may be supposed to

46. Hom. *Iliad*. lib. i. ii. ix.

47. Hom. *Iliad*. lib. ii. vi. et seq. Of this spirit examples are
numerous; but two will suffice to exemplify it. " Agamemnon
" came forward with speed, and thus upbraided his brother;" who
had consented to spare the life of Adrastus, a young Trojan, on
the promise of a valuable ransom:—" O soft in temper! What
" pity hath seized thy soul, Menelaus!—Well have the Trojans
" deserved of thee!—Their friendship in thy halls has been
" known!—Let none from destruction escape; none elude the
" death in our hands. Not the lisping infant in the mother's arms;
" not *he* shall escape with life. All her sons must with Ilion fall, and
" on her ruins unburied remain" (*Iliad*. lib. vi.). The aged Nestor
was near, and thus urged the Argives aloud:—" O friends, O heroes
" of Greece! fierce followers of Mars in arms, let none stop behind for
" the spoil; with rich plunder to return to the ships. Let us first the
" warriors slay; then strip, at leisure, the dead." Id. ibid.

have

PART I.   have collected a large store of provisions[48]. The hardships they had suffered, the trophies they had won; a desire of revisiting their native country, and of enjoying in their several homes the booty they had gained, all stimulated them to seek a speedy termination to their arduous enterprize; while ambition, honour, revenge, the sense of shame, the love of glory, and the lust of plunder, forbade them to look toward any alternative but death or victory[49]. Troy must be taken, or every Greek must perish beneath its walls[50].

The

48. That they had collected such a store appears from the plenty they enjoyed in their camp, after they returned to the siege (Hom. *Iliad*. passim.). There we find abundance of corn, bullocks slaughtered in profusion, and wine copiously drank (Id. ibid.). The wine of Agamemnon, and no doubt of other Grecian chiefs, was readily brought from Thrace (Hom. *Iliad*. lib. ix.); and purchased with the spoils of Asia Minor. The Greeks indulged freely in this good liquor, and also in the luxury of the table (Hom. *Iliad*. passim.); though their feasts, suitable to the service in which they were engaged, were more substantial than delicate (Id. ibid.). Nor did they inconsiderately give way, like many barbarians, to excess in liquor: they were systematically luxurious. We do not find they even went too far, in gratifying a social disposition. "Command the Argives," said the prudent Ulysses, " to take the repast: let them take food and wine; " for these are strength and valour in war! He that is filled with wine, " whose sinews are strengthened with food, will unceasing through " the day urge the fight. Undaunted is his soul in his breast, unfa- " tigued remain his stout limbs." Hom. *Iliad*. lib. xix.

49. Hom. *Iliad*. lib. ii. "Even he," says Ulysses, "who but for a " month is detained from his spouse, bears ill his untoward fate. " But to us the ninth year is rolling round, since on this shore we " lay in arms, yet here so long to remain, and disappointed to return, " would cover Greece with lasting disgrace." Id. ibid.

50. From the speech of Nestor, in the second book of the Iliad, it appears they had taken an oath to this purport. " When the Argive " ships assembled in Aulis, bearing destruction to Troy, and the holy " altars flamed to the gods," in consequence of a favourable omen, they mutually bound themselves to accomplish the object of their enterprise. " Just God!" said the grey haired king, in the debate on returning home, after Achilles withdrew his forces;—" how have " vanished all our vows? Whither fled are the oaths we made? The

" league

The Trojans foresaw their danger, and had pre-pared themselves to meet it. Like the Greeks, they were become expert soldiers, by the long and constant use of arms. Their numbers were less diminished, by reason of their being more under cover; and they had received strong auxiliary aids from many nations of Asia Minor, and even from Europe[51].

Hector, Priam's eldest son, the Trojan commander in chief, was a brave and warlike prince, adorned with every manly virtue, and distinguished by each heroic quality[52]. He was seconded by other leaders of tried courage, zealous in the common cause, and burning with resentment against the invaders[53]. But the Trojans and their confederates, whose ardour prompted them to frequent sallies, must soon have been cooped up within their walls, or have sunk under the steady valour, and collected force of the hardy

" league with solemn rites confirmed?—The plighted faith that binds
" mankind?—This I affirm, and all must know, That on the day
" when Greece ascended her ships, full on the right was heard the
" thunder of Jove; and his auspicious signs came abroad on the
" winds." Hom. *Iliad.* lib. ii.

51. Hom. *Iliad.* lib. ii. et seq. Among the European auxiliaries of Priam were numbered the Hellespontine Thracians, and the Pæonians, a Macedonian tribe (*Iliad.* lib. ii.). His Asiatic auxiliaries were from so many districts, that Agamemnon says (Id. ibid.) the " *aids* of *Troy* " *wielded* their *spears* from an *hundred states.*" And the poetical historian makes Iris, " the messenger of Ægis-bearing Jove," say " many " are the aids that wander through the wide city of Priam; *varying,* " each tribe, *in their tongue,* as they mix in the streets of Troy" (*Iliad.* lib. ii.). The most distinguished of these tribes, or nations, were the Paphlagonians, Halizonians, Mysians, Phrygians, Mæonians, Carians, and Lycians (Id. ibid.). I give them in the order in which they are mentioned by Homer, without regard to their eminence.

52. Hom *Iliad.* passim. The character of Hector, as a warrior, is finely marked by Diomedes, the gallant leader of the *Argives,* properly so called: " O friends! not unjustly we Hector admire; match-" less at launching the spear, to break the lines of battle bold. Ever " near him stands one of the gods, to turn aside the deadly point!" *Iliad.* lib. v.   53. Id. ibid.

Greeks,

Greeks, if discord had not found its way into the camp of Agamemnon[54].

Achilles, the most valiant of the Grecian chiefs, who led the Myrmidons and other warlike tribes from Thessaly[55], and who had been peculiarly successful in reducing the Trojan towns[56], dissatisfied with the division of the spoil, but more especially irritated at being deprived of a fair captive, named Briseis, withdrew himself from the army of the besiegers, and carried with him his victorious bands[57].

The

54. Hom. *Iliad.* lib. ii. et seq.

55. Hom. *Iliad.* lib. ii. " *Myrmidons, Hellenes, Achæans* the war-" riors were called." Id. ibid.

56. Hom. *Iliad.* lib. viii. ix. xx. " He drove me," said Æneas, " from Ida of streams, when descended the chief on our herds ; when " he levelled the high-built Lyrnessus, and Pedasus smoked on the " ground" (*Iliad.* lib. xx.). And Achilles himself boldly declared, that with his fleet he destroyed twelve towns ; and, " by land, level-" led eleven with the dust" (*Iliad.* lib. ix.). " Much *spoil* I gathered " in all," added he ;—" but all I brought to the son of Atreus. He " remained at his ships, remote from danger, received the spoil" (Id. ibid.). Here it is worthy of remark, That while the Greeks were dispersed, in collecting provisions and spoil, the Trojans and their allies, it appears, were so fully occupied in defending their property, in their various districts, that no attack was made upon the Grecian camp, though then unfortified.

57. Hom. *Iliad.* lib. i. The speeches of Achilles to Agamemnon, on this occasion, are highly characteristic of the manners of the age, as well as of the haughty spirit of that chieftain, " the bulwark of Greece," and the terror of Troy. " Rolling wrathful eyes on the king, Achilles thus replied : " Ha! lost to shame ; who henceforth will obey thy " commands ?—Who move afar at thy nod ?—Who here face thy foes " in fight ?—I came not to war with Troy ; to slay her gallant sons. " They never injured Achilles ; never drove away his herds, or seized " his warlike steeds. They trod not the harvests of fertile Pthia. Thee, " O lost to decency and shame ! thee we have followed to gladden thy " soul ; to punish the Trojans for thy brother, and for thee, ingrate !— " But on thee our favours are lost ; no value thou hast placed on our toil. " In being ungrateful, thou art unjust. Thou threatenest to take away " my prize ; the prize for which I laboured in bloody fields, the prize " that applauding Greece bestowed. Nor shared I ever equal with thee,

" when

The defection of so great a captain, and the absence of the gallant troops accustomed to conquer under his command, beside infusing discontent into the minds of the Greeks, wonderfully encouraged the Trojans[58]. The patriotic Hector, no longer overawed by superior prowess, led out his countrymen with various success against the besiegers[59]. Æneas his kinsman, leader of the Dardanians; Sarpedon, commander in chief of the Lycians; Glaucias, who commanded under Sarpedon, and other Asiatic chieftains, also greatly distinguished themselves[60].

To these were opposed the most illustrious Grecian warriors: Idomeneus, king of Crete; Meriones, who commanded under him; Ulysses, king of Ithaca, Cephalonia, Zacynthus, and other islands in the Ionian sea; Menelaus, king of Lacedæmon; Agapenor, king of Arcadia; Diomedes, leader of the Argives; Telamonian Ajax, from Salamis; Tlepolemus, from Rhodes[61]; and Agamemnon, commander in chief of the armament; who not only directed the operations of war, but animated the Greeks by his example[62]. Now more equally matched, the contending nations strug-

---

" when the populous towns of the Trojans lay smoking beneath our
" swords. The greater portion of fight is mine: the shock of battle
" falls on my hands; but when the division of plunder *comes*, the
" largest portion is thine" (*Iliad.* lib. i.). " Another thing I will tell
" thee, and thou record it in thy soul; for a woman these hands shall
" never fight, with thee nor with thy foes. Come, seize Briseis! ye
" Argives take the prize ye gave; but beware of other spoil which
" lies stowed in my ships on the shore. I will not be plundered
" farther!—If otherwise thy thoughts, Atrides! come in arms; a
" trial make; and these very slaves of thine shall behold thy blood
" pouring around my spear". Id. ibid.

58. They soon discovered that, " nor of stone were the bodies of
" the Argives formed, nor of steel unknowing to yield; to turn the
" sharp point of the spear, to strike the shivered sword from the
" hand?—Nor Achilles lifts the lance: in his ships the hero lies,
" brooding over the wounds of his pride" Hom. *Iliad.* lib iv.

59. Hom. *Iliad.*. lib. iv—vii.   60. Id. ibid.

61. Hom. *Iliad.* lib. ii.   62. *Iliad.* passim.

gled

gled hard for mastery; now was seen the shock of armies, the single combats of heroes, and the bloody rencounters of chieftains at the head of their followers[63].

A new perfidy had inflamed this hostile fury. Menelaus having vanquished Paris in single combat[64], the Trojans, contrary to solemn treaty, persisted in refusing to deliver up Helen, or fulfil other stipulations[65]. The Greeks accused them of *breach* of faith[66];

---

63. Hom. *Iliad*. lib. iv.—vii.   64. *Iliad*. lib. iii.

65. Hom. *Iliad*. lib. iii. iv. et seq. What these stipulations were, we are informed in the words of the *treaty*, and also in the *demand* of Agamemnon, after Paris had escaped from the field; in which the words of the treaty are literally repeated, as far as they regard the *stipulations*. I shall, for the sake of conciseness, give only the demand. " Hear me, O warriors of Ilion! Dardanians, and allies of Troy," said Agamemnon :—" with victory crowned, Menelaus possesses the field; " restore, therefore, Argive Helen, and all the treasure she brought. " Pay also a just fine to the Greeks, memorial for future years" (Hom. *Iliad*. lib. iii. sub. fin.). It must however be owned, that the slaying of one or other of the combatants, seems always to be implied as a condition of the treaty. Yet a compact so solemnly ratified could hardly, in those rude times, have been framed to turn upon a particular expression: victory must have been meant. As a proof of this, we do not find that the Trojans, in answer to the demand of Agamemnon, ever made use of such evasion, as an apology for not fulfilling the treaty. The religious rites, with which the ratification of this treaty was accompanied, afford a curious view of the sacred ceremonies anciently used on such occasions (*Iliad*. lib. iii.). There we see prayer united with sacrifice : two lambs slain by Agamemnon; " wine poured in libations to Heaven, and holy vows made to the " gods who forever live" (Id. ibid.). The prayer in which the two armies joined is too remarkable to be omitted. " O Jove most au- " gust! thou greatest in power, and ye the other deathless gods! let " those who first the treaty break, let their blood flow, like this " wine upon the ground ; their blood, and that of all their race; and " may their wives mix in love with their foes." Hom. *Iliad*. lib. iii.

66. *Iliad*. lib. iv. " Nor unpunished their oaths shall pass," said Agamemnon ; " nor plighted faith which binds mankind. Though " Jove his wrath may defer, the hour of visitation will come. The " great son of Saturn, who sits aloft; the dweller in the highest " heavens shall over them shake his dreadful ægis, awakened to rage " by their recent crime. Their broken faith shall not pass unheed- " ed." Id. ibid.

and

and thus prosecuted the war with fresh vigour, and all the rancour of roused revenge[67].

Hector, stung with that reproach, and seeing no end to hostilities, challenged the most redoubted of the Grecian chiefs to meet him in arms[68]. Nine warriors stept forwards, each willing to encounter the guardian of Troy[69]. By the advice of Nestor, the aged king of Pylos, recourse was had to lots for the choice of a champion. Each of the nine warriors marked his lot, and threw it into the helmet of Agamemnon. Nestor shook the whole in the helmet, and forth flew the lot of Telamonian Ajax[70]. The two heroes engaged in sight of the two armies. Each launched his spear twice at his antagonist; each threw at the other a large stone: both unsheathed their swords, and advanced to close fight; when the hearlds, "sacred messengers "of men and Jove! one from the Trojans, and one "from the Greeks, interposed[71]."

67. *Iliad.* lib. iv.—vii.

68. Hom. *Iliad.* lib. vii.

69. Id. ibid. "First arose the king of men, the far-commanding "Agamemnon; next the son of Tydeus, Diomedes in battle renowned. "The Ajaces then arose, both in matchless valour cloathed; the great "Idomeneus, and Meriones equal to Mars in arms. Eurypylus succeeds "to these the gallant son of the great Euæmon. Thoas started up "with speed, the warlike offspring of Andremon. Last arose divine "Ulysses. All these stept forward in arms, bent on godlike Hector "to lift the spear." Hom. *Iliad.* ubi sup. 70. *Iliad.* lib. vii.

71. Id. ibid. "But let each some gift exchange," said Hector, on the interposition of the heralds;—"some fair memorial to future "times; that the sons of Ilion may say, These fought for renown "alone! then in friendship departed from war" (Hom. *Iliad.* ubi sup.). "Thus, as he spoke, he gave his sword, distinguished with silver "studs. With its scabbard, he stretched it forth; with its belt "wrought curious with art. Ajax his girdle gave, bright with Phœ- "nician red." Hom. *Iliad.* lib. vii.

In

In consequence of this interposition, a truce for burying the dead, took place between the contending nations[72]. And Agamemnon made use of that temporary suspension of hostilities to fortify the Grecian camp—with a wall flanked with towers, and a ditch defended by stakes[73].

At the expiration of the truce, the hostile powers again assumed their arms; and the fight raged more fiercly than ever. " Shield is harshly laid to shield : ", spears grate on the brazen corslets of the combatants. " Bossy buckler with buckler meets: loud tumult rages " over all. Groans are mixed with the *boasts* of war- " riors[74] ; the slain and slayers join in the noise: the " field floats with blood[75]." From morning till noon, the event of the battle remained doubtful. Then victory began to incline to the Trojans ; and before sun-

72. Hom. *Iliad.* lib. vii. This truce was proposed by the Trojans; who, at the same time, offered to restore the Spartan treasure. And to that Paris agreed to " add rich treasures of his own ;" but *Helen* he still refused to restore. The Greeks, therefore, disdainfully rejected the offer. Id. ibid.　　　　　　73. Id. ibid.

74. The boasts and insults of the Greek and Trojan warriors, but especially of the former (*Iliad.* passim.), savour strongly of barbarism. Not Telamonian Ajax, the most manly and honest-hearted of the Grecian heroes, was free from *boasting;* nor the noble-minded Hector, the pride of Troy. " Ajax came forward near the foe, bearing his " shield, like a tower on high; his brazen shield, covered with the *hides* " of seven bulls : bearing his shield before his breast, the son of Tela- " mon advanced. Standing near the godlike Hector, he threatening " began aloud : Hector; now singly engaged, thou shalt know, what " leaders the Greeks have in war, beside Achilles the breaker of lines, " the lion-hearted Achilles!—To him great Hector replied, Ajax " descended of Jove ! son of Telamon, leader of armies, attempt not " me like a boy to affright. I know to the right to raise my shield; " to wield it to the left, I know. In standing fight to dare I am " taught; to set my steps to the clamours of Mars. On the car I have " learned to launch the spear; ,from my steeds to hurl forward the " war. But thee by stratagem I will not strike; for brave thou art " and great in arms. No course shall be followed by Hector, but " open force on such a foe." *Iliad.* lib. vii.

75. Hom. *Iliad.* lib. viii.

set

set the Greeks were driven with great slaughter into their camp in spite of their most vigorous efforts to maintain their ground[76]. Nor did their entrenchments seem sufficient to protect them. Hence " un-" willing Troy saw the falling light; but grateful was " shady night to the vanquished Argives[77]."

Hector, exulting in his decisive victory, called a council of war on the field; and explained to the Trojans and their allies his purpose of remaining under arms all night, in order to prevent the Greeks from putting to sea, and escaping before morning. " For " night," said he, " has chiefly saved the Argives, and " their navy on the shore of the main[78]." His resolution was applauded, and all the measures he proposed adopted[79]. Heralds were sent to Troy, to order the youths under the military age, the old men, and even the women to keep watch in " the lofty towers," and to kindle fires, " lest a hostile band should surprise " the city, during the absence of the troops[80].

Fires were also ordered to be kindled on the spot where the Trojans passed the night, " between the " river Scamander and the Grecian fleet[81];" and strict watch there was kept[82]. " Much elated, the " warriors, in arms, sat by their martial tribes. Sheep " and beeves are brought from Troy; bread is " brought, and generous wine. The wood is gather-" ed round in heaps : the winds bear the smoke to the " skies. A thousand were the fires in the field;" and " round each fifty warriors sat[83]. Their faces bright-
" ened

76. Id. ibid.   77. *Iliad.* ubi sup.   78. Hom. *Iliad.* lib. viii.
79. Id. ibid.   80. *Iliad.* ubi sup.
81. Hom. *Iliad.* lib. viii.   82. Id. ibid.
83. *Iliad.* lib. viii. sub. fin. The *number* of the Trojan forces, consequently, was *fifty thousand.* That the allies of Priam were *not* included
in

" ened to the beam. Their steeds stood near at their
" cars; with oats, and yellow barley fed[84]."

Meanwhile Agamemnon had assembled in coun-
cil the chiefs of the terror-struck Greeks[35]; and as no
hope remained of their being able to " take in arms
" the wide-streeted city of Troy," he proposed that
they should " obey the pressure of the times," and
" fly, in their ships, to the loved shore of their native
" land[86]." The motion was opposed by Diomedes,
the gallant son of Tydeus, and by the voice of the
whole council[87]. Nestor, king of Pylos, became mediator between the commander in chief, " the king of
" Men," and the Grecian leaders. By his advice, a
nightly guard was appointed to defend the fortifications of the camp, and Agamemnon gave a feast to the
chiefs in his tent[88]. There it was resolved, through
the counsel of the same venerable prince, to send an
humble deputation to the quarters of Achilles, bearing the offer of many rich presents, and the restitution

in this number, appears from the information given to Ulysses by
Dolon, the Trojan spy, whom he had made prisoner. From that information we learn, That " the allies collected afar, gave all the night
" to repose;" and that, on this occasion, " the native Trojans only kept
" awake" (Hom. *Iliad.* lib. x.). It also appears that the allies lay on
the other side of the Scamander. " By the main lie the Carians,"
said Dolon;—" the Pæonians, skilled at the bow. Near are the Leleges,
" the Caucones, the Pelasgi. Toward Thymbra lie the Lycian bands.
" The haughty Mysians stretch their lines by their side. There the
" Phrygians, breakers of steeds; there the Meonians, who fight in
" their cars. The Thracians are the farthest of all; newly come, apart
" from the rest. Rhesus, their king, lies in the midst, the gallant son
" of great Eoneus" (*Iliad.* lib. x.). The Thracians, afterward noted
for barbarism, seem at this time to have been a rich and polished people. " His steeds," said Dolon, in speaking of Rhesus, " are the most
" beautiful these eyes ever beheld; the best, and the largest in size.
" His car is adorned with gold; with silver plated, high laboured
" with art. He came to the field in arms of gold; huge, wondrous,
" and bright to behold; such as no mortal should wear: they suit
" only the deathless gods." *Iliad.* lib. x.   84. Id. ibid.
85. Hom *Iliad.* lib. ix. init.   86. Id. ibid.
87. *Iliad.* ubi sup.   88. Hom. *Iliad.* lib. ix.

of

of his loved Briseis[89]; in order to induce him to rejoin the army, in that season of danger and dejection, " when broken, troubled and dark, were the minds of the Grecian powers[90]."

This deputation was formed of three of the most respectable Grecian leaders; Phoenix, chief of the Dolopians, Telamonian Ajax, and sage Ulysses[91]. The son of Laertes strongly represented the perilous situation of the Greeks, and enumerated the proffered presents[92]. Phoenix endeavoured to soften the offended hero by shewing the duty of forgiveness, and urging

ing

89. Id. ibid. " The rich presents to all I will name," said Agamemnon : " seven tripods untouched by the flame; ten talents of purest gold ; twenty chaldrons of burnished brass. To these twelve " steeds I will add, already victors in the race. Seven blameless " damsels I also will give; all Lesbians skilled in female arts. These " in peopled Lesbos I chose, when it fell by the hero's sword. In " beauty, in form divine, the damsels the race of women excel. These " I will give to the chief; and, leading these, the white bosomed " Briseis, whom by force I have torn from his arms. An awful oath " I will add. That I never ascended her bed, nor mixed in love with " her glowing charms. All these he shall now receive. Hereafter " should the gods lay in dust the lofty city of noble Priam, with " gold, with brass, he his navy may load, when we shall divide the " spoil; twenty Trojan dames let him also chuse, next to Argive " Helen, in beauty and form" (Hom. *Iliad*. lib. ix.). Agamemnon farther offered to give to Achilles the choice of his daughters, on the return of the Greeks to their native land; and "without price," with " such presents as father never gave to a child. Seven cities shall " call him their lord," said the king, " near the limits of sandy " Pylos. Rich are the dwellers in flocks, abounding in lowing " herds." And the territory of Pedasus, one of those cities, was also " renowned for its vines." Id. ibid.

90. Id. ibid. 91. Hom. *Iliad*. lib. ix. They found Achilles " unbending his mind at the harp; his beautiful, his polished harp : " its neck of silver on high ; a part of the spoils of Eetion, when fell " his lofty town by the foe. With this his mighty soul he soothed, " and sung the actions of chiefs to the sound." Id. ibid.

92. Hom. *Iliad*. lib. ix. " To him the godlike Achilles replied, " Noble son of Laertes! Ulysses for prudence renowned, it behoves " me to open my soul, to unveil my heart, to declare my resolves; " to put, at once, an end to requests; to remove suits like these from mine

PART I. ing the example of the gods[93]. Ajax to argument
added reproach. " Unfeeling chief!" exclaimed he,
" a brother receives the price of a brother's blood. Fá-
" thers for their slain sons are appeased. The murderer
" pays the high fine of his crime: and in his city unmo-
" lested lives[94]. The heart of the parent relents; the
" roused rage of his soul subsides. To thee alone, son

" mine ears. A foe to my soul is the man, detested as the regions of
" death, who hides one design in his mind, and produces another in
" words. Nor Agamemnon will bend my heart, nor all the other
" Greeks in tears. Defrauded as I am by your king, let him cease,
" let him despair me to persuade. But let him, Ulysses! with thee,
" with other chiefs consult, how best he can turn the hostile fire from
" the ships of Greece. Much already has he done, much performed
" without my aid!—A mighty wall the king has built; a broad deep
" ditch is sunk around: with stakes its bottom is lined. But all
" these fail to repel the foe; to sustain the force of bloody Hector.
" Whilst I led in battle the Greeks, not remote from his walls he
" roused the war! Id. ibid.

　93. Hom. *Iliad*. lib. ix. " Subdue, O chief! thy mighty soul,"
said Phoenix:—" it becomes thee not to harden thy heart. The gods
" themselves are bent with prayer. The deathless gods, the first in
" force, in honours first, and the greatest in power, by solemn sacri-
" fice are won, by softly breathing vows are gained. For libation,
" for the favour of victims, they avert their flaming wrath from
" mankind. The suppliant, indulgent they hear; the repenting they
" ever forgive. *Prayers are the daughters of Jove!*—O Achilles, re-
" vere the daughters of Jove; yield to the goddesses: they have ever
" bent the souls of the brave!—Had Atrides no gifts proposed, had
" he named no future reward; had he still his folly retained, nor I
" would have bid thee thy rage allay, nor aid would for Greece
" have desired, though broken and distressed in war. But he at
" present gives thee much; in future he promises more: he sends as
" suppliants to thy knees the chosen chiefs of the Greeks. Let them
" not have come hither in vain. Till now thy resentment was just,
" henceforward thy wrath is a crime" (Id. ibid.). " To him great
" Achilles replied, Phoenix, aged chief, beloved of Jove! disturb
" not my soul with these complaints; melt not my heart with tears,
" to gratify the son of Atreus. To favour him becomes not thee:
" it becomes thee to think like thy friend; to make a foe of the man
" I abhor." *Iliad*. ubi sup.

　94. From this, and other passages in the Iliad, we learn, that in
Greece, at the time of the Trojan war, murder was not punished
with death.

of

" of Peleus! the gods have given an inflexible mind;
" a heart relentless, unswayed, and unkind!—And
" whence is this stubborn wrath?—For one captive
" woman, the slave of thy sword, seven beauteous in
" form we propose: and to these add gifts unequalled.
" Clothe in mildness thy soul; thy dwelling, son of
" Peleus! revere.   Beneath thy roof we the Greeks
" represent.   Above others, we regard thy renown[95]."
The haughty chieftain remained inexorable[96].   He
rejected the presents with disdain[97], and enjoyed the
distress of the Greeks[98].

Agamemnon, mortified at the fruitless supplication
he had made, and anxious for the safety of the army
under his command, could not enjoy the blessing of
sleep.   " Wild rolled his soul in the breast of the shep-
" herd of his people[99].   Frequent burst the deep sighs
" of the king: his stout heart greatly heaves with its
" cares[100].   Starting from his bed, round his ample
" body his vest he drew.   The stately buskins he bound
" on his feet.   Over his broad shoulders the shaggy
" hide of a lion he threw: large and tawny fell the
" rough spoil to his heels.   He grasps the long spear
" in his hand[101]."

Menelaus was agitated with " equal cares.   Sleep
" weighed not his eyes to repose.   Much he dreaded

95. Hom. *Iliad*. lib. ix.

96. Id. ibid. " Son of Telamon, leader of armies !"—Achilles replied, " all from thy soul thou seemest to have said.   But my heart
" swells with wrath unappeased." *Iliad*. ubi sup.

97, " Hateful are the gifts of Atrides to me," said Achilles, in
answer to the speech of Ulysses ;—" not if as many presents he gave,
" as sands crowd the shores of Troy—not with all should he sooth
" my wrath, or bend to his purpose my soul." *Iliad*. lib. ix.

98. Hom. *Iliad*. lib. ix. xi.

99. This expression is applied by Homer to all good kings. *Iliad*.
passim.   100. Hom. *Iliad*. lib. x.   101. Id. ibid.

" new

" new woes to the Greeks, who had crossed the wide
" main in his cause; who had come in his quarrel to
" Troy, rolling war to her troubled shores[102]." He
also rose, and went to wake Agamemnon. Him he
found, " at his own dark ship," putting on his armour.
The two brothers waked the chiefs in whom they
could most confide: Telamonian Ajax, Idomeneus,
and Nestor. The aged king of Pylos awaked
Ulysses and Diomedes. Other chiefs started from
sleep; and, having found the guards vigilant, the
" whole body of chieftains passed the ditch, and
" held a council of war on a spot unsoiled by the
" slain," between the Grecian camp and the Trojan
army[103].

There it was proposed by Nestor, to send a chief
to reconnoitre the state of the enemy; and to learn, if
possible, their designs. The dangerous service was
undertaken by Diomedes; who, being allowed the
choice of an associate, prudently requested that Ulysses
might accompany him[104]. The two chiefs accordingly set forward on their perilous enterprise. And
fortunately, before they had occasion to exercise their
sagacity, they met with a Trojan spy, named Dolon,
whom they made prisoner[105]. By him they were informed that the Trojans only kept watch; and that
the allies of Priam had consigned themselves to repose[106]. Thus instructed, they slew Dolon, and advanced to the quarter where the Thracians lay.
There they found no warrior awake. Diomedes slew
Rhesus, the Thracian king, and twelve of his leaders[107]. His famous horses stood unharnessed at his

---

102. *Iliad.* lib. x.
104. Hom. *Iliad.* ubi sup.
106. *Iliad.* lib. x.

103. Id. ibid.
105. Id. ibid.
107. Id. ibid.

car.

ear. These the compatriot chiefs untied, and carried them unmolested to the Grecian camp[108].

Encouraged by the success of this nocturnal adventure, the Greeks resolved to persevere in the war, and boldly to face all its dangers. No longer afraid of the thundering *Hector*, " to them more pleasing battle " became, than to return in their hollow ships[109] to " the loved shore of their native land[110]." Hence the struggle between the contending nations grew fierce even to desperation, and was maintained with a degree of vehemence unparalleled in the history of mankind.

" Dreadful swells the voice of Atrides: his commands to arm ascend the winds. He clothes himself in burnished steel. Before him he reared his all-covering shield; strong, beautiful, of various work.   On his head the bright-clasped helmet he placed: four horse-hair crests adorn it, and dreadfully nod aloft. Two spears the king grasps in his hand: pointed were both with steel[111].

108. Hom. *Iliad*. lib. x. The return of these chiefs affords a lively picture of the manners and accommodations of the Greeks in their camp on the Trojan shore. " When they came to the tent of Tydides, " with thongs they bound the steeds in their place; to the manger " they are all tied, where stand the fleet steeds of the king, with " purest corn in order fed. They bathed their bodies and limbs in the " main. But when the wave had washed off the blood, and cleansed " the sweat and dust away, to their polished baths sprung the he- " roes; and refreshed their souls, as they lay. Over their limbs they " threw the oil; they all their sinewy joints anoint. To the joyful " repast they sit down. From the urn, to the brim filled with wine, " they pour the rich libation to Pallas." Id. ibid.

109. From this, and other expressions of Homer, the Grecian ships, at the Trojan war, appear to have had holds of considerable depth and capacity. In them the chiefs stowed their plunder: in them they had their beds, as well as in their tents; and to them they seem to have retired in seasons of danger. *Iliad*. lib. ix. x. et seq.

110. Hom. *Iliad*. lib. x.   111. Id. ibid.

" Each Grecian hero to his driver issues forth his commands, to hold the steeds in order along the trench. In arms, they rush on foot to the field. Ere yet the morn confirmed her light, wide spread the clamour of arms. First the foot are ranged in their line ; the cars arranged, sustain the rear[112].

" The Trojans, on the other side, form their lines on the rising ground. Great Hector the battle arrays : Polydamus, blameless in soul ; Æneas, who among the Trojans[113] was honoured as a deathless god ; the three sons of great Antenor; Polybus, the noble Agenor, and youthful Acmas[114]. Hector, in the front, lifts aloft his broad shield ; as a baleful comet, by night, glides red behind the broken clouds : now it bursts forth in full blaze, now it hides in darkness

112. *Iliad*. ubi sup.

113. Here we discover that Æneas, the leader of the Dardanians, was considered as a Trojan. The distinction between the Dardanians and Trojans is not easily marked. They were certainly the same people (Hom. *Iliad*. lib. xx.): The Trojans were Dardanians (Id. ibid.) ; and the Dardanians were the subjects, not the allies of Priam (Hom. *Iliad*. passim.). From the allies they are always distinctly classed (Id. ibid.). From the Trojans they are only distinguished by name: in the same manner as the Lacedæmonians were distinguished from the Spartans ; the latter being the inhabitants of the capital and its territory, from which they proudly took their name; the former, the great body of the people of the state, living in different districts. The name of *Dardanians*, however, appears to have been more particularly applied to the people inhabiting mount Ida; where Dardanus, the founder of the Trojan kingdom, had built the city of *Dardania* (Hom. *Iliad*. lib. xx.); and where Anchises, the father of Æneas, a branch of the Dardanian royal family, seems to have held dominion under Priam, the head of the elder branch of that family, and great-grandson of *Tros*, from whom the city of *Troy* took its name. It was also called *Ilion* (as I have had occasion to observe), from *Ilus*, the son of *Tros*, by whom it was built (Strabo, *Geog*. lib. xiii. p. 593. edit. Lutet. Paris, 1620). Ilus removed the seat of government from the mountain to the plain (Id. ibid.) ; near the mouths of Simois and Scamander, and opposite the island of *Tenedos*.

114. Hom. *Iliad*. lib. xi.

its

its awful head. Thus Hector appeared, now in the front, now sunk behind, as he formed the dark lines. All over flamed the chief in his steel, like the lightning of father Jove[115].

" As reapers, ranged at either end of a field, hasten to meet as they cut down the corn, or wheat, or the golden barley, successive fall behind them the ears—thus the Greeks, thus the Trojans advance; bounding on, each other they slew. Neither host thinks of shameful flight; equal fell the youths on each side. Like wolves they rush wildly along[116]. While morning beams on the hosts, while encreases the day, shafts fall equal on each side: the combatants tumble in death, on the field. But at the hour when the woodman prepares his light repast, in the mountain groves; when his hands are relaxed with toil, in felling the trunks of lofty trees, a languor pervades his soul: the pleasing thoughts of repast fill his breast. Then with their valour the Argives, rousing each other, broke the line of the foe[117].

" Agamemnon bounded forward the first: he slew the shepherd of his people, Bianor. His friend the hero also slew, Oileus, the ruler of steeds. Through his forehead, as he came, passed the lance. The brazen helmet withstood not the point: through the skull rushed the deadly spear. Subdued he fell in the dust. There the king of men left the chiefs, after he had torn their armour from their shoulders;—right onward he passed in his arms, and slew four youthful warriors; two sons of Priam,

---

115. Id. ibid. 116. *Iliad.* lib. xi.

117. Id. ibid. The Trojans, though inferior in prowess to the Greeks, seem to have understood the order of battle better. " They " fell at once into ranks, forming themselves with speed to the " charge." Hom. *Iliad.* lib. xii.

and

PART I. and two of the warlike *Antimacus*[118]. These also
he left in death on the field; where the thickest engaged, he rushed. Behind him followed the Argives
in arms. Foot slew the foot, as they fled; horse on
horse advanced in blood. The dust was roused in
clouds from the field, by the high sounding feet of the
steeds. The king pressed, and slew the flying: loud
swelled his urging voice to the Argives[119].

"As when devouring fire falls on the withered
groves, this way and that it roaring moves, borne
wide by the veering winds, the boughs fall in the
strength of the flame, the huge trunks are in ruin involved: thus beneath the son of Atreus fell the warriors of Troy, in their flight. Many were the high-
maned steeds that bore their empty cars through the
lines; their sounding cars they bore along; now deprived of their gallant drivers, who lay prone on the
earth[120].

"The son of Atreus hung forward on Troy. The
flying host reached the tomb of Ilus. Half the plain
they had passed, with eager speed, in their flight.
The king roaring followed the wild rout. Dust and
blood stained his irresistible hands; for, above measure, he raged at the spear. But, when he approached
the town, to the foot of its lofty wall; then Hector,
who had withdrawn from the shafts, from the dust,
from the deaths of the field; bounds forward in all
his arms. Two spears fill the hands of the chief:

118. It was through the influence of this chief, bought by Paris,
that the Trojans " suffered not the beautiful Helen to be restored to
" the great Menelaus" (Hom. *Iliad*. lib. xi.). He even "advised, in
" council, the Trojans to slay Menelaus; when he, with Ulysses,
" bore to Troy the demands of Greece." *Iliad*. lib. xi.

119. Hom. *Iliad*. lib. xi.   120. Id. ibid.

through

through the army he greatly moves, urging the Trojans
to fight. Dreadful havock he wakes around. From
flight they at once turn their face, and stand forward
against their pursuers. The Greeks strengthen their
lines restored: battle is renewed over the field[121]."

"Iphidamas, the son of Antenor, great in battle,
large in size; bred in the fertile Thrace, the mother
of flocks and herds, now advanced on Agamemnon.
When near to each other the warriors drew, bending
in the martial strife, the spear of Atrides from his antagonist strayed: wide it flew of its aim. Iphidamas
struck the king on the belt. Beneath the breast-plate,
the lance he urged; hurled with all the force of his
powerful arm. But it pierced not the varied belt,

121. Hom. *Iliad.* lib. xi. Here I shall take occasion to observe,
That both the Greeks and Trojans, but especially the Greeks, greatly
laboured under the influence of superstition; and that both had, by
this time, learned to take advantage of it. Before Hector attempted
to stop the flight of the Trojans, he saw the lightning beginning to
burst from the thunder-cloud on the summit of mount Ida; or, to use
the allegorical language of Homer, "then the father of men and gods
" sat on the tops of the streamy Ida. Just descended from heaven, he
" sat: the thunder kindles, as it grows in his hands" (Hom *Iliad.* lib.
xi.). This Hector perceived; hence Jupiter is said to have sent Iris
with a message to him (Id. ibid.). The Greeks also saw it (*Iliad.*
ubi sup.); and as they knew the Trojans had a temple to Jupiter,
their tutelary god, at Gargarus on mount Ida (*Iliad.* lib. viii.), they
thought as usual, that the son of Saturn was warring against them
(*Iliad.* lib. xi.). The thunder on mount Ida seems generally to have
broken forth about noon (*Iliad.* passim.): about that time also the
sun became too powerful for the Greeks to maintain the fight; hence
Apollo, as well as Jupiter, is said to have constantly favoured the
Trojans (Id. ibid.). Panic-struck by the voice of the cloud-compel-
ling Jove, or smote with the darts of *Phœbus,* the Greeks during their
summer campaign, in the ninth year of the war, were, therefore, generally driven to their ships before sunset; when roaring *Neptune,* or
the waves of the sea, often came to their aid, and repelled the Trojans (*Iliad.* passim.). The army of Priam, however, was less alarmed at the rage of the earth shaking god, than the host of Agamemnon at the wrath of the thunderer.

The

.The king of men seized the spear in his hand: with all his strength he drew forward the lance, and wrenched it from the grasp of the foe. He then struck the neck of Iphidamas with his sword: his limbs at once were unbraced; he slept the iron sleep of death[122].

" The son of Atreus despoiled the slain chief, and bore his beauteous arms through the line. Coon beheld the mournful deed; Coon, renowned among men, the eldest born of Antenor. Sudden sorrow overshadowed his eyes, for a brother slain by the foe. Unseen he stood by the side of the king: he struck in the middle of his arm. Below the elbow entered the lance: through and through passed the point of steel. The king of men shrunk with pain at the wound, but he ceased not from battle and blood. On Coon the hero rushed, holding forward his long spear in his hand; Coon was dragging his slain brother along, Iphidamas, of the same parents born. He held the dead by the foot, and called aloud for the aid of the brave. Him the king struck, as he drew the slain, below the bossy shield: his limbs are unbraced in death. On Iphidamas, lopped off by the sword, the head of his brother fell in blood[123].

" Thus the two sons of Antenor, beneath the arm of the great Atrides, fulfilled the decrees of fate, and descended to the regions of death. Through the ranks of the foe rushed the king, with spear, with sword, with weighty stones; so long as from the gaping wound gushed forth, in its warmth, the blood. But when the wound grew dry, racking pain pervaded his frame. He bounded into his polished car, and turned his steeds to the fleet of the Argives[124]."

122. Hom. *Iliad.* lib. xi.　　123. Id. ibid.　　124. *Iliad.* lib. xi.

Agamemnon,

Agamemnon, however, before he quitted the field, thus incited the Greeks to fight :—" O friends, chiefs, " and leaders of Argos ! turn the foe from the navy " of Greece. Oppose the tide of battle in its course; " for prescient Jove to me denies to contend through " the day with the foe."—" He spoke, the driver urged the steeds to the hollow ships of the Argive powers. Not unwilling they flew along. They poured the white foam on their breasts ; with dust their sweaty sides were stained, as they bore from the strife of heroes the pain-invaded king[125].

" Not unperceived by Hector the son of Atreus forsook the field. He swelled his loud voice on the winds, and urged *Lycia* and *Troy* to fight. " O Tro- " jans ! gallant Lycians ! Dardanians, fighting hand " to hand ; shew yourselves warriors, O friends ! recal " the wonted force of your souls. The bravest of the " foe has retired. Great Jove covers me with renown: " right forward urge your steeds on the Argives ; add " fresh glory to your fame[126]."—He spoke, and roused the soul of each chief. In the front of the battle he himself strode large, exulting in his mighty soul. He descended with fury to the fight ; like a blast that, bursting from Heaven, falls in wrath on the deep. Seven chiefs the hero slew ; unnumbered fell the crowd by his hand[127].

" Then had ruin come apace ; then had the Greeks been rolled back to their hollow ships, had not Ulysses waked to fight the great son of warlike Tydeus. " Son " of Tydeus !" the hero said, "why forget we our " wonted strength ?—Advance, O friend ! support " my side." To the chief the son of Tydeus replied, " I will remain, and thee support; but vain is our

125. Id. ibid.   126. Hom. *Iliad.* ubi sup.   127. Id. ibid.

" prowess

" prowess in war. The cloud compelling Jove is our " foe: he wishes to give Troy success; to cover us " with lasting woe." He spoke, and from his lofty car, threw in death Thymbræus on earth. Ulysses the warlike driver slew, Molion, the friend of the hapless chief. They left the dead in their blood, having stopt their progress in war, and broke the Trojan ranks as they moved[128].

" Hector perceived the chiefs: he rushed furious on both in his arms; resounding he came along. The Trojan columns tread the path of the king. Tydides shuddered as the hero he beheld, and thus spoke to Ulysses: " Destruction rolls on us apace. All furi- " ous great Hector is near; but let us his rage oppose, " and sustain the storm as it comes." He said, and threw his quivering lance. Nor strayed the long spear from the foe: on his head, on the helmet it fell. Stopt short is the steel by the steel: the point pierced not through to the skin: the long triple helmet forbade. Staggering the horo fell backward, and mixed with the warrior crowd. On his knees half inclined he fell. His hands robust sustained the chief, while sudden night arose on his eyes[129].

" The son of Tydeus advanced to his spear: through the warriors, as they fought in front, he advanced to where it fixed remained in the ground. The spirit of great Hector returned. His car again the hero mounts, and drives amain amidst the crowd. The son of Tydeus rushing on with his spear, sent before him his voice to the chief:—" From death thou " hast now escaped!—Sure near thee advanced was " Fate; but Apollo stretched over thee his hand. To " him thy vows are paid, when thou issuest to the

---

128. *Iliad.* lib. xi.   129. Id. ibid.

                                    " clangour

" clangour of spears. But thou shalt not escape from
" this lance, should we meet hereafter in fight. Others
" I now will pursue, such as Fortune shall bring to
" my arm[130]."

But the brave Diomedes, the son of Tydeus, was
wounded in the foot with an arrow by Paris, while
stripping " the slain son of Paeon," and obliged to quit
the field[131]. Ulysses also was wounded, and encircled
by the Trojans[132]. Ajax came to his assistance, and
Menelaus led him through the crowd, till the driver
approached with his car[133]. " Great Ajax issued forth
on the foe; slaying steeds, laying warriors in death.
Nor heard illustrious Hector; in the left wing of the
battle engaged, near the bank of the roaring Scamander. There chiefly fell the heads of the brave : there the
loudest tumult arose, round the great Nestor in arms ;
round Idomeneus, renowned at the spear. Through
their lines Hector winds his deadly course. Dreadful

130. Hom. *Iliad*. lib. xi.

131. Id. ibid. " His bow the warrior bent on the shepherd of his
" people, Tydides : behind a pillar he stood; the tomb of Dardanian
" Ilus, a hero renowned in former years. Paris (or *Alexander*) drew
" the horns of his bow ; nor in vain flew the shaft from his hand. He
" struck the right-foot of the chief: through and through the arrow
" passed, and sunk its point in the ground below. On the plain the
" hero sat down, and from his foot drew the barbed shaft. Bitter
" pains creep through all his joints. The polished car he ascends,
" and drives amain to the ships." *Iliad*. lib. xi.

132. Hom. *Iliad*. ubi sup. The situation of Ulysses, on the retreat
of Diomedes, was such as demanded the firmest courage. " No Argive
" remained by his side, for wide spread the panic over all. Deeply
" sighing, in his distress, the chief thus spoke to his mighty soul :—
" Ah me! what course shall I take ?—Great the shame, if from num-
" bers I fly; yet worse the peril, if alone I remain. The Argives
" have left the field: Jove has turned others to flight!—But why thus
" argues his soul with Ulysses ?—To stand firm is the part of the
" brave; whether they fall in their blood, or hurl death on the rush-
" ing foe." *Iliad*. lib. xi.   133. Id. ibid.

were the deeds of his hand; whether he wasted the ranks of the warriors on foot, or threw the beamy lance from his car[134].

" Nor yet had the Argives given way had not Paris removed from the fight the shepherd of his people, Machaon. His right arm he struck with his shaft. Fear seized the Argives, breathing strength, lest the warrior should fall by the foe. Straight Idomeneus advanced through the lines, and thus addressed Nestor divine:—" O Nestor! son of Neleus, great glory of " Achaia in arms, haste! ascend with speed thy car; let " Machaon ascend by thy side; turn thy swift steeds " to the navy of Argos, A physician equals in value " an host; whether to cut the shaft from the wound, or " pain to expel by his art[135]."—He spoke, nor Nestor

---

134. *Iliad*. lib. xi.

135. Id. ibid. Æsculapius, who acted both as a physician and surgeon, was deified by the pious gratitude of the Greeks (Strabo, *Geog*. lib. viii. et seq.). He appears to have been a Thessalian by birth, and of the district of Estiaeotis; whence his two sons, Podalirius and Machaon, carried their troops in thirty ships to the Trojan war (Hom. *Iliad*. lib. ii.). He grew so famous in his profession, and performed so many wonderful cures, in cases esteemed desperate, that he was reputed to have raised many from the dead (Diod Sicul. *Biblioth*. lib. iv.). Hence mythologists say, That Pluto complained to Jupiter of Æsculapius, for weakening his empire in the regions below, by diminishing the number of the dead. At this Jupiter was so much incensed, that he slew Æsculapius with a thunder-bolt (Id. ibid.). These circumstances are finely touched by Ovid, in the prophecy of Ochirroe, relative to the future growth of the infant Æsculapius.

" Hail, great physician of the world, all hail!
" Hail, mighty infant; who, in years to come,
" Shalt heal the nations, and defraud the tomb.
" Swift be thy growth, thy triumphs unconfined;
" Make kingdoms thicker, and increase mankind.
" Thy daring art shall animate the dead,
" And draw the thunder on thy guiltless head.
" Then shalt thou die; but from the dark abode
" Rise up victorious, and be twice a god."

disobeyed:

disobeyed: he mounted the polished car: Machaon placed himself by his side; the son of the great *Æscu-lapius*, renowned for the healing arts[136].

" Cebriones, as he sat in the car, by the side of illustrious Hector, beheld the Trojans on the right broken. To the chief he addressed his words :—" Hector!" the warrior began; "while here we wind "through the Argive lines, on the distant edge of re-" sounding war, the Trojans afar are dispersed; horse " mix with foot in the rout. Ajax dissipates their " ranks. Well I know his tremendous shield: let us thither drive the fleet steeds[137]." He spoke, and struck the high-maned steeds: beneath the lash they drew forward the rapid car. Between the Greeks and Trojans they rushed; treading bodies, treading shields. In blood the whole axle is drenched: the car itself is stained with blood, which flew wide from the feet of the flying steeds. Much the hero wished to advance; to break the solid ranks of men, to bound with death upon the foe. Dreadful tumult he raised on the Argives: nor ceased he to rage with his spear. He winds his course through other lines; with lance, with sword, with weighty stones; yet he shuns the battle of the son of Telamon[138].

" But *Jove*, as aloft on Ida he sat, threw terror on the soul of Ajax: astonished he darkly stood. Over his shoulders he placed his seven-fold shield. Shuddering

136. The *mild* character of Æsculapius bore so much resemblance to that of Jesus Christ, that the Gentiles accused the first christians of having stolen their healing god (Cyril. *Cont. Julian.* lib yi.). And the character of Apollo, the reputed father of Æsculapius (Diod. Sicul. *Biblioth.* lib. iv.), bore in some respects a still stronger resemblance to that of the Messiah, the great physician of souls; as he not only healed the body, but illuminated the mind. Hygin. in *Fab.* cap. L

137. Hom. *Iliad.* lib. xi.   138. Id. ibid.

the

the hero retreats : he often bends his wild looks on
the foe : he often turns his dreadful face, then slowly
lifts his limbs along.   Behind him the Trojans pour.
Opposed to them all was the chief ; and he stopt their
progress to the navy of Argos[139]." The Greeks came
to his assistance ; and the hostile nations, " mixed in
crowds, fought with the rage of devouring flames[140],"!
But many of the Grecian chiefs having been wounded
in the former part of the day[141], and obliged to quit
the field, victory finally declared for the Trojans.
And the Greeks were forced to seek shelter in their
camp[142].

" Nor now the foss sustains the charge, nor lofty
wall protects the Argives.   The bulwark of the navy
fails; the wide trench, which around was drawn to
save the swift ships from the foe; to save the mighty
spoil within[143]." The Greeks, however, made a gallant defence, though subdued by the scourge of Jove.
" Around the firm-built wall fierce battle and clamour
arose.   Mighty Hector, the fierce awaker of flight,
fights with a whirlwind's rage. To pass the foss, loud
swelled his lofty voice to his friends[144]."

139. *Iliad.* lib. xi.   140. Id. ibid. et lib. xii. init.

141. Beside those already mentioned, Eurypylus " the gallant son
" of the great Euæmon," who carried his troops from the neighbourhood of mount Pelion, in " twice twenty dark ships," to the Trojan
war, (Hom. *Iliad.* lib. ii.), was wounded in the thigh by Paris, with
an arrow, " as he spoiled the dead" (Hom. *Iliad.* lib. xi.). And here
I cannot help remarking, That this rage of spoiling the dead afforded opportunity for most of the wounds the Grecian chiefs received ;
and that it was neither restrained by the most pressing danger, nor
regulated by the maxims of military prudence. Like hungry savages,
the most illustrious Greeks rushed upon their prey, regardless of consequences; and in the exposed situation, into which their rapacity
threw them, they were often slain. *Iliad.* passim.

142. Hom. *Iliad.* lib. xii.   143. Id. ibid.

144. *Iliad.* lib. xii.

The

The Trojans crowded around their illustrious commander: the bravest of their allies also came forward; and the Grecian camp was regularly stormed. By the advice of the wise Polydamas, who " of all the host " alone foresaw the future by weighing the past," the chiefs descended from their cars. Hector shewed the example. " On the bank of the foss profound, they fell at once into ranks; forming themselves, with speed, to the charge. Into five bodies the warriors divide: before each strode its leader in arms[145]."

The bravest, fiercest Trojan youth; those who longed most to engage, to ascend the walls in assault; to slay before their ships the foe, formed behind Hector. The second band was led by Paris; the third by the hero Asius, the son of Hyrtacus, who Sestos and Abydos possessed; the fourth was led by Æneas, the dauntless son of great Anchises. The renowned allies were led by Sarpedon, by Glaucus, by great Asteropæus. These, to the godlike Sarpedon, seemed of all others the bravest and best, next to the hero himself; for all the allied chiefs he in all excelled[146].

" These covered with their arms, raising aloft the solid orbs of their shields, rushed on the Greeks in their valour. Nor long they deemed the foe would stand; they already saw them slain at their ships. The other warriors of Ilion—the allies, who came from afar, obeyed in all the prudent Polydamas[147]. The Argives stood aloft in the well-built towers: huge stones flew in showers from their hands. For themselves, for their tents they fought; for the ships, which should bear them away[148]. As falls the snow on the ground, borne along by the boisterous winds; when

145. Id. ibid.   146. Hom. *Iliad* ubi sup.
147. Id. ibid.   148. Hom. *Iliad.* lib. xii.

the blast bursts the laden clouds, and pours the thick-
flying flakes on the world; so thick flew the darts from
each side; from the hands of the Argives, from the
Trojans renowned in arms[149]."

While thus the battle raged, Polydamas foreseeing that the forcing of the Grecian entrenchments
would be attended with difficulty and danger, went to
Hector, and told him that he had seen an unlucky
omen: "the high-flying eagle of Jove dividing the
host to the left." He, therefore, sagely observed,
"though the gates we should force, and break through
this wall in our strength; though the Greeks should give
way in the fight, not victorious shall we return, or
tread back the same path to our friends. Many Trojans we shall leave in their blood, many will fall by
the spears of the foe; when, in fury, they fight for their
ships[150]. Thus," added he, "the augurs will explain
the portent, thus the skilled in each omen divine. Let
them speak, and the host will obey[151]."

" Turning sternly on the chief, the various helm-
ed Hector replied, " Polydamas, not grateful are thy
" words to mine ear. Well thou knowest better coun-
" sel to give; some advice more happy to frame.
" Wouldest thou bid me to forget father Jove?—The
" high thunderer's promise confirmed?—Wouldst
" thou bid me the god forget, to follow birds that wan-
" der on the winds? These nor sway my thoughts nor
" my deeds: I care not to what quarter they fly; whe-
" ther they sail to the right, to the sun, to rising morn,
" or spread their broad wings to the left; to the west,
" all in darkness involved. Let us follow what great

149. Id. ibid. 150. *Iliad.* ubi sup.

151. *Iliad.* lib. xii. Here we find divination by augury prevailing
in early ages; and the operation of armies regulated by augurs among
the ancient Trojans, nearly in the same manner as among the Romans, their reputed descendants.

" Jove

" Jove decrees : he who reigns over mortal men, whom
" all the deathless gods obey. One augury is ever
" the best : it is for our country to fight[152]."

" Thus saying, the hero advanced : with loud clamour the Trojans followed amain. Darkly came forth
from above the thunder delighted Jove. On the summits of streamy Ida he waked a gust of squally wind :
it bore forward the dust on the ships. He broke the
yielding souls of the Argives : he gave glory to Hector
and Troy[153]. Confiding in the omens of Jove, and
much confiding in their strength ; the Trojans strove to
burst the walls of the Argives ; they strove to break
into the camp. The towers they struck with their
hands, the battlements they tore away : they sapped
with bars the projecting piles, which the Argives had
driven in the earth ; the stable stays of their lofty towers.
These they wrenched with force in their hands ; they
hoped to draw in ruins the wall. Nor yet did the
Argives give way : their battlements they lined with
their shields, and poured death on the foe from above[154].

" Nor had the Trojans broke open the gates, nor
great Hector broke asunder the bars, if prescient Jove
had not roused on the Argives his son beloved, the
mighty Sarpedon. Like a lion the hero rushed forth :
he held aloft the wide orb of his shield ; beauteous,
brazen plated over ; which the artist had finished with
care, and placed the thick hides between its plates. This
before him the hero held : two spears shine aloft in his
hands. Forward the hero strides in his strength ; to
the wall, to the bulwarks of Argos[155].
                                            " The.

152. Hom. *Iliad.* lib. xii   153. Id. ibid.
154. *Iliad.* lib. xii.
155. Id. ibid. The speech of Sarpedon to Glaucus his associate, on
this occasion, is highly characteristic of the manners of early times.
                                            " Glaucus,"

' " The battlement is seized by Sarpedon. He wrenched it with his hand robust: it followed his force; down it fell. Bare is the wall above; wide open is the way for the foe. Ajax, Teucer, both assail the chief with their pointed steel: this with the barbed arrow, that with the spear. On the splendid thong, by which hung his broad shield, fell with force the eager shaft. Ajax struck Sarpedon's shield in his might. Through and through passed the lance, and harshly drove him back in his course[156]. A small space from the wall he fell back; yet not wholly retreats the chief. Urged by his own great soul, by his ardent desire of renown, loud swelled the voice of the king, as to his Lycians he turned:—"O sons of Lycia!" " he said; why abates the wonted force of my friends? " —Hard is the task for me alone, though the wall be " broken down by my hand,—hard is the task for your " king to open wide a path to the ships. Advance! " follow me, all in arms: the work demands the hands " of all[157]."

" He spoke; they revered the voice of the king; around their illustrious leader they crowd, and bear forward on the foe with their might. The Argives, on the other side, strengthen their lines within the wall. Within its huge shade they from; for great was the safety they derived from their works. Nor could the

" Glaucus," the hero began, " why are we the most honoured by all? " why with the chief seat at the feast? with the flesh, with the flow- " ing bowl!—Why in Lycia look all on our steps, as on the tread of " heaven-descended gods?—Why possess we sacred portions of land " on the banks of the gulfy Xanthus?—Beautiful fields that bear " the vine, over which waves the golded grain!—It becomes us for " these, O Glacus! amid our Lycians conspicuous to stand: to be " the first to urge the fight; to equal our honours with deeds" (Hom. *Iliad.* lib. xii.). Glaucus, in obedience to the request of his friend, advanced to the wall of the Grecian camp; but was instantly wounded in the arm by Teucer, the brother of Telamonian Ajax, and obliged to retire. Id. ibid.

156. Hom. *Iliad.* lib. xii.   157. Id. ibid.

Lycians

Lycians burst the wall, and force their way to the
ships; nor could the Argives drive the foe from the
lofty wall. Death passes from side to side. The broad
shields are torn on each breast: through and through
the light bucklers are pierced. Many are the mutual
wounds. Wild rushes the steel from the combatants:
dark fate in every form appears; the flying, the standing are slain. The former through their backs are
pierced; the latter receive death through their shilds.
The towers are all distained with gore; the battlements
are drenched in blood; on each side horrid slaughter
is seen. The Argives fall, the Lycians are slain.
Nor could the foe force the Greeks to fly: in equal
scales the battle hung[58].

"Thus victory inclined to neither side, till Jove
with superior renown had clothed Hector, the great
son of Priam. Loud swelled the voice of the king, as
he urged the Trojans to fight:—" Assail with fury the
" foe; car-ruling Trojans, advance! burst the falling
" wall of the Argives; on the ships throw devouring
" flame[59]."—" All heard the loud voice of the king:
right forward they rushed on the wall; the battlements
they seized in their hands, stretching before them their
pointed spears. Hector raised from the ground a stone,
which lay before the spacious gate; heavy, vast, rugged. He bore it forward in all his strength to the well-
compacted portal. Double-leafed and high was the
gate: behind were passed two solid bars, which stretched from side to side; fitted both with a lock within.
Near this gate stood the dreadful chief. Firmly
spreading his limbs, he urged forward the stone with
all his force. In the centre it struck the wide door:
both the hinges it broke in twain. Within fell the
stone, with horrid crash. Shrilly creaks the bursting

158. *Iliad.* lib. xii.   159. Id. ibid.

gate: the bars, the boards give way at once; and wide
fly the splinters in air[160].

"Great Hector bounded forward with rage. Dark
as night seemed the rushing chief: frightful blazed,
over his body, his arms. Two spears he grasps firm
in his hands. None but the gods could then oppose
the wrathful king, as he bursts through the gate.
Awful blazed the living flame from his eyes: loud
swelled to his people his voice. He bade the Trojans
to rush, to follow his steps; and they, with eager speed,
obeyed. Some clamber over the lofty wall, others
crowd in arms through the gate. The Argives fly
amain to their ships. Horrid tumult resounds over
the shore[161]."

Having thus forcibly entered the Grecian camp,
the Trojans "hoped to take the navy of Argos," and
"to slay all the Greeks at their hollow ships[162]." But
"the world-surrounding Neptune, emerging from the
depth of his main, urged the Argives to battle and
blood. He filled with valour their rising souls, and
made their limbs light in the fight[163]. They formed
deep around the two Ajaces:" the great son of Telamon and the swift-footed son of Oïleus, renowned at the
spear; the elder and younger Ajax:—"firm rose their
warlike ranks to the foe. Nor Mars descending to the
fight, nor Minerva could the martial form of the lines
despise. For the bravest, the chosen of Greece, all
skilled in each movement of war, waited the coming
of Hector[164]. Spears crowd on spears, as they rise;
shield to shield is closed; buckler its buckler supports,
helmet its helmet, and man his man. Crowded the

160. Hom. *Iliad.* lib. xii.   161. Id. ibid.
162. Hom. *Iliad.* lib. xii. init.   163. Id. ibid.
164. *Iliad.* lib. xii.

horse-hair crests arise : the plumes mix, as they wave in the wind ; so thick stand the warriors in arms. The lances vibrate in their hands, touching as they stretch them to blood. Right-forward they move to the foe; their souls burn for the fight[165].

"The gathered Trojans pour, in force, on the Greeks. All-furious great Hector precedes; like the wasteful force of a falling rock, which the torrent rolls large from the mountain's brow, when the rugged steep is sapped by the ceaseless showers of high thundering Jove. He deemed that he could reach the tents, and wade in blood to the ships of the Argives. But when to the phalanx he came, he stopt; leaning forward with all his strength. Thick rattle the spears on his mail; the swords fall crashing on every side. The Greeks shove him away with force : with blows staggering the chief retreats. Loud swells his voice to his troops, urging them to fight :—" O Trojans, and Lycians renowned; " O Dardanians, fighting hand to hand, stand firm to " your arms !—Not long, O friends ! shall the Greeks " sustain this spear, though firm the phalanx they " present[166]. Even now, I judge, they will yield to " my arm ; if I am, in truth, urged to the fight by " the most powerful of all the gods, the high-thunder- " ing husband of Juno [167]."

This speech kindled valour in the souls of the Trojans and their renowned allies, who charged in the centre. But there they were vigorously opposed by the

---

165. Id. ibid.   166. Hom. *Iliad.* ubi sup.   Of all the engagements described by Homer, this at the ships is the most regular. Here we see both the Greeks and Trojans display a considerable share of military skill in forming their troops; and, subduing their rage for spoil and blood, steadily preserve the order of battle.

167. *Iliad.* lib. xiii.

Greeks

PART I. Greeks under the Ajaces; and under Teucer, " skilled at once to bend the bow, and to launch the spear
in standing fight." These employed the force of
Hector. In vain did he attempt " to overpower their
strength, or to cut through their invincible bands his
wasteful path to the navy of Argos[168]." Meanwhile
Idomeneus and Meriones bent their course with the
Cretans to the left wing; where the Greeks were
sorely pressed by the Trojans under Deiphobus, one of
the younger sons of Priam. On the approach of the
king of Crete, Deiphobus called to his assistance Æneas,
his kinsman. Other chiefs, on both sides, joined battle: the fight raged with fury, in all quarters; and
the Trojans, wisely dispersed over the field, were in
danger of being broken and routed, when Hector, by
the advice of Polydamas, agreed to call a council of
war[169]. Before the council was assembled, however,
he moved along the front of the line; and finding
Paris hotly engaged in the left wing, the two brothers
" took their rapid way where most flamed the fight"
in the centre; where " successive the Trojans, troop
after troop, gleaming in steel advanced. Before each
squadron strode its chief. Hector first came on. From
side to side the hero ranged. He sought for a breach
in the deep formed phalanx, as tall he stalked behind
his shield. But he disturbed not the souls of the Argives; and great Ajax defied him to arms[170]."

By this time Polydamas had collected the Trojans
and their allies into one great body; and it seems to
have been resolved by their chiefs, in council, to make
a last effort to break the Grecian phalanx, and destroy
the ships[171]. About the same time it was resolved by
the wounded Grecian chiefs, to whom Nestor had

168. Id. ibid.　　　169. *Iliad.* lib. xiii.
170. Id. ibid.　　　171. Hom. *Iliad.* ubi sup.

communicated

communicated the danger of the navy, "to move to the field." "Let our words," said Diomedes, "give "the aid our arms deny. They who stand apart let "us urge, and push onward the sluggish in war[172]."

Now the thunder having ceased to roar, and the lightning to flash on the summits of mount Ida, a delightful calm succeeded the storm. The air became mild, and the sky serene; but the rolling of the waves increased. Hence Jupiter is allegorically said to have sunk to sleep in the arms of Juno[173], while Neptune aroused the Greeks to bolder exertions[174].

172. Hom. Iliad. lib. xiv.

173. The mythology of Homer contains such a mixture of physical and moral allegory, mixed with traditional fable, that it is impossible, in every particular, to reconcile it to reason; though the general meaning is commonly obvious. The present instance will serve as an example. Juno having borrowed the cestus of Venus, and conscious of the power of her charms, artfully pretended, that she was going to visit the utmost bounds of the habitable earth. To her the high ruler of storms: "O Juno! some other time urge thither thy rapid "way; but let us now dissolve in love: give all our souls to its joys. "Never did such fierce desire, for goddess or for mortal dame, pour "its lambent flame through my heart, as that which now subdues my "soul; not when I mixed with the charms of Ixion's glowing spouse, "who bore the valiant Perithous, equal in council to the gods; not "when Danæ I pressed, the fair-limbed daughter of great Acrisius; "the mother of godlike Perseus, the most renowned of mortal men; "not thus I burned for the beautiful daughter of Phœnix, who "brought forth the prudent Minos and Rhadamanthus, equal to gods. "Nor felt I thus in my soul for the Theban Alcmena, the mother of "magnanimous Hercules; nor for Semele, who bore Bacchus divine, "the joy of mortal men. Nor burned I thus for stately Ceres, grace- "ful queen! with golden locks; nor for the splendid charms of La- "tona, nor even for thy majestic self; as now I feel love in my soul, "and soft desire pervading my frame" (Hom. Iliad. lib. xiv.). Juno yielded to his wishes. "The eager son of Saturn threw his arm "round his glowing consort. They lay on their fragrant bed. "Around them poured their cloud of gold; their beauteous cloud, "from which distilled the lucid drops of the dew of heaven. Thus "Jove sunk in repose on the summit of his own dark hill. With "love, with sleep he lay subdued, and held his heaving spouse in his "arms." Id. ibid.

174. Iliad. lib. xiv.

"They

"..They all obeyed the voice of the god. The wounded kings restored the martial ranks; the son of Tydeus, the great Ulysses, and Atrides, the sovereign of men. Moving through the forming lines, they changed, with their commands, the arms; the strong are bestowed on the strong, and the light assigned to the feeble in fight[175]. Now cloathed in all their burnished steel, gleaming moves the army along. The earth-shaking Neptune precedes the line[176].

" Opposed to the god was mighty Hector: he also formed his own firm lines. Then dark swelled the war on each side. Both poured it forward; the blue-haired king of the ocean, and Hector illustrious in arms. This aided the Trojans in fight, that urged the Argives to blood. Behind the tents and hollow ships highswelled the hoarse waves of the main. The hosts plunge in dreadful conflict; horrid clamour ascends the sky. Not so loud resounds the wind in the leafy tops of the lofty oaks, when the storm over the echoing hills wings its course, as the shouts of the Trojans and Argives; when roaring they rushed to battle, and poured their whole strength in the shock[177].

" Illustrious Hector the combat renewed: he first threw his spear on Telamonian Ajax. Right-forward stood the face of the chief; nor from his body strayed the lance. It fell where the two thick belts each other crossed on his manly breast: one sustained his broad shield, the other his deadly sword. These now saved his body from wounds. When Hector saw that the rapid spear flew in vain from his hand, back he turned to the troop of his friends; avoiding death from the hands of the foe[178].

175. Id. ibid.
177. Id. ibid.

176. Hom. *Iliad.* lib. xiv.
178. Hom. *Iliad.* ubi sup.

" Great

" Great Ajax perceived the warrior, as he retired, and raised a huge stone from the earth; for many lay where the foes engaged, to prop the hollow ships on the sounding shore. One of these the chief heaved from the ground. It struck Hector above the orb of his shield: on his neck fell the forceful weight: he fell, he lay along the ground. From his hand, he dropt the brazen lance; from his arm, the wide orb of his shield; the helmet from his head[179].

" With dreadful clamour advance the Greeks: they hope to drag the chief to their line. Thick fly the shafts from their hands; but none, at a distance or hand to hand, could touch the shepherd of his people with steel. His valiant friends stood formed around; Polydamas, the godlike Æneas, Agenor the divine, Sarpedon the great leader of the Lycians, and Glaucus blameless in soul. Nor any warrior neglected the chief: all held before him the wide orbs of their shields. His friends bore him in their arms from the fight, till they came to his bounding steeds. Behind the war they stood remote, with their driver and various car. They slowly took their way to Troy. Deep groaned the king as they moved[180]."

" When the Argives saw Hector subdued, with rising spirit they rushed on the Trojans. They remembered the dismal fight[181]." After a hot contest, in which many warriors were slain on both sides, "pale terror wandered over the lines of the Trojans. Each looked around in his fear, and searched where flight could bear him away from death[182]." The routed Trojans repassed " the lofty wall and the trench profound. Many fell beneath the hands of the Argive

---

179. Id. ibid.
181. Id. ibid.
180. *Iliad.* lib. xiv.
182. Hom. *Iliad.* lib. xiv.

powers ;

powers; by the hand of Ajax, the swift son of the great O'ileus. None could equal the chief in speed, when he hung on the flying foe[183]."

But the sea retired, and Hector recovered his strength before morning. The sun rose with portentous aspect; which threw terror into the souls of the Greeks, and inspired the Trojans with fresh courage[184]. Hector, having roused his warriors, led them again to the fight; "gleaming bright, as he winds through the lines; when each Argive had hoped, that slain he lay beneath the strength of Telamonian Ajax. Their hearts sunk in sudden dismay[185]."

While the Greeks, who so lately hung forward on the flight of the Trojans, stood thus panic-struck, Thoas, the valiant leader of the Ætolians, offered prudent counsel to his brother chiefs. "O Argives!" said he, "attend to my words; listen to the thoughts of " my soul: dismiss the crowd to the hollow ships; " command the main body to quit the field; and let " us, who surpass others in valour and fame, stand " forth, in a band, raising high our pointed spears, and " try to repress the rage of the foe. Though burning " for fight, Hector will dread to enter the phalanx of " Argos[186]."

His advice was approved. The Grecian chiefs " formed their deep ranks in the front. Round the strength of godlike Ajax, round Idomeneus, king of Crete; round Teucer and great Meriones; round Meges, equal to Mars in arms, they formed the bravest warriors. From wing to wing the chiefs were convened. Opposed to daring Hector they stood; to all

---

183. Id. ibid.
185. Id. ibid.

184. Hom. *Iliad*. lib. xv.
186. *Iliad*. lib. xv.

his

his Trojans tried in arms, while backward the crowd
retired to the ships of the Argive powers[187].

" The thick-formed Trojans advance. They first
pour their strength on the foe. Before moved Hector,
with mighty strides; but before him rushed Phœbus
Apollo, with his shoulders wrapt in a cloud. He held
aloft the ægis of Jove, wildly tossing its orb in the sky;
the dreadful ægis, rough and shaggy on every side[188]:"
—or, in plain language, a thick and frightful halo or
haze surrounded the sun, and obscured his rays. "Yet
the Argives, deep-formed in their arms, sustained the
shock: as long as Phœbus Apollo held the ægis un-
moved, so long fell the mutual spears; and equal fell
the foes on each side. But when, right in the face of
the Argives, he shook the broad ægis on high, and
waked above them his tremendous voice;" some un-
usual noise in the air;—"their souls were unmanned:
they forgot their wonted valour in fight[189]."

In consequence of this portentous appearance, and
alarming sound, "over the wall fled the Argive powers;
over the stakes, and the trench profound, they urged
their scattered flight. Hector roused the Trojans to
battle; loud swelled his voice in their ears: he bade
them rush on the ships, and leave the bloody spoils on
the field. "Him whom I shall find apart," said he,
" whom these eyes shall loitering behold, I shall in-
" stantly send to the shades. Nor brother, nor sister in
" tears, shall procure him at death the funeral pile[190].
" Dogs shall tear his wretched corse; before our city,

187. Id. ibid.   188. Hom. *Iliad.* ubi sup.   189. Id. ibid.
190. *Iliad.* lib. xv. From this and other passages in Homer (*Iliad.*
lib. vii.), we find that the Trojans, as well as the Greeks, had in this
early period adopted the custom of burning their dead; a custom
which also prevailed among the Romans, the reputed descendants
of the Trojans.

" he shall bleach in the winds[191]."—" He spoke; over the shoulders of his steeds the high-raised lash re-sounded amain. He urged the Trojans, through all their lines. With threatening clamour they advanced with the chief; with dreadful tumult they drove their cars. Before them moved Phœbus Apollo[192]."

But the Greeks, though " driven over their works, stood firm near the ships. They urged each other to fight. Their hands they raised to all the gods: each poured, with loud voice, his prayer; but chief arose the voice of Nestor, the guardian of Achaia in arms. The aged prayed to the first of the gods, stretching forth his hands to the heavens[193]. Loud thundered prescient Jove; to his ears on high came the prayer of the son of Neleus. The Trojans heard the awful sound: they deemed it the heavenly sign of Jove's sacred will to their arms. With growing fury they rushed on the foe: battle raged over all their line. Their steeds they drove amain to the ships: at their stern burned the dreadful fight[194].

" Hand to hand both parties urged their spears. The Argives their dark vessels ascend: with long poles they gall the foe; poles, which lay stowed in their ships, formed to wage the naval war[195]; sheathed at the point with steel. With firmness they sustained the rushing

---

191. Id. ibid.   192, *Iliad.* lib. xv.

193. Id. ibid. " O, Father Jove!" the aged said, " if in Argos, " abounding in corn, any warrior departing for Troy, burning the " thighs of a sacred bull, or offering the first fruits of his field, prayed " to thee for his safe return; if thou hearest, if thou promised to grant " his request, remember these in their sore distress. Turn, awful lord " Olympus! turn away the evil day; suffer not the Argives to fall: " repress thou the hands of the sons of Troy." *Iliad.* lib. xv.

194. Hom. *Iliad* lib. xv.

195. Id. ibid. Here we find that naval engagements were in use before the Trojan war, and that the Grecian vessels were not merely transports, but also ships of war.

force

force of Troy." But after a furious conflict, in which many warriors fell, thundering Jove again interposed: " he roused the Trojans to battle and blood. They advanced on the ships, like lions that tear their prey; and the Greeks yielded to heaven-sent flight[196].

" Within the first line of the ships, the routed Argives convey their flight. The farthest ships, on the shore of the main, walled them in from behind to their tents. With loud tumult pursued the foe. At their tents behind the first line, the Greeks stood gathered. Shame and terror confine them to war. Loud exclaiming they each other exhort, but chiefly the voice of Nestor arose; the ardent voice of the guardian of Argos. " O friends! be men," he said; " let each recal " to his mind his children, his spouse beloved: his wide " possessions at home, the parents whom much he re- " veres; whether living, they breathe the air, or dead, " they reside in the tomb. By them I adjure you all! " though absent, they speak in my voice: they bid you " stand [197]."

" Thus Nestor speaking, roused to strength, and awakened the souls of all. Minerva dispersed from their eyes the thick cloud that had hovered around; the heaven-sent darkness, which had shrowded their fight; bright bursts upon them the day; from the ships, from the field rushed the light. They beheld Hector, so great in the fight; the warring friends of the chief they beheld: they saw the troops that behind stood from war; they saw those engaged at the ships. The whole field rose at once to their view. No longer it pleased the stout heart of magnanimous Ajax to stand still in his arms, where the other warriors of Achaia stood. From deck to deck the hero rushed, stretching

196. *Iliad*. lib. xv.   197. Id. ibid.

wide

PART I. wide his mighty strides. He wielded the huge pole in
his hands; a weapon of death in the naval fight, twenty-
two cubits in length, bright studded with steel around.
His loud voice ascended the sky: unceasing he exclaimed to the Greeks, and urged them to defend their
camp[198].

" Again burned the dreadful battle: death flew from
side to side. Unfatigued wouldst thou have thought
the foes; unbroken and new in the field: so fierce
they met in the shock. With fury they urged the fight;
but different was the state of their souls. The Argives
apprehended they could not escape: they provoked the
death which they saw no means of eluding. The
minds of the Trojans were roused with hope: they
thought they could burn the fleet, and drench with
the blood of heroes the shore[199].

" Hector seized with his daring hand the dark stern
of a hollow ship; the beauteous ship, which over the
main brought the hapless Protesilaus. For this, hand to
hand, the hostile nations contended. Now they nor
dreaded the flight of shafts from afar, nor darts coming
down from the winds. Hand to hand, and face to face,
with one mind they waged the war. With axes, with
pikes they fought; with mighty swords, with steel-
pointed spears. Many bright swords fell on the earth;
with dark handles, with large polished hilts; and glit-
tered as they lay in the dust. Confusion spread with
tumult around: the earth floated with blood[200]."

But Hector never quitted his hold of the ship.
" On the stern are spread his broad hands, while thus
he eagerly swells his voice:—" Haste! bring the fire,

" urge

198. Hom. *Iliad.* ubi sup.   199. Id. ibid.
200. *Iliad.* lib. xv.

" urge the fight; pour at once your gathered force
" on the foe. This is the day, the happy hour, in
" which Jove delivers us all. Let us seize the hateful
" fleet, hither come against the will of the gods.
" The fleet which has covered us with woes, through
" the cowardly counsels of age. Me the elders thus
" long have kept back, though burning to fight at
" the ships : they restrained the whole army from
" war[201]."—" He spoke, and with fiercer rage the Trojans rushed on the Argive powers.

" No longer Ajax himself sustains the fight : over-
whelmed with darts he retires. He left the deck of
the equal ship : to the banks of the rowers he retreated. There stood the chief and eyed the foe ; with his
spear he turned the Trojans away : he drove away
whoever came with the flame. Ceaseless swelled his
dreadful voice on the winds ; ceaseless he urged the
Argives to battle. " O friends, O heroes of Argos!"
he said, " once followers of Mars in arms, shew your-
" selves men ; recal your wonted valour of soul. Deem
" ye that aids are behind, that a bulwark ascends
" in the rear? Have you any other protecting trench,
" any wall to turn destruction away? No city of ours
" is near ; no lofty towers, to annoy the foe. We have
" no place of defence; no town, in succession, to
" guard : on the shores of the bright-mailed Trojans
" we stand, inclosed by the main. Between the wave
" and the foe we are hemmed. Distant far is our na-
" tive land : our safety is placed in our hands. Certain
" ruin must attend on our flight[202]."

" He spoke, and furious exalted his spear. Whoever of Troy's hapless sons rushed forward on the
ships with the flame, to gain the favour of Hector, on

---

201. Id. ibid.   202. Hom. *Iliad.* lib. xv.

his

his spear Ajax received: hand to hand, he pierced them with his lance. Twelve Trojans, thus advancing with fire, lay slain at the stern of the ship[203]." But the strength of Ajax was at length exhausted. " Dreadful sounds the bright brass on his head, smote on every side by the foe. His left shoulder is relaxed with toil, in holding high his firm shield to the war. Yet could they not drive him along, though leaning forward with all their spears. High heaves with short-breathing his breast; sweat wanders over all his limbs. Nor rest nor respite he finds, on every side assailed[204]."

Still, however, the dauntless chief maintained his station, until deprived of his deathful weapon. " Hector struck with his wide-beaming sword the ashen spear of the godlike Ajax, where joined the wood with the steel. Through and through passed the eager blade. The son of Telamon wielded in vain the pointless staff in his mighty hand. Wide flew the bright head of the spear, resounding as it fell to the ground. Then the hero shuddered in his soul: he retreated beyond the darts. The foe threw the devouring fire: wide over the ship spreads the flame[205]."

Before the Greeks were pushed to this extremity, the gallant but mild Patroclus, who commanded under Achilles, had resolved to use his influence to rouse the hero to fight. " Who knows," said he, " but I " may move his relentless soul?—For powerful is the " voice of a friend[206]." Embarrassed, however, in what manner to disclose his purpose, he "stood before Achilles: wide rushed the warm tears down his cheek.

203. Id. ibid.   204. Iliad. lib. xvi.
205. Id. ibid.   206. Hom. Iliad. lib. xv.

The.

The great son of Peleus saw his grief. Pity rose in his
mighty soul; and thus, with winged words he began:
" Why fall thy tears, O Patroclus? Bringest thou tid-
" ings of dire import to the Myrmidons or to their
" king? Hast thou heard aught of sorrow from Phthia?
" —or mournest thou the fate of the Argives, because
" they fall at their hollow ships for their injustice to
" me? Speak! conceal not thy soul; let us both know
" the cause of thy grief [207]."

" Deeply sighing, the car-borne Patroclus said, O
" Achilles! thou first of the Argives in arms, reproach
" me not for these tears; for deep the woes that over-
" shadow the host.   All the bravest have retired
" from the fight: their hands unwilling have ceased
" from the strife of spears.   Wounded they lie sad
" in the ships.   Them the skilled in the healing arts
" attend, and dress their deep wounds.   But thou,
" O Achilles! relentless remaineth: nothing heals
" the wounds of thy pride!—If still thou refusest to
" turn certain ruin from thy country and friends, me
" at least send forth to fight; submit thy forces to my
" command.   Let the Myrmidons take their spears,
" and light may perhaps arise on our friends.   Give
" me to wear thine arms; to cloath myself in thy
" wonted steel.   The Trojans, by the likeness de-
" ceived, will in terror desist from the fight, and the
" Argives will breath from their toil [208]."

" Ah, Patroclus!" the godlike son of Peleus replied, " heavy woe sits deep on my heart: still wrath
" wraps in tempest my breast.   Much have I suffered
" in soul.   But let the past be forgot: it becomes not
" man forever to rage, to cherish endless strife. Assume

207. *Iliad.* lib. xvi.   208. Id. ibid.

then

" then my splendid arms, be thou the leader of my
" troops to the fight.   Conduct my Myrmidons
" along, as the dark cloud of the Trojan powers has
" girt the ships with all their strength.   Hemmed in
" to the shore of the main, small the space which
" the Argives possess. The whole city pours on them
" amain: full of confidence the Trojans fight.   No
" longer rages the spear in the hands of the mighty
" son of Tydeus; no longer the hateful voice of Aga-
" memnon comes with force on mine ear. But I hear
" the voice of Hector: his urging voice ascends the
" winds: the Trojans hear it over their lines; they
" possess the whole field, and slay in battle the war-
" riors of Argos. Rush forth in thy valour, O Patroc-
" lus! and turn destruction away from our ships.
" Prevent, O friend! the hostile flame, lest our hopes
" of return should be lost [209]."

While Achilles was giving instructions to Patroclus, " not to urge the strife too far; not to push the
" war to Ilion," he saw the *whole stern* of the contested
ship *involved in flames.*   He *smote his manly thigh* and
thus exclaimed, " Arise in thy strength, O Patroclus!
" valiant ruler of steeds, arise! I see at the fleet of
" the Argives the *rapid force of resistless fire.* Haste!
" assume the bright arms: I myself will convene the
" troops [210]."   He spoke, and Patroclus obeyed: he
armed himself in burnished steel [211].   He took two

---

209. Hom. *Iliad.* lib. xvi.   210. Id. ibid.

211. " First the beauteous greaves on his legs he drew, with silver
" clasps fastened before; then he placed on his manly breast the cui-
" rass of the noble Achilles; various, starry, bright flaming with
" gold. Round his shoulders he suspended the sword, distinguished
" with silver studs. On his arm he raised the shield; a wide, and
" solid, bossy orb. On his gallant head he placed the dazzling hel-
" met: the horse-hair waved on high in the wind; and dreadful
" above nodded the crest," *Iliad.* lib. xvi.

strong.

strong spears in his hands, which fitted well his manly
grasp; but he took not the long, heavy, strong spear
of Achilles, which none of all the Argives but he could
wield in fight: the Pelian ash, cut from the brows of
Pelion, a destruction to heroes in war[212].

" The hero ordered Automedon to join the steeds
to the car; Automedon, next to Achilles, the breaker
of armies, and whom he honoured most. Firm in
fight was the chief, to sustain the assault of the foe.
The warrior obeyed the high behest; whilst Achilles,
rushing tall through his troops, roused them all over
the tents to their arms. They issued forth like devouring wolves, in whose breasts dwelt resistless force. In
the midst stood the son of Peleus, urging forward the
deep ranks of his bright-shielded men. Fifty were his
hollow ships on the shore, which he brought over the
ocean to Troy. In each, fifty warriors came, skilled
all at the oar as in arms. Five were the leaders in
fight[213]; chiefs trusted by their daring lord. He
himself was the first in command, as the first in the
bloody field[214]."

212. Hom. *Iliad.* ubi sup.

. 213. Id, ibid. It is not a little remarkable, That *two* of these *five*
leaders were *bastards* and the reputed *sons of gods* (Hom. *Iliad.* lib.
xvi.). Achilles himself was the reputed son of a goddess (Hom. *Iliad.*
lib. i. et seq.): And his mother, the bright-moving Thetis, was probably the daughter of some Phœnician merchant, who had come to
trade on the coast of Phthiotis; and whom Peleus had carried off, or
purchased from her father. For to use her own words, " Me only
" of the daughters of Ocean, Saturnian Jove submitted to the arms of
" a man!—He gave me, much unwilling, to Peleus. I sustained a
" mortal's hated embrace" (Hom. *Iliad.* lib. xviii.): Or, in vulgar
language, she was *compelled* to *marry* a man she *did not like*, and who
was so far inferior to her in accomplishments, that she is represented
by Homer as a goddess, and he as a mere mortal, though a renowned
warrior.

214. *Iliad.* lib. xvi.

PART I. When Achilles had formed his warlike troops
behind their leaders, he thus issued his commands :—
" Forget not, Myrmidons! the threats ye oft poured
" in mine ears; your threats, in these hollow ships
" against the sons of lofty Troy, in the safe season of
" the wrath of your lord. Now the huge work of
" battle appears : the season which you love is arriv-
" ed. Let each follow his own daring heart, and turn
" on the Trojans the war[215]." " He spoke and awakened their strength: he kindled valour over all their
souls. More thick became their lines, when they
heard the awful voice of their king. Buckler its buckler supports, helmet its helmet, and man his man.
Crouded the horse-hair crests arise, the plumes mix
as they wave in the winds; so thick stand the warriors
in arms. But before the rest stood two heroes unmatched in their force; Patroclus and warlike Automedon, having both but one soul in their breasts. Tall
they stood in the front of the line. Great Achilles
entered his tent; he opened a beauteous chest, the
high-wrought gift of the bright moving Thetis. Within
was a laboured bowl, as it came from the artist's hands,
never touched with the lips of man; never stained
with the dark-red wine: nor yet in libations used to
the gods, unless to father Jove. This from the coffer
he took : he purged it with sulphur: in clear water he
washed it: he cleansed his hands, and drew the dark
wine. In the sacred circle he stood; steadfast eying
the broad face of the sky, he poured the libation with
prayer.

" Jove, awful king of Dodona!" he said ;—" Pe-
" lasgic, O far-dwelling Jove !—O thou that pre-
" sidest on high, heretofore thou hast heard my

215. Id. ibid.

" prayer;

" prayer; thou hast opened thine ears to my voice:
" grant again success to my vows!—Here in my
" ships I remain, but my friend I send forth to war;
" to battle I send him forth, amid many warriors in
" arms. With him send victory, O Jove! ruler of
" tempests: confirm his stout heart in his breast.
" Grant, after he drives from the ships the dreadful
" strife and the clamour of fight, that to me he may
" safe return: that the chief may return in all his
" arms, with his close-fighting friends in the war[216]."
" Thus praying the hero spoke. Jove heard him on
Ida of streams: the father of gods granted half his
request, and half he gave to the winds.

" Right forward moved the troops in their arms,
with Patroclus undaunted in soul. Close-compacted
in order they move, and rush with mighty force on
the foe. Patroclus raised his manly voice, and thus
urged his friends to fight:—" O Myrmidons! daunt-
" less in war; gallant friends of the great son of
" Peleus, show yourselves men. Recal the wonted
" force of your souls; let us honour the mighty
" Achilles; by far the bravest of the Greeks, and
" who over the bravest extends his command. Let
" the son of Atreus his errors learn; let all-com-
" manding Agamemnon repent, that he has not
" honoured in aught the first of the Argives in
" arms[217]." " He spoke, he awaked their strength;
he kindled valour over all their souls. Deep-formed,
they rushed on the foe: loud echoed the navy around,
as the Argives shouted for joy. But when the Trojans saw the gallant son of the brave Menætius, and
his partner in war rushing on, the souls of all within
them sunk. They deemed that the swift son of Peleus

216. Hom. *Iliad*. lib. xvi.   217. Id. ibid.

had

had thrown from his soul his wrath; wildly staring they turned their eyes, each searching a quarter for flight[218].

" Then first Patroclus threw his bright lance through the air: in the midst of the Trojans it fell, where amain raged the tumult of arms; near the stern of the beauteous ship, that bore Protesilaus to Troy. He drove from the navy the foe, and extinguished the raging flame. Half-burnt the ship is left on the sand; to flight the Trojans are turned: with dreadful tumult they scour away. The Argives pour wide from their ships; loud clamour ascends the sky. As when Jove from the lofty summit of a mountain, that rears its dark brow to the skies, dispels with his bolt the thick cloud that had settled on high; bright rise all the rocks to the view, the broken ridges of the hills appear, the forests wave their heads in the light; clear opens wide heaven to the eye: thus the Argives distinct appeared, when the flame they repelled from the ships, and rolled the hostile smoke away. A short space they all breathed from their toils. Nor yet ceased wholly the fight: nor yet, over the length of their lines, the foes turned their back on the ships before the rushing force of the warlike Argives. Some resisted the turning war, and unwillingly quitted the fleet[219].

" But suddenly dispersed is the battle: each leader a leader slays, and man pursues man with his spear. Patroclus urged forward his steeds, where thickest over the field fled the foe: beneath the axles the heroes fell; prone they lay on the earth, pressed by the wheels. The crashing cars are overturned as they fly. From bank to bank of the trench bound the

---

218 *Iliad.* lib xvi.   219. Id. ibid.

coursers

coursers of the mighty Peleus, the *splendid gift of the gods!* eager to urge all their speed. His soul roused the hero on Hector: he wished to strike the chief with his spear; but his steeds bore him away. As when beneath the rain-laden winds, the whole world is wrapt in thick gloom; when, in the season of autumn, Jove, shrouded in impetuous showers descends in his rage on the earth, and pours his dreadful wrath on mankind; when the laws are perverted by force; when justice is expelled from her seat; when judges unjustly decide, regardless of the vengeance of Heaven, the rivers swell beyond their fixed bounds, and spread the dark deluge amain[220]; the torrents bear away, in their course, the falling sides of the echoing hills; red-rushing from the sounding mountains the streams roar wide to the deep, and levelled are the works of men: so impetuous, so noisy, so dark, is poured the flight of the Trojans. The steeds groan, as they rush along: the whole field is tumult[22]."

Patroclus having thus broken the Trojans in battle, drove back his eager steeds toward the ships; nor permitted the remains of the hostile army to return to the town, though bent on flight. "Between the navy, the river, and the wall, he hemmed them in with furious force. Wildly flew many deaths from his hand: he took on many revenge. Heaps on heaps they crowded the ground. When Sarpedon beheld his friends laid low in death, subdued by the mighty hands of the gallant son of Menætius, he raised his urging voice in the fight, and thus chid his Lycians:— "Whither fly the renowned in arms?—Now your

220. From these allusions we discover, that in the days of Homer regular forms of jurisprudence were established; and that the unjust decisions of judges, and the forcible obstruction of the operation of laws, were thought worthy of divine vengeance.

221. Hom. *Iliad.* lib. xvi.

"valour

" valour show: I will meet this warrior in fight, that
" I may learn why he thus prevails in the strife.
" Many woes has he laid on the Trojans; many stout
" limbs has the hero unbraced [222]."

" He spoke, and bounded to earth from his car, in
the harsh sound of all his arms. Patroclus, on the
other side, beheld the king, and leaped from his car.
As two vultures on a high-towering rock, with clench-
ing talons and crooked beaks, screaming aloud engage
in fight; so the heroes with clamour advanced, rushing
forward to mutual wounds. Sarpedon strayed wide
from the foe: his shining lance flew guiltless through
the air; over the left shoulder of his antagonist it
passed. Patroclus then urged his steel; nor in vain
flew the shaft from his hand. He struck the king on
his manly breast, where the fibres involved the strong
heart: he fell like some stately oak, or poplar, or lofty
pine; which the woodmen cut down on the hills, to
form the dark ship for the main [223]."

" Thus slain by the spear of Patroclus, lay the
leader of the Lycians in arms. He groaned from his
indignant soul, and called his loved friend by his
name. "O Glaucus!" he said, "O warrior among
" warriors renowned, now it behoves thee to fight; to
" urge the battle with daring hand. Now must the
" war be thy care, if undaunted in war is thy heart.
" Urge, Glaucus! my people to fight; urge the leaders
" of the Lycians in arms: send thy voice through the
" lines; O bid them for Sarpedon to fight!—Nor only
" bid but act, O friend! stretch over me thy gleaming
" steel. To thee hereafter I shall be a disgrace, a dire
" reproach to my friend: shame shall cover all thy
" future days, should the Argives possess my arms;

222. Id. ibid.   223. *Iliad.* ubi sup.

" should

" should they strip me before the hollow ships[224].
" Boldly urge the dreadful fight, rouse all my people
" to arms[225]." As groaning he spoke, shadowy death
arose on his eyes: the foe placed his foot on his breast :
he withdrew from his body the spear. The bloody
fibres followed the point; with the lance issued forth
his great soul. The Myrmidons detained his steeds,
as they snorted, and wished to fly[226].

" Glaucus straight roused to the fight the Lycian
leaders over all their lines. Furious he rushed through
the ranks: he bade them contend for the mighty Sarpedon; then moving forward, with majestic strides,
he called the Trojans to defend his friend. He called
the godlike Polydamas, he called Agenor divine; he
rushed to the dauntless Æneas, to Hector clad in
mail. "Approach, O my gallant friends !" he said ;—
" throw resentment, throw rage in your souls ; pre-
" vent the foe from dishonouring the dead. The
" Myrmidons the slain will disgrace, enraged for the
" Argives who fell; who sunk in blood, beneath our
" spears at the ships [227]." The Trojans are invaded
with grief. The pillar of their city, Sarpedon was,
though born in a foreign land. Many and brave were
the hero's troops, but he himself was the bravest of

---

224. Thus we find, that it was considered as a great indignity for
the body of a hero to be stripped of his arms, and dishonourable for
his friends to suffer such disgrace. Hence the obstinacy with which
the Greeks and Trojans fought, not only to preserve the bodies, but
the arms of their fallen friends ; and the avidity of the victors to
seize them. For to carry off the arms of a fallen hero was regarded
as matter of triumph, independent of their value (*Iliad,* passim.).
But the rapacity of the Greeks for spoil hurried them far beyond what
glory required; and proved, as I have already had occasion to observe,
the cause of many of their misfortunes. Hector was also obliged to
repress, at times, the rapacity of the Trojans. *Iliad,* passim.

225. Hom. *Iliad.* lib. xvi.　　　　226. Id. ibid.
227. *Iliad.* lib. xvi.

all.

all. Right-forward they rushed on the foe. Hector led, in wrath, the fierce attack[228]."

Meanwhile " the stout heart of Patroclus urged the warlike Argives to arms. He first spoke to the Ajaces, already prompt in their souls to fight. " O " Ajaces!" he said, " now place the fight in your " souls: stand forth to repel the foe ; be what in war " you have been; even add to your former fame. " The man lies slain in his blood, who first scaled the " wall of the Argives ; Sarpedon lies in death. Now " let us disgrace the slain, by stripping his corse of his " arms. And O that with steel we could lay some " gallant friend of the hero on earth[229]!" He roused them thus, already prompt. The firm ranks are formed on each side, the Trojan and the Lycian powers ; the Myrmidons and warlike Argives. Fierce they met in fight over the dead. Dreadful the clamour ascended the winds, as heard afar is the sound of the woodmen felling the forest amain, on the lofty tops of the echoing hills : so spread the horrid crashings of war over all the wide resounding plain ; the sound of steel, of battered shields, struck with swords, pierced with spears. The whole field is one tumult, one noise. Death darkly bounds from line to line. Nor could the skilful eye of a discerning man now distinguish the noble Sarpedon. With darts, with blood, with dust overspread, the hero lay. Ceaseless crowd around him the foe[230].

" The breast of Hector was filled with dismay. He ascended his car in his flight; he exhorted the Trojans to fly. Nor even the gallant Lycians now sustained the fight. All turned their backs to the foe. Their king they saw pierced through the heart, lying beneath

228. Id. ibid.　　229. Hom. *Iliad.* ubi sup.　　230. Id. ibid.

the

the heaps of slain. Many had fallen on his corse.
The Greeks stript of his arms the great Sarpedon; his
brazen, his bright-beaming arms. The gallant son of
Menætius gave the splendid spoils to his friends to be
borne to the navy of Argos[231].

" Patroclus, urging his deathless steeds; urging
Automedon to arms, pursued the Lycians and Trojans.
Above measure raged the chief with his spear. First
he slew Adrastus; then Autonous, and gallant Eche-
clus. Perimus fell by his spear; Epistor, and brave
Melenippus. Elasus he also slew; Mulius, and godlike Pylartes. These he transfixed, as they fled. The
whole hostile army is poured over the plain. Then
had the sons of the Argives taken Troy with *lofty-gates*,
beneath the hands of Patroclus; but Phœbus stood in
the high tower:" or, in other words, the sun was
too hot for such an arduous enterprize, after the fa-
tigues which the Greeks had sustained. " The god
aided Troy, and entertained dreadful mischief against
the son of Menætius. Thrice he strove to ascend the
wall, thrice Apollo threw him back to the ground."
After a fourth attempt " Patroclus retired: he dreaded
the wrath of Apollo, who shoots from afar[232]."

Now Hector, who had hitherto stood at the Scæan
gate, in doubtful suspense, whether to renew the
fight or to command his troops " to defend the wall,"
ordered brave Cebriones " to drive his car right on
the foe. Apollo entered the line of the Argives: he
roused destructive panic; he gave glory to Troy.
Hector neglected the rest of the Greeks: he slew them
not with his deadly spear: but on the warlike Patroclus
drove forward his bounding steeds. Patroclus, on
the other side, bounded from his car to the ground.

In his left-hand is his beamy spear: in his right he wields aloft a stone; white, rugged, of enormous size. He grasped it in his hand robust: he threw it forward with all his might; nor strayed he far from the chief. The weight flew not in vain from his hand: he struck the driver of Hector's car; Cebriones the son of illustrious Priam, his offspring by a secret bed. He struck him as he held the reins: on his forehead fell the sharp stone; both his brows were crushed by the weight: the skull yielded; like a diver, he tumbled to earth, and his soul left his corse on the plain[233].

" Patroclus rushed, in his might, on the hero slain by his hand. He bore along a lion's force; a lion, whom his own courage destroys. Hector, on the other side, leaped from his car to the ground. Like two lions, they fought for the slain; two lions, who on the mountain's bleak brow, both raging with hunger, each other assail for some slaughtered hind in her flowing blood. Thus for the fallen Cebriones fought the two authors of dreadful fight; Patroclus, the son of Menætius, and the illustrious Hector. Each wishes from his inmost soul to pierce the other with ruthless steel[234].

" Hector seized the slain by the head, nor quitted the hero his hold. Patroclus, on the other side, dragged the fallen chief by the foot. The hostile armies meantime engaged in fight. The Trojans and Argives are drenched in blood. Death darkly bounds from line to line: loud tumult rolls together the field; as when the east and southern winds, descending from the heavens, contend in the leafy groves of the echoing hills; bending the thick woods in their rage. Over the mountain the forest resounds: harshly crash

233. *Iliad.* lib. xvi.   234. Id. ibid.

the

the trunks of trees, as they break. Thus the Trojans
and warlike Argives; fiercely bounding on each other,
engage. Mutual were the deaths and the wounds:
neither side thought of shameful flight. Many sharp
spears are fixed in the earth round the slain offspring
of aged Priam; many winged arrows came sounding
along, rushing from the nerves of the bows; many huge
stones flew through the air, and crashing fell on the
bossy shields, as wildly raging fought the foes round
Cebriones laid in his blood. But he lay largely, extended in dust, unmindful of his bounding steeds[235]!

" Whilst the sun rolled his bright orb over half the
heavens, mutual were the wounds of the foes: the people fell equally on each side; but when he veered his
slant beams to the west, then the Argives victorious
remained: they rose superior to fate. They drew the
hero Cebriones from the heaps of dead and of darts,
from the tumult of Troy in fight: they stripped the
fallen chief of his arms[236]. Patroclus then, with hostile
soul rushed forward on the foe with his spear. Thrice
he rushed, like brazen Mars: dreadful swelled his voice
on the winds: thrice he nine warriors slew. But when
he made the fourth assault, bounding on with the force
of a god, then Phœbus met him in dismal fight: dreadful was the course of the god!—Behind the hero he
stood: his broad shoulders he struck with his hand:
a dizziness seized his bright eyes. Phœbus threw his
helmet to the ground; bright rolled the sounding brass
on the earth, through the feet of the bounding steeds.
His spear hung loose in his nerveless hand; his heavy,
huge long spear he scarce could drag along the dust.
His shield fell from its thong on the ground: the cuirass
on his breast was loosened, by the hand of the son of
Jove. A sudden stupor invaded his mind. His limbs

---

235. Hom. *Iliad.* lib. xvi.   236. Id. ibid.

were unbraced: dizzy and astonished he stood. Between his shoulders a Dardan warrior, approaching
behind, drove his spear; Euphorbus, the son of Pan-
thus. He struck, but could not subdue: he withdrew
his ashen spear from the wound; he retreated, and
mixed with his friends [237].

" He could not sustain Patroclus, though exposed
he stood in the fight. But the hero subdued by the
stroke of the god, by the sharp-pointed javelin subdued,
retreated to the troop of his friends; avoiding death
from the hands of the foe. And when Hector perceived the great Patroclus thus retreating, wounded,
he rushed upon him through the ranks of the foe;
Hand to hand he urged the spear: through his nether
belly it passed: resounding he fell to the earth. Dreadful sorrow shades the host of the Argives. Hector
withdrew from the wound the bright spear, *placing his
foot on the slain.* He threw the corse supine from his
lance: he rushed on the great Automedon, the godlike friend of the swift son of Peleus. Much he wished
to slay the chief. Him his bright steeds bore away;
the deathless steeds of the warlike Peleus, the splendid
gift of the gods [238].

" Not unseen by the son of Atreus, by Menelaus
renowned in arms, Patroclus lay subdued in the dismal fight. He moved through the front of the line,
bright-sheathed in his burnished steel; round the corse,
in defence, he moved, like a heifer around her young.
He stretched his bright spear before him; he raised
the bright orb of his shield, ready to consign to death
the foe that should dare to approach the dead [239]."
In this defensive situation he stood, when Euphorbus,
who first smote the fallen hero, advanced and struck

237. *Iliad.* lib. xvi.   238. Id. ibid.
230. Hom. *Iliad.* lib. xvii.

the wide round of his shield. "But he penetrated not
the solid brass; bent back is the point on the orb.
The son of Atreus urged next his bright spear, addressing a prayer to Jove. He struck the throat of
Euphorbus, as he turned away. With all his force he
urged the point: through and through he pierced his
neck. The steel appeared in blood behind. Resounding he fell to the earth: on his body crashed harshly
his arms[240].

"Then had the son of warlike Atreus stript the
slain of his beauteous arms; but Phœbus Apollo envied
the spoils to the king. He roused on him Hector
divine, in force equal to impetuous Mars. The deep
ranks of the Trojans advanced. Hector preceded in
all his might. Unwilling the king retired; often turning, as he quitted the slain, his manly face to the foe.
When he came to the line of his friends, over the
ranks he rolled his eyes in search of the great Telamonian Ajax. The hero he soon descried; far in the
left of the line, confirming his warriors in fight, and
turning their force on the foe. Over them had spread
a panic divine, raised by Phœbus Apollo in wrath[241].

"Forward to the chief strode the king; near the
hero he stood, and began: "Hither, Ajax! come
"hither, O friend! let us haste, let us fight for the
"fallen Patroclus! let us bear his corse to Achilles.
"His naked corse! for his martial arms, I deem, are
"possessed by Hector."—"He moved the soul of the
chief. Ajax stood across the front of the fight: Menelaus attended his steps." Meantime Hector, having
stript Patroclus of his arms, "dragged the slain hero
along, resolved to lop the head from the trunk; to give
the mangled corse a prey to the dogs of Troy. But Ajax

240. Id. ibid.   241. Iliad. lib. xvii.

came

came near, raising his shield aloft like a tower : Hector retreated amain, and mixed himself with the ranks
of his host. He ascended with a bound his car : he
gave the beauteous arms to his friends ; to bear them
to the high-walled Ilion, to add to his mighty renown[242].

" Meanwhile Ajax stretched forth his broad shield
over the slain son of Menætius. He stood like a long-
maned lion, who stalks around defending his young ;
a lion, when bearing his whelps along, surrounded by
the hunters within the woods. He rolls his flaming
eye-balls in strength ; dark sink his dreadful brows
on their glare, and half cover their fire as they burn ;
so stalking round the hero Patroclus, Ajax covered
his bleeding corse. On the other side the warlike
Menelaus stood in arms, indulging his grief for his
friend, and increasing the cloud on his soul[243]." But
Hector, having urged his troops to battle, " retired
from the flaming strife. Bounding forward with eager
speed, he soon overtook his friends : he came along
on the steps of those, who bore to lofty Troy, the
burnished arms of the great son of Peleus. Standing
apart from the mournful fight, the awful hero changed
his arms. He gave his own to the warlike Trojans,
to be borne to sacred Ilion ; and he assumed the immortal arms of great Achilles, the son of Peleus ;
the arms, which the deathless gods gave to his father
beloved[244].

" The armour fitted Hector divine. Dreadful
Mars breathed on him his force. His limbs with
fresh vigour are braced ; new strength pervades his
frame. To his gallant friends, in battle, he rushed.
Like Achilles, he seemed to them all ; as flaming he

242. Id. ibid.   243. Hom. *Iliad*, ubi sup.   244. Id. ibid.

strode

strode over the field, in the arms of the great son of
Peleus. Winding his course, through all the line, he
roused the chiefs of the people to fight. "Hear me!"
he said, "ye hundred tribes, who border on sacred
"Troy: nor I, in want of numbers at home, nor to
"cover our fields with an idle crowd, have roused you
"from your distant homes, or called you to the walls
"of Ilion. To defend the Trojans ye came, to shield
"their wives and infant sons; to enter battle with
"willing hearts, to chace a valliant foe from the land.
"Let each therefore turn his face to the Greeks,
"whether safety or death presents[245]!"—"Right forward they rushed, with all their gathered force, on
the Argives. They raised before them their spears.
Much they hoped to force the dead from the mighty
grasp of the great Telamonian Ajax. Fools that they
were!—many pierced by his dreadful spear, poured
forth their souls on the corse[246]." But as Hector had
collected the storm of war, and poured it dark over the
field, Menelaus "swelled his loud voice on the winds;
he thus called the bright-mailed Argives:—"O friends!
"O leaders of Argos! O princes of the nations in
"arms! Ye who, with the sons of Atreus, quaff at
"large the public wine; ye who command your tribes,
"who derive your sacred honours from Jove, let some
"issue forth of their own accord; let them feel rage
"in their souls, that the great, but fallen Patroclus,
"should become a sport to the dogs of Troy[247]."

"He spoke—and the son of Oïleus, the swift-
footed Ajax heard. He first came forward in steel,
resounding as he rushed through the fight. Idomeneus
followed the chief, and the friend of the great Idomeneus; Meriones equal to Mars the destroyer of armies.

---

245. Hom. *Iliad.* lib. xvii.   246. Id. ibid.
247. *Iliad.* lib. xvii.

But who can name all the chiefs, all the warriors that came in their arms, when the Argives renewed the fight round the corse of the fallen Patroclus?—The gathered Trojans rushed first to battle. Hector preceded in arms. As when, in the echoing mouth of a river, descending from father Jove, huge tumbles the roaring wave, and rolls back in its channel the stream; so loud was the clamour of Troy. But silent stood the Argives arrayed: they stood around the son of Menætius, having but *one* soul in their breasts; walled round with their shields, they stood[248]." Yet the Trojans shook "the ranks of the deep-formed Argives; they removed them from the slain: they dragged the bloody corse over the field. But not long remained distant the Greeks; straight Ajax turned their face to the foe: Ajax in figure, in deeds, in arms, the first of the Greeks in fight, next to the blameless son of Peleus. He broke the firm front of the Trojans.

"In his strength like a mountain-boar, who disperses with ease, on his hills, the youthful hunters with all their hounds; so illustrious Ajax dispersed the Trojans, when he poured upon them his force[249]. Already they had surrounded Patroclus: they hoped to drag to their city the slain, to cover their arms with renown. Him Hippothous seized by the foot, the illustrious son of Pelasgian Lethus; he dragged the dead through the burning fight, binding round the ancle a thong. He pleased Hector and Troy by the deed; but sudden fate hovered over his life. None could turn death from the chief, though eager to ward it away. The son of Telamon, bounding amain, struck the hero hand to hand with his spear. On the brazen helmet fell the lance. Split is the casque in twain. The point passed near the horse-hair cone, forceful driven

248. Id. ibid.   249. Hom. Iliad. ubi sup.

by

by a sinewy arm. The brain, where entered the eager steel, rushed bloody to the earth from the wound; his strength is at once unbraced. He dropt the foot of the slain on the ground: on his face he fell on Patroclus; prone he lay, in death, on the dead[250].

" But Hector launched on the godlike Ajax his spear, that shone bright as it flew. Ajax saw the gleaming steel as it came ; and, inclining, avoided its point: but the spear fell on warlike Schedius, the magnanimous son of Iphitus, by far the bravest of all the Phoceans. Him the hero struck in the throat: through his shoulder appeared, in blood, the eager point of the fatal lance: resounding he fell to the earth; over his body crashed harshly his arms. And Ajax struck the warlike Phorcys, the son of Phænops, illustrious in arms. Through his body passed swiftly the lance; the steel broke the cuirass in twain, and mixed its point with the entrails behind. Extended large he lay on the earth, and grasped the dust with his dying hand[251].

" The foremost of the ranks of the foe give way: illustrious Hector himself retires. Loud swell the shouts of the Argives: they drag the slain heroes away ; Phorcys and the valiant Hippothous. From their bodies they tore their arms. Then had the Trojans in flight, driven headlong before the Argives, ascended to lofty Ilion; then the Argives had won renown, by their own proper courage and force, if Apollo had not roused Æneas to battle. Bounding forward in his arms, he stood far advanced beyond the line; and the Trojans turned their face from shameful flight: they

250. Id. ibid. "From the *fertile Larissa* far," adds Homer (*Iliad.* lib. xviii.): Hence we learn, that a Pelasgian colony had been there planted before the Trojan war.

251. *Iliad.* lib. xvii.

rushed

rushed onward against the Argives. Æneas launched with force his bright spear: he struck Leocritus, the gallant friend of the great Lycomedes. Before the slain Lycomedes stood in steel: he launched his beaming spear on the foe; he struck the shepherd of his people, brave Apisaon. Through his liver rushed eager the lance; straight his limbs are unbraced in death. From the fertile Paeon he came; and, next to the great Asteropæus, he was the bravest of his people in fight[252].

" Him, as he fell in his blood, pitied the mighty Asteropæus. Right onward he urged his course, ready to launch his spear on the Argives; but no opening appeared for his steel. Covered over with their bucklers they stood: they formed a circle round the fallen Patroclus, and stretched forward to the Trojans their spears. Through their lines rushed the godlike Ajax. He urged them to the battle with words, with deeds he urged them to fight. He permitted none to retreat from the dead; none to rush forward from his line on the foe. He commanded all to stand firm; to close round his spear their close ranks: hand to hand to urge their bright points[253]. Such were the orders of mighty Ajax. The earth is drenched with purple blood; heaps on heaps sink the foe to the ground. The Trojans, with their allies renowned, fell mixed with the falling Argives. Nor the latter urged the fight without blood, though fewer they sunk in death. They remembered the words of the chief: close compacted the warriors stood and warded off death by their mutual aid[254].

" Thus fought the foes on the field, with all the rage of devouring flames. Deep darkness involved the

252. Id. ibid.
254. Id. ibid.
253. Hom. *Iliad*. ubi sup.

fight: in a cloud stood concealed the foes; who pushed their spears through blood and death, round the fallen son of Menætius[255]. The other warriors of lofty Troy, and the Argives, bright-covered with mail, fought free in the air serene. Spread over them is the splendour divine, the sharp light of the blazing sun. Nor cloud arose from the ample field, nor mist inwrapt the mountain's head. At intervals they fought dispersed; avoiding, with mutual care, their deadly spears as they flew. But the foes, who in the centre engaged, suffered woes, and wounds, and death; involved in battle, in darkness, in night[256].

" Then arose amid the crowd, in words like these, the voice of some Argive in arms; "O friends! urge
" onward the war: it becomes not, we must not re-
" treat. It were now disgraceful to fly to the ships:
" here rather let the earth open wide, and closing over
" us conceal our shame!—This were better for our
" fame, than to suffer the car-ruling Trojans to drag
" Patroclus hence to their lofty city, and to cover with
" renown their arms." Then some Trojan exclaimed,
" O friends! here let us urge the war; let none turn
" his foot from the fight, though all were destined to
" fall in death on the corse of the hero slain."—" On
either side such words were used. The souls of the warriors are awakened; death rages amain over the field. The horrid clangour, the tumult, the noise of arms, swelled on the air, and rose to the brazen concave of heaven[257].

" Hector hurled his bright lance through the air, at the breast of the great Automedon. He saw the gleaming steel, as it came, and stooping forward avoided its point. Behind him it stood fixed in the ground;

255. Hom, *Iliad.* lib. xvii.   256. Id. ibid.
257. *Iliad.* lib. xvii.

the

the staff quivered as it sunk in the earth; but soon the strong spear remitted its force, as it shook. Then hand to hand had the heroes closed; then with their swords had they urged the fight, but the Ajaces rushed in between. They parted the combatants, as they glowed to engage[258]. Avoiding the battle of the chiefs, the leaders of Troy retired; Hector, the great Æneas, and Chromius in form like the gods. They left Aretus," whom Automedon had slain, "in all his blood; mangled, torn, he lay on the ground. Automedon divested the slain of his arms; and glorying over the warrior thus, began: "This, at least, has lessened my grief for the fall of the son of Menætius; a part of the cloud of woe is dispelled, though less than his the renown of the slain."—"He spoke, and placed aloft in the car the bloody spoils of the hapless Aretus. Stained with gore are his feet and his hands. Like a lion the hero seemed, when drenched with the blood of some slaughtered bull[259].

"Again over the fallen Patroclus is kindled the dismal fight. Blue-eyed Pallas awaked the fierce strife. Inwrapt in a purple cloud she shot from heaven to the field. She entered the nations of Argos; she roused the soul of each chief to the fight. First she spoke to the son of Atreus, to Menelaus renowned in arms. A chief there was among the Trojans, Podes the son of Ætion; in wealth abounding, brave in war: the most honoured by Hector of all the warriors, who fought for Troy; his companion, his guest beloved: him, as he turned to flight, the yellow-haired Menelaus struck with his spear. Near the belt passed the eager steel: through and through rushed deadly the lance. Resounding he fell to the earth. The foe dragged the slain from his friends, to the deep ranks of

258. Id. ibid.   259. Hom. *Iliad.* lib. xvii.

the

the Argive powers [260]." But then Hector, encouraged by Apollo, " advanced to the front of the battle, gleaming bright in his burnished steel; then Jove took his dreadful ægis, he hung it forward a gleaming portent: all Ida he wrapt in a cloud. His bolts issued forth from the gloom, and awful rolled his loud thunders on high. The whole mountain he shook as he launched: he gave victory to Troy, and turned the Argives to flight [261].

" Not unperceived by magnanimous Ajax, by Menelaus renowned in arms, Jove had inclined the scale, and given the changing victory to Troy. With words like these began aloud Telamonian Ajax, " Would " that some friend were near to bear the tidings to the " great son of Peleus!—He I deem, knows naught " of our state: the mournful tale has not yet reached " his ear, that his friend beloved has fallen in the war, " Nor can mine eyes perceive a chief, a fit bearer of " news to Achilles. Oppressed with darkness we fight; " our steeds, ourselves are involved in clouds. O " Father Jove! remove the gloom; free from dark- " ness the sons of Argos:—restore the sun!—Give us " to see with our eyes: destroy us at least in the light! " as destruction seems good to thy soul [262]."—" He spoke, and Jupiter heard: he pitied the hero's tears: straight he dispersed the darkness, he removed the cloud from their eyes. The sun shone from his sky; the whole battle is covered with light [263]."

Then it was resolved to send Antilochus, prudent Nestor's magnanimous son, to the illustrious son of Peleus, to let him know, " that fallen beneath the hand of the foe, lay slain the most beloved of his friends." Meantime it was found necessary, to give up the idea

260. Id. ibid. 261. *Iliad.* lib. xvii.
262. Id. ibid. 263. Hom. *Iliad.* ubi sup.

of

of repelling the Trojans, and to attempt to carry off
the corse of Patroclus by flight. This desperate service
was undertaken by Meriones and Menelaus. "They
raised the corse in their arms: aloft they reared it with
all their force; loud swelled the shout of the Trojans,
when the Argives raised the body from the earth.
Right forward they rushed, like hounds pursuing a
wounded bear; but when the Argives turned their
face, the colour changed over their features through
fear. None sustained the fight for the corse of the
chief [264].

" Thus with spirit they bear amain the hero's corse
toward the ships of the Argives. Dreadful battle
swells behind them, with noise; like a fire which in-
vades, in its rage, the wide streets of well-peopled
towns. Sudden it bursts to sight; the lofty domes sink
dark in the broad-skirted flame. Resounding it spreads
along, beneath the force of the roaring winds; such the
horrid sound of bounding steeds, of men rushing forward in arms, when collected they poured on the flight
of the Greeks [265]. Behind the two Ajaces broke the
rushing tide of the foe. Yet the foe pursued amain.
Two godlike heroes led them on; Æneas, the great
son of Anchises, and Hector, illustrious in arms [266].

" Ah me! what change is this?"—cried Achilles,
as he sat alone near the lofty sterns of the hollow ships:
—" Why again fly the long-haired Argives?—Why
" turn they their flight to the ships?—Much I dread,
" that the deathless gods have fulfilled the mournful
" fears of my soul [267]."—" While thus he turned his
dismal thoughts, came Nestor's illustrious son. Wide
poured the warm tears from his eyes: he told at once

264. Id. ibid.   265. *Iliad.* lib. xvii.
266. Id. ibid.   267. Hom. *Iliad.* lib. xviii.

the

the mournful tale. On the son of warlike Peleus a
dark cloud of sorrow arose. He raised the ashes in both
his hands: he poured them on his head, and disfigured
his graceful face. To his garments the dark dust ad-
hered on every side. Large he is spread on the earth;
covering a wide space, as rolling he lies. He tears his
heavy locks with his hands. The captive maids issue
forth from their tents, the bright prizes he had gained
in war; which Patroclus had won in the field. Sad
in soul they issued forth. Their mournful voice arose
round the chief: they struck their white breasts with
their hands. Their lovely limbs were unbraced with
woe. Antilochus joined his grief to their tears: he held
the mighty hand of Achilles; for deep he groaned from
his inmost soul. He dreaded that the chief, in despair,
would raise the steel against his life [268]."

As soon as the son of Peleus had given vent to his
grief, he went, unarmed, to the trench beyond the wall
of the Grecian camp. " There standing he raised his
voice. When the Trojans heard, over their lines, the
brazen voice of the all-subduing Achilles, the souls of
all shrunk with fear in their breasts [269]. Back they
turned their sounding cars, presaging dreadful woes in
their souls [270]." Then the Greeks " placed on a bier
the mangled corse of the hapless Patroclus. His friends
beloved stood wailing around. They bore him away to

268. Id. ibid.

269. On this occasion Homer introduces the *simile* of the *trumpet;*
which certainly was not in use in Greece or Asia Minor, at the time
of the Trojan war, as he never mentioned it in any of the charges to
battle. Hence the merit he constantly ascribes to a *loud voice.* Yet
was he not unacquainted with the importance of that spirit-stirring
instrument; for he tells us, " so *shrilly loud arose the voice* of the
dauntless son of the car-ruling Peleus, as swells the sound on the
winds, when the clear voice of the trumpet ascends; when ruthless
foes surround with battle a town, and roll amain their whole force on
its walls." *Iliad.* lib. xviii.   270. Hom. *Iliad.* lib. xviii.

the

the ships. Great Achilles followed their steps. Warm poured the dark tears down his cheeks [271]."

This happened about sun-set; or, to use the mythical language of Homer, "Juno graceful, with large rolling eyes, now sent the unwearied sun, unwilling, to the waves of the main [272]. His splendid orb is sunk in the west. The godlike Argives cease from their toils: from the perils of the bloody fight; from the labours of all-equalling war. The Trojans, on the other side, removed themselves from the dismal fray, and loosed their rapid steeds from their cars. To council they all convened. Even before the repast was prepared, the council was standing held: none dare to sit down on the plain; for terror had seized the Trojan host, when great Achilles presented his form to view [273]." To them the prudent Polydamas began to raise his warning voice. Polydamas of Hector the faithful friend: on the same night were the heroes born: the former in council superior rose, the latter excelled at the spear. With soul devoted to the host, Polydamas thus began:

271. Id. ibid.

272. In JUNO, Homer seems *generally* to *personify* the *lower region of the heavens*, the atmosphere of our earth; and in JUPITER, the *ethereal region* or *higher heaven;* where reside the *seeds of fire*, and whence *Juno derived her generative power.* Hence the learned Blackwell remarks, "No wonder the *mighty agent* that keeps up the round of generation, should assume a thousand forms to accomplish his ends; and as little that the active mass which surrounds the globe, the AIR whose *elastic spring produces such convulsions* at the approach of FIRE, should be *frequently embroiled* with her imperious mate" (*Mythol*. Lett. xii.). But when Homer *adapts himself* to *vulgar apprehension*, he uses a *legendary language* suited to *vulgar prejudices*, and represents, by Jupiter and Juno, the *two great immortal beings* supposed by the Greeks to preside in the heavens; and thought to govern, in conjunction with the other deities, the affairs of men. I have formerly, however, had occasion to observe, and I here repeat the remark, That *physical* and *moral allegory* are so *blended*, in the writings of Homer, with *traditional fable*, that there is often no reducing his mythology to any *measure of common-sense*.

273. Hom. *Iliad.* lib. xviii.

" Weigh

" Weigh with caution our state, O friends! to every
" side send the thoughts of your souls. As for me,
" I advise to retreat; this instant to march to the
" town: for distant far we remain from our walls.
" Whilst Achilles retained his wrath; whilst he raged
" against Atrides, less heavy was the weight of the
" arms of the foe: the Argives were less dreadful in
" fight. I then rejoiced to pass the night near their
" dark hollow ships; my hopes then arose to conquest:
" in thought, I saw their navy destroyed. But now
" other terrors arise: much I dread the great son of
" Peleus. Fierce, impatient, is the soul of the chief.
" He will not his valour confine to the field, where
" the Trojans and Argives have long tried the equal
" fortune of Mars. For the city the hero will fight;
" for our wives, for our tender dames. Let us, there-
" fore, return to Troy: obey my voice! believe my
" words.

   " If ye will obey my words, though sore dismayed
" and mournful in soul, through the night we may, in
" council, provide for the defence of ourselves and
" Troy. Our lofty towers shall protect the town; our
" high gates repel the force of the foe: our gates fitted
" with massy planks, long, polished, and compacted
" with art. At morning our towers we will man, and
" stand in arms on our lofty walls. With disadvan-
" tage, if he comes, he shall fight: fruitless battle he
" shall urge round our town; again the chief will re-
" turn to his ships, after tiring his high-maned steeds
" in various circles round our walls. Though great
" his valour, he never will attempt to force our gates;
" he can never succeed[274]."

274. Id. ibid.

Hector treated this sage advice with disdain. "Poly-
" damas!" the hero said, "displeasing are thy words
" to my soul. Dost thou advise us to return, again
" to shut ourselves up within our walls?—Is it not
" enough, O friends! that so long we have been cooped
" in our towers?—But cease, imprudent man! dis-
" perse not thy fears through the host. Yet none of
" the Trojans will hear, I will not suffer them to hear.
" Listen all! attend to my words; let all obey the re-
" solves of my soul. Prepare the supper through the
" host; let the army, by their tribes, take repast.
" Remember the nightly guard! Watch all in your
" martial arms. At morning, with the earliest light,
" ranged thick, we shall wake the dreadful strife be-
" fore the hollow ships of the foe. If in truth the hero
" is roused, if Achilles descends to the fight, I shall
" not shun him in the field; I will oppose him hand to
" hand; or he shall mighty honour gain, or renown
" shall cover my spear[275]." Thus spoke the illustrious
Hector: the Trojans shouted over their host[276].

In consequence of this approved resolution, the
Trojans remained in arms on the field, and "took repast. But the Argives, throughout the long night,
raised the voice of grief for the fallen Patroclus. To
them the son of godlike Peleus, deep-groaning began
the woe. He laid his slaughtering hands on the breast
of his friend beloved; while, from the depth of his
soul, frequent broken sighs arose. "Vain was the pro-
" mise, ye gods!" exclaimed he, "which I made on
" that fatal day, when I confirmed in his lofty halls the
" soul of the hero Menætius. I told the hero, that to
" Opuntia his high-renowned son should return laden
" with his portion of spoil, after Ilion lay in ruins on
" the earth. But Jove fulfils not, in all, the hopes of

275. *Iliad.* lib. xviii.   276. Id. ibid.

aspiring

" aspiring man!—Yet since thee I survive, O Patro-
" clus! I will not cover thy corse with earth, till hither
" I shall bring in these hands the head of Hector.
" Twelve Trojan youths I will also slay, a bloody
" offering at thy pyre!—Meantime thou thus shalt lye
" in death, in mournful state before the ships. Around
" thy corse the daughters of Troy, and deep-bosomed
" Dardanian dames, shall over thee raise their mourn-
" ing voice. Night and day shall descend their tears.
" Our bright conquests in war shall mourn; the maids,
" whom in arms we acquired, while wealthy states
" fell subdued by our deadly spears[277]."

But as soon as " Aurora, clad in saffron robe, rose
bright from the ocean," Achilles, having got a new suit
of armour[278], " strode along the shore of the roaring
main,

---

277. Hom. *Iliad.* lib. viii. The Grecian chiefs seem to have been
great favourites with the Asiatic ladies; as they, though violently
seized by the blood-stained hands of the invaders of their country,
could not only reconcile themselves to their condition, but feel a fond
affection for the slayers of their husbands and brothers (Hom. *Iliad.*
passim.). It may also be observed, that the Grecian warriors, though
ferocious even to a degree of savage barbarity, were tender of their
female captives (Id. ibid.); and so much addicted to women, that
every chief had a kind of seraglio in his tent (*Iliad.* lib. ix. et seq.).
Even aged Nestor had his fair bed-fellow.

278. This armour is said to have been formed by Vulcan, *the workman divine!* and procured for, and presented to Achilles by his mother,
Thetis (Hom. *Iliad.* lib. xix.); probably because it was brought by sea
from Lemnos, where the limping god was fabled to have his forge, and
whence the Grecian army before Troy was supplied with wine (*Iliad.*
lib. vii. sub. fin.). And as whole fleets arrived at the Grecian camp
from that island (Id. ibid.), the Greeks would, no doubt, be furnished
with whatever the Lemnians could supply them. In exchange, some
gave brass, some steel; some the hides of oxen, some oxen themselves;
others purchased wine with slaves (Hom. *Iliad.* lib. vii. sub. fin.).
The sovereignty of Lemnos was then held by Euneus, the son of Jason (Id. ibid.); the friend, if not the kinsman of Achilles (Strabo,
Geog. lib. i. p. 45, edit. sup. cit.). If the island of Lemnos had not
been

main, and roused to council the heroes of Argos.
Dreadful rose the loud voice of the king. From wing
to wing the army heard. Even those that formerly remained remote from battle at the ships of the Argives; the pilots, who led them over the ocean; they,
who held the helms in the main; they, to whom the
stores were in charge; the dispensers of victuals and
wine: all these to the assembly repaired, as great
Achilles, who had so long abstained from fight, again
made his appearance [279]."

At the council, a reconciliation took place between
Achilles and Agamemnon. The presents formerly
proffered were delivered. "Seven tripods the Grecian
chiefs brought from the tent of Atrides," by his command, "twenty caldrons of burnished brass, and twelve
coursers unmatched in the race: they brought seven
bright-blushing maids, graceful in form, and expert in
female arts; the eighth was the blooming Briseis. Ulysses, preceding the other chiefs, bore ten talents of gold.
Behind in long order came, bearing gifts, the young
chiefs of the Argives. In the midst of the assembly
the whole treasure is placed [280]. Then rose the great
Agamemnon. Talthybius, endowed with voice divine,
held the victim-boar in his hands. Atrides drew forth
the knife, which always hung by the large sheath of his
deadly sword. He cut the bristles from the head of
the boar: with hands uplifted to Jove he prayed. All
the Argives sat in silence around. Beginning his
prayer, he said, eying the spacious face of the sky!

" Bear witness, O Father Jove! best and greatest
" of gods; hear, O Earth! O Sun, attend!—hear,

---

been famous in early times for the forging of metals, the Greeks
would not have degraded the Egyptian and Phœnician god, FATHER-
FIRE, the opificer of the universe, to the character of a blacksmith,
and made it his work-shop.

279. Hom. *Iliad.* lib. xix.   280. Id. ibid.

" ye

" ye furies, that dwell under ground, and punish per-
" jured mortals at death! that I laid not my hand in
" force on the charms of the stately Briseïs; that I as-
" cended not by persuasion her bed. Untouched she
" remained in my tents, unsullied are her beauties di-
" vine. If Atrides swears falsely in aught, may the
" gods heap on him the woes, that overwhelm the
" perjured in soul [281]."—Talthybius threw the victim,
with speed, in the vast stream of the hoary main.
Then Achilles arose, amid the Argives, and thus spoke
aloud:—O Father Jove! from thee are derived the
" weighty woes of mortal men. Nor had the son of
" Atreus ever moved my heart with his words, nor
" had he torn from my side the maid, but that Jove
" ordained it all. He decreed, by his councils divine,
" to urge so many souls of Argos to the goal of destruc-
" tive death.—But haste! partake the strengthening
" repast, that sudden we may issue to war [282]."

" He spoke, and the council dissolved. The chiefs
departed, each to his own hollow ship. But the magnanimous troops of Achilles took in charge the rich
treasure bestowed. The wealth they placed in the
hero's tents: they conducted to their place, the maids;
the coursers, to the stud of his steeds [283]." As soon
as this service was performed, and the whole army had
taken food and wine, "the Argives poured from their
ships on the plain; so thick, that to heaven ascends the
dazzling gleam from the brightly-burnished helmets of
men; from the bossy orbs of rattling shields, the firm
breast-plates, the steel-pointed spears. The crash of
touching arms is heard. The ground hoarsely groans
as the warriors move [284]!

281. *Iliad.* lib. xix.
283. Hom. *Iliad.* lib. xix.
282. Id. ibid.
284. Id. ibid.

" In

" In the midst of the martial host, Achilles arms himself. He grinds his teeth in his dreadful rage. His eyes flash, like two flames of fire. With wrath relentless his soul burns, and grief resistless pervades his heart. In his fury against the Trojans, he puts on his armour; the splendid work of the artist divine [285]!—First the beauteous greaves on his legs he drew [286], fastened before with silver clasps. The breast-plate on his breast he placed [287]: round his shoulders he threw his sword; beaming forth, with its studs of gold. Before him he reared his all-covering shield; large, solid, and strong over its round [288]. It sent its bright beams afar, like the broad orb of the moon. His strong helmet on his head he placed: like a comet it shone. Dreadful nodded the plumes of gold, which Vulcan had poured thick on the crest [289].

" The hero tried himself in his armour; whether it fitted his body aloft, or lay with ease on his manly limbs." And, finding it every where easy and firm, "he took from its place his father's spear; the long, heavy, strong javelin of Peleus, which none of all the Argives but

285. See note 278.

286. These greaves must have covered both the legs and thighs; for, otherwise the thighs would have been left entirely naked, as we find no other armour provided for them. And that the thighs of the Greeks and Trojans were not so exposed, appears almost certain, from the few wounds inflicted on them, though less perfectly secured by the shield than the belly. In what manner the armour of the legs and thighs, if in one piece, could be fitted for walking, is not my business here to inquire.

287. The breast-plate or cuirass, seems to have come as low as the belt or girdle, which secured the loins (*Iliad. passim.*). In the arming of Achilles no mention is made of the girdle. His vulcanian armour must, therefore, have been complete without it. But, like all the armour of those times, it seems to have been open at the back.

288. This shield, like that of Idomeneus, and those of some Trojan chiefs, was formed wholly of metal. I forbear to say any thing of the figures said to have been wrought upon it. These I consider as poetical ornaments. 289. Hom. *Iliad.* lib. xix.

Achilles

Achilles could wield in fight: the Pelion ash, which
Chiron gave to his sire. Automedon, and Alcimus
brave joined to the car the steeds. The studded bridles
are placed in their mouths: the reins extend behind,
to the well-compacted seat of the car. Seizing the
bright whip in his hand, Automedon leapt at once on
the chariot: behind bounded aloft great Achilles, ready
for war. Bright in his arms he stood like the beams
of the high rolling sun[290]. Around the son of Peleus
pour the Argives. The sons of Troy, on the other
side, form darkly on the rising ground[291].

A furious engagement took place[292], in which the
Greeks were victorious, and Achilles made dreadful
havoc among the Trojans. " He slew the flying as they
fled : the dark earth floated around with their blood.
The whole axle of his car is stained with blood : the
seat itself is drenched with gore ; as sprinkled it bursts,
on each side, from the feet of the coursers, from the
steel-surrounded orbs of the wheels. Aloft sat the son
of Peleus, eager to acquire renown. His invincible
hands, as he stretches them forth to deaths, are stained
with dust, with clotty blood[293]!"

In this bloody pursuit, Achilles slew many distinguished warriors ; and many more would have fallen
by his hand, if the rivers Scamander and Simois, had

---

290. Id. ibid.   291. Hom. *Iliad*. lib. xx. init.

292. This engagement was accompanied with a frightful uproar of
the elements, poetically called the battle of the gods. " Dreadful thundered, from above, the father of men and of gods. Beneath, Neptune
struck the earth with his waves; the mountains all shook their lofty
heads; streamy Ida trembled to its base; its cloudy summits nodded
on high. Troy tottered over all her walls: the navy shook, on the
rocking shore. Struck with fear was the king of the dead; lest Neptune, as he shook the huge world, should burst the earth, and lay
open to gods and men the secrets of his gloomy halls. *Iliad*. lib. xx.

293. Hom. *Iliad*. lib. xx.

not been suddenly swelled by a thunder-storm, accompanied with an earthquake, and choaked with the bodies of the slain. " He bounded with his spear in the stream of Scamander, or Xanthus : roused to wrath is the mighty god," to use the allegorical language of Homer; " furious he rears his high-swollen waves. From his channel he throws the dead; the bodies mangled by the steel of Achilles. These he threw, as he raged, ashore; loud bellowing, like an hundred bulls. The living he saved with his beauteous streams, forming around them a watery wall: but dreadful round great Achilles the troubled water swelled and roared. Leaning forward on his broad shield, he turned the current with the orb. But upborn are his feet by the stream. He seized a branchy elm in his hands; and issuing from the channel, with force, urged his flying steps over the plain. Nor yet desisted the river god : he reared his current above its banks; darkening its colour, his flood arose. He resolved to turn Achilles from fight, to save the Trojans from ruin and death[294], Loud roaring rushed along, with foam, with blood, with heroes slain, the purple wave of the Jove-descended stream[295] !"

The waters, however, having subsided, in consequence of the action of the sun, wind, sulphureous fire, and the clearing of the stream of Scamander of dead bodies, " Achilles hung forward on Troy. He slew the people, he slew the steeds. In the lofty tower of the Scæan gate the aged Priam trembling stood. He saw the large form of the son of Peleus, and before him the flying Trojans : broken, scattered, they fled over the plain. "Much I fear," said hé, "this dreadful chief will burst his way through our sacred walls.["] And he ordered the guards to hold wide-open the gates, to receive the flying troops. " Right to the city

294. *Iliad.* lib. xxi.   295. Id. ibid.

their

their way they held, parched with heat and whitened
with dust. They crowded with joy through the gates.
They breathed within their walls from toil. The whole
city is filled with the host[296]."

Having " cheared with cooling draughts their
souls," the Trojans " manned their battlements; leaning forward with their steel to the foe[297]." Hector
alone disdained to take refuge within the walls: he
took his station " before the Scæan gate[298]." Meantime Achilles, who had been engaged, under the burning heat of the sun, in pursuit of a chief that he could
not overtake, while the Trojans entered their gates[299],
" bright strode toward the city; blazing, like a baleful
star!—Him Priam beheld: forth broke, in mournful
accents, the aged king. He struck his head with uplifted hands: he shrilly raised his wailing voice, in en-
treaty to his beloved son; but his son stood darkly at
the gate. Much burned the soul of Hector, to mix in
fight with Achilles[300].

" O Hector !" said Priam, stretching forth his
withered hands, " stay not unsupported; meet not in
" fight this warrior, who in force excels thee far.
" Destructive chief!—would that he were as little
" loved by the gods, as by Priam!—Then bloody
" hounds his corse should soon tear, and vultures flap

296. Hom. *Iliad.* lib. xxi.   297. *Iliad.* lib. xxii.   298. Id. ibid.
299. So I understand his pursuit of Apollo, under the form of
Agenor. Smote by the piercing rays of the sun, and rendered almost frantic, Achilles pursued a Trojan warrior, or a phantom, far
beyond the line of battle, when his whole attention ought to have
been turned to the town. Hence the reproach of Apollo, in the true
spirit of ancient allegory. " To thee was not given to discern the
power divine in human form. Ceaseless fury has distracted thy soul !
—The enemy is lost to thy spear: safe-inclosed is the foe in his walls;
whilst thou in idle pursuit hast hither diverted thy speed." Hom.
Iliad. lib. xxii.   300. Id. ibid.

" round him their wings. A gleam of joy would arise
" on my heart, bitter sorrow would half quit my soul.
" Of many sons he me has deprived, of many gallant
" sons; or slain, or sold captives to distant isles. Two
" meet not now mine aged eyes, Lycaon and young
" Polydorus[301]. If wander their souls in the regions
" of death, sorrow will lie deep on my heart: much
" their hapless mother will mourn; but for thee a
" whole people will mourn! the Trojans defenceless
" and lost, shouldest thou yield thyself to death, sub-
" dued by the son of Peleus. Yet enter thou the wall,
" my son!—O save the Trojans, the Trojan dames;
" save thine own important life: give not to Achilles
" renown. Pity me, worn down with ills; pity, while
" yet my senses remain, pity an unhappy king! whom
" Jove, in the last extremity of age, has doomed to
" misfortune's bitterest woes[302]."

" Thus the aged monarch spoke in his grief. He
tore his hoary hair with his hands; but he changed
not Hector's mighty soul. Hecuba, his mother, raised
her parent voice; loud-wailing and drowned in her
tears. With one hand she laid her bosom bare, with
the other her breast exposed: "O Hector! my be-
" loved son," she said, " if ever with this parent-breast
" I settled thine infant cries, oppose these lofty walls
" to the rage of the ruthless foe!—Enter the gate, too
" daring chief! stand not to contend in arms with
" Achilles. Alas! shouldest thou fall by his hand,
" never shall these parent-eyes drench thee with tears
" on the mournful bier. Far, ah! far remote from
" her that bore thee, Hector! far remote from thy
" high-born spouse, thee hostile dogs shall tear, at the
" ships of the Argive powers[303]."

301. Both these Achilles had slain, since his reconciliation with
Agamemnon. Hom. *Iliad*. lib. xx. xxi.

302. *Iliad*. lib. xxii.   303. Id. ibid.

" Thus

" Thus addressed they the voice of woe, their suppliant voice to their son beloved: nor bent they Hector's daring heart. Resolved, he stands firm in his
place. He waits the near approach of the mighty
Achilles. Against a tower the hero leaned, on the
bright orb of his spacious shield. Indignant rolled his
thoughts within, and thus he spoke to his mighty soul:
" Ah! what course shall I take?—shall I enter this
" gate and these walls?—I dread the reproach of the
" Trojans, of the Trojan dames with sweeping trains;
" I dread the voice of cowardly men. Thus, perhaps,
" they will say in mine ear, Hector trusting to his
" strength," as he had rejected the advice of Polydamas, "lost his people, and his country destroyed!—
" Thus they will speak aloud; for me then it were
" better far, or to return, having slain Achilles; or,
" for the city to fall by his hands[304]."

" Whilst this he revolved in his soul, near him
advanced the great Achilles; like Mars, shaking high
his bright helmet. Over his right-shoulder, shook
aloft the Pelion ash: dreadful gleamed the brazen
point. All his dazzling arms shot flame, like the lightning of father Jove; like fire, that burns with ceaseless
rage; like the beams of the rising sun!—Mighty Hector, struck with fear at the sight, sustained not the
hero's approach. Leaving the lofty gate behind, round
the walls of Troy he fled. The son of Peleus darts
forward with eager speed, Hector quick-moves his
active limbs[305].

" Beyond the high watch-tower they passed; beyond the fig-trees, that resound in the winds. They
came to the river's copious source, to the two-fountains
of gulphy Scamander: one hot issues forth to the light,

304. Hom. *Iliad*. lib. xxii.   305. Id. ibid.

smoaking

smoaking as it rolls along! the other, even in summer, flows cold as hail or driven snow, or water congealed into ice. Into ample cisterns fall the streams; beauteous, wide, of marble formed. There the dames of the warlike Trojans; there their daughters, of splendid charms, used to wash their graceful robes, in the quiet season of peace, before the Argives came to Ilion [306]. Beyond these the heroes bounded amain. One fled, the other hung on his flight. Nor for the victim, nor for its extensive hide; nor for any wonted prize of the race, the heroes urged their rapid steps: they ran for the gallant soul of Hector, the breaker of steeds [307].

" As often as the son of Priam turned his long strides to the lofty Dardanian gates, when right forward he urged his course to the well-built Ilion towers; that his townsmen aloft, from the walls, might pour their flying darts on the foe: so often the great son of Peleus rushed between, and drove him afar; for he turned ever his steps near the wall of his much-loved town!—But Achilles gave a sign to his warlike troops: he suffered them not to launch their pointed shafts on the flying chief: lest another should share the renown which he wished wholly to enjoy [308]. When near each other the heroes came, bending forward with all their arms, Hector first silence broke, waving high his various helmet:—" No more, son of godlike Peleus," said he "I fly thy steps or decline the fight. Thrice round " the lofty city of Priam have I fled, nor sustained thy " rage; but now his soul bids Hector stop. I now " oppose thee, chief! in arms; determined to slay or " be slain. But let us call to witness the gods; for " they the best witnesses are: they are guardians of

---

306. Every particular in this circumstantial description, bears such strong marks of truth, that we cannot doubt but Homer copied it from nature, and drew his accompanying facts from authentic information.

307. Hom. *Iliad.* lib. xxii.   308. Id. ibid.

"oaths

" oaths and leagues. Thy corse I shall not dishonour
" in ought, should Jove grant success to my spear,
" and call forth thy soul round my steel. Stripping thee
" of thy beauteous arms, I shall restore thy corse to
" the Argives. This also do thou, Achilles[309]!"

" Sternly turning his eyes on the chief, the mighty
son of Peleus replied, " Hector, most detested of
" men! speak not of leagues to me. As faithful trea-
" ties can never subsist between mankind and beasts
" of prey; as the wolf and timid lamb can never
" agree: so no friendship, no compact, no league,
" can ever subsist between Hector and me. One or
" other, this instant, shall glut with his blood fierce
" Mars. Rouse then all thy knowledge in fight;
" shew thyself dauntless and firm; a warrior unyield-
" ing and strong."—" He spoke and threw his forceful
lance. Illustrious Hector beheld, and shunned the
gleaming point, as it came. Stooping forward, he
avoided the death: above flew resounding the spear;
and quivered as it sunk in the earth[310]. Minerva
drew the lance from the earth: she restored it to Achilles, unknown to Hector[311].

" The chief elated into hope, and thus addressed
the great son of Peleus: " Thou hast wandered from
" thine aim Achilles!—Now, in thy turn, avoid the
" brazen point of my deadly spear."—" He spoke, and
threw his mighty lance; nor strayed the bright point
from its aim. He struck the shield of Achilles; resulting flew the lance from the orb. Rage darkened

309. Hom. *Iliad.* lib. xxii.   310. Id. ibid.

311. It is difficult to say, what we should understand by this ma-
nœuvre; whether the address of Achilles in recovering his spear, or
the slight of some of the myrmidons, in secretly conveying it to
him. But it has much the appearance of fraud; and, in consequence
of it, Hector fought under great disadvantage.

the

the soul of the chief, that the spear had rushed in vain from his sinewy arm. He dejected in countenance stood, and thus desponding spoke: "Alas! the hour " of Hector is nigh. Near me hovers destructive fate: " No resource remains, no hope of escape!"—"This saying, his sword he unsheathed; his heavy sword, which hung loose by his side. High-bounding, he rushed on the foe, raising his beamy sword. Achilles, all-furious advanced: he filled his soul with savage rage: he stretched before his ample breast his high-wrought, solid shield. His four-coned helmet, with awful gleam, nodded high on the brows of the king. The mighty spear shook aloft in his hand. Eager wandered his eyes over illustrious Hector in search of a place for the wound. His beautiful body impervious remained; covered wholly with the brazen armour, which he had torn from the strength of the fallen Patroclus. A place, at last appeared to the chief, where the shoulder joins the neck, near the throat; where death enters with fatal ease. Through this Achilles drove, with mighty force, his spear. Through and through the neck, passed the eager point of the deadly lance. But the ashen spear divided not the windpipe in twain. The power of speech still remained to the unhappy chief[312].

"I entreat thee," said Hector, now languid and faint, " by thy own great soul!—by thy knees, by thy " parents beloved, not to leave me a prey to dogs at " the ships of the Argive powers. But receive thou " the rich stores of brass, receive high-valued gold; " which my father will lay at thy feet, my mother " now mournful in years. Restore thou my corse to " my house, that the Trojans and Trojan dames may " lay me, in death, on the pyre[313]."

312. Hom. *Iliad.* lib. xxii.   313. Id. ibid.

" To

" To him Achilles sternly replied, " Wretch! en-
" treat me not by these knees, by my parents revered
" and beloved: would that my fury and rage could sti-
" mulate my heart so far, as piece-meal to devour thee
" wholly; for the woes thou hast thrown on my soul.
" But none shall drive from thy corse the hungry dogs
" or birds of prey: no! should they lay at my feet ten,
" twenty-fold, the wealthy stores which Troy contains
" within her walls; and to their presents add the pro-
" mise of more, no! should Dardanian Priam weigh
" thy body against his gold; not for all should thy mo-
" ther revered weep over thee, laid in death on the
" lofty bier. But thee shall the birds of prey, and
" hungry dogs devour on the plain [314]."—" Well I
" know thee," dying Hector replied, " deaf to pity,
" implacable fierce; wholly steel is thy savage breast.
" But thou, inexorable chief! take heed; for me the
" wrath of some god may arise."—" Thus, as he
faintly spoke, the shades of death involved the hero.
His soul, heaving his graceful body, descended to the
regions below; mourning his untimely fate, his vigour,
his valour, his youth [315],

" To him, whilst even in death he lay, Achilles
thus spoke: "*Die thou!*—I shall receive my fate, when-
" ever it shall please the storm-ruling Jove, and the
" other immortal gods."—" He spoke, and withdrew
from the slain his spear. Apart he placed the bloody
lance, and loosed from the shoulders of the hero his
arms. The rushing Argives poured around him.
With wonder they surveyed the form, the awful beauty
of Hector!—Nor stood an Argive near the chief that
inflicted not a wound on the dead [316].

314. Hom. *Iliad.* lib. xii.　　　315. Id. ibid.
316. *Iliad.* lib. xxii.

" When

. " When Achilles had spoiled the dead of all his arms, he thus began, standing in the midst of the Argives.: " O friends! O leaders of Argos! princes " of the nations in arms! now as the gods have sub- " dued this man beneath my deadly spear; this man, " more destructive to Greece than all the sons of Troy " combined! now let us haste in our arms, let us at " once assail the town; that we may learn the state of " the Trojans, their present disposition of soul: whe- " ther, as slain lies their hero, they will abandon their " lofty city: or whether, though Hector has ceased to " live, they will still maintain it[317]."

This speech was dictated by sound policy; and if the council it offered had been followed, the Trojan capital, in all probability, would have been instantly taken. But the soul of Achilles was little under the government of political prudence. He soon recollected that, " at the ships lay the mangled Patroclus unburied. " Him I shall never neglect," said he, " while life " informs with motion my limbs." He, therefore, proposed that, instead of attacking Troy, " the youths " of assembled Achaia, singing pæans should return to " their ships."—" Let us drag the slain along," added he : " we are covered with mighty renown. We have " slain Hector; to whom the Trojans, over all their " state, paid their vows, as to a present god[318]."

" He spoke, and formed, in his wrathful soul, a deed unworthy of Hector. He bored his sinewy ancles behind, and through them inserted a thong. To the car he bound them aloft. The hero's head dragged along the ground. Placing the arms in the seat, Achilles ascended his car. He lashed his coursers to speed; not unwilling they flew over the plain. The sand rose in

---

317. Id. ibid.   318. Hom. *Iliad.* lib. xxii.

clouds

clouds around the dead; his dark-brown locks were trailed on the earth. His whole head, so graceful before! now lay involved, and soiled with dust. Great Jove had forsaken the chief: he gave him to the insults of foes: a sight of woe, in his native land[319].

"Thus soiled with earth, dragged Hector's graceful head. His mother tore her hoary hair from the roots: she threw afar her splendid veil; loud rose the screaming voice of her grief, when thus she beheld her son. Deeply groaned his father beloved[320]. The whole people raised one cry of woe: over the town spread one general lament!—Not greater could their sorrow have been, had lofty Ilion, wrapt wholly in flame, sunk down to its base in their sight[321]."

This consternation evinces the probability, that Achilles might have taken Troy, if he had led the Myrmidons immediately to the assault, on the fall of Hector. But he wasted so much time, in celebrating the funeral of Patroclus[322], that the Trojans had leisure

319. Id. ibid.

320. *Iliad.* lib. xxii. Andromache was not yet informed of the death of Hector. "But when she came to the tower, to the mournful troop of her friends, she stood wildly eying the field!—She beheld him dragged to the ships of the Argives. A sudden night obscured her soul; backward falling, she breathless remained. Wide poured from her graceful head the beautiful braids which bound her hair; the fillet, the net woven wreath; the veil that shaded her beauty!— the veil, which golden Venus gave, on the day illustrious Hector brought her blushing from the halls of Ætion, giving many nuptial gifts to her sire. Around her stood her sisters in tears. They held her raving in their hands, and eager for death through woe." Hom. *Iliad..* lib. xxii.

321. *Iliad.* lib. xxii.

322. Hom. *Iliad.* lib. xxiii. The description of this funeral abounds with many curious traits of ancient manners, customs, and opinions, which I shall afterward have occasion to notice. Here I shall only offer a few particulars, intimately connected with the history of the

sure to recollect themselves. He secretly sold the
body

Trojan war. "The Greeks loosed their bounding steeds from the
yoke. All convened around the ship of the godlike son of Peleus.
He furnished the splendid funeral feast, in honour of his friend beloved. Many snow-white fatted beeves are stretched on earth by the
force of the steel; many sheep are laid in death; many screaming
goats are slain; many boars with snow-white tusks, high fed, and
abounding in fat, are extended on spits before Vulcan's resounding
flame (Id. ibid.). But Achilles is conducted by the leaders of Argos to Agamemnon, the divine. Scarce persuaded, he moved along,
still raging in his soul for his friend. When they came to the lofty
tent of Agamemnon, the sovereign of all, the king commanded the
loud-voiced heralds to surround a mighty tripod with flame; and to
entreat the son of Peleus to wash the gore of foes from his hands.
Inflexible, the chief refused, adding a binding oath: " No, by al-
" mighty Jove! the greatest and the best of the gods, I will not ap-
" proach the bath ; nor water shall be poured on my hands till I place
" on the pyre Patroclus, till I strew these locks on the dead !—When
" those rites shall be performed, grief will lessen its weight on my
" heart. Yet now, though sad, the feast I will share with the kings.
" But thou, with early morn, O Agamemnon! command the host to
" bring the wood; to rear aloft the mighty pile! such as is fit to send
" the dead to the dark region of mournful death." Hom. *Iliad.*
lib. xxiii.

The wood was cut on mount Ida, and chiefly carried on mules.
When the huge pile they had reared, Achilles commanded all his
troops to cover themselves with bright arms; to join each his bounding steeds to the car. " Obedient, at once they arose. They cloathed
themselves in burnished steel. They mounted their chariots with
speed. Both the warriors and the drivers ascend. The cars moved
slowly before, behind a cloud of infantry moved. In the midst, his
most beloved friends bore the corse of the hapless Patroclus. With
their shorn locks they covered the dead. Last of all came Achilles,
bearing the head of his friend !—When they came to the destined
place, the great son of Peleus stood apart from the pile, and cut his
yellow locks amain; his golden locks, which he had nourished with
care" (Hom. *Iliad.* lib. xxiii.). " An hundred feet spread the pile
on each side. High on the top they laid the dead. Many fatted sheep
were slain, many beeves lay in death at the pyre. Stript of their
hides they lay. Achilles wraps with their fat the dead. From head
to foot involved he lay, the flayed carcases ranged on each side. He
placed jars of honey and oil, low bending over the lofty bier. Four
high necked steeds he threw in the pile. Of nine dogs that belonged
to the chief, he slew two to attend their lord. He transfixed, with
steel,

body of Hector to Priam[323]: and twelve days were allowed for the celebration of his funeral[324]. Before that
term was elapsed, the Trojans may be supposed to
have taken precautions for the defence of their city.
Achilles fell beneath its walls[325]; and the remaining
Greeks found much trouble in reducing it.

The particulars of the siege, after the death of
Hector, I shall not attempt to relate; as here Homer
fails us, the only author who can be depended on, for

steel, twelve youths, a bloody offering to the slain; twelve Trojans
of parents renowned! so dreadful was the wrath of his soul." Id. ibid.

323. *Iliad.* lib. xxiv. As soon as Priam had resolved to go, under
night, to the quarters of Achilles "from the bridal chamber they
bore, and placed aloft on the polished wain, the rich price of the
corse of Hector" (Id. ibid.). The several articles are thus enumerated: " twelve beauteous robes, the venerable monarch withdrew
from his stores; twelve single mantles, of ample size; twelve car-
pets, twelve beauteous cloaks; as many vests of glossy hue; ten
talents of the purest gold; two burnished tripods, and four caldrons.
A high-laboured bowl he produced; which Thrace, in solemn embassy, had bestowed on the sovereign of Troy: a mighty gift! but
this the aged king spared not within his lofty halls; for much he
wished, from his inmost soul, to redeem his son beloved" (*Iliad.* ubi
sup.). Achilles accepted the ransom (Id. ibid.); and it appears, that
he had not only saved the body of Hector from dogs, but preserved it
from corruption, in expectation of such a ransom (Hom. *Iliad.* lib.
xxiv. passim.). His dragging it round the tomb of Patroclus is no
contradiction to this remark.

324. That term Priam requested. " It shall be so," Achilles
replied: " Aged Priam! thy commands are obeyed. For so long
" I will hinder the fight, and grant the request of thy soul." *Iliad.*
lib. xxiv.

325. For so saying we have the general consent of tradition, and
the authority of Homer; who perpetually anticipates the death of
Achilles, and even hints at the manner of it (*Iliad.* passim.). But
the most pointed passage, in regard to that event, is found in the
speech of the ghost of Patroclus to the son of Peleus. " Me destruc-
" tive fate has involved," said (or seemed to say) the empty shade of
the chief;—" the fate appointed at my birth. Even over thee, O
" Achilles! hovers fate. Thou art destined to fall before the walls of
" the high-born Trojans." Hom. *Iliad.* lib xxiii.

what

what relates to the Trojan war[326]. It appears, however, from this venerable author, that Troy was taken in the tenth year of the war, and burnt, by the Greeks[327]. And that all the Trojans were slain, or carried into slavish captivity[328]. In a word, as passion, inflamed by the prospect of plunder, not policy, had dictated the Trojan war, every stage of it was marked with cruelty and blood. And the issue of the sanguinary enterprise proved almost alike fatal to the victors, and to the vanquished.

The Greeks, who survived the subversion of the kingdom of Troy, took no measures for establishing· dominion over the country they had conquered: they did not so much as attempt to settle a colony in any part of it. Having accomplished their vengeance, and recovered the wife of Menelaus[329], they embarked for Europe immediately after the division of the spoil[330]; and freed the remaining nations of Asia Minor from the terror of utter extirpation.

The

326. The farther progress of the siege may be seen in Virgil (Æneid. lib. ii.) and in Tryphiodorus (*Ilioy. Alosis*.); but as these authors lived too long after the Trojan war, to be regarded as historical evidence, I shall make no use of them here.

327. Hom. *Iliad.* lib. xii. xx.   328. *Iliad.* lib. xxiii. xxiv.

329. Hom. *Odissey.* lib. iv. Helen again appears with all the dignity of a queen in the court of Sparta (Id. ibid.); and although she affects the character of a penitent, we discover the wanton through the fine disguise. She declares that "her pleased bosom glowed with secret joy," when Troy was taken by the Greeks; and that she then was conscious of remorse and shame, for "the effects of that disastrous flame, kindled by the imperious queen of love, which forced her to quit her native realm" (Hom. *Odissey*, ubi. sup.): but she lays no blame on Paris. She respected Menelaus as a brave warrior, and a worthy and indulgent husband; but the libertine son of Priam was the man of her heart.

330. *Odissey*, lib. iii. Agamemnon, indeed, stayed to offer sacrifices to the gods, for his victory (Id. ibid.); and "half the Greeks respectfully obeyed the king of men" (Hom. *Odissey*, ubi sup.). But the most distinguished chiefs "unmoored at rising morn their ships, and

brought

The victorious chiefs were anxious to revisit their own dominions, where the greatest disorders had prevailed during their absence [331]. But from their ignorance of navigation; their eager desire of reaching their several homes by the nearest course, and the bad state of their vessels, many of them were shipwrecked: some were thrown on unknown shores; and scarce one of them entered his destined port, but after a tedious and disagreeable voyage [332]. On their arrival, several princes were obliged again to put to sea, in quest of new territories; their paternal dominions having been seized by usurpers, or occupied by invaders [333]. The fate of others was yet more deplorable.

Agamemnon, whose passage home appears to have been the quickest of any of the Peloponnesian chiefs, was murdered, soon after his return to Mycenæ, by his wife Clitemnestra, and her paramour Egisthus, who seated himself on the Argive throne [334]. But they were not suffered to enjoy in peace the fruits of their atrocious crime, or to indulge unmolested their guilty passion. Awful justice overtook them. A blow, from an unexpected arm, left mankind, in their punishment, a lesson to correct the dangerous example. Orestes, the son of Agamemnon and Clitemnestra,

brought their captives and their stores on board" (Id. ibid.). And Menelaus speedily followed them, and "joined their fleet in the Lesbian bay" (Hom. *Odissey*, lib. iii.). Nor did Agamemnon remain long behind. *Odissey*, lib. iv.

331. Hom. *Odissey*, lib iii. iv. Thucydid. lib. i. cap. xii.

332. Id. ibid. The wanderings of Ulysses are well known; and Menelaus, having lost his pilot (*Odissey*, lib. iii.), was driven on the coast of Egypt, where he was long detained by calms and contrary winds. Hom. *Odissey*, lib. iv.

333. Hom. *Odissey*, passim. Thucydid. lib. i. cap. xii.

334. Hom. *Odissey*, lib. iii. iv. xi.

who

who had fortunately escaped the sword of Egisthus, returned privately to Mycenæ, after an exile
of some years; and, in revenge of his father's
death, slew both the bloody usurper and traiterous
adultress [335].

By this signal act of vengeance, which put him in
possession of his father's dominions, and a marriage
with the daughter of Helen and Menelaus, Orestes
added the kingdom of Sparta to that of Argos and
Mycenæ [336]; and became the most powerful prince
that ever had reigned in Peloponnesus. He found it
necessary, however, in order to establish his character, and clear himself from the imputation of guilt,
in having laid violent hands on his own mother, to
submit his cause to the court of Areopagus at
Athens [337]. That famous tribunal gave a decree in
his favour [338], and all Greece was satisfied with the
equity of the decision.

The great power of Orestes, if not the vigour of
his administration, preserved his dominions from the
disorders that afflicted Greece, for sixty years after the
termination of the Trojan war; a period in which piracy and rapine universally prevailed, and when several states repeatedly changed masters [339]. That licentious spirit, however, began to subside; and order
and tranquillity were generally restored. But the return of the *Heraclidæ*, or descendants of Hercules,
into Peloponnesus, during the reign of Tisamenes,
the son of Orestes [340], threw all things again into

335. *Odissey*, lib. iii.
336. Pausan. lib. ii. p. 60, edit. sup. cit.
337. Pausanias, lib. i. p. 27.   338. Id. ibid.
339. Thucyd. lib. i. cap. xii.
340. Pausan. lib. ii. p. 60.

confusion

confusion in Greece; and entirely changed the face of affairs in that part of Europe, and also in Asia Minor.

This matter will require explication, my lord, and furnish subject for another letter.

LETTER

LETTER IV.

A GENERAL VIEW OF THE AFFAIRS OF GREECE FROM THE
FINAL INVASION, AND CONQUEST OF PELOPONNESUS BY
THE HERACLIDÆ, TO THE ABOLITION OF REGAL POWER
AT ATHENS; WITH AN ACCOUNT OF THE SETTLEMENT
OF THE GRECIAN COLONIES IN ASIA MINOR.

PART I.

WE have formerly seen[1] in what manner
Hercules was excluded the succession to the kingdom of Mycenæ, by the selfish policy of his grand
uncle Sthenelaus, who gave the princely inheritance to
his own son, Eurystheus. The toils and perils to which
Eurystheus exposed this hero, in hopes of getting rid
of so dangerous a rival, are well known under the
name of the *labours of Hercules.* The reputed son of
Jove, however, surmounted every difficulty. But not
being proof against the shafts of fate, he died in great
agony about the fiftieth year of his age, in consequence of a poisoned shirt, ignorantly sent him by
his wife Deïaneria, and left behind him many children
by various mothers[2].

The children of Hercules were reared by different
princes, who respected the memory of their father:
but his legitimate sons solely by Ceix, king of Tra-
shine. Unfortunately, however, the generous guardianship of Ceix, and the youthful valour of the sons of
Hercules, awaked the jealousy of Eurystheus, who
threatened to make war upon that prince, should he

1. Lett. II.   2. Apollod. lib. ii. Diod. Sicul. lib. iv.

yield

yield them any longer an asylum at his court[3]. The
Heraclidæ saw the necessity of quitting Trachine ; and,
in this extremity of their affairs, they applied for protection to all the states of Greece. Athens alone
durst afford them shelter[4]. Eurystheus led an army
against that city. He was met by the Heraclidæ,
supported by the Athenians, and commanded by Hyllus, the eldest son of Hercules by Deianeira, and by
Theseus, king of Attica. The two armies joined battle, and Eurystheus was defeated and slain[5]; in consequence of which events, the kingdoms of Argos and
Mycenæ passed, as formerly noticed[6], from the family
of Perseus into that of Pelops.

Elated with their success, the Heraclidæ entered
Peloponnesus. There they were joined by a number
of adherents, and made themselves masters of many of
the capital towns and districts in that peninsula[7]. But
these conquests were soon abandoned. the country
being afflicted with a desolating plague, the Heraclidæ
consulted the Delphic oracle, in regard to the means
of putting a stop to so terrible a calamity. The Pythia
or priestess replied, that in order to avert that calamity, they must desist from their enterprise, but might
renew it after three crops[8]. they obeyed, and returned at the end of three years, which they conceived to
be the time fixed by the oracle.

Atreus, the eldest son of Pelops, who had succeeded Eurystheus, his father-in-law, in the kingdoms of Argos and Mycenæ, collected a strong force
to oppose the invaders[9]. When the armies of the
two parties came within sight of each other, Hyllus,

3. Id. ibid. 4. Issocrat. *Panathen.*
5. Apollod. lib. ii. Diod. Sicul. lib. iv. Strabo, lib. viii.
6. Lett. II. 7. Apollod. et Diod. ubi sup.
8. Id. ibid. 9. Diod. Sicul. lib. iv.

the leader of the Heraclidæ, proposed to decide the dispute by single combat, in order to save the effusion of blood. The offer was accepted, and a regular agreement made, That, if Hyllus was victorious, the Heraclidæ should immediately enter into possession of the contested kingdoms; but, if he was vanquished, that neither he, nor any of his kinsmen, should return into Peloponnesus for an hundred years. Hyllus was slain by the champion of Atreus, and the Heraclidæ withdrew according to treaty[10].

The descendants of Hercules, however, never lost sight of their hereditary claims. The recovery of their rightful inheritance, and even the conquest of the whole Grecian peninsula, continued to occupy their thoughts, and to fill their ambitious hearts with hope amid the wilds of Oeta and Parnassus, where they had obtained the rocky district of Doris: and at the expiration of the stipulated number of years, Temenus, Cresphontes, and Aristodemus, great grandsons of Hyllus, having collected a formidable body of Dorian and Ætolian followers, invaded Poloponnesus by sea[11].

Tisamenes, the son of Orestes, at that time king of Argos and Lacedæmon, attempted to dispute the pretensions of the Heraclidæ, but without effect. He was vanquished in battle, and the gallant invaders made themselves instantly masters of his dominions[12]. Corinth, Elis, and Messenia, also submitted to their arms[13].

Having now no enemy to contend with, the Heraclidæ, according to the custom of the times, di-

---

10. Pausan. lib. ii. Diod. Sicul. ubi sup.
11. Pausan. lib. iii. Strabo, lib. viii.   12. Apollod. lib. ii.
13. Pausan. et Strabo, ubi sup.

vided

vided their conquests by lot. The kingdom of Argos
fell to the share of Temenus: Cresphontes obtained
the territory of Messenia; and Laconia was set apart
for Eurysthenes and Procles, the infant sons of Aristodemus, who had died in the course of the war[14]. Elis
was given, by the surviving leaders, to an Ætolian
chief named Oxylus, who had contributed to the success of their enterprise. They bestowed Corinth on
Aletes, one of their kinsmen; and they spared Arcadia for friendly reasons; Cresphontes having married
Merope, the king's daughter[15].

Such of the subjects of Tisamenes, as discovered a
resolution to maintain their independency, were politically permitted by the Heraclidæ to settle in the maritime district, which afterward became famous under
the name of Achaia. The rest were driven into exile,
or reduced to slavery; and their possessions were
divided among the Dorian and Ætolian adventurers,
who claimed them as the reward of their valour[16].

Thus did the descendants of Hercules recover their
rightful inheritance, and the sovereignty of Peloponnesus return from the family of Pelops to the blood
of Perseus. Nor did that peninsula alone feel the
effects of this revolution. The Grecian states and
countries beyond the Corinthian isthmus, suffered almost equally with those within it, from the return of
the Heraclidæ, as the Dorian conquest of Peloponnesus
is commonly called. The people first dispossessed,
threw themselves upon their neighbours; and they, in
their turn, carried desolation into more distant territories. The stronger every where drove out the weaker.
Like the waves of an agitated sea, the Grecian tribes

14. Apollod. lib. ii. Pausan. lib. ii. Strabo, lib. viii.
15. Pausan. lib. iv.   16. Issocrat. *Panathen.* et in *Archidam.*

shocked

shocked upon one another, in continual succession, for almost half a century [17].

During that turbulent and fluctuating period, when all security of possession was lost, and consequently all attachment to country, the first Grecian colonies in Asia Minor were planted. A body of Ionians, originally established in Attica, but afterward settled in Peloponnesus, had there remained in tranquillity till the last invasion of the Heraclidæ; when the Achæans being driven from the territory of Laconia, fell upon them, and forced them to quit that peninsula [18]. They sought refuge in Attica, their former country. But finding, in a course of years, the lands assigned them insufficient to support a growing population, they embarked with some Athenian adventurers; and landing on the coast of Asia Minor, between the river Hermus and the promontory of Posideion, took possession of a district then bounded by Lydia and Caria; and which, in succeeding times, was from them called IONIA [19]. There they built Ephesus, Miletus, Teos, Colopon, Clazamena, Smyrna, Phocæa, and other cities [20]. They also took possession of the islands of Chios and Samos, which were included in the Ionian confederacy.

Ant. Ch.
1184.

The establishment of this colony had been preceded by other settlements on the Asiatic coast, scarce less famous in history. A body of Ætolians, having been driven from their possessions in Peloponnesus by the Dorians, who accompanied and supported the Heraclidæ in their conquest of that peninsula, found them-

17. Strabo, lib. ix. Pausan. lib. v. vii.   18. Id. ibid.
19. *Parian. Chron.* Epoch. xxvi. Pausan. lib. vii. Strabo, lib. xiv.
20. Id. ibid. Smyrna was originally built by the Ætolians, but afterwards destroyed, and rebuilt by the Ionians. Herodot. lib. j.

selves -

selves obliged to look out for new lands. They accordingly put themselves under the conduct of Penthilius, one of the sons of Orestes, who had taken refuge in the island of Euboea; and after rambling, for some time, unsuccessfully over the northern provinces of Greece, under his command, they crossed the Hellespont under his son Echelatus, and settled on the coast of Asia Minor, between Ionia and Mysia[21]. There gradually extending their population, from the river Hermus to the Hellespont, they gave to that maritime district the name of Æolia. In Æolia stood Cume, Lampsacus, Abydos, Larissa, and many other celebrated cities[22].

A third colony passed from Greece into the Lesser Asia during the same restless period. It was composed of a body of Dorians, who had been put in possession of the district of Megara by the Heraclidæ. Seized with the roving spirit of the times, and hard pressed by the Athenians, the greater part of the Dorians quitted that territory, and seated themselves in a promontory of Asia Minor, between Lycia and Caria, to which they gave the name of *Doris*, or DORIA[23]. There they founded Halicarnassus, Cnidus, and several other cities. They also spread themselves into Rhodes, Cos, and the smaller contiguous islands[24].

As these emigrations were made about the time the republican spirit began to predominate in Greece, the adventurers carried with them the same spirit into their new territories. And that spirit, which taught the Asiatic Greeks bravely to spurn the chains of oriental despotism, may be said not only to have saved

---

21. Strabo. lib. ix. xiii.   Vell. Patercul. lib. i.
22. Herodot. lib. i.   Strabo, lib. xiv.
23. Strabo, lib. xiv.   Pausan. lib. vii.   24 Id. ibid.

their

their mother-country from becoming a province of the
Persian empire, but eventually to have subjected Asia
to the sword of Alexander.

Though the Grecian cities in Asia Minor and the
contiguous islands, like those on the European continent, were frequently governed by ambitious citizens,
who, under the odious name of *tyrants*, had usurped
the supreme power, the basis of their interior policy
was every where republican; each city having its senate
and popular assembly. They had also their general
assemblies, where affairs of national importance were
discussed. The delegates of the Ionian cities, as we
shall have occasion to see, met in the Panionian council; and the Æolian and Dorian cities had assemblies of
a similar nature. Every public measure, in a word,
wore the appearance of freedom in Asiatic Greece,
however much particular states might be oppressed
with civil tyranny.

These observations naturally lead me to speak of
the abolition of royalty among the Grecian states in
Europe; and to notice the most remarkable circumstances with which that general revolution was attended.

The monarchical government which, in early times,
universally prevailed in Greece, was extremely limited.
The king or the head of the tribe, being no more than
chief magistrate of the state, or rather the most eminent citizen in the community, could take no resolution but in conjunction with the heads of the principal
families; nor adopt any public measure without consulting the body of the people[25]. But moderate as

25. Arist. *Polit.* lib. iii. Diod. Halicarnas. lib. v. Homer, Odyss.
lib. viii.

that

that government appears to have been, it was always considered as an irksome restraint upon the volatile genius and ardent temper of the Greeks, which strongly tended toward democracy[26]. And no sooner had the invasion of the Heraclidæ disturbed the regular order of succession, and consequently weakened the respect for regal authority, than the slightest incident was laid hold on to introduce the desired change; or even the smallest approach toward it, in hopes of at last perfecting the plan of equal freedom and independency. Kingly government, which had in many places degenerated into tyranny, was accordingly abolished, by degrees, in every Grecian state except Lacedæmon.

Two events, preparatory to this change of government, are not a little interesting, exclusive of the consequences by which they were followed.

A quarrel having arisen between the Thebans and and Athenians concerning the possession of a frontier town, the armies of the two nations were preparing to decide the dispute by a general engagement, when Xanthus, king of Thebes, proposed to settle the matter by single combat; in order to save the loss of lives as a great number of men must otherwise fall on both sides. But Thymætes, king of Attica, though of the blood of Theseus, declined the hostile competition. He was deposed, in consequence of his cowardice; and the Athenian sceptre was given to a Messenian prince named Melanthus, who had bravely accepted the challenge, and slain the king of Thebes[27].

The Thebans were deeply mortified at the death of their king; an incident which, joined to a long train

26. Homer, Iliad. lib. xvi. Plut. *Vit. Theb.*
27. Strabo, lib. ix. Pausan. lib. ix. Polyæn. *Stratag.* lib. i.

of

of misfortunes that had afflicted their sovereigns, gave them a strong aversion against regal power, at the same time that it afforded them an opportunity of indulging their passion for freedom. They accordingly adopted a republican form of government[28]; resolved that their happiness and misery should no longer depend upon the good or ill-fortune of any one family, or their liberties on the will of any one man.

But the Thebans, in abolishing royal authority, lost their political consequence. A long night of obscurity involved Bœotia. It was split into many petty republics, among which a kind of confederacy subsisted; but which were jealous of each other's prosperity, and often hostile to the general interest[29]. The Athenians were more fortunate in their change, of government. And that change, which took place soon after the foregoing, was occasioned by a similar circumstance.

The Heraclidæ, after the conquest of Peloponnesus, saw with a jealous eye the growing power of Athens, under Melanthus. He had afforded refuge to a number of Ionian and Messenian fugitives, expelled the Grecian peninsula by the Dorians, and still thirsting for revenge. No sooner, therefore, did the descendants of Hercules find themselves firmly seated in their new territories, than they declared war against the Athenians[30]. Codrus, the gallant son of Melanthus, then filled the throne of Attica. His heroic valour was equal to the defence of his country, but the superstition of the times gave a new direction to his patriotism. The Heraclidæ having consulted the Delphic oracle concerning the success of their enterprise, had received for answer, " That the

28. Pausan. lib. ix.   29. Pausanias, ubi sup.
30. Strabo, lib. ix. Justin, lib. ii.

" party

" party whose leader should be slain by the enemy, " would prove victorious." In consequence of this response, they issued, at the head of their army, an express order, that none of their men should kill the king of Athens [31].

Informed of that order, and also of its cause, Codrus generously resolved to sacrifice himself for the safety of his people. The love which they bore to their prince made them keep a watchful eye over him, suspecting his patriotic purpose. In order to elude their affectionate vigilance, as well as to deceive the enemy, he cloathed himself in the habit of a peasant; entered the hostile camp in that mean disguise, with a faggot on his shoulder, and a pruning-hook in his hand; provoked a quarrel with a soldier; smote him, and fell by the sword of his humble antagonist [32].

The tumult occasioned by the death of Codrus produced inquiry. His body was known. And the Heraclidæ believing on the equivocal response of the oracle, that nothing but misfortune could now attend their undertaking, they withdrew their forces without hazarding a battle [33].

The pious patriotism of Codrus, in leaving Attica without a king, furnished the Athenians at once with a pretext for abolishing monarchy, and an occasion of indulging their violent love of liberty, by establishing a commonwealth. Disposed, as they pretended, to give that generous prince a successor in the throne, but unable to find one worthy of such honour, they declared Jupiter alone to be thenceforth sovereign of Athens [34].

31. Id, ibid.   32. Pausan. lib. vii. Val. Max. lib. v.
33. Id. ibid.   34. Pausan. lib. vii. Strabo, lib. xiv.

They

They chose, however, Medon the eldest son of Codrus their chief magistrate, under the name of *Archon*, and declared, that this high office should remain hereditary in his family; but that he and his successors should be accountable to the assembly of the people, for the due administration of public affairs [35].

The government of Sparta also experienced a change in this age of innovation. Eurysthenes and Procles, the two sons of Aristodemus, to whom the kingdom of Lacedæmon fell, in the distribution of the conquests of the Heraclidæ, instead of dividing the territory of Laconia between them, or reigning alternately, like some Grecian sovereigns in ancient times, were persuaded to reign jointly, and with equal power. They accordingly chose the city of Sparta as their common capital or seat of government; each of them bearing the title of *king of Lacedæmon*, and being acknowledged as such [36].

But although royal authority was thus fully established at Sparta, in the descendants of Aristodemus, and subsisted in both branches of the reigning family, for seven hundred years, the state soon felt the enfeebling effects of divided sway [37]. Each of the kings, in order to strengthen his administration, found it necessary to court the favour of the people. This competition made the people too sensible of their importance; and eventually gave birth to the most daring licentiousness, upon which there was no curb. Anarchy the worst of tyrannies, proved the consequence of unbridled liberty. The kingdom of Lacedæmon was continually split, into two factions, which frequently came to blows. Even royal blood had been spilt, in these popular tumults [38]; and all the springs of govern-

35. Id. ibid.   36. Pausanias, lib. iii.
37. Plut. *Vit. Licurg.* Strabo, lib. viii.   38. Plut. ubi sup.

ment

ment seemed to be dissolved, when the wisdom and
virtue of one man gave compactness and vigour to the
political machine.

Your lordship will readily perceive, that I allude to
the illustrious Lycurgus. The establishment of the
institutions of the Spartan legislator forms a memorable
æra in the history of Greece. But before we enter
upon the investigation of that subject, which will open
to our view many important objects of inquiry, and
lead us to speculations of great moment in the science
of human affairs, I must make a pause.

LETTER

PART I.

THOUGH Greece, as we have had occasion to see, was peopled by colonies from various countries, government and manners, in all its different states, were nearly the same during the heroic ages. This similarity continued till after the conquest of Peloponnesus by the Heraclidæ. Then the republican spirit, which every where sprung up, gave diversity to government, and government had a necessary influence upon manners. The change, however, was hardly perceptible for a while. That variety, and even contrast of manners, which prevailed among the Greeks in later times, beyond what has been known among any other people, ancient or modern, bearing one common name, and speaking the same tongue, was little obvious until the laws of Lycurgus began to produce their effect upon the character and manners of the Lacedæmonians, and those of Solon upon the temper and spirit of the Athenians.

These reflections naturally lead us to inquire after the origin of the institutions of the Spartan legislator, as an introduction to the subsequent part of the history of that celebrated state.

Lycurgus

Lycurgus, son of Eunomes king of Lacedæmon, the fifth in descent from Procles, and the tenth from Hercules, is said to have succeeded to the joint sovereignty on the death of his elder brother Polydectes, and in the seventh year of the reign of his colleague Archelaus. His virtues and talents gave promise of a just and able administration. But an unexpected, though natural circumstance, deprived his countrymen of that hope, and involved himself in a variety of difficulties. The widow of Polydectes declared herself pregnant. Yet more ambitious to retain the honours of a queen, than desirous to experience the tender cares of a mother; inflamed with amorous passion, or unwilling to suffer the neglect of widowhood, she secretly intimated to the new king, That, if he would agree to marry her, no child of his late brother should ever disturb him in the possession of the Spartan throne [1].

Lycurgus, who had laid aside the ensigns of royalty, and assumed the title of *protector*, as soon as he was made acquainted with the queen's pregnancy, thought it prudent to conceal his abhorrence of her atrocious purpose. He seemed even to enter into her views; begged that she would take nothing that might injure her health, or endanger her life; for he would so concert matters, that the fruit of her womb should be no bar in the way of their mutual wishes. And having thus quieted her anxiety on that delicate point, he took care, when the time of her labour drew nigh, to place trust-worthy servants about her person, with strict orders, that if she brought forth a son, they should convey the child instantly to *him;* but, if a daughter, to leave the infant with her women [2].

1. Plut. *Vit. Licurg.*   2. Id. ibid.

The

The politic and generous protector was supping with the principal Spartan magistrates, when the queen was delivered; and the child, proving to be a son, was presented to him according to his commands. He took the boy in his arms, and said, addressing himself to the magistrates, "Spartans! a king is born to you;" then placed the infant prince in the royal seat, and named him *Charilaus*, or "the people's joy;" in allusion to the pleasure expressed on the occasion, by the company, at his own wise and liberal conduct, rather than at the birth of a king [3].

Generous and wise, however, as the conduct of Lycurgus was, and high as it placed him in the esteem of all good men, it failed to dissipate the dark suspicions raised by his enemies, and infused into the minds of the corrupted populace. Their selfish hearts, incapable of feeling the disinterested sentiments by which he was actuated, ascribed his magnanimous prudence to sinister motives. They imputed to him a design upon the liberties of the state [4]. In order to belie these suspicions; to avoid the resentment of the slighted queen, by whose adherents they had been excited; and fully to vindicate the honour of his character, Lycurgus condemned himself to a voluntary banishment.

Whether this sage patriot had conceived, before his departure from Sparta, the idea of reforming the constitution of his country, antiquity has left us to conjecture. We are only told, on good authority, that he visited Egypt and Crete [5], where government and legislation were supposed to have attained the highest degree of perfection. And it appears, from his institutions, that he must have carefully studied the

3. Plut. ubi sup.   4. Id. ibid.
5. Plut. *Vit. Lycurg.*

Egyptian

Egyptian polity, and that the Cretan constitution was the model after which he framed the Spartan.

While Lycurgus was contemplating that famous system of government, the work of the elder Minos (which we have formerly had occasion to consider[6]), and storing his mind with political maxims, the kingdom of Lacedæmon was a prey to internal dissensions. The people were turbulent, and the magistrates without authority. Even regal sway was set at naught, by the licentious multitude. Archelaus was a weak prince, Charilaus a minor. All subordination was lost, and lawless anarchy reigned triumphant.

These disorders made the Spartans severely sensible of the value of their late protector; who, during his short but vigorous administration, had restored domestic tranquillity. They accordingly sent deputies to solicit his return[7]; indirectly declaring themselves willing to submit to any body of laws, which he should think necessary for the reformation of the state. All orders of men joined in the request[8].

After having received several embassies to this purpose, Lycurgus returned to Sparta! and, in compliance with the general wish of his countrymen, assumed the high character of legislator. But he found, on entering upon this arduous and dangerous office, more obstacles to surmount than his sagacity had foreseen; more changes to effect, and consequently more prejudices to combat. He discovered that, instead of some partial innovations it would be necessary to new-mould the constitution of the state, in order to accomplish the desired reformation[9]. With that view, he boldly digested his celebrated political system; which had for

Ant. Ch.
1784.

---

6. Lett. II. of this work.　　7. Plut. *Vit. Lycurg.*
8. Id. ibid.　　9. Plut. ubi sup.

its object the perfecting of government, by an equal
division of power and of property.

The Spartan legislator, however, aware of the difficulty of establishing institutions, which would militate
so strongly against the selfish and voluptuous passions
of man, bethought himself of a happy expedient for
silencing all opposition. Well acquainted with the influence of superstition upon the human mind, and
with the awe inspired by divine authority, he went to
the oracle of Apollo at Delphos, before he made
known to his fellow-citizens that plan of government
which he meditated, and fully opened his purpose to
the sooth-saying god. The pythia saluted him with
the title of " *companion of the gods!* and rather god
than man;" assured him that Apollo was propitious to
his undertaking, and that the state which he should con-
stitute, under the auspices of the prophetic divinity,
would prove the most illustrious in Greece[10].

Ant. Ch.
1784.

Fortified with this famous response, Lycurgus gave
the name of RHETRÆ to his institutions; thereby in-
sinuating, that he had received them from the oracle[11].
And having thus added the voice of heaven to the
veneration of his country, he proceeded without obstruction to the execution of his plan. His first and
grand step toward a new constitution was, the establishment of a senate; in order to maintain an equili-
brium of power between the Lacedæmonian kings and
people, and to repress the usurpations of either. This
senate consisted of twenty-eight members, chosen by
the legislator from among the leading men, in whom
he could most confide. But the future election of
senators, who commonly held their seats during life,
was committed to the assembly of the people[12].

10. Plut. *Vit. Lycurg.*   11. Id. ibid.
12. Arist. *Polit.* lib. ii. Xenoph. *Rep. Lacon.*

The

The Spartan government, after the establishment
of the senate, was, properly speaking, neither monarchical, aristocratical, nor democratical, but mixed,
like the British constitution; a compound of all
the different forms. The two kings remained, but
their sway was very limited. They were only the first
citizens in the state[13]. They had, however, the power
of peace and war; were entitled to receive ambassadors, and entrusted with the superintendence of religion[14]. As commanders in chief of the armies of the
republic, they had the honour of leading the van, in
all military expeditions, and of bringing up the rear
on their return[15]; and beside being first served at the
public meals, each had a double portion of victuals assigned him[16].

The kings of Lacedæmon, among their other prerogatives, enjoyed that of being perpetual presidents
of the senate: and the importance of this prerogative
was not small. The senate alone had the right of proposing and investigating public measures. No debate
on any such subject could originate in the assembly of
the people. But to the people belonged the power of
deliberating on the resolutions of the senate, and of
ultimately sealing with approbation, or putting a negative upon every such resolution[17].

The Spartan senate, however, notwithstanding that
check upon its proceedings, was found to possess too
extensive powers, and to lean too much toward regal
authority. In order to counteract this dangerous tendency, and effectually counterbalance the preponder-
ation of the aristocratical part of the constitution, Lycurgus constituted the ephori[18]; five annual magi-

13. Id. ibid.   14. Herodot. lib. vi.   15. Id. ibid..
16. Herodot. ubi sup. Plut. *Vit. Lycurg.*
17. Xenoph. *Rep. Lacon.* Plut. ubi sup.
18. Herodot. lib. vi. Xenoph. ubi sup.

strates,

strates, whose proper business it was to protect the rights of the people, and watch over the administration of government[19]. These magistrates were chosen by the people in full assembly, and generally from among the most vigilant citizens[20].

The privileges of the ephori were many; and their controuling power was so strong, that it might be called the bridle, and they themselves, by their combining and invigorating influence, the sinews of the Spartan state[21]. To them it belonged to convoke, prorogue, and dissolve, the less and greater assemblies of the people; the former composed of the inhabitants of the capital, the latter of the free inhabitants of the country, including its several towns and villages. They could expel, imprison, and even punish with death, any obnoxious senator[22]. They monthly exchanged with the kings, whom they could fine or put under arrest, solemn oaths of fidelity: the kings swearing, in their own name, to govern according to the established laws and customs; and the ephori, in the name of the people, to support the authority, and protect the persons of the princes of the blood of Hercules, while they should so reign and rule[23].

Such was the system of government founded by Lycurgus at Sparta; a system which, although composed of seemingly discordant parts, remained longer entire, than the constitution of any other Grecian state. This permanency it chiefly owed to that equitable distribution of power, which it contained; and which, by a happy temperament, kept alive the jealous spirit of liberty, without suffering the shocks of the dæmon of anarchy. The vigour, and even the union of the Spartan state, was preserved, according to the

---

19. Plato, de *Leg.* lib. iii.   20. Arist. *Polit.* lib. ii.
21. Xenoph. et Plato, ubi sup.   22. Xenoph. *Rep. Lacon.*
23. Id. ibid.

intention

intention of the legislator, by the perpetual emulation and competition that animated the breasts of its citizens; and which may be called the *two brands*, by which their public virtues, their courage, and patriotism, were kindled and fed with fire.

From the equitable distribution of power, Lycurgus proceeded to the more equal division of property; aware that no people, how well balanced soever their government, can long retain either liberty or independency, unless some sense of national dignity and personal equality inform the mind of every free citizen. Property, in the kingdom of Lacedæmon, was then very unequally shared. A large proportion of the people had truly no honest means of subsistence[24]. The rich wallowed in abundance, while the necessitous, if not predatory poor, were at once debased and oppressed[25].

In order to remedy these evils, Lycurgus, after numbering the people, divided the whole territory of Laconia into thirty-nine thousand equal shares; nine thousand of which he appropriated to the citizens of Sparta, as their particular domain; and the remaining thirty thousand shares, he assigned to the inhabitants of the country[26]. Desirous yet farther to abolish the distinctions of rich and poor, but sensible of the impracticability of a division of moveable property, the Spartan legislator prohibited the use of gold and silver coin; called in, as far as possible, all that was in circulation; and ordered that thenceforth iron money, which he took care to get stamped and issued, should only be received in payment of any debt, or as the value of goods[27].

24. Plut. *Vit. Lycurg.*   25. Id. ibid.
26. Xenoph. *Rep. Lacon.* Plut. *Vit. Lycurg.*
27. Id. ibid.

Nor did the austere vigilance of Lycurgus stop here.
That concealed wealth might not enable any man to
indulge in luxury at home, nor such indulgence excite
the desire of riches, he commanded all the male citizens
to eat together in public, as in Crete; and each, in
turn, to contribute his monthly quota toward the common meal[28], fifteen messing together at one table[29].
And these public tables, beside repressing luxury, became so many schools of public virtue and political
wisdom; the old and young freely conversing together
on all subjects of national interest or national glory[30].

Having thus provided for the internal stability of
the state, the Spartan legislator took measures for securing it against foreign enemies. He had already
in a manner annihilated private property, in order
to eradicate luxury: he now proscribed the usual
means of acquiring wealth. Still keeping his eye on
the Cretan constitution, without servilely copying the
institutions of Minos, he committed not only the labours
of husbandry, but the exercise of all mechanical arts,
solely to slaves, who bore the name of helots[31]; re-

28. In this particular, the ordinances of Lycurgus, with respect to
eating in public; differed from those of Minos: the Cretan public
meals, perhaps more wisely, were furnished at the expense of the
state. Those of Sparta, regulated by public authority, were however sufficiently meagre. The most exquisite dish was a kind of
pottage, known by the name of *black broth*. Plut. ubi sup.

29. Plut. *Vit. Lycurg.*   30. Xenoph. *Rep. Lacon.* Plut. *Vit. Lycurg.*

31. The most received opinion concerning the origin of this name
is; That Helos, a Lacedæmonian town, having attempted to establish
its independency, was reduced by force; that the inhabitants, as a
punishment for their temerity, were condemned to the most humiliating slavery, and precluded the possibility of ever recovering their
liberty, by a law of the Spartan council, forbidding them to be eman-
cipated or sold to foreign states; and that their posterity thus multiplying, and being generally dispersed over Lacon a, the name of *helot*
became common to all the Lacedæmonian slaves, afterward acquired by
conquest or otherwise. Vid. *Acad. des Inscript.* tom. xxiii. et auct. cit.

serving

serving to the Lacedæmonians, or free inhabitants of Laconia of all descriptions, no profession beside that of arms, nor any care but the welfare of the community [32].

In conformity with this fundamental law, which constituted the Lacedæmonians a nation of soldiers and politicians, Lycurgus framed a number of regulations for making them superior in prowess, and keen-sighted in whatever concerned the interests of their country, beyond every other people in Greece. And what is still more to his praise, they became, in these particulars, as we shall have occasion to see, the very men he wished to form them; unequalled in political sagacity, military courage, conduct, discipline, and the whole science of war. But they grew, at the same time, insolent, haughty, ambitious, and cruel, as might have been foreseen; turning against their neighbours, without any regard to justice or humanity, those arms and that hardy valour, which were meant for their own defence. Yet must I not omit the singular, if not in all respects praise-worthy ordinances, in the code of manners, which gave them eventually the power, as well as the inclination, of committing such violences; and which have all a remote reference to a state of hostility.

The attention of Lycurgus to the personal qualities of the people, on whose minds he meant to ingraft his institutions, discovers a truly philosophic spirit, unfettered by vulgar prejudices. He encouraged marriage, and even enjoined it, as a duty; but the parties

32. Herod. The Romans, who recruited their legions chiefly from the sturdy class of husbandmen; and who allowed patriotism to spring naturally from the happy possession and free use of private property, while they laid a wider basis for power, raised a firmer column of public security.

were

were not allowed to contract it until they had attained the age of maturity, that they might produce strong and healthy children[33]. Yet farther to promote this great end, the Lacedæmonian virgins, instead of the sendentary employments of the loom and the needle, common to the other young women of Greece, were ordered to occupy themselves, like the youths, in running, wrestling, and throwing the quoit or javelin[34]. These exercises they generally performed *naked*, the better to tone their fibres. And on certain high festivals they danced publicly in the same shameless condition, in order to provoke the desires of the men; and, conscious of the influence of their charms, leeringly dispensed praise and blame to their admiring lovers[35].

Nor did the care of the sage legislator for improving the breed of the Lacedæmonians stop here. As a check upon the excess of desire, and to prevent the new-married men from emasculating their vigour in the arms of their active and full-formed brides, they were commanded to sleep in the common dormitory, along with their male companions, and durst only visit their wives by stealth[36]. The early matrimonial commerce of the Spartans was, therefore, a kind of perpetual intrigue; both sexes being obliged to contrive occasions of meeting one another secretly, and of retiring without being observed[37]. So that their passions, thus held in play, were kept from languishing; while their constitutions were preserved from suffering, by too frequent indulgence.

All these ordinances, however, were not thought sufficient by Lycurgus, for giving to the bodies of his

33. Plut. *Vit. Lycurg.*   34. Xenoph. et Plut. ubi sup.
35. Plut. *Vit. Lycurg.*   36. Id. ibid.
37. Plut. ubi sup.

countrymen that health, symmetry, and vigour, which
he wished them to possess, and esteemed essential to
the welfare of the community. He had already sacrificed female delicacy on the altar of patriotism, in
commanding the young women to wrestle and dance
publicly without any veil to modesty: he next offered
up conjugal fidelity to the same idol; and with it all
jealousy in the intercourse of the sexes. Married
women, like all other property, may be said to have
been held in common at Sparta. Husbands were permitted to borrow each others wives; and even required, under certain circumstances, to lend the partners
of their bed, for the purpose of *mending* the *breed*[38].
And this pretence was so easily forged, that young
and handsome married persons, who happened to be
less fortunately matched, found little difficulty in reci-
procally contributing to the support of the state, while
they indulged their mutual wishes.

But the perfecting of the Spartan breed demanded
a yet higher sacrifice than either virgin modesty or the
sanctity of the marriage bed; a sacrifice over which
humanity must ever mourn, though strictly enjoined
by the laws of Lycurgus. All children, as soon as
born, were ordered to be carried to a public office,
where certain aged persons were appointed to examine
them; and if they happened to be diseased, feeble, or
deformed, they were thrown into a deep cavern in the
neighbourhood of mount Tygetus. But if they were
well-shaped, strong and healthy, they were delivered
to nurses provided by the state[39]; and who by their
skill, in judiciously co-operating with nature, became
famous over Greece, and perhaps saved as many lives
as the severity of the legislator destroyed.

38. Xenoph. *Rep. Lacon.* Plut. *Vit. Lycurg. et Numa,*
39. Id. ibid.

At

PART I.

At seven years of age the boys were taken from their parents, and put under public preceptors; no Lacedæmonian being permitted to rear, or educate his children, but according to the mode prescribed by law. The preceptors were chosen from among people of the first consideration, and seem to have regarded themselves as fathers of the children of the state. Accordingly their chief object, in educating the Spartan youths, was to mould the passions, sentiments, and ideas of their pupils, to that form which might best assimilate with the constitution of the republic; and so to exercise the powers of both body and mind, as to raise them to the highest possibilty of performing every thing useful to the community; to make them bold, vigilant, and skilful warriors, yet obedient soldiers; with a strong sense of honour, stimulated to heroic deeds by the desire of applause and apprehension of shame, but ever ultimately governed by the love of their country, which might be considered as the main spring of their souls[40].

The Spartan education and discipline could scarcely be said ever to cease. After twelve years of age the boys, whose former mode of life had been abundantly austere, were permitted to wear only one garment, and that equally in winter as in summer; to sleep on no better beds than reeds, which they themselves must gather: and they were compelled to go barefooted at all seasons. As they approached manhood, their discipline was increased in austerity; their stated labours, which left them hardly a vacant hour in the day, being augmented, in order to curb the impetuous passions of youth[41]. Nor was there found any remission of those labours, unless during military service. Then many indul-

40. Xenoph. et. Plut. ubi sup.
41. Plut. *Vit. Lycurg*. Xenoph. *Rep. Lacon.*

gences

gences were wisely allowed; and to such a degree, that the camp might be regarded as a scene of ease and luxury by the Lacedæmonians, who there took pleasure in adorning their persons, and seemed to give up their hearts to mirth[42]. Before the age of thirty, no man was allowed to take part in public affairs at Sparta. For ten years later, it was not reputable for the Lacedæmonians to devote themselves to political or juridical business; and sixty years of persevering virtue were necessary to entitle any candidate to a seat in the senate[43].

To these civil ordinances Lycurgus added certain military maxims, or laws, in the same spirit. He forbid the Spartans to surround their city with walls, lest security should lead them to remit their vigilance in its defence; and he enjoined them not to pursue, after battle, a flying foe, for various reasons—lest their ardour should blind them against latent danger; the utter destruction of their enemies unstring the nerve of their courage, or the thirst of conquest incite them to covet extensive dominion, which his institutions were not calculated to preserve[44]. He also forbid them to make war by sea; which, as he had cut the sinews of their commerce, in abolishing the use of the precious metals, he knew they could not support: and he desired them to beware of continuing hostilities long against the same people, lest they should teach their adversaries their method of fighting[45]. He made it shameful for them to fly before an enemy, how superior soever in force; so that death or victory, in battle, was the lot of every Lacedæmonian; or a fate worse than death, disgrace! an infamy that excluded them from all civil and military employments[46].

42. Id. ibid. 43. Xenoph. ubi sup. 44. Plut. *Vit. Lycurg.*
45. Id. ibid. 46. Xenoph. *Repub. Lacon.*

    . In order to enable the Lacedæmonians to maintain, in the field, that high military character, which the tone of their bodies and the temper of their minds, as formed by the laws of Lycurgus, were so well fitted to support, their forces were arranged in a masterly manner, and nearly resembling the disposition of the armies of modern Europe[47]. The Spartan army was formed into a certain number of moræ or brigades, composed each of four lochoi or regiments. The lochos, which consisted of five hundred and twelve men, was divided into four pentecostyes, and each pentecostys into four enotomies[48]. All these different bodies, from the mora downward, were commanded by officers subordinate in rank to each other; and the whole army, by one of the joint kings of Lacedæmon[49].

The Spartan troops were uniformly cloathed in red, by the direction of Lycurgus; in order to prevent the soldiers from perceiving their loss of blood, or the enemy from discovering their wounds[50]. Their arms consisted of large bucklers, pikes or spears of moderate length, and strong short swords, with two edges[51]. They advanced to battle with the greatest alacrity, yet most exact regularity, keeping time with their steps to the sound of flutes or fifes[52]; and so perfect was their discipline, that through the hottest engagement, they preserved unbroken that beautiful order with which they began the action, and which enabled them to give a celerity to all their evolutions, and an im-

47. Xenophon ascribes the military, as well as the civil code of Sparta, to Lycurgus. But that enlightened philosopher and historian lived in too late an age to be able to judge, with any degree of accuracy, what arrangements were made by the sapient legislator, and what might be attributed to subsequent improvements.

48. Thucyd. lib. v. et Xenoph. *Repub. Lacon.*   49. Id. ibid.

50. Xenoph. *Repub. Lacon.*   51. Id. ibid.

52. Xenoph. ubi sup. Plut. *Vit. Lycurg.*

pulse to their efforts, that filled their enemies at once with admiration and terror[53].

But the austere institutions of Lycurgus, which, in raising to such a height the political and military virtues of the Lacedæmonians, paid no regard to the milder qualities, to the culture of the heart; and which, by inspiring a ferocity of disposition, that threw a kind of horror over their manners, may be said to have debased, instead of enobling the character of man, were very unfriendly to general happiness.

Attentive only to the safety of the state, the Spartan legislator, in forming a community of patriotic soldiers, always ready for action, forgot that they were free citizens, who had a right to taste of every social delight, and to dispose of their time and their talents as they thought proper, unless in a season of danger; not the hireling bands of a despot, whose interest it is to extinguish every sentiment of humanity, and strangle every finer feeling in its birth, in order to render the instruments of his tyranny more fit for their barbarous service. For the Lacedæmonians in the full enjoyment of political freedom, were the slaves of their own legislative system; which, by a bold effort of speculation, may be said to have founded the welfare of the republic on the misery of the individuals that composed it

As in forming a community of soldiers Lycurgus forgot that they were citizens, in forming citizens he forgot that they were men, endowed by nature with many generous passions, and capable of reciprocating many noble sentiments, beside those that concerned the state; he therefore not only endeavoured to re-

53. Xenoph. Repub. Lacon.

move

PART I.

move to a distance every thing that might minister to luxury or effeminacy, but to crush in the bud all the softer sympathies, and leave the Lacedæmonians no other passion but the love of glory and of their country. He attempted to make them superior to interest, to pleasure, and even to pain[54]; to stifle in their breasts the voice of natural affection, with all the charities of father, son, and brother[55]. The Spartan and the patriot swallowed up every inferior relation, and with them all the domestic virtues, and all the sweets of private life.

Private happiness, which cannot subsist without the affectionate discharge of domestic duties, is however the only solid foundation for public virtue, national prosperity, or public happiness. And true patriotism, and true heroism, are intimately connected with humanity of disposition and generosity of spirit. But the Spartans, of all people ever dignified with the appellation of *civilized*, were perhaps the most obdurate and illiberal. And that complexion of heart and mind was the necessary effect of their austere education and political system. Having properly no employment but that of arms, to which they were trained from their infancy, and few tender cares, they lost all compassion for the sufferings of their fellow-creatures; or if they retained any sympathetic affection, it was only for the

54. On the annual celebration of a festival, instituted by Lycurgus, in honour of Diana Orthia, all the Spartan boys were whipped, until the blood ran down upon the altar of that cruel goddess. And this flagellation was performed in presence of the magistrates of the city, and under the eye of fathers and mothers; who, instead of compassionating their children, ready to expire from the severity of the lashes, to which they frequently fell martyrs, exhorted them to suffer patiently the discipline inflicted, and without seeming to be conscious of any uneasy sensation. Cicero, *Tuscul.* lib. v. Pausan. lib. iii. *Plut. Vit. Lycurg.* 55. See what was formerly said concerning the inquest upon new-born infants, &c.

companions

companions of their dangers and toils. For the unarmed helots, by whose industry they subsisted, they
had no bowels of pity.

Never was human nature so degraded, as in the
abject condition of this miserable class of men, who
might have envied the lot of labouring cattle. As if
their dog-skin cap, and sheep-skin vest, had not been
sufficient to remind them of their servile state, they
were compelled to submit, once a day, to a certain
number of stripes, without having deserved them from
their imperious masters[56]. They were prohibited every
thing liberal or manly, and every thing humiliating,
and even debasing, was commanded them[57]. A stately
figure, or graceful mien, if discovered in any of their
young men, was equal to a sentence of death : the ill-
fated youth was instantly dispatched, and his master
was fined for too much indulgence[58]. The helots, in
a word, were at once the slaves of the public and of
private persons. They were accordingly lent in common; and, to complete their misfortunes, any one
might wantonly punish them for the smallest fault, and
to any degree, as they had no power of claiming the
protection of the laws[59].

We must not, however, ascribe to the disciplined
inhumanity of the Spartans, all the cruelties practised
upon the wretched helots. Some of these may be imputed to a radical defect in the political arrangements
of Lycurgus, rather than to the austerity of life imposed by his institutions. By committing the labours of
husbandry, and the exercise of all mechanical arts,
exclusively to slaves, instead of sharing them with, if
not assigning them solely to an inferior order of free

56. Athen. lib. vi. xiv.   57. Plut. Vit. Lycurg.
58. Athen. ubi sup.   59. Id. ibid.

men, who would have augmented the power of the state, and become its firmer support in every season of danger, he raised up, in the accumulating numbers of the helots, a formidable body of internal enemies ; ever watchful of an opportunity to recover their freedom, and take vengeance on their oppressors.

The jealous fears, and alarming apprehensions, necessarily resulting from such a perilous situation, made the Lacedæmonians have recourse to many cruel measures for breaking the spirit, and thinning the growth of the helots. One atrocious expedient, or rather institution, for the latter purpose, named the *crypitia*, or ambuscade, is too singular, and well attested, to be omitted in the history of this extraordinary people, though humanity shudders at the recital.

The public preceptors occasionally ordered some alert Spartan youths, selected for that horrid purpose, to disperse themselves in the country, armed with a dagger, and furnished with some necessary provisions. The better to execute their barbarous commission, they commonly concealed themselves in unfrequented places through the day; and sallying forth at night, assassinated all the helots they could find. At other times, they wantonly fell upon these unarmed men, and unhappy victims of political jealousy, in the fields by day, and put to the dagger the strongest and most comely of them[60].

But this horrid institution (which is ascribed by Aristotle to Lycurgus), and every other occasional expedient, being found insufficient to prevent the overgrowth of the helots, it was usual for the ephori, we are told, in entering upon office, to declare war

60. Plut. *Vit. Lycurg.*

against

against them, and to massacre them under pretence of
law [61].

Much honour is, however, due to Lycurgus, after
every deduction from the merit of his institutions. He
is the only legislator, in ancient or modern times, who
has made the breed of the human race an object of national policy; and if he had paid as much attention to
the moral, as to the physical qualities of man, he
would have been the greatest cultivator of his species
the world ever knew. For the age in which he lived,
he was a prodigy of civil wisdom, political sagacity,
and military skill. And his country soon experienced
the salutary effects of his laws. They gave such a tone
to the Spartan constitution, that the Lacedæmonians,
lately a distracted and divided people, began instantly
to act with concert and vigour, and secretly aspired at
dominion over the neighbouring states.

Iphitus, king of Elis, attentive to the progress of
this ambition, and sensible of his inability to contend
with the Spartan power, ingeniously contrived to secure his territory, and promote the welfare of his subjects, by a policy very different from that of Lycurgus.
Taking advantage of a tradition, that the Heraclidæ,
in bequeathing to his ancestor Oxylus the country of
Elis, or Elia, and the guardianship of the temple of
Jupiter at Olympia, had consecrated this district to
the presiding divinity, he endeavoured to interest all
the descendants of Hercules, and even all Greece in
its protection. In order to confirm the received tradition, and thus encircle his kingdom with a wall of
sanctity, he applied to the oracle of Apollo at Delphos,
for the renewal of certain sacred games which had, in
more ancient times, been occasionally celebrated on

[61] Arist. *Polit.* lib. ii.

the

the fertile banks of the river Alpheus, near the city of Pisa, in honour of the Olympian god[62].

The ministers of superstition, ever willing to extend its sway, readily listened to the request of Iphitus. He obtained a response, as favourable to his purpose, as he could have wished. The discontinuance of those *sacred* games, he was told by the pythia, or supposed divinely inspired priestess, having drawn down the indignation of Jupiter, and of Hercules, his deified son, by whom they were first celebrated, had been the cause of all the calamities, with which Greece had long been afflicted[63]. The king of Elis was, therefore, commanded by the oracle to proclaim a truce, or general cessation of arms, to all the Grecian states, that were willing to partake in the Olympian festival, or desirous of averting the vengeance of the offended god[64].

Invested with such high authority, Iphitus took measures, for not only renewing the Olympic games, but connecting them intimately with the most solemn religious ceremonies, and rendering their celebration perpetual and regular; every fifth year, or after an interval of four complete years[65]. And the spirit of the times, and the genius of the Grecian people, happily conspired with the views of the Elian prince.

Ant. Ch.
776.
Olymp. I. 1 No sooner was the armistice proclaimed, than all men, desirous of distinguishing themselves by feats of strength or agility, repaired to Olympia. There hostile animosity being laid aside, the subjects of the several states of Greece joined in one common sacrifice to Jupiter, and emulously contended for the palm of

62. Pausan. lib. v.   63. Id. ibid.
64. Pausan ubi sup.   Phlegon. ap. Euseb. *Chron.*
65. Id. ibid.

glory

glory in various kinds of gymnastic exercise[66]. And so strong was the passion of the Greeks for athletic competitions, that the Olympic games continued to be celebrated with splendor for more than a thousand years; and with such regularity, that the Olympiad became the great canon by which the Greeks computed time. Hence the rapturous exclamation of the learned Scaliger:

" O how fortunate was it that the ancient Greeks
" should think of celebrating, with so much devotion,
" every fifth year, their Olympic games! Hail, vene-
" rable Olympiad! thou guardian of dates and æras!
" assertrix of historical truth, and curb upon the wild
" licentiousness of chronologers!—But for thee, all
" things would still have been covered under the
" thick veil of darkness[67]."

The *civil* and *political influence* of those games upon the *whole* Grecian people, to whom their perio-

66. The five gymnastic exercises most celebrated by the ancients, and which were exhibited in succession at Olympia, when the games had attained their perfect form, consisted of running, leaping, wrestling, throwing the disk or quoit, and boxing. To these were added, in more polished times, two equestrian exercises; the chariot-race, and common horse-race (Pausan. lib. v. vi.). Iphitus is said to have at first revived only the foot-race, or *stadium;* so called from the length of the course, which consisted of the eighth part of a Grecian mile, or about an hundred and twenty-five English paces. See West's *Dissertat. on the Olympic Games*, et auct. cit. and M. Burette, *Memoire* dans L'Academie Royal des Inscription et Belles Lettres.

67. Scalig. *Chron. Euseb.* Chronologers in general, however, do not compute the Olympiads from the institution of the Olympic festival by Iphitus, but from the twenty-eighth celebration, when Corœbus is said to have been victor in the foot-race, one hundred and eight years later. But as no memorial is preserved of any transaction in Greece, either civil or military, during that long interval, sir Isaac Newton seems fully justified in striking it out, and affixing the same date to both events; namely, the year 776 before the christian æra. And his chronology, in *this particular*, has here been followed, in preference to that commonly received.

dical celebration, at Olympia, supplied the want of a common capital, and became a centre of social and sacred union, as well as a field of generous emulation, was great beyond the example of any similar institution in the history of the human race [68]. But this subject I shall afterward have occasion to illustrate in tracing the progress of society in Greece. Here it will, therefore, be sufficient to observe, that the *institution* of the Olympic festival was followed by *particular* political advantages, which far exceeded the most sanguine hopes of Iphitus. It served not only to protect the little territory of Elis against the dreaded invasion of more powerful neighbours, but gave a kind of sacred character to the inhabitants, as the hereditary priesthood of Jupiter. War could never approach their country, without drawing down upon the impious invaders the wrath of Heaven [69]. Hence they neglected to fortify their towns, and devoted themselves chiefly to agriculture and the pleasures of a country life [70].

But the lands of every people in Peloponnesus were not, like those of the Elians, protected by sacred bulwarks. The Lacedæmonians therefore, in finding the growth of their power, under their austere institutions, and in projecting the consequent enlargement of their territory, cast their eyes upon other adjacent states; and, after trying their arms and new discipline against the Arcadians and Argives, who

68. See West's *Dissertat. on the Olympic Games*, sect. xvii. et auct. cit.
69. Strabo, lib. viii.
70. Polybius, lib. iv. Nor could they engage in *offensive war*, as we learn from Phlegon (ap. Euseb. Chron.), without violating their sacred character. Being disposed to take part in such a war, they sent to Delphos to know the sense of the Oracle of Apollo. The pythia answered, in the name of the god, " Defend your own country, if " attacked, until the return of the fifth year, which brings peace with " it ; but refrain from war, being yourselves the examples and arbiters " of amity and concord in Greece." Phlegon. ap. Euseb. *Chron.*

zealously

zealously united in defence of their respective boundaries, the kingdom of Messenia was finally marked out
by the disciples of Lycurgus as the object of Spartan
ambition [71].

That fertile country, which lay to the west of Laconia, and on the coast of the Ionian sea, was still
governed by the descendants of Cresphontes; to whom
it had fallen, as formerly related, in the division of
the conquests of the Heraclidæ [72]. But neither a sense
of this common consanguinity, nor a consciousness
that the people of the two states were of the same
Doric origin, could prevent the kings of Lacedæmon
from forging various pretences for quarrelling with
their Messenian neighbours. Repeated injuries accordingly took place on both sides, and were repeatedly retaliated by each party.

At length the Spartans, having secretly completed
their military preparations, and bound themselves by
oath not to desist from hostilities until they had accomplished their purpose, invaded the Messenian territory
without any declaration of war; and, as an awful prelude to the projected conquest, took possession of
Ampheia, a frontier town, after putting the unarmed
inhabitants to the sword [73].

Roused, rather than discouraged, by that unexpected blow, Euphaes, king of Messenia, pursued the
most efficacious measures for defeating the designs of
the enemy. Sensible of his inability to contend, in
the field, with the disciplined valour of the Lacedæmonians, he ordered his subjects to take refuge in the
fortified towns, and watch every opportunity of sally-

---

71. Justin, lib. iii. Pausan. lib. iv.   72. Lett. IV.
73. Pausan. lib. iv.

ing

PART I.   ing out upon the barbarous invaders of their country,
          For four years did he adhere to this plan of defensive
          war, before he ventured to collect his forces.   At
          last, thinking the Messenians sufficiently trained to
          arms, he placed himself at their head, and led them
          toward the frontiers of Laconia.

Ant. Ch.   Elated with the prospect of a decisive trial of
739.   strength, which they had so long sought in vain; and
Olymp. x.2
          of ascertaining, by a general engagement, the issue of
          a tedious war, the Lacedæmonians, who had remitted
          their ineffectual efforts to reduce the Messenian towns,
          eagerly flew to arms; and marched to meet their ex-
          asperated enemies with all the confidence of victory.
          The Messenians did not decline the combat. But the
          martial ardour of both armies was checked by certain
          unforeseen circumstances; by the sudden swelling of
          a rivulet, that intersected the plain between them,
          and the subsequent interposition of night.   And next
          morning, the Spartan generals found the Messenian
          camp so strongly fortified, that they judged it prudent
          to lead home their disheartened troops, without at-
          tempting to storm it [74].

          The austere fathers of the senate, enraged at the
          pusillanimous behaviour of their younger countrymen,
          reproached them with the violation of their oath, and
          ordered them again to take the field.   The disgrace
          was felt by every order in the state, and the most vigor-
          ous measures were taken for wiping it off.   The
          whole military force of Laconia was assembled; and,
          after setting aside a sufficient number of free men for
          the internal safety of the country, an offensive army of
          twenty thousand combatants was mustered.

                    74. Pausan. lib. iv.

                                        This

This formidable body, commanded by Theopompus and Polydorus, the two kings of Lacedæmon, was opposed by the Messenian army under Euphaes, in the neighbourhood of Ampheia. Though conscious of his inferiority in numbers and in discipline, the Messenian prince resolved to give battle to the enemy; trusting for success to the intrepid valour inspired by patriotism, to the thunder-cloathed arm of vengeance, and the gigantic efforts of despair. Filled with that heroic sentiment, he thus addressed his faithful subjects, and the associates of his danger: "It is not only for your "king and country that you are to fight, as the me- "lancholy fate of Ampheia will inform you: it is for "your lives and liberties, and for those of all that are "dear to you; of your fathers, brothers, wives, and "children[75]."

At these words the Messenians rushed into action, agitated by all the passions that can inflame hostile animosity, or give perseverance to fortitude. The Spartans, yet in the bloom of youthful manhood, received their impetuous antagonists with the cool courage of experienced veterans. But the Spartan phalanx, although firm, wanted strength to sustain the collected blows that were hurled against it by the Messenian column. The call to exertion was not equal. Ambition, the love of glory, and the fear of shame, were feeble incitements, in comparison of the motives by which the Messenians were actuated. The ranks of the Spartans were accordingly broken by the vigorous impulse of their more awakened competitors, whose rapid shock was irresistible.

The discipline of Sparta, however, in this extremity, gave her troops an advantage, which discipline

75. Id .ibid.

alone

alone can confer: it enabled them again to form, and dispute the field with the seemingly victorious enemy. But during the momentary confusion, the strength of individuals had been tried; personal injuries and insults had been given and received; and the pride of personal prowess was now added to martial ardour. Even the contending kings were fired with this passion. Regardless of the laws of war or the dictates of humanity, man encountered man with the ferocity of the lion and the tyger, and with all the rancour of private revenge. The battle raged more hotly than ever. No quarter was given, no mercy was craved. The dying warrior spent the last effort of his strength in dealing vengeance, or in animating his companions to inflict it on the foe. The carnage on both sides was dreadful; yet was the contest maintained with unabated courage by both, when night put a stop to the business of death. And, what is not a little remarkable, neither party laid claim to victory; but each, when morning appeared, craved a suspension of arms for the purpose of burying the slain[76]. The Spartans afterward retired, without offering to renew the struggle for dominion; nor did the Messenians attempt to lift a sword, for the farther establishment of their independency[77].

But although the bloody conflict was thus left undecided, the state of the contending powers was very different after the battle. If the Spartans had not cause to rejoice, they had great room for consolation, and even for hope. They had lost the flower of their army; but that loss could soon be repaired by a community of soldiers. The Messenians had suffered no less severely; and they could not recruit their forces

76. Pausan. lib. iv.   77. Id. ibid.

with

with the same facility. Nor was this the only disadvantage under which that gallant people laboured.

In consequence of the former inroads of the Lacedæmonians, who had industriously destroyed the fruits of the earth, and cruelly cut off the husbandman with his hopes, the Messenians in the fortified towns had been reduced to the necessity of subsisting upon unwholesome food; and famine was now followed by pestilence, its usual attendant, which rendered the inhabitants of the smaller towns unable to resist the renewed assaults of the ravaging enemy. As a desperate remedy for these evils, Euphaes ordered his people to abandon those abodes of misery, and take refuge with him among the mountains of Ithome; in a place strongly fortified by nature, and which he surrounded with works that made it impregnable in that age[78].

The first public measure which the Messenians took, after sheltering themselves in Ithome, was to consult the Delphic oracle concerning their future destiny, and the means of appeasing the anger of the gods; they being still apprehensive of famine, and afflicted with the contagious distemper it had occasioned. The pythia, who is supposed to have been under Spartan influence, replied, that they must sacrifice a virgin of the royal race, in order to procure the intercession of Apollo. The lots were accordingly cast; and the daughter of Lyciscus, sprung from Æpytus, the son of Cresphontes, was marked out as the victim. But the paternal affection of Lyciscus proved stronger than his public virtue. Although the diviner declared that *reputed daughter* to be supposititious, and, therefore, not a proper sacrifice, he went secretly over to the enemy,

---

78. Pausan. ubi sup.

instead

instead of waiting the issue of the captious dispute, and carried his daughter with him[79].

Alarmed at this desertion, the desponding Messenians were ready to sink under their superstitious terrors, when Aristodemus, the head of a distinguished branch of the royal family, patriotically offered to sacrifice his amiable and undisputed daughter, for the preservation of his distressed country. But against that cruel sacrifice new objections were urged. An enamoured youth, to whom the maiden had been betrothed, insisted that she was not at her father's disposal but his. And finding this argument disregarded, he daringly affirmed, in order to save his beloved bride, that the daughter of Aristodemus, not being a virgin, could not satisfy the requisition of the oracle; protested that she had yielded to the ardour of his passion, although their marriage rites had not yet been celebrated; and that she was now pregnant, in consequence of such criminal indulgence.

Enraged at the impudent attempt to fix a stain upon the honour of his daughter, and blind to the generous motive, the indignant father slew her with his own hand; and publicly ripped up her womb, in proof of her innocence[80]. That innocence was pathetically acknowledged by the sighs and tears of the agonizing multitude, who imprecated vengeance on the impious calumniator. The Messenian priests, however, demanded another victim, as this had not been regularly sacrificed. But Euphaes, supported by the voice of all the families of the Herculean race, declared that the command of the oracle had been fully complied with, as the blood of a royal virgin had been shed; the manner of sacrificing being of no importance[81].

79. Pausan. lib. iv.   80. Id. ibid.
81. Pausan. ubi sup.

And

And his naturally brave people, believing their peace with heaven was made, prepared themselves resolutely to defend Ithome to the last extremity.

The perseverance of the Messenians in this resolution, and the obstinacy of the Lacedæmonians in pursuing their utter destruction, awakened more strongly the attention of the people of the neighbouring states. The Arcadians and Argives, who had long been jealous of the domineering spirit, and ambitious views of the disciples of Lycurgus, came to a resolution to support the king of Messenia; while the Corinthians, a maritime and commercial people, whose interests did not interfere with those of Sparta, leagued themselves with that republic.[82]

In consequence of these alliances, the war in Peloponnesus became more general. Emboldened by the presence of their confederates, the Messenians ventured again to quit their fortifications, and face the exulting enemy in the field. In the first regular engagement, they gained an advantage over the Lacedæmonians, but lost their gallant king. He was mortally wounded in animating his men by his heroic example, and his body was with difficulty recovered[83].

Euphaes, having left no issue, was succeeded in the Messenian throne by Aristodemus; whose valour and conduct justified the choice of his fellow-citizens, in conferring on him the disputed sceptre. For five years did he baffle all the efforts of Sparta to subvert the liberties of his country; and, in one great battle, he defeated the united forces of the Corinthians and Lacedæmonians. But the difficulty of supporting his army in a country that had been so long the scene of

82. Pausan. in Lacon. et Messen. 83. Id. ibid.

war, and which was still ravaged by the barbarous invaders, who were constantly reinforced with fresh troops, drove him at last to despair. He stabbed himself on the tomb of that daughter, whom he had ferociously slain[84].

The Messenians, now destitute of a leader, in whose abilities they could confide, abandoned Ithome, after sustaining a siege of five months. The more resolute spirits sought independency among their allies, in Arcadia and Argos, or in more distant countries; and the remainder of the people, dispersed over that territory, which was now become an accession to the kingdom of Lacedæmon, were forced to submit to such conditions as the haughty victors thought fit to impose upon them[85]. They were required to pay to their conquerors, after taking an oath of allegiance, one half of the annual produce of their lands: and, as a mark of their subjection, a certain number of both sexes were ordered to appear at Sparta, in mourning, on the death of her kings and senators[86]

Such was the issue of the first Messenian war; after which, Greece appears to have enjoyed profound peace for several years, and an uncommon degree of internal tranquillity. Population rapidly increased; and the adventurous Greeks, not having sufficient room at home, continued to diffuse themselves in colonies. Beside their successful emigrations to the neighbouring islands, and the coast of Asia Minor, already mentioned, they had early established settlements in the islands of Cyprus, Sicily, and Sardinia; and in the southern division of Italy, afterward known by the name of *Magna Græcia*[87]. But these

---

84. Pausan. lib. iv.   85. Id. ibid.   86. Pausan. ubi sup.
Strabo, lib. viii.   87. Dion. Halicarnas. lib. i. Strabo, lib. v. vi.

first settlements were of small consideration, in comparison of those that succeeded them.

The Corinthians now founded in Sicily the famous city of Syracuse, which quickly rose to eminence, and became the capital of a wealthy and powerful state. They also planted a colony in the island of Corcyra, in the Ionian sea; and that colony soon spread itself to the neighbouring continent, and founded in Illyricum, the cities of Epidamnus and Apollonia[88]. Meanwhile, a body of emigrants from Chalcis, in Euboea (an island on the coast of Attica, and early peopled by the Athenians), under the conduct of a Messenian chief, and supported by a band of his brave, but unfortunate countrymen, gave a beginning to the renowned city of Rhegium; seated on the extreme point of Italy, which narrows the Sicilian strait[89]. And Tarentum, no less distinguished among the towns of Magna Græcia, was founded during the same tranquil period, by a body of Spartan refugees[90]. The circumstances which occasioned this last emigration, are sufficiently curious to merit a short detail.

The first Messenian war having been protracted beyond expectation, the Spartan wives became impatient at the absence of their husbands; and represented to them, that the state would be ruined unless population was continued, should they even prove ultimately successful in their enterprize. In order to provide against that danger, without violating the oath by which they had bound themselves, at setting out on the second expedition, " not to return home until they had subdued " their enemies," these inflexible warriors came to a singular resolution. They sent back, with the consent of the senate, all the young men in the army who were

88. Strabo, ubi sup.   89. Strabo, lib. vi.   90. Id. ibid.

under

under the military age at the time the oath was taken, and enjoined them to cohabit promiscuously with the married women[91].

The boys that sprung from this irregular commerce were distinguished by the names of Parthenians, in allusion to the condition of their mothers[92]. And little delicate as the Lacedæmonians were, in regard to the integrity of the persons of their wives, they were not so devoid of all moral sentiment, as to overlook the public stain in the birth of the Parthenians. After the close of the war, these unhappy children of lust, and political necessity were, therefore, held in contempt by the conquerors of Messenia. As they knew not their fathers, they belonged to no family, and could claim no inheritance, although entitled to all the other privileges of Spartan citizens.

This despised and neglected condition induced the Parthenians to associate closely together in youth; and, when they arrived at the age of manhood, even to league themselves in confederacy with the depressed helots. A plot, which they had formed against the state, was discovered; yet were they treated with singular lenity. Instead of being punished in proportion to the degree of their criminality, they were only expelled the community; and, in order to remove them to a greater distance, and thus effectually prevent their future machinations, they were furnished with every thing necessary for establishing a settlement beyond the limits of Peloponnesus[93]. They accordingly emigrated under the conduct of Philanthus, their leader in the abortive conspiracy; and, having crossed the Ionian sea, they landed on the south-east coast of Italy,

Ant. Chr.
714.
Olymp.

91. Pausan. lib. iv. Strabo, lib. vi. Justin, lib. iii.
92. Aristot. Polit. lib. v.   93. Strabo et Justin, ubi sup.

and

and there built the city of Tarentum, at the bottom of the delightful bay, to which it had the honour of giving the same name[94].

After the expulsion of the Parthenians, the Lacedæmonians enjoyed almost thirty years of public and domestic peace. And during the greater part of that term, as well as during the ten years immediately preceding it, the Messenians quietly submitted to the hard conditions imposed upon them by their imperious masters. But their servitude became, at length, too grievous to be patiently borne, by men who had not lost all memory of their former independency, or to whom any hope remained of recovering the rights of a free people. The boldest youths of the second generation, who had not experienced the calamities of war, and whose indignant hearts beat high with martial ardour, looked therefore anxiously around for a determined leader; under whom they might renew that generous struggle, in which their unfortunate fathers had failed, and gloriously attempt to regain their station among the Grecian states. Such a leader they found in Aristomenes; a young man distinguished by every mental and personal quality that can exalt the character of a hero, and who had the advantage of deducing his descent from Hercules, through a long line of Messenian kings.

The Messenians, however, were not so transported by their zeal for liberty, as to lose sight of the dictates of political prudence. Before they ventured to appear in arms, they privately sent deputies to gather the sentiments of the Arcadians and Argives, the former allies of the Messenian state. Both nations encouraged them by the most flattering promises of assistance, in

94. Id. ibid.

their

their purpose of throwing off the Spartan yoke. Aristomenes accordingly assembled a body of his countrymen, and attacked the Lacedæmonians at the village of Daræ.   There an obstinate battle was fought; and although the victory was left undecided, the Messenians were so much pleased with the gallant behaviour of their leader, that they saluted him on the field with the title of *king*[95]. Aristomenes declined the invidious honours of royalty, but accepted the office of commander in chief, with the appellation of *general;* which, in that age, implied a superiority in military prowess, as well as in rank, and in the conduct of armies.

The Messenians had no reason to repent their generosity, nor Aristomenes to blame his moderation. They committed to him the whole conduct of their affairs; and he proved himself worthy of their confidence, by a guardianship, regulated by the most disinterested patriotism, and distinguished by acts of the most exalted heroism.   Immediately after the battle at Daræ, he performed an exploit almost too bold for historical credibility.   Sensible of the influence of an auspicious omen, at the beginning of a war, he hastily travelled to Sparta in disguise ; entered that city by night ; and hung up in the temple of Minerva a shield, with an inscription upon it, intimating, that Aristomenes dedicated that offering to the warlike goddess, from the spoils of the Lacedæmonians[96].

The fame of this adventure was followed by the consequences Aristomenes had foreseen. It inspired the Messenians with the most romantic courage, which they displayed in many enthusiastically valorous deeds; while it filled their enemies, apprehensive of having lost the favour of Pallas, with superstitious terrors.

95. Pausan. lib. iv.　　　　96. Id. ibid.

In

In order to avert the misfortunes they feared, the Spartans consulted the oracle of Apollo at Delphos. The pythia replied, That they must demand a general from Athens, to conduct the future operations of the war.

No response could have been more mortifying to the pride of Sparta; yet was she forced to make the humiliating request. And the jealousy of Athens, although little willing to contribute to the exaltation of a rival's power, durst not oppose the injunction of the oracle. But the Athenians, in complying, attempted to defeat the end proposed by obedience. They sent to Sparta a lame man, named Tyrtæus, who had never been distinguished by any military exploit, or invested with any command; and who had hitherto exercised the profession of a schoolmaster[97].

The Lacedæmonians, however, received him as a leader appointed by heaven; and a poetical talent, which he possessed, seemed to mark him out to them as the peculiar instrument of Apollo, sent for their exaltation.

Meanwhile Aristomenes, after having garrisoned the sea-ports of Pylus and Methone, had collected into one body, all the Messenians able to bear arms. And that formidable army of native troops was reinforced with succours, not only from Arcadia and Argos, but also from Elis and Sicyon, which had acceded to the confederacy: and by Messenian refugees, from various countries. The Lacedæmonians had likewise assembled their whole forces, under Anaxander, one of their joint kings, and Tyrtæus the Athenian. And the united strength of Laconia was augmented by the auxiliary aid of the Corinthians, the former allies of the Spartan state, and by the friendly assistance of the citizens of Lepara, who had thrown off the authority

97. Pausan. ubi sup.

of

of Elis[98]. These combined armies met in the large
plain of Stenyclara, on the frontiers of Messenia;
where, in three successive engagements, the field was
obstinately disputed, but in each of which the Lacedæmonians were forced to give ground, notwithstanding
their dependence upon divine assistance.

The last and most bloody of those engagements was
fought at a place called *the Boar's Monument*. There,
both parties charged with the most determined courage; and the issue of the battle appeared doubtful,
when Aristomenes, at the head of a chosen band of
Messenian youths, attacked the principal division of
the Spartan army, commanded by the king in person,
and broke it or cut it in pieces. He afterward attacked
a second, and even a third body that remained firm,
and with equal effect. The Lacedæmonians and their
allies yielded in every quarter to the shock of their
antagonists. They fled; were pursued with great
slaughter; and a decisive victory remained to the
Messenians[99].

The rapid success of Aristomenes, however, instead
of inducing him to relax his military efforts, served
but to inflame his patriotic zeal. He not only followed the fugitive enemy beyond the boundaries of
Messenia, but deeply invaded Laconia, and pillaged
several towns. Astonished at such a reverse of fortune, and humbled by the loss of a gallant army, the
Lacedæmonian kings, and the venerable fathers of the
Spartan senate, remonstrated against the farther prosecution of the war; and seemed disposed to permit the
Messenians to enjoy that liberty and independency,
which they had so gloriously recovered. The same
opinion was adopted in the assembly of the people, and
approved by the allies of the Spartan state. Tyrtæus

---

98. Id. ibid.   99. Pausan. lib. iv.

alone

alone remained firm: he reprobated the disgraceful resolution, and urged the revival of hostilities with so much warmth, that all ideas of peace were laid aside [100].

Awakened to a sense of national honour by the poetical effusions of the Athenian bard, whose sacred character attracted veneration, the Lacedæmonians were fired anew with the spirit of conquest. Ashamed of having listened for a moment to the suggestions of timid councils, they speedily recruited their broken forces, and again entered the territory of Messenia. Though assisted only by a small body of Arcadians, under Aristocrates prince of Orchomenus, who was secretly in the Spartan interest, Aristomenes bravely advanced to meet the formidable enemy.

The Spartan troops did not seem to decline the combat. But instead of that gay courage with which they were wont to be animated on the approach of battle, the memory of their recent defeats filled them with melancholy reflections. They lamented the number of men that must fall; and whose bodies, lying in mangled heaps on the field, would be dragged to one common funeral pile, without being recognised by their relations, or honoured with solemn rites.

Now was the time for Tyrtæus to exert his poetical talents: and they did not fail him on the occasion. He sung, at the head of the Spartan army, the exploits of ancient warriors, the renown awaiting on valour, the joy and the rewards of victory; and, as a farther encouragement to desponding spirits, he directed each man to tie round his right arm some token, by which his body, however disfigured by wounds, might be known to his kindred or friends [101]. These heroic songs, and this animating device, had the desired effect.

100. Id. ibid.
101. Pausan. ubi sup. Justin. lib. iii. Strabo, lib. viii.

The

The Lacedæmonians laying aside all gloomy apprehensions, eagerly longed for an opportunity of retrieving the glory of their country; and when that opportunity was offered them, they advanced to the charge with the firm aspect of men resolved to conquer or perish.

The Messenian general, who had drawn up his forces at a place called the Great Ditch, was prepared to meet the most vigorous efforts of the enemy. But all his measures were disconcerted by the perfidy of the Arcadian prince. When the two armies were ready to join battle, Aristocrates led off his division; and, in order to make his defection more evident, he crossed the front of the Messenian line. Aristomenes attempted, but in vain, to keep his troops in their ranks. Astonished at a treachery so flagrant, the Messenians quitted their ground, and endeavoured to bring back their allies. The Lacedæmonians took advantage of their confusion. They were totally routed, surrounded, and almost all cut in pieces[102].

Aristomenes, whose presence of mind never forsook him, and whose patriotic courage only shone more conspicuously through the cloud of misfortune that involved his country, finding he could no longer keep the field against the enemy, pursued the same policy formerly adopted by Euphaes, in similar circumstances. Still accompanied by the chosen band of warriors, who fought near his person; who were foremost in every station of danger, and who had hitherto remained unbroken, he collected the scattered remains of his ruined army. With these tried soldiers, and such of the defenceless inhabitants of the open towns, as were fit to bear arms, he occupied the fortified post of Eira; strongly situated among mountains on the southern shore of Messenia, and accessible only toward the

102. Id. ibid.

friendly

friendly harbours of Pylus and Methone, whence it
could receive a ready supply of provisions[103].

In this fortification, which soon became a large
town, and in the two neighbouring sea-ports, that
maintained a constant communication with Eira,
the Messenians preserved their liberty and indepen-
dence for eleven years, in spite of all the exertions of
Sparta to bring them again under her dominion. During that period, the valour and conduct of Aristomenes were displayed in many wonderful exploits.
Not satisfied with repelling the assaults of the enemy,
or with cutting off their foraging parties within the
Messenian territory, he frequently passed the Spartan
frontier, and came home loaded with plunder, after
having laid waste the country.

Emboldened by these successful expeditions, Aristomenes ventured to penetrate into the heart of Laconia.
While the Lacedæmonians were fully employed in
the siege of Eira, he surprised, by a rapid nocturnal
march, the populous town of Amycle, situated on the
banks of the Eurotas, and only a few miles distant
from Sparta; seized a large booty before any force
could be assembled to oppose him, and returned unmolested to his strong hold[104].

But this splendid enterprise, added to a series of
fortunate adventures, had almost proved fatal to the
Messenian hero. It rendered him negligent, through
excess of confidence, while it excited the vigilance of
his enemies. In making a new irruption into the
Spartan dominions, he was attacked by a large body of
troops, commanded by the two kings of Lacedæmon.
Finding his retreat intercepted, he made a vigorous
defence, surrounded by a band of gallant companions,

---

103. Pausan. et Strabo, ubi sup.　　　104. Id. ibid.

But

PART I. But his little party being overpowered by numbers, he
was at last made prisoner, and carried in chains to Sparta
with fifty of his brave associates. There considered as
audacious rebels, who had not only dared to throw
off the yoke, but to lift the sword against their
conquerers, they were all condemned to be thrown
into a horrid cavern, called the Ceada; the common
dungeon in that capital, for the most atrocious criminals.

In suffering this ignominy, all the associates of
Aristomenes are said to have been killed or disabled by
the shock. He alone survived unhurt, in consequence
of having been indulged the privilege of retaining his
shield; a weapon of defence held in peculiar honour
by all ancient warriors, and which, by striking against
the sides of the cavern, had broken the force of his fall.
Two days did he remain in this frightful charnel ex-
pecting death, his face covered with his cloak. On
the third morning, about dawn, he heard a noise;
when uncovering his eyes, and looking around him,
he saw a fox feeding upon the bodies of his companions. Fortunately conjecturing that this animal must
have entered by some secret passage, he allowed it to
approach him; caught hold of it: and, while it strug-
gled to get loose, followed it, until it made its way
through a crevice in the rock. Here, favoured with
a glimpse of side-light, he gradually worked his way;
and, at length, accomplished his escape[105].

The unexpected appearance of Aristomenes at Eira
filled his countrymen with joyful astonishment. They
considered him as a deliverer, miraculously restored to
them by heaven. And his first exploit had a tendency
to infuse the same idea into the minds of his enemies;
who had pushed the siege with great vigour during his

105. Pausan. lib. iv. Polyæn. Stratæt. lib. ii.

confinement,

confinement, and hoped soon to get possession of the
place. Informed that a body of Corinthian troops was
marching to join the besiegers, he secretly went out,
and lay in ambush for them; attacked their camp under cover of night; routed them with great slaughter;
and returning, loaded with plunder, offered to Messenian Jove, for the third time, the hecatomphonia [106]:
or tremendous sacrifice of an hundred victims, which
he alone was entitled to perform, who had, with his
own hand, slain an hundred of his enemies in battle.

This severe blow, connected with the wonderful
escape of Aristomenes, of which it was the immediate
consequence, and the obstinate defence to be expected
from his future exertions, made the Lacedæmonians
almost despair of being able to make themselves masters of Eira. The Delphic oracle was again consulted, and a favourable response obtained: the fall of Eira
was solemnly denounced. But the prediction of Apollo
though finally fulfilled, was not accomplished merely
by Spartan valour and perseverance. The devoted
city, when thought to be least in danger, was betrayed
to the besiegers by a Spartan deserter.

That traitor had formed an intrigue with a Messenian married woman, whose house was under the walls
of Eira, and whom he was accustomed to visit, while
her husband was upon duty in the citadel. One even-
ing, however, the amorous couple met with an unsea-
sonable interruption in their pleasures. Just as they
had got into bed, the centinel returned, and loudly
knocked at the door. After having provided for the
safety of her gallant, the wife admitted her husband,
and insidiously welcomed him with the warmest expressions of joy; inquiring, with seeming anxiety, by

106. Id. ibid.

what

what happy turn of fortune she was so unexpectedly favoured with his company. He innocently told her, That Aristomenes being wounded, the soldiers on guard, at the out-posts, knowing he could not walk the rounds, as usual, and fearing nothing from the enemy, had agreed to retire to their several habitations, in order to avoid the inclemency of the weather, as the night was excessively wet and stormy.

The trembling deserter, having listened to this conversation, stole from his lurking-place, and carried the important intelligence to Empiramus, the Spartan general, whose attendant he had formerly been, and to whose generosity he trusted for pardon and reward. The hostile army was accordingly put in motion by Empiramus, both the kings being absent; and, by Ant. Ch. 671. Olymp. xxvii. 2. planting ladders against the defenceless posts, the Lacedæmonians entered Eira without resistance, in the eleventh year of the siege[107].

The fate of that last resort of Messenian liberty, however, was not yet decided. The alarm being instantly spread, Aristomenes, seconded, by the bravest and most active of his fellow-citizens, endeavoured to dislodge the enemy. But it was impossible for the Messenians, during a night of darkness, thunder, and tempest, to act with vigour or concert. Their boldest efforts, therefore, failed to produce the desired effect; and, when morning appeared, they found the Lacedæmonians so strongly posted, that all hope of expelling them vanished. Consequently the only alternative which remained to the gallant garrison of Eira, was to attempt to break the Spartan battalions, or submit to the law of the conqueror. The former choice was universally adopted; every one resolving to perish with

107. Pausan. ubi. sup.

the

the freedom of his country, rather than live under the degrading tyranny of Sparta. The women joined the men in this heroic resolution, and both sexes seemed inspired with more than mortal prowess. Maidens, widows, wives, and mothers, fought by the side of their sons, husbands, lovers, and brothers, for every thing that is dear to humanity.

Three days and nights was the furious conflict maintained with unabated courage. At length, on the fourth morning victory began to declare for the Lacedæmonians; who, having sent back to their camp a division of the army, which had wanted room to act, were constantly supplied with fresh troops. But the Messenians, even in the ruin of their country, enjoyed a kind of triumph. Aristomenes, finding it was now become necessary to abandon Eira, collected into one body as many of his troops as were still able to sustain the combat. In the centre of that body he placed the old men, women, and children: his son Gorgus commanded in the rear, he himself conducted the van; and advancing against the enemy with his spear poised, at the head of his tried companions, shewed he was determined to perish or penetrate through the hostile ranks. The Spartan general saw his purpose; and afraid to encounter his despair, opened him a passage, and allowed him to lead off the remains of his brave countrymen unmolested [108].

Aristomenes, after bursting from Eira, directed his march toward Arcadia. And there was exhibited a striking instance of the hospitality and generosity of ancient times. The Arcadians, loaded with cloaths and provisions, met their unfortunate allies at mount Lycæa, on the frontiers of the two states; and not

108. Id. ibid.

only

only afforded them present shelter, but offered to divide with them their lands, and to give them their daughters in marriage [109].

This kind reception encouraged Aristomenes to form one of the boldest, and best conceived enterprises, recorded in the annals of Greece. Finding he had still five hundred Messenians fit for the most arduous service, he resolved with these fearless and hardy troops to surprise the city of Sparta; while its bravest defenders were employed in pillaging Eira, or in reducing Pylus and Methone. Three hundred Arcadian volunteers instantly joined themselves to that gallant body; and before the Messenian leader could have reached the heart of Laconia, his little army would have been augmented with many Argian adventurers, ambitious of sharing in his danger, and of humbling their haughty neighbours. The enterprise must have been crowned with the most glorious success, and future heroes and patriots would have envied the fortune of Aristomenes.

But the best laid schemes are often rendered abortive, by accidents which human wisdom could not foresee; or defeated by such acts of perfidy and baseness, as noble minds are incapable of imputing to human beings. Aristocrates, the Arcadian prince, who had formerly deserted Aristomenes in the field of battle, but who had afterward been trusted by that generous hero, on pleading a momentary panic, retarded, under various pretences, the projected expedition against Sparta; and, in the meantime, communicated to the enemy the design of surprising their capital. The treachery was discovered by an intercepted letter from Anaxander, one of the Spartan kings, whom I

109. Polyb. lib. iv.

have

have already had occasion to mention; acknowledging the favour of the past, and present services of Aristocrates. And this betrayer of the liberties of a free people, of his engagements as an ally, and his trust as sovereign, was deservedly stoned to death by his own subjects[110]. A column was erected on the spot to perpetuate his infamy, with an inscription denoting his crime and its punishment[111].

The failure of this favourite enterprise seems to have broken the unconquerable spirit of Aristomenes. We do not find him afterward taking any arduous share in the future fortunes of his countrymen; nor have we any satisfactory account of the subsequent part of his life. We are indeed told, that his implacable hatred against Sparta remained, and that he travelled into Lydia, and even into Media, in order to raise up enemies against that warlike state[112]. But the Medes were then utterly unknown to the Greeks, and the Spartan power was yet too inconsiderable to be supposed capable of alarming the jealousy of the Lydian monarchy. It appears, however, by the general concurrence of historians, that the Messenian hero, soon after the conquest of his country, retired to the island of Rhodes, and there probably ended his days in honourable ease; having married his youngest daughter to Damagetes, king of the town and territory of Ialysus, in that island[113].

But to return to the order of historical events. Immediately after that fatal treachery, which so deeply affected Aristomenes, and which was followed by the death of Aristocrates, he conducted to Cyllene, a seaport of Elis, the most active and enterprising Messeni-

110. Pausan. lib. iv. Polyb. ubi sup.   111. Id. ibid.
112. Pausan. lib. iv. Plin. lib. xi.
113. Pausan. et Plin. ubi sup. Val. Maxim, lib. i.

ans who had taken refuge with him in Arcadia : leaving the aged and infirm to the protection of their generous allies.   On his arrival at this port he found, according to previous agreement, his fugitive countrymen, from the maritime towns of Pylos and Methone, ready to receive him, and furnished with every thing necessary for establishing a settlement on a foreign shore ; they having taken shelter on board their ships, as soon as they heard of the reduction of Eira, with all their most valuable goods and furniture.   Aristomenes approved of their resolution of planting a colony in some distant region, but declined the honour of leading it forth. That arduous service he relinquished to his son Gorgus, assisted by Manticles ; a young man of great merit, and the son of a distinguished patriot, who had fallen in the cause of his country [114].

While the Messenians were deliberating on this subject, and before they had fixed upon any particular place for the establishment of their projected colony, they received from Anaxilas, prince of Rhegium, descended from their ancient kings, an invitation to come and settle in his dominions ; that city having been partly founded, as we have seen, by Messenian refugees, on the termination of the former war.
Ant. Ch.
670.
Olymp.
xxvii. 3.
In consequence of this invitation, the Messenian adventurers embarked for Rhegium.   But when they arrived there, they found the friendship of Anaxilas to be less generous than they had believed.   He was engaged in hostilities with the Zancleans ; an Æolian colony that practised piracy, and possessed a delightful territory on the opposite coast of Sicily.   Against this enemy, likely to prove too strong for him, he craved their aid. The Messenians, who were prepared for any desperate enterprise, readily embraced

114. Pausan. lib. iv.

the

the proposal. The Zancleans were speedily vanquished. The Messenians took possession of the conquered country, and became one people with the Æolian colonists; whom their humanity had saved from the sword, and their generosity preserved from servitude [115]. And Zancle, the former capital, changed its name to that of Messene, which it still, with little variation, retains.

In consequence of this large emigration, and the retreat of Aristomenes to Rhodes, the Lacedæmonians found themselves absolute and undisputed masters of the territory of Messenia. Such of the native inhabitants, as chose to remain in that territory, were reduced to the condition of helots, and compelled to cultivate, for their conquerors, those lands which had formerly belonged to themselves or their ancestors [116]. From a condition so degrading, it might be supposed they could never emerge; and that their sufferings would have extinguished in their minds all hope of recovering their ancient freedom or independency. But slavery could not break the firm spirit of the Messenians. They still considered themselves as a Grecian people; and, after two hundred years of servitude, we shall see them again throw off the Spartan yoke.

Meantime the power of Sparta was great in Peloponnesus, and formidable even to the states beyond the Corinthian isthmus. That Grecian peninsula, formerly comprehending seven, now contained only six independent states. And the Lacedæmonians, after the conquest of Messenia, occupied one third of Peloponnesus. The remaining two thirds were possessed, in unequal divisions, by the Corinthians, Eleans, Achæans, Arcadians, and Argives [117]. The Corinthians, beside the terror of their naval force, and

115. Pausan. ubi sup. Strabo, lib. vi.   116. Pausan. lib. iv.
117. Strabo, Geog. lib. viii.

the

the resources which their extensive commerce yielded, were protected against the Spartan power by their impregnable situation, as the Eleans were by their sacred character. The Achæans had early associated themselves under a democratical form of government, in twelve independent cities, which had one common interest and bond of union; and in which they long enjoyed their independency. The Arcadians, secure in a mountainous district, where they led the life of herdsmen or shepherds, were farther defended by their hardy valour, and ancient renown[118]. The Argives, no less brave, and more warlike, were engaged in perpetual hostilites with Sparta. And their intimate alliance with Arcadia, founded on the sense of a common danger, only could have preserved them from sinking under the arms of the ambitious disciples of Lycurgus.

The politic Lacedæmonians, however, sometimes found means to engage the Arcadians to remain neuter; and then the most vigorous exertions of martial prowess generally proved too feeble, to enable the Argives to repress the encroachments of their usurping neighbours. One of those separate wars was distinguished by events sufficiently memorable to merit particular notice; though we know not, with certainty, the æra when they happened.

Sparta, in the course of her usurpations, had asserted a claim to the city of Thyrea and its territory, which lay on the frontiers of Argolis and Laconia; and had violently taken possession of it[119]. The Argives collected the largest army they had ever sent into the field, in order to support their right, and recover the contested district; while the Lacedæmonians advanced

118. Id. ibid.   119. Herodot. lib. i.

with

with an equal or superior force, to maintain their conquest [120]. But when the armies of the two states were preparing to engage, it was agreed, in a conference between the hostile leaders, that the dispute should be decided by three hundred men selected from each army: and that, during the awful combat, the main body of both armies should withdraw, lest the troops of either party should be prompted to interpose in behalf of their countrymen [121].

In consequence of this agreement, the six hundred champions joined battle, and fought with such intrepid courage, and so equal a degree of strength and skill, that when night came down, and arrested the sword of death, only three combatants were left alive; two Argives, named Chromius and Alcinor, and one Lacedæmonian, the renowned Orthryades [122]. The Argive champions, thinking themselves undisputed masters of the field, or desirous of escaping from such a scene of carnage, hastened to the camp of their countrymen, with the news of their hard-earned victory. Meantime Orthryades, though wounded, collected into one heap the spoils of his slaughtered enemies, and rested upon the spot [123].

Next morning, when the commanders of the two armies, at the head of their forces, went to view the

---

120. Pausanias (lib. x.) places this war in the latter part of the reign of Theopompus, king of Lacedæmon; and, consequently, between the first and second Messenian wars. But Herodotus, who lived much nearer to the time of the hostile competition, represents it as happening one hundred years later, and only just brought to an issue when Cyrus the great invested the Lydian capital, and Croesus sent ambassadors to crave assistance from Sparta (Herodot. lib. i.); in the year five hundred and forty-eight before the christian æra, agreeably to the date in the margin.

    121. Id. ibid.   122. Herodot. lib. i. · Pausan. lib. x.
    123. Id. ibid.

slain,

slain, and determine the dispute, the Argives saw, to
their astonishment, this solitary warrior enjoying his
melancholy triumph; having written with his own
blood, in the last runnings of ebbing life, his name
upon the trophy which he had raised [124]. The Lacedæmonians accordingly claimed the victory. The
Argives denied their pretentions, and both armies
joined battle. The conflict was fierce, obstinate and
bloody. At last the superior discipline and strength
of Sparta prevailed. The Argives were totally routed
and Thyrea remained with the conquerors [125].

But the Lacedæmonians, although thus victorious
over their most warlike and powerful neighbours, were
long restrained, by various circumstances, from attaining that weight of dominion, or high arbitration, at
which they so eagerly aspired. Fortunately for the
liberties of Greece, a rival power was now rising up,
ambitious to dispute with Sparta the pre-eminence in
arms and political importance.

124. Pausan. ubi sup.

125. Herodot. lib. i. The Argives were so much mortified at this
defeat, that the men cut off their hair; the women divested themselves of their jewels; and a solemn decree was passed, and an awful
vow taken by both sexes, "That no man should suffer his hair to
" grow, nor any woman wear ornaments of gold, until Thyrea should
" be recovered." Herodot. ubi sup.

LETTER

LETTER VI.

HISTORY OF ATHENS AND THE NORTHERN STATES OF
GREECE, FROM THE DEATH OF CODRUS, THE LAST
KING OF ATTICA, TO THE EXPULSION OF THE PISI-
STRATIDÆ; INCLUDING AN ACCOUNT OF THE RISE OF
THE GRECIAN ORACLES; OF THE EXTENSION OF THE
INFLUENCE OF THE AMPHICTYONIC COUNCIL; OF THE
ISSUE OF THE FIRST SACRED WAR, WITH THE INSTI-
TUTION OF THE PYTHIAN GAMES; AND A VIEW OF
THE ESTABLISHMENT OF THE LEGISLATION OF SOLON.

WHILE Peloponnesus was shaken by those
long and barbarous wars, which terminated in the
subversion of the liberties of Messenia, the Grecian
states beyond the Corinthian isthmus, either enjoyed
the blessings of peace, or felt but lightly the inconveniences of hostile discord.   The bickerings between
the petty northern republics, though frequent, were
attended with little bloodshed, and followed by no important consequences.   The Thebans having lost all
vigour and concert with the abolition of royalty, Bœotia
being broken into twelve rival townships, were in no
condition to act offensively.   And the Athenians, after
adopting a republican form of government (on the
death of Codrus, as formerly related [1]), lived in such
harmony under their perpetual archons, for almost
four centuries, that their affairs furnished few materials for history.   The subsequent period was less
tranquil.

LETTER
VI.

Ant. Ch.
1069.

1. Lett. IV.

Become

PART I.

Ant. Chr.
754.
Olymp.
vi. 4.

Ant. Ch.
684.
Olymp.
xxiv. 1.

Become impatient of the very shadow of royalty, the citizens of Athens, on the death of the hereditary archon Alcmæon, raised Charops to the archonship, on condition of holding it for ten years only. Six decennial archons followed Charops. After the expiration of those sixty years, a farther and greater change was made in the Athenian government. It was resolved that the office of archon should be annual, and that nine persons, instead of one, should be appointed to execute its duties [2].

These magistrates, however, were not vested with equal authority, nor were the same functions common to each. The most exalted in dignity, called Archon Eponymus, or simply Archon, by way of eminence, represented the majesty of the republic; the second in rank, who had the title of Basileus or king, was head of the Athenian religion; and the Polemarch, who was third in rank, had the chief direction of military affairs. The remaining six archons, who bore the general appellation of Thesmothetæ, or "guardians of the laws," presided as judges in the ordinary courts of justice, as the former three did in the superior tribunals; and the whole nine, when convened, formed the council of state [3]. The archons were usually chosen by lot, from the highest class of citizens; but sometimes the assembly of the people, with which resided the right of legislation, assumed the power of naming them [4].

An authority so temporary and limited, as that possessed by the annual archons, was not sufficient to restrain the restless spirit of the Athenians, agitated by factions, and jealous to excess of their political free-

2. Pausan lib. vii.   3. Arist. *Polit.* lib. iv. vi. et Frag. *de Civit. Ath.* See also Potter, *Archæolog. Græc.* book. 1. chap. xii. 4. Plut. *Vit. Aristides.*

dom.

dom. Athens accordingly became a scene of anarchy, violence, and injustice. At length, made severely sensible of the inconveniences of such an unstable government, and of an unsettled jurisprudence (the Athenians having yet no regular code of laws), all parties saw the necessity of reforming the state; and especially of regulating the administration of justice. For the execution of this great work, they cast their eyes upon the archon Draco; a man of rigid morals, and incorruptible integrity, but unfortunately of a mind not equal to the important and arduous undertaking.

As if conscious of his political inability, Draco seems to have left the Athenian constitution nearly in the same state that he found it. He confined his innovations chiefly to juridical matters. And, even in these, he shewed himself little capable of accommodating his ideas to the circumstances of the times; to the character of the people, who had intrusted him with the high office of legislator, or to the general temper of mankind. He made capital almost all crimes, which came under the cognizance of his laws [5].

The very severity of such a jurisprudence defeated its own end, the *reformation of manners.* When conviction must necessarily have proved fatal to the culprit, few witnesses would appear against persons accused of inferior crimes; and as the humanity of the judge was interested in saving, where the evidence against such offenders was complete, it followed of course, that all crimes passed unpunished except those of the most atrocious nature [6]. The laws of Draco, therefore, instead of remedying the evils of which his countrymen complained, may be said to have increased them. But they served to compose the minds of the

5. Plut. *Vit. Solon.* Arist. *Polit.* lib. ii. 6. Id. ibid.

Athenians

Athenians for a time, and happily paved the way for the
reception of laws and institutions of a very different
description; for those of Solon, which were as mild as
his predecessor's were severe[7]. And all their assuasive
lenity was necessary, to insure their operation.

The condition of no people perhaps ever exhibited
a deeper scene of trouble and disorder, than that of
the inhabitants of Attica, when the virtues and abilities of this extraordinary man were called to their relief.
The magistrates plundered the public treasury; and
often betrayed, for bribes, the cause of justice. The
rich oppressed the poor: and the wretched populace,
practised in robbing, and driven to despair, were ripe
for rebellion[8]. Descended from an ancient and honourable family, Solon had, in early life, been distinguished
at Athens for his love of learning and his talent for
poetry[9]. And the misfortunes of his country soon
brought forward to notice those political powers, which
afterward enabled him to reform the constitution of
the state.

Perceiving the weakness of the Athenian government, the people of Salamis (an island in the Saronic
gulf), had revolted, and leagued themselves with those
of Megara. The Athenians made several attempts to
recover that island; but, in all, they failed of success.
And so great had been their loss, on those mortifying
occasions, that the assembly of the people passed a law,
making it a capital offence in any person, whatever
might be his rank, his office, or his character, to propose a renewal of the unfortunate enterprise[10]. But

7. As an apology for this severity, Draco cynically replied, "Small
"crimes deserve death, and I can find no greater punishment for the
"most heinous." Plut. *Vit. Solon.*

8. *Fragm. Solon.* ap. Demosth.   9. Plut. *Vit. Solon.*
10. Id. ibid.

although

although no one durst openly require the repeal of
this rash law, it became the cause of shame and dissatisfaction among the younger and braver Athenian
citizens.

Of the latter number was Solon. He, therefore, bethought himself of an artifice for evading the penalty,
yet inducing the people to annul their own act. Having circulated a report, that he was subject to temporary fits of madness, he accordingly composed an in-
flammatory poem, entitled *Salamis;* and rushing out
into the market place, mounted the heralds-stone, and
recited his performance to the crowd. The people
were filled with sorrow and indignation at the pusillan-
imity of their desponding law, for relinquishing that
island. The obnoxious statute was repealed; and it
was instantly resolved, that a new armament should
be sent against Salamis. The command of the expedition was committed to the party that Solon had
embraced. It was conducted with ability, and crowned with success. Salamis was recovered without much
bloodshed[11].

Ant. Ch.
601.
Olymp.
xliv. 4.

The fortunate issue of this enterprise acquired
Solon considerable influence at Athens; and other
events conspired to spread the fame of his sagacity and
promptitude over all Greece. Those events I must relate, and point out his connection with them, before I
speak of him in his legislative capacity.

I have already had occasion to mention the establishment of the council of Amphictyons, and its superintendance over the oracle of Apollo at Delphos.
But I have hitherto found no opportunity of relating
the rise of that oracle, or of noticing the extension of

11. Plut. ubi sup.

the

the Amphictyonic council, in consequence of the conquest of Peloponnesus by the Heraclidæ. I shall now, therefore, offer these subjects to your lordship's attention, by way of introduction to the history of the first *Sacred War*, which furnished Sôlon with new occasions of discovering the strength of his genius.

"All mankind," says Homer, in the person of Nestor, "have need of the gods[12]!" A sense of this need, which seems intuitive in the human mind, or a consciousness of our own weakness, that leads us to look up for protection to superior powers, may be considered as the *natural cause* of all *religion*. And a desire of penetrating the will of those gods, the supposed dispensers of good and evil, has, among various nations, given birth to divination, soothsaying, and oracular responses. The Grecian oracles are said to have derived their origin from Egypt and Crete, the two great nurseries of heathen superstition: and thence the Greeks had also received their popular creed.

The most ancient of the Grecian oracles was that sacred to Jupiter at Dodona[13], the rise of which is thus accounted for by Herodotus. A Phœnecian ship-master, in a voyage to Egypt, having carried off with him from the city of Thebes on the Nile, one of the priestesses, or female attendants, belonging to the temple of Jupiter there, sold her as a slave in Thesprotia;

---

12. *Odyss.* lib. iii. ver. 48.   13. Herodotus, lib. i. cap. lii. Strabo, lib. vii. p. 327, edit. Lutet. Paris, 1620. M. Hardion (*Prim. Dissertat. sur l'Oracle de Delph.*) endeavours to prove, that the Oracle of Delphos was more ancient than that at Dodona; because the Pelasgi were in Thesprotia, when the Dodonian oracle was established (Id. ibid.). But the Pelasgi were spread over Greece and the contiguous countries in the most early times (Herodot. lib. i. cap. lvi. lvii. et. seq. Strabo, lib. vii. p. 327—329, edit. sup. cit.): and they had their name not from Pelasgus, as M. Hardion supposes, but from their wandering character. Strabo, lib. viii. p. 397.

a mountainous

a mountainous district, on the south-west coast of Epirus. Though here reduced to a state of servitude, and ignorant of the language of the country, this woman soon attracted the veneration of the rude natives. Her sagacity, acquired by living among a more cultivated people; her foreign aspect, and mysterious carriage, suited to the habits of Egyptian superstition, made them all conclude she must hold private converse with some divinity. She encouraged their easy credulity; and, well instructed in the means of taking advantage of it, occasionally chose her station under the dark shade of an aged oak, near the village of Dodona; whence she gave answers, in a broken dialect, to every one who came to consult her[14]. These answers she delivered in the name of the god Jupiter, with whose secret councils she pretended to be intrusted. Her prophetic reputation daily increased. She at length spoke in the Greek tongue; or with a *human voice*, to use the words of the admiring Thesprotians[15]. Her success gained her associates, who became her successors. And a temple, famous for its oracular responses, rose to Dodonean Jupiter in the centre of the grove, where the Egyptian captive had first taken her stand.

Similar institutions were attempted, and established in different parts of Greece. But the oracle of Apollo at Delphos early acquired, and long maintained a reputation superior to all other oracles in the heathen world. This celebrity it owed to the following circumstances.

On the southern side of the winding ridge of mount Parnassus, which divides the districts of Phocis and Locris, and at no great distance from the sea-ports of

---

14. Herodot. lib. ii.   15. Id. ibid.

Cirrha

Cirrha and Crissa, was formed by nature a kind of amphitheatre, encompassed with stupendous rocks. In the midst of that almost inaccessible spot, was hollowed a deep cavern, the crevices of which emitted a vapour that strongly affected the brain[16]; and as phrenzy of every kind, among the Greeks, was supposed the effect of divine inspiration, the incoherent speeches of the herdsmen, who had approached that cavern, were regarded as prophetical, and ascribed to the immediate impulse of some god residing in the place[17].

In consequence of this notion, an assembly of the neighbouring inhabitants was convened at Delphos, or the solitude, as the word imports, in order to deliberate on the means of best receiving the inspiration, and uttering the responses of the divinity. For these purposes, it was resolved by that assembly to appoint one person, a virgin prophetess, whose safety should be provided for by a frame placed over the principal chasm, whence the maddening vapour issued; as several of the superstitious multitude, who had resorted to Delphos for information concerning futurity, had fallen into the cavern, while intoxicated with its effluvia, and there perished[18]. The frame was made to rest on three feet, and thence called a tripod. On that frame the prophetess, who obtained, in very early times, (from Python, one of the titles of Apollo) the name of Pythia or Pythoness, was seated when she had occasion to exercise her sacred function[19].

The interposition of public authority gave new importance to Delphos, and made way for a farther establishment. A rude temple was built over the hallowed cavern; priests were instituted to determine,

16. Strabo, lib. ix. Diod. Sicul. lib. xvi.   17. Id. ibid.
18. Diod. Sicul. ubi sup.   19. Pausan. lib. x. Diod.
Sicul. lib. xvi. Strabo, lib. ix.

on what occasions the pythia should mount the sacred
tripod, in order to imbibe the prophetic steam; as well
as to collect and digest her frantic ravings, confusedly
poured forth, while under the supposed influence of
the inspiring god. And ceremonies were prescribed,
and sacrifices performed, to the presiding divinity,
under various names[20]. At length some pious adventurers from Gnossus in Crete, landed at the port of
Crissa, and proceeding up the bold declivity of mount
Parnassus, placed the temple at Delphos immediately,
under the auspices of Apollo[21]; by whose command
they declared they had acted, and whose priests they
there became[22].

Under this new and permanent deity, through the
skill of his Cretan ministers, the reputation of the
oracle rapidly increased; and Delphos, which had the
singular advantage of being nearly in the centre of
Greece, was represented as the centre of the world,
and the appellation of *navel of the earth* was bestowed
upon it[23]. The size of the holy city became early
considerable, and the riches and splendour of the temple of Apollo proverbially great.

The institution of the Amphictyonic council, which
was particularly intrusted by its founder (as I have formerly had occasion to observe[24]) with the protection of
the territory of the soothsaying god, added much to
the wealth and magnificence of Delphos, by spreading
the fame of the oracle. No business of any consequence was undertaken in Greece, either by states or
individuals, without consulting the pythia. On such
occasions a present was always necessary: and the opulent endeavoured to conciliate the favour of Apollo,

20. Id. ibid.   21. Homer, *Hymn. ad. Apol.*
22. Id. ibid. Apollo was then a deity of high reputation in the
Grecian islands, and in Asia Minor, but yet of small fame on the con-
inent of Greece.   23. Strabo, lib. ix.   24. Lett. II.

by

by offerings of high value[25]. Vanity was called in to the aid of superstition. The names of such as sent or brought valuable presents were carefully registered; and when statues, tripods, vases, or other ornaments, of precious metal or curious workmanship, were offered at the shrine of the god, they were publicly exhibited in honour of the community, prince, or private person, by whom they had been bestowed. An emulation in donations took place, and the treasury of the oracle became immensely rich and great[26].

As Delphos had acquired an increase of wealth and fame from the early guardianship of the council of Amphictyons, that council, and consequently the oracle, obtained more extensive influence from the conquests of the Dorians under the Heraclidæ. Formerly constituent members of the Amphictyonic assembly, the Dorians continued to send deputies to its meetings after they had established themselves in Peloponnesus; and the people of all the provinces which the Heraclidæ had conquered, within the Corinthian Isthmus, gradually assumed the same privilege[27]. Thus the Amphictyons became a representative body of the whole Grecian people; consisting not only of the three principal tribes, Ionians, Dorians, and Æolians, but of the several subdivisions of those tribes, and of the various communities formed from their promiscuous cohabitation, and their combination with other ancient tribes, as well as with foreign invaders[28]. The most distinguished of these mixed communities were the Athenians, of Ionian extraction partly; the Lacedæmonians, of Dorian descent; and the Bœotians, of Æolian origin.

25. Vid. *Dissert. sur l'Oracle de Delph.* par. M. Hardion, et anet. cit. 26. Id. ibid.

27. See Dr. Leland's *Preliminary Discourse* to the *Hist. of Philip of Macedon*, and Mitford's *Hist. of Greece*, chap. iv. sec. iii. and the authors there cited. 28. Id. ibid.

Each

. Each independent Grecian state, with some few exceptions, had thenceforth a right to send two deputies or representatives to the Amphictyonic council. One of these deputies, whose office was to attend to the civil affairs of his constituents, under the title of pylagoras, was elected by the suffrages of the people; the other, called hieromnemon, from his exclusive privilege of superintending the business of religion, was appointed by lot[29]. The central city of Delphos, so famous for its oracle, which had been politically placed under the protection of the Amphictyons, as we have seen, was now chosen as the place for holding their vernal meeting. The autumnal council continued to assemble at Thermopylæ[30].

But neither the augmented consequence, and immediate superintendance of the Amphictyonic council, nor the sacred respect inspired by the extended and growing influence of the Delphic oracle, could restrain lawless rapacity from concerting a project for plundering the shrine of Apollo. That impious project was formed and executed by the Crisseans; whose territory lying to the south of Delphos, and comprehended in an extent of about twenty-four miles in length, and fifteen in breadth, contained three large and flourishing cities; Crissa, Cirrha, and Anticirrha[31].

A soil comparatively fertile, an advantageous foreign commerce, and a lucrative inland trade, instead of satisfying the desires, served only to increase the avidity of this highly favoured people. They first exacted heavy contributions from all merchants who went to expose their goods to sale, and afterward from persons of every description, who resorted to the holy

29. Leland, ubi sup.   30. Id. ibid.
31. Strabo, lib. ix. Pausan. lib. x.

PART I.

Ant. Ch.
600.
Olymp.
xlv. 1.

city[32]. Their vicinity to that city rendered familiar to them the woods, the grottos, the ministers, and the worship of the prophetic god. Reverence was thus diminished, and avarice excited. The temple of Delphos was robbed, in a moment, of all the accumulated treasure, and rich votive offerings, lavished by the profuse bounty of superstition for ages[33]. As the minds of men were not prepared for such a horrid sacrilege, no measures had been taken to prevent it, Nor were any immediately adopted, for punishing the offenders: so that the Crisseans were permitted not only to seize but to secure their booty; to add murder to robbery; and to defile the sacred groves with the most abominable lusts[34].

It belonged to the council of Amphictyons to punish the perpetrators of these atrocious enormities, which its vigilance had failed to prevent. But the deliberations of that assembly were formal and indecisive. And it was not without difficulty that Solon, one of the Athenian delegates, could induce the majority of his associates to adopt the obvious and necessary resolution, under such circumstances, of taking vengeance on the aggregated crimes of the Crisseans; and, by so doing, to vindicate the offended majesty of religion, and resent the affront offered to the august Amphictyonic body[35].

Nor were the measures taken, in consequence of this resolution, which gave a beginning to the sacred war, either prompt or vigorous. The forces first brought into the field by the Amphictyons were not equal to the enterprise for which they had been levied. They therefore attempted in vain, during nine years, though furnished with various reinforcements, to make

32. Pausan. ubi sup. Æschin. in *Ctesiphont*.   33. Id. ibid.
34. Pausan. lib. x.   35. Pausan. ubi sup. Plut. *Vit. Solon*.

themselves

LETTER
VI.
Ant. Ch.
591.
Olymp.
xlvii. 2.

themselves masters of any of the devoted towns[36]. In the tenth summer of the war, Crissa was carried by assault. Its fortifications were demolished, in obedience to the command of the oracle; the houses were consumed with fire; and the inhabitants were treated with a severity proportioned to the degree of their guilt, and to the hostile rage of the victorious besiegers, boiling with holy indignation. They were all either put to the sword or committed to the flames[37].

The object of the sacred war, however, was not yet fully accomplished; nor was the vengeance of Apollo completely executed, in the destruction of the Crissean capital. A remnant of that impious community still subsisted in the strong maritime town of Cirrha. And as it was found that the reduction of this place would be attended with many difficulties, recourse was had to the advice of the oracle. "You "shall not overturn," said the pythia, the instrument of the ministers of the Delphic god, "the lofty towers "of Cirrha, until the foaming billows of blue-eyed "Amphitrité beat against the resounding shores of "the Holy Land[38]."

This answer appeared absolutely inexplicable, as the success which it promised was made to depend upon a seemingly impossible circumstance; for, how could the sea be conveyed, for several leagues, over rocks and mountains, so that its waves might dash against the craggy precipices, which bounded the territory of Delphos;—That difficulty no one was able, for a time, to obviate. The inhabitants of Cirrha, therefore, flattered themselves with the hope of perpetual security; and the majority of the members of the

36. Id. ibid. Strabo, lib. ix. Thessal. *Orat. ad Athen.*

37. Æschin. in *Ctesiphont.*
38. Pausan. lib. x.

Amphictyonic

Amphictyonic council thought there was reason for relinquishing an enterprise, which seemed so unpropitious to the god by whose order the war had been undertaken, and whose insulted divinity it was meant to avenge.

While these desponding sentiments prevailed in the camp of the besiegers, Solon, the Athenian delegate, who had first roused the Amphictyons to arms, ventured to offer more spirited council. His superior sagacity enabled him to penetrate the mysterious meaning, or at least to give a favourable turn to the response of the oracle. To bring the sea to the boundary of the Holy Land, he admitted to be impossible for man; but the Holy Land, he ingeniously observed, might be made to communicate with the sea, by extending that boundary. In order to accomplish this junction, it was only necessary to consecrate the intermediate space, with the same ceremonies which had formerly been observed in dedicating to Apollo the Delphian territory[39].

Solon's happy explication of the answer of the oracle was honoured with the unanimous approbation of his associates, and preparations were instantly made for carrying the suggested expedient into execution. The property of the Cirrhean plain was accordingly surrendered to the incensed god, with the most pompous formality, by the Amphictyons; and the soldiers, animated with new courage by that pious ceremony, assailed the walls of Cirrha with resistless fury. The place was taken, and the dependent town of Anticirrha submitted at the same time. The sacrilegious citizens were either put to the sword, or carried into slavish captivity[40]. Such was the issue of the *first sacred war*.

39. Id. ibid.   40. Pausan. Æschin. et Thessal. ubi sup.

The

The community of Crissa, formerly so rich and powerful, was forever extirpated. Its lands were laid waste, its cities were demolished. The harbour of Cirrha alone was allowed to remain entire, as a convenient port for Delphos[41]. Condemned to perpetual sterility by the oracle, the Crissean territory long lay in an uncultivated state; for the Delphians, abundantly furnished by superstition with the conveniencies, and even with the luxuries of life, were under no necessity of ploughing or sowing the ground for subsistence[42].

The fortunate termination of this war, which strengthened the authority of the Amphictyonic council, and procured new respect to the Delphic oracle, at the same time that it exalted the character of Solon, was distinguished by the re-establishment of the pythian-games, or festivals in honour of Apollo. These games, which had been interrupted by a long train of hostilities and calamities, were now celebrated with a pomp worthy of the occasion. The Amphictyons bestowed on the victors, instead of the scanty rewards usually offered to gymnastic combatants at such public solemnities, the most precious spoils of the Crissean cities[43].

Nor was this the only innovation made by the Amphictyons, on the restoration of the pythian festivals. They proposed prizes for competitors in instrumental music, unaccompanied with poetry: and thus separated the sister-arts, which had hitherto been united in all musical competitions at the Grecian festivals; the laurel crown being always adjudged to the poetic

41. Id. ibid.   42. Lucian. in *Phalar.*
43. The victors in the Olympic games received only an olive chaplet or crown, and a branch of palm. See West's *Dissertat. on the Olymp. Games*, Sect. xvi. et auct. cit.

musician

musician, who animated the effusions of his genius with the sound of his voice and lyre[44].

How far that separation was beneficial or hurtful to the advancement of those arts, I shall afterward have occasion to consider, in tracing the progress of Grecian poetry and music. At present, my lord, we must investigate a more important subject.

Before the conclusion of the sacred war, Solon had been chosen archon, and entrusted, by his countrymen, with the reformation of the laws and constitution of the Athenian state. Aware of the difficulties he had to encounter, Solon began his archonship with composing the minds of the people, and predisposing them for the changes necessary to be made in the government. With a view to the first of these objects he endeavoured to quiet the rival factions of Cylon and Megacles, by which Athens was then distracted, and which had their origin in a very extraordinary proceeding.

During the first year of the sacred war, Cylon, a powerful citizen, and son-in-law to Theagenes, tyrant of Megara, was encouraged by his flatterers, and an equivocal response of the Delphic oracle, to usurp the supreme power. In prosecution of this ambitious project, being furnished with a body of troops by Theagenes, he seized the acropolis or citadel of Athens. The people, among whom he seems to have formed no party, instantly flew to arms. They were joined by the inhabitants of the country ; and Cylon, seeing no prospect of relief, privately made his escape[45]. His adherents, thus deserted, and pressed by famine, sat

44. See Blackwell's *Inquiry into the Life of Homer*, and Gillies's *Hist. of Greece*, chap. v. et auct. cit.   45. Thucyd. lib. i.

down

down as suppliants by the altar of Minerva in the citadel[46]. Persuaded by Megacles, then archon, to quit
their sanctuary, under a promise of personal safety,
they were, notwithstanding, put to death by order of
that magistrate and his colleague[47]: and some of them
were slain, even at the shrine of the goddess[48].

In consequence of this sacrilegious breach of faith,
these magistrates were called the accursed of the goddess[49], and became the objects of public hatred[50].
Meantime the secret adherents of Cylon, united with
such of his avowed partizans as had escaped the general slaughter[12], gathered new strength and confidence,
and loudly demanded justice on the associates of Megacles; he himself, it should appear, being removed
from that inquest by death. The influence of the family of Megacles was great in Athens. But there was
no withstanding, among a superstitious people, the cry
against the crime of unexpiated sacrilege; to which the
friends of Cylon artfully imputed all the misfortunes
that afflicted, or those that threatened the state. Solon
was, therefore, able to persuade such of the accused
magistrates as remained alive to stand trial. They were
found guilty, by a grand jury of three hundred citizens of the highest class, and driven into exile[53].
Nor was this punishment thought sufficient to satisfy
the vengeance of the offended deity. The bodies of
the dead were dug out of the grave, and conveyed beyond the limits of Attica[54].

While Athens was agitated with the violent disputes which preceded the trial of those obnoxious

46. Id. ibid.   47. Plut. *Vit. Solon.*
48. Id. ibid. Thucyd. ubi sup.   49. Thucyd. lib. i.
50. Plut. *Vit. Solon.*
52. Those who applied to the wives of the magistrates, Plutarch
tells us, were spared. *Vit. Solon.*
53. Plut. ubi sup.   54. Id. ibid. et Thucyd. ubi sup.
                                        magistrates

magistrates, and which enfeebled the councils of the state, the people of Megara retook Salamis. This loss augmented the superstitious fears of the Athenians; and Epimenides, a pious sage, deeply skilled in religious mysteries, was sent for from Crete. On his arrival, he contracted an intimate friendship with Solon, and smoothed the way for the reception of the institutions of that legislator[55]. By expiations and lustrations, he hallowed and purified the city of Athens, and made the people more observant of justice, and more inclined to union[56].

Solon, however, conducted himself with great caution, in the exercise of that high authority with which he was vested. He resolved to make no innovations but such as appeared absolutely necessary, and which he had reason to think would be approved by the majority of his fellow-citizens. Hence his liberal answer to those who questioned him in regard to his legislation, That if he had not given the Athenians the best possible laws, he had given them the best they were capable of receiving[57]. Conformably to this mild and moderate principle, wisely tempering coercion with lenity, he began the exercise of his legislative function with repealing all the bloody laws of Draco, except those concerning murder. He next struck at the root of the reigning evil; the *unequal division of property*; which enabled the rich to tyrannize over the

55. Plut. *Vit. Solon.*   56. Id. ibid.   When Epimenides was ready to take his departure, the Athenians offered to load him with honours and rewards; but he would only accept of a branch of the sacred Olive that grew near the temple of Minerva in the acropolis, and which was said to have sprung out of the earth at her command (Plut. et Diog. Laert. *Vit. Solon.*). This was a present worthy of disinterested wisdom and superior sanctity, and which could not fail to spread the reputation of both, with the influence of Epimenides, over the minds of men.

57. Plut. *Vit. Solon.*

poor

poor, incited the poor to alarm the rich for their safety, and both to embroil the state[58].

To relieve the former party, without offending the latter, was a delicate business; and it was skilfully managed. Solon got both parties to join in a common sacrifice, called *seisach theia*, or "the feast of deliverance from burdens[59];" a pious prelude to a general insolvent act, or full release of persons and things, which enabled him to accomplish his purpose, and in a manner that gave satisfaction to the more liberal minded Athenians of all ranks, as well as to the multitude[60]. He maintained the former division of property, but abolished debts, and reduced the legal interest of money, while he made effectual provision, that an insolvent debtor should not, in future, become the slave of his creditor; be compelled to deliver up his children to servitude, or to sell them for the discharge of any debt[61].

Having surmounted this grand difficulty, and established such preliminary ordinances as seemed im-

58. Id. ibid.   59. Diog. Laert. *Vit. Solon.*

60. For, as Aristotle sagely observes, "Solon innovated no farther "on ancient establishments, than seemed necessary to promote and "secure the enfranchisement of the people" (*Polit.* lib. ii.). Some of the poor, indeed, thought he did too little for them, and many of the rich, that he did too much; but his justice and moderation were admired by the great body of his fellow-citizens. Plut. et Diog. Laert. *Vit. Solon.*

61. Aristot. Plut. et Diog. Laert. ubi sup. But the Athenian slaves, after all the citizens were enfranchised, greatly exceeded the number of free men. Toward these degraded fellow-creatures, the disgrace of Greek and Roman policy, Solon could only extend his humanity, by framing regulations for their better treatment. Their servitude was accordingly henceforth more gentle, and their condition in all respects more eligible in Athens, than in any other Grecian state (Demosth. *Philipp.* iii.). They were placed under the protection of the laws, and might prosecute their masters for ill usage. Athenæus, lib. vii.

PART I. mediately necessary for public peace, the Athenian legislator proceeded to balance the constitution of the state. With this view, he divided the citizens, or free inhabitants of Attica of native origin, together with such foreigners as had been naturalized, into four classes, regulated solely by a census of the annual produce of their lands[62]; so that an open course was left for hope and emulation, as a citizen of any of the inferior classes might, by frugality and honest industry, obtain a place in the highest, and consequently a title to all the honours and offices connected with it[63].

The first class consisted of such citizens as had an annual income of at least five hundred *medimni*, or measures of liquid, as well as of dry commodities; namely, corn, wine, and oil; equivalent to between five and six hundred pounds sterling, according to the present value of money. The second class was composed of such as had an income of three hundred measures; the third class, of such as had an income of two hundred measures; and the fourth, and by far the most numerous class, of such as either possessed no property in land, or the annual produce of whose estates was below two hundred measures[64].

To Athenians of the first class Solon confined the arconship, with other offices of expence and dignity;

---

62. Plut. *Vit. Solon.*   63. Aristotle, in forming his idea of a *citizen*, seems to have had his eye on the Athenian constitution, as reformed by *Solon*. "Generally speaking," says he, "a "citizen is one partaking equally of subordination and power." The definition may be extended to different states, but in one the best constituted, a citizen is a subject competent to, and occasionally candidate for every office, in proportion to his estimation and good life. *Polit.* lib. iii.

64. Plut. *Vit. Solon.* The attic *medimnum*, the measure here computed by, was equivalent, according to the computation of Dr. Arbuthnot, to four pecks and six pints, or somewhat better than an English bushel.

to,

to those of the second and third classes, he appropriated the inferior magistracies, with the municipal and
military offices ; reserving only to those of the fourth
class an equal voice in the assembly of the people, with
all the other common privileges of citizens[65]. And
that voice, and these privileges, were sufficient to give
this class, by reason of its numbers, an ascendency
over the other three, notwithstanding their official superiority. To the collective body of the Athenian citizens, legally convened, belonged not only the right
of electing and judging magistrates and ministers, entrusted, for a limited time, with public authority, but
also the power of deciding ultimately in all cases, legislative, executive, and juridical[66]. They only could
contract or dissolve alliances, and with them remained
the alternative of peace and war[67].

Aware of the danger of thus devolving sovereignty
into the hands of the people, though on the generous
principle, that the few ought not to command, and the
many obey, Solon instituted, for the support of his political system, a new council or senate; consisting of
four hundred members, annually chosen from the four
tribes into which the Athenians were then divided,
one hundred out of each tribe, and from the three
higher classes of citizens[68]. Such an assembly, he con-

65. Plut. ubi sup. Aristot. Fragm. de Civit. Athen. et Polit. lib. ii.
66. Solon directed, that in the Athenian courts of justice, both civil
and criminal causes should be decided by a set of men taken, in the
manner of an English jury, from the body of the people, the archons
only presiding as judges. Id. ibid.
67. Aristot. ubi sup. et Xenoph. Polit. Athen.
68. Xenoph. ubi sup. et Plut. Vit. Solon. The Athenians were afterward divided into ten tribes, and then fifty senators being chosen out
of each tribe, the whole number became five hundred; whence the
senate was commonly called the Council of Five Hundred, or simply
The Five Hundred.

cluded

cluded, would hold a sway, which the college of archons had not been able to maintain.   He, therefore,
committed to the senate many of the executive powers
that had formerly belonged to those magistrates, as a
council of state ; and, among others the sole right of
equipping fleets and armies, beside such high privileges
as were peculiar to its constitution ; the prerogative of
convoking the popular assembly, of examining and ap-
proving all matters of debate before they could be proposed in that assembly, and of enacting laws which had
force during a year, without requiring the consent of
the people[69].

The weight of this senate, which assembled every
day, except on festivals, infused a considerable mixture
of aristocracy into the Athenian constitution.   And,
Solon endeavoured to raise an additional and powerful
counterposie, in order to preserve, yet more steadily,
the balance of state, against the hazards attending the
uncertainty and turbulence of democratic rule[70]. That
he in some measure effected, by restoring and augmenting the consequence of the court of areopagus,
which the institutions of Draco had almost annihilated.
By those of Solon it was invested, beside its criminal
jurisdiction, with a general inspection over the laws
and religion, as well as over the manners of the citizens[71]. Composed solely of those magistrates, who
                                                    had

69. Id. ibid. Before the expiration of that term, the good or evil
tendency of any law would become obvious to the multitude, and
might be more safely annulled or confirmed. Nor would the multitude be often wrong, when unprejudiced. For, as Aristotle justly
remarks, " although the constituent members of a popular assembly,
" each and by himself, shall judge worse than a well-educated man,
" yet the whole and together shall decide better, or certainly not
" worse, than a council of statesmen." *Polit.* lib. iii.
  70. Plut. et Aristot. ubi sup.
  71. Id. ibid. " Rather adapting his laws to the state of his coun-
                                                    try,"

had passed through the office of archon with credit,
and stood the scrutiny of the people, the areopagus
was entitled to assume not only a censorial, but in critical times, even a sort of dictatorial power[n]. It was
the only Athenian tribunal in which the judges held
their seats for life, and from whose decrees there lay
no legal appeal to the popular assembly[73].

Having thus secured the government of the republic by the senate and areopagus, as by two firm an-
chors, Solon fondly hoped, that it would not thenceforth become the sport of the waves of popular fury.
He found himself, however, mistaken. The giddy
Athenians set no bounds to their desire of innovation.
They were perpetually soliciting the legislator for some
new regulation or amendment[74]. In order to avoid
their eager importunities, he resolved to travel. But

try," says Plutarch, "than his country to his laws, and perceiving
" that the territory of Attica, which but poorly rewarded the labours
" of the husbandman, was far from being sufficient to support a lazy
" multitude, Solon ordered that *trades* should be accounted *honourable;*
" and that the council of areopagus should examine into every man's
" means of subsistence, and chastise the idle." Plut. *Vit. Solon.*

72. Isocrat. *Orat. Areopag.*

73. Id. ibid. See also Potter's *Archæolog. Græc.* book i. chap xix.
et auct. cit. Such was the political system established at Athens by
Solon. To enter into a detail of his civil regulations, would be devi-
ating from the object of this work; especially as most of his laws are
now become familiar, by being adopted into the Roman code, and
thence conveyed into the jurisprudence of most nations in modern
Europe. Some of them, however, are sufficiently memorable to merit
particular notice. " Let no man," says he, " stand neuter, in times
" of sedition, under penalty of banishment and confiscation; let no
" son be obliged to maintain a father, who has not taught him some
" trade; let not a guardian live in the same house with the mother of
" his ward. If an archon is found in public intoxicated with liquor,
" let him be put to death. If a man detects his wife in adultery,
" and lives with her afterward, let him be accounted infamous."
Plut. et Diog. Laert. *Vit. Solon.* Demost. et Aul Gell. passim.

74. Plut. *Vit. Solon.*

before

PART I.   before his departure, he procured a promise from the
whole body of citizens, solemnly confirmed by oath,
that they would abolish none of his institutions for
ten years[75]. After such a term of experience, he
wisely conjectured, that whatever alterations should
seem necessary, might be made with greater certainty
of contributing to public happiness[76].

. But the Athenians, though not utterly regardless
of their oath, paid little respect to the institutions of

75. Herodot. lib. i.   Proclus, in *Timæo*.

76. " Governments ever should be constituted," says Aristotle,
" with a view to the *happiness* of the *constituents*" (*Polit*. lib. vii.).
This axiom I have endeavoured to confirm in treating of the Spartan
government; the deficiency of which, with respect to internal felicity, cannot be more strongly marked than in the words of Alcibiades.
" There is nothing singular," he was wont to say, " that the Laceda-
" monians should die fearlessly in battle; for, considering the mise-
" ries they suffer under their rigid institutions at home, they may
" well choose a glorious death in the field, in exchange for such a
" life" (Ælian, *Var. Hist*. lib. xiii. chap. xxviii.). The spirit of the
institutions of Solon was in almost all respects, the reverse of that of
Lycurgus; and an equal contrast of character, of austerity and mildness, was observable between the people of Athens and those of Sparta,
as we shall have occasion to see in tracing the history of the two
states.   Moral and intellectual improvement, justice, humanity, and
mutual sympathy, were the leading principles of Solon.   He did not
attempt to force, but to cultivate the nature of man.   And the great
object of his policy was the union of self-love and social, by direct-
ing equally the hopes and fears of the Athenians, the reason and passions of *all* to the security of *all*.   Hence his celebrated answer to the
question, " How may injury and injustice be excluded from human
" society ?"—" By teaching all," replied he, " to feel the injuries done
" to each" (Diog. Laert. *Vit. Solon*.).   " He imagined and reduced to
" system," to use the words of a respectable modern author, " a com-
" monwealth, wherein virtue, wherein property, and every substan-
" tial discrimination, from character or profession, was acknowledged
" and preserved; and wherein the best principles of aristocratic and
" popular government were combined, by institutions equally fa-
" vourable to subordination and to liberty; to civil gradations, and
" to the rights of mankind."   Young. *Hist. Ath*. book i.

Solon,

Solon, during his absence[77]. Soon after his departure, the three factions or parties, into which the people of Attica had been formerly divided, made again their appearance; namely, those of the lowlands, the highlands, and the coast; or, in other words, the aristocratical, democratical, and moderate parties[78]. The latter party received strong support from Megacles, representative of the opulent and powerful family of the Alcmæonids. At the head of the aristocratical party stood Lycurgus, the son of Aristolaides, also a man of ancient family, and of great wealth and consequence. The democratical party was governed by Pisistratus; a distinguished young man, who traced his high descent from the patriotic Codrus: and who added to superior talents and accomplishments—to the most persuasive eloquence and the deepest political discernment, a daring spirit, and engaging manners[79]. He had been successful in several naval and military enterprises, in which his valour and conduct were equally conspicuous; and seemed naturally formed for sway[80]. Meanwhile he affected the greatest moderation, and captivated the hearts of the populace by his affability and liberality[81].

These three parties, and their leaders, divided and distracted the Athenians of all conditions, when Solon returned to his native city; after he had spent the number of years, mentioned at his departure, in visiting

---

77. Plut. Vit. Solon.   78. Id. ibid.

79. Plut. ubi sup. Herodot. lib. i. v. vi.

80. Herodot. et Plut. ubi sup.

81. Id. ibid. He was always attended by two or three slaves, carrying bags of money, in order to enable him to relieve the necessities of the poor. At the same time, he reproved idleness, and encouraged industry (Meurs. in *Pisistrat.*). And he carried his seeming love of equality so far, as to order the gates of his gardens and orchards to be left open, that the fruit might be common to all. Id. ibid.

various

various countries, and had resided some time in Egypt, in Cyprus, and in Lydia[82]. The venerable legislator was received, on his return, with the most profound respect by his countrymen. Yet, violent as the storm was, which agitated the state, it does not appear that his experienced wisdom was solicited by the majority of any party, to guide the helm of government. He endeavoured, however, though ineffectually, by his personal influence, to reconcile the heads of the different factions, and to appease the animosity of their adherents[83]. But their prejudices were become rooted; and their opposition having assumed the semblance of principle, pride and shame equally conspired to prevent a coalition. Solon, therefore, could only watch, with parental care, over the safety of that constitution which he had framed, without attempting to administer a remedy for its disorders.

82. Plut. *Vit. Solon.* During the residence of Solon in Lydia, is supposed to have happened that famous conversation with Croesus, which has been retailed by so many historians, and which had for its object the instability of human greatness, admirably illustrated by Herodotus in the history of the Lydian monarch (*Historiar.* lib. i.). Plutarch, fond of story-telling, has repeated it in his *Life of Solon,* because of its celebrity, as he says, notwithstanding the disagreement of the pretended interview between Solon and Croesus with certain chronological tables, from which some writers had attempted to prove it to be fictitious, but which he represents as not to be depended upon (Plut. *Vit, Solon.*). And this artful apology for blending truth and falsehood, has been considered by a multitude of modern authors as a proof of the uncertainty of all ancient chronology, as Plutarch could not rely on it. To me, however, it appears only a proof, that the conversation alluded to was considered as fabulous by the more judicious ancient historians, and that the old man was disposed to relate it, for the purpose of embellishing his narrative. I cannot therefore help expressing my surprise, that so judicious a writer as Dr. Gillies, who places the usurpation of Pisistratus (universally allowed to have happened after the return of Solon to Athens) in the year 578 before the christian æra, and the accession of Croesus to the Lydian throne sixteen years later, in the year 562 before the same æra (*Hist. Greece,* chap. vii. and chap. viii. xiii.), should ingraft this conversation into the page of history. 83. Plut. *Vit. Solon.*

Pisistratus

Pisistratus, who was related to Solon by the mother's side, and whose mind had been early formed by the instructions of that legislator, strove to blind his vigilance by the most sedate deportment, and the warmest declarations of his love of liberty and equal freedom. The keen eyes of Solon, however, penetrated the fine disguise, and read the real designs of his too aspiring pupil[84]. But before he could concert any measures for defeating them, Pisistratus, by a bold artifice, or brave and fortunate escape from a conspiracy against his life, became master of the republic. Having wounded himself, and the mules that drew his chariot, says Herodotus; but more probably being actually wounded by assassins, as he declared, in his way to his country seat, he returned to the city, and drove violently into the agora or market-place[85].

Filled with compassion for the lacerated condition of their engaging demagogue, the people crowded about him; while he, in a pathetic speech, ascribed the impotent vengeance of his envious and cruel enemies—the ills he had suffered, and those he had to fear, solely to his disinterested patriotism and friendship for the poor. Deeply affected, alike by what they heard and saw, the enraged multitude were ready to fly to arms. In order to quiet them, a general assembly was summoned; and that assembly, at the motion of a popular leader, in spite of all the arguments of Solon, and the opposition of the two rival factions, appointed Pisistratus a guard of fifty men[86]. This guard he took the liberty to augment, under various pretences, without exciting the jealousy of the people[87]. At length, finding himself sufficiently strong for accomplishing his purpose, he threw off the mask; took

84. Plut. ubi sup.   85. Herodot. lib. i. Plut. Vit. Solon.
86. Id. ibid.   87. Plut. Vit. Solon.

possession of the acropolis, and usurped the government of the state[88].

During the commotion raised by that revolution, Megacles and his principal adherents sought safety in flight. Nor does it appear that Lycurgus and his partizans took any measures for restoring the liberties of Athens. But Solon, although old and unsupported by any faction, was true to his principles. He one while upbraided the Athenians with cowardice; and, at another, exhorted them to attempt the recovery of their freedom. " It would have been easier," said he, " to have repressed the growth of tyranny; but " now when it has attained some height, it will be " more glorious to cut it down[89]." Finding, however, that none of the people had courage to take arms, he returned to his own house; and having laid aside all thoughts of making any other public effort, placed his weapons at the street-door, exclaiming with conscious pride, in the hearing of his fellow-citizens, " I have " done all in my power to defend, from despotism, my " country and its laws[90]!"

But

88. Herodot. et Plut. ubi sup.   89. Plut. Vit. Solon.
90. Id. ibid. Thus consoled, the Athenian legislator passed his few remaining years as a wise man ought, be the accidents in life what they may: in social converse with his friends; and in the exercise of his intellectual powers; but especially of his poetical talent, which he seems at all times to have cultivated, and employed as a resource amid the rubs of fortune. Hence the following manly sentiment:

" For vice, though plenty fills her horn,
" And virtue sinks in want forlorn;
" Yet ne'er shall SOLON meanly change
" His *truth* for *wealth's* most easy range!
" Since virtue lives, and truth shall stand,
" While wealth eludes the grasping hand.
The same talent served to dissipate the langour of old age.

" I grow

But Pisistratus, in assuming regal dignity, and Investing himself with supreme power, made no change in the forms of the Athenian constitution, as established by Solon. He allowed all its assemblies, its magistracies, its offices civil and military, to remain; and he enforced the due execution of law and justice not only by his authority but his example; readily obeying a citation to appear in the court of areopagus, on a charge of murder, for which he was acquitted[91]. Hence the frequent saying of Solon: " Lop off only "his ambition, cure him of the lust of sway; and " there is not a man more disposed to every virtue, or " a better citizen than Pisistratus[92]."

All the virtues of this accomplished prince, however, added to his high renown in arms, could not reconcile the Athenians to kingly power. Twice was Pisistratus obliged to seek refuge in exile, and as often did he recover the sovereignty of Attica, by his superior talents; his courage, his conduct, and captivating manners[93]. The causes of these revolutions, and the circumstances with which they were attended, were thought sufficiently important by Herodotus to be particularly enumerated in his narration: and he was a good judge of such matters. But to the ancient Greeks, many things relative to their own affairs appeared important, which would seem altogether frivolous to an inhabitant of modern Europe. I shall, therefore, my lord, only offer to your consideration a few leading facts, intimately connected with the character of Pisistratus, and the state of the people of Attica during his domination.

" I grow in learning as I grow in years."
Says he; and afterward adds, with much good humour:
" Wine, wit, and beauty, still their charms bestow;
" Light all the shades of life, and cheer us as we go."
Excerpt. in Plut. Vit. Solon,

91. Plut. Vit. Solon.   92. Plut. et Diog. Laert. ubi sup.
93. Herodot. lib. i.

The

The only crime imputed to this famous usurper, or Athenian tyrant, as he is commonly called, was an excess of political caution. He confined the honours and offices of the state almost exclusively to his own partisans[94]. Enraged at finding themselves and their adherents deprived of all power and consequence, Megacles and Lycurgus, the leaders of the two depressed parties, united their strength against their exulting rival, and expelled him the republic[95]. Megacles, however, dissatisfied with the anarchy that ensued, sent proposals of support to the banished chief. His alliance was accepted, and Pisistratus again took possession of the government[96]. But Megacles, on a fresh disgust, turned against him the whole weight of the Alcmæonids; and they being joined by the partisans of Lycurgus, with whom a reconciliation had taken place, obliged the tyrant once more to divest himself of his authority, and quit his native country[97].

Pisistratus retired to Eretria, in the island of Eubœa. There, though in banishment, he possessed so much personal interest, and was held in such high consideration by the neighbouring states, that he was able, in the eleventh year of his exile, to enter the territory of Attica at the head of an armed force, and make himself master of Marathon[98]. Here he erected his standard. Partizans flocked to him from all quarters; and he soon found himself strong enough to venture to march toward Athens[99]. The Alcmæonids

94. Meurs. in *Pisistrat.* Thucydid. lib. vi.

95. Herodot. lib. i.   96. Id. ibid.

97. Herodot. ubi sup. The word τυραννος or tyrant, among the Greeks, had no relation to the abuse of power, the meaning now commonly affixed to it. It was employed solely to denote a citizen who had usurped the government of a free state, whatever use he might make of his authority. But that such authority was generally abused, must also be admitted. And hence the modern acceptation of the word.

98. Herodot. lib. i.   99. Id. ibid.

met him with a formidable army, before he reached the metropolis. But they allowed themselves to be surprised, and their forces were instantly routed[100].

Now was the season for Pisistratus to display his clemency: and his presence of mind, setting aside his humanity, was too great to let slip the opportunity. He ordered his two sons, Hippias and Hipparchus, to ride after the fugitives, and tell them, in his name, that they had nothing to fear, if they would go quietly to their several homes[101]. That message had the desired effect. The Athenian militia, relying on the unimpeached faith of their virtuous but too ambitious fellow-citizen, utterly dispersed themselves and never more assumed the form of an army; so that Pisistratus entered Athens without resistance, and took a third time possession of the government[102].

The slaughter, however, was considerable, notwithstanding the politic interposition of the generous victor. And in order more effectually to secure his sway, as well as to provide against the future effusion of blood, the mild usurper judged an act of severity necessary. He demanded, as hostages, the sons of all those citizens who had been most active in arms against him, and who had not fled their country; and sent them to the island of Naxus, which he had formerly conquered. He also retained, for the support of his authority, part of his foreign troops[103]. By these wise precautions, and an equitable administration, Pisistratus remained undisturbed master of Attica, till his death; and transmitted the tyranny, or supreme power, to his two sons Hippias and Hipparchus[104]

Hipparchus

---

100. Herodot. ubi sup.   101. Herodot. lib. i.   102. Id. ibid.
103. Herodot. lib. i.
104. Id. ibid. I have not concealed the great or the good qualities of Pisistratus; yet can I not ascribe all his beneficent actions to liberal

' Hipparchus, although represented by the accurate Thucydides as the younger brother[105], appears to have succeeded his father in the government of the Athenian state[106]. He was a munificent patron of learning and the liberal arts, and drew around him men of genius from all parts of Greece. In imitation of his illustrious sire and predecessor, he adorned the city of Athens with many splendid buildings, while he cultivated the morals and polished the manners of its inhabitants; encouraged industry, and rewarded

ral motives. A man whose popularity, acquired by many blandishments, enabled him, and whose ambition prompted him to assume the mastery over his fellow-citizens; and who found it necessary to maintain his power, not only by a military force, but by a perpetual attention to the favour of that populace by which he had acquired it, would often be obliged to dissemble his sentiments, and even to affect those which he did not feel. He must frequently have had recourse to both simulation and dissimulation; not only in words and exterior behaviour, but in actions or public conduct, whatever might be the natural probity of his disposition, or the sincerity of his private friendships.

I cannot therefore believe, because Pisistratus furnished the Athenians with the first complete collection of Homer's poems, that " he was zealous to diffuse among them the liberal and manly sentiment of that divine poet" (See Dr. Gillies's *Hist. of Greece*, chap. xiii.). I rather think he was desirous, like every politic usurper, of furnishing them with amusement, that they might not perceive he had left them only the shadow of liberty, in the forms of their free constitution, and attempt to recover the substance; that they might have less leisure or inclination to plot against his arbitrary government.

With the same view, he greatly encouraged industry and agriculture, in preference to commerce, or such mechanic arts as might augment the population of the factious city of Athens (Meurs. in *Pisistrat.* Ælian, *Var. Hist.* lib. ix. cap. xxv.). In a word, Pisistratus was a most seductive orator, a consummate politician, and an accomplished prince; and, as such, I have represented him. No absolute sovereign, in ancient or modern times, appears to have been a more perfect master of the art of reigning, though he never assumed the title of king.

105. Thucyd. lib. vi.

106. Plato in *Hipparch.* Ælian, *Var. Hist.* lib. viii. cap. ii. Meurs. in *Pisistrat.*

　　　　　　　　　　　　　　　　　　merit

merit[107]. He was slain by Harmodius and Aristogiton, in resentment of a private injury[108]. And
notwithstanding his public virtue, and an administration, which, in the language of panegyric, is said to
have revived the memory of the *golden age*, so strong
was the detestation of the Athenians against regal
power, after they had recovered their freedom, that
his murderers were long celebrated as the deliverers
of their country from tyranny[109]: and many statues
were erected to perpetuate the memory of the perpetrators of the crime[110]!

The tyranny at Athens, however, did not, properly
speaking, commence till after the death of Hipparchus. Hippias, highly incensed at the assassination
of his brother, and alarmed for his own safety, put to
death many of his fellow-citizens, beside Harmo-

107. Id. ibid.

108. Thucydid. lib. vi. Harmodius being in the bloom of youth
and beauty (says the Greek historian), Aristogiton, an Athenian
citizen, of a more advanced age, doated upon him (according to the
abominable *love of the Greeks*), and had him in his possession, to use
the plain language of Thucydides (lib. vi.). Hipparchus, who was
addicted, it seems, to the same unnatural lust, eagerly solicited the
favours of Harmodius. But although unsuccessful, he did not chuse
to make use of force (Id. ibid.). Meanwhile Aristogiton was inflamed
with jealousy, and filled with terror, at the advances of so powerful
a rival; and the *lover* and the *beloved*, roused to resentment by an
aggravating circumstance, not connected with this infamous amour
—an attempt to disgrace the sister of Harmodius, concerted and accomplished the murder of the Athenian prince. Thucyd. ubi sup.

I shall leave others (See Young's *Hist.* of *Athens*, book i. chap.
viii. and Gillies's *Hist. of Greece*, chap. xviii.) to mantain the purity
of such connections; for to me they have always appeared suspicious.
Plutarch has endeavoured to shade them under the veil of virtuous
friendship; but, in relating facts, he forgets his general reasonings.

109. Thucyd. lib. vi. Demost. *Orat. in Leptin.* Plin. *Hist. Nat.* lib.
xxxiv. cap. viii.

110. A crime, which Thucydides affirms, arose from "a competition in love;" and in that love which nature abhors. Thucyd. lib.
vi. cap. liv.

dius

dius and Aristogiton[111]. All whom he hated or feared fell victims to his severity[112]. Yet farther to secure his power, and even to provide a retreat, in case of necessity, he looked around him for foreign aid; and having married his daughter Archedice to Æantides, son of Hippoclus, tyrant of Lampsacus, with whose family he entered into a close political alliance[113], he thenceforth governed the Athenians with all the rigour of despotism[114].

The exiled Alcmæonids and their adherents, ever watchful of an opportunity to recover possession of their family-estates, and to re-establish the liberties of their native country, beheld with satisfaction the discontents occasioned by the tyranny of Hippias. During their banishment, they had engaged in their interest the oracle of Apollo at Delphos; by rebuilding, in a magnificent manner, the temple of the prophetic god, which had been consumed by fire[115]. And they were now able, with the assistance of a body of Lacedæmonian forces, procured them by the favourable responses of the oracle, to accomplish their design.

Ant Ch.
510.
Olymp.
lxvii. 3.

Victorious over the army of Hippias in the field, the confederates entered Athens, and besieged the tyrant in the acropolis. That citadel was of sufficient strength to have long baffled all the efforts of the

111. Herodot. lib. v. Thucydid. lib. vi. Plato in *Hipparch*. Ælian. *Var. Hist*. lib. xi. cap. viii. 112. Id. ibid.

113. An epitaph, found at Lampsacus, on the lady, who formed the basis of this league, is recorded by Thucydides, and worthy of being preserved to the latest posterity.

" From Hippias sprung, with regal power array'd,
" Within this tomb Archedice is laid;
" By father, husband, brothers, sons, ally'd
" To haughty tyrants, yet unstain'd with pride."

Thucyd. lib. vi.

14. Herodot. et Thucydid. ubi sup. 115. Herodot. lib. v.

besiegers;

besiegers; especially as the Lacedæmonians were under the necessity of soon returning home. But accident and natural affection accomplished what force and military skill seemed unable to effect. Anxious for the safety of their offspring, whom they had conveyed out of the fortress, and who had fallen into the hands of the Alcmæonids, Hippias and his partizans, on condition of having their children restored, agreed to surrender the acropolis, and to quit the territory of Attica within five days[116].

In consequence of this revolution, the Athenians recovered their political freedom, after they had been governed by the ambitious family of Pisistratus for sixty-eight years. And notwithstanding the many struggles they were obliged to maintain, in order to preserve their liberty and independency, against the attacks of ambitious neighbours, and the conspiracies of usurping citizens, they acquired a degree of importance in Greece, amid the turbulence of democracy, which they had never reached, nor ever could have attained, in the repose of monarchy. For, as Herodotus judiciously remarks, so great is the spring communicated to the faculties of men by the equal distribution of power, that their most vigorous efforts under a master are feeble and languid, compared with their strong exertions in a state of perfect freedom; where every one, in acting for the good of the community, may be said to act for himself, and considers his own interest, and even his own honour, to be at stake[117].

These reflections, suggested by the expulsion of the Pisistratidæ, and the prosperity of the Athenians under a republican government, your lordship will find more fully confirmed and exemplified in the history

116. Id. ibid.   117. Herodotus, lib. v.

PART I. of another great people ; in the banishment of the
Tarquins from Rome, and the rapid rise of the Romans to grandeur, after the establishment of their commonwealth. I shall therefore turn your eye toward Italy, before we trace farther the advances of liberty in Greece. But we must, in the meantime, take a view of the progress of society in this celebrated country.

LETTER

LETTER VII.

THE PROGRESS OF ARTS, MANNERS, RELIGION, AND LITE-
RATURE IN GREECE, FROM THE HEROIC AGE TO THE
FULL ESTABLISHMENT OF THE ATHENIAN REPUBLIC.

IN inquiring into the origin of the Grecian LETTER VII.
states, and deducing their progress in policy and arms,
I have had occasion to notice the introduction of the
more useful and necessary arts among the people of
the growing communities[1]. The arts of elegance and
design, with the abstract sciences, properly belong to
the subsequent period. But the formation of the manners, the religion, and the popular literature of the
Greeks, appertains to the present.

The arts introduced into Greece from Egypt, Phœnicia, and Asia Minor[2], though they induced the roving and barbarous natives to live in fixed habitations,
had made small progress before the Trojan war. And
the disorders in the Grecian states, occasioned by that
war, prevented the surviving adventurers, on their
return to their several homes, from successfully cultivating the conveniencies of life[3]; whatever new ideas
they might have acquired, during the prosecution of
their foreign enterprise, by viewing the improvements
of a more polished people[4].

The subsequent invasion and conquest of Peloponnesus by the Heraclidæ, threw all things again into
confusion[5]; while the fermentation produced by the
rising passion for liberty, before the general abolition

1. See Lett. II.   2. Ibid. et auct. cit.
3. See Lett. III.   4. Ibid.   5. See Lett. IV.

of

PART I. of monarchy in Greece, yet farther retarded the advances of the arts of peace[6]. But after these events had taken place, and the Grecian states had discharged, with their surplus of population, their restless spirits in colonies; planted on the coast of Asia Minor, in Italy, Sicily, and in the islands of the Ægean and Ionian seas; society made rapid progress in Greece[7], and in all the communities speaking the Greek tongue.

This progress was accelerated by the periodical celebration of the Isthmian, Nemean, Pythian, and Olympic games[8]: but more especially the latter. At those games, denominated *sacred*, the Greeks assembled from all their various states, and from all the continents and islands in which they had planted colonies. There, appearing as the people of one great nation, they entered upon a generous competition of mental talents, as well as of personal abilities and accomplishments. Poets, orators, historians and philosophers, appeared among the candidates for fame[9].

Never had emulation a more glorious field, or social intercourse a wider theatre, than at the sacred games of Greece. Mind caught fire from mind, and a general rivalship took place; not only between indivi-

---

6. Ibid. et auct cit.   7. See Lett. IV. V. et auct. cit.

8. Of the institution and celebration of the Olympic and Pythian games an account has already been given (Lett. V VI.). The Isthmian games were celebrated, once in five years, at the isthmus of Corinth; and the Nemean, once in three years, at Nemea in Argolis. These games were all of a similar nature, and the same kind of gymnastic and equestrian exercises were performed in all, though not in the same order; namely, running, leaping, wrestling, throwing the disk, boxing, driving the chariot, and riding the single horse. West's *Dissert. on the Olympic games*, sect. vii.—xvii. and the authors cited. See also, on the same subject, *Mem. Dissertat. et Recherches*, par. M. Burette et M. l'Abbe Gedoyn, dans *Choise des Mem. de l'Academie Royale des Inscript. et Belles Lettres*, tom. i.

9. Lucian. in *Herodot.*

duals

deals but communities[10]. The effects were answerable, and such as have astonished all succeeding ages. There the Grecian manners were polished, while Grecian policy was perfected[11]. A laudable desire of elegance, in dress and accommodation, was diffused; and, in consequence of that taste, better houses were built by the rich; stately temples were reared to the gods; religious ceremonies were multiplied, and theatrical exhibitions invented.

But the advances of refinement were very unequal in the different states of Greece. Sparta, hedged round by the austere institutions of Lycurgus, and in a manner excluded from all intercourse with foreigners, was backward in admitting the approaches of elegance, and late in adopting the improvements most intimately connected with the happiness of human life. The axe and the saw were long the only tools employed by the Lacedæmonians in finishing the timber-work of their houses[12]. Their architecture and furniture were proportionably rude[13]. Gymnastic exercises were their chief amusements; and the maxims of policy and war, which formed their literary code, were, at Sparta, the sole objects of a liberal education[14].

10. West, ubi sup.

11. Id. ibid. The amusements which the Greeks shared in common at Olympia, or Pisa, and other places where those games were celebrated, naturally disposed their minds to gaiety and good humour. They had daily occasion to mingle freely, to see and converse with each other. They seemed to be in a manner inhabitants of the same city: they offered, as one people, sacrifices to the same God, and participated the same pleasures (Strabo, lib. ix:). By these means popular prejudices were rubbed off; animosities were softened; the causes of umbrages were explained and removed; and the people of the different Grecian states, having thus an opportunity of learning each others strength and disposition, as well as the force and preparations of their common enemies, were enabled to provide for their security, and to encourage each other to guard and maintain their common liberties.

12. Plut. *Vit. Lycurg.*   13. Id. ibid.

14. Xenoph. *Rep. Lacon.*

The

The aspect of things was very different at Corinth. Early enriched by commerce, and habituated to an extensive intercourse with foreign nations, the Corinthians indulged themselves in all the delicacies of Asiatic luxury, and even imitated the pomp of oriental opulence[15]. Their city was accordingly filled with temples, palaces, theatres, porticoes, and private houses equally admirable for their structure[16]. They gave birth, during the period under consideration, to the order named Corinthian, the most superb in architecture, and adorned their public buildings with columns and statues of the most exquisite workmanship[17].

The Athenians, though yet less wealthy than the Corinthians, discovered an equal, if not superior taste

15. Thucyd. lib. i. Strabo, lib. viii. xvii. Plin. lib. xxv. · 16. Id. ibid. 17. Plin. et Strabo, ubi sup. Contrary to the opinion of Winkelmann (*Hist. de l'Art de l'Antiquite*, liv. vi. chap. i.), I am disposed to believe, that the early progress of architecture and sculpture at Corinth was partly occasioned by the longer continuance, or revival of regal goverament, in that city and its territory. Absolute princes have ever been fond of magnificent buildings, the most munificent patrons of statuaries and painters, and the greatest encouragers of all the arts that can contribute to the splendour of a palace; but unfriendly to the higher strains of poetry, and the bolder effusions of eloquence, which require the utmost freedom of thought and sentiment; and still more so to history, which delivers, or ought to deliver, without a veil, truths they are afraid to hear. The courts of such princes are also favourable to polished manners; as the delicate disguises of the passions become necessary, to save their pride from mortification; and the play of wit and conversation, to contribute to their amusement, and to flatter their vanity. In order to establish this position, I have no occasion to advert to modern times, or to anticipate the events in ancient history. As the Corinthians owed their first advances in elegance and refinement chiefly to their famous tyrant Periander, who lived in the sixth century before the christian æra (Diogen. Laert. *Vit. Periand.*), the people of Samos were, in like manner, indebted for their early progress in civility to Polycrates, as we shall have occasion to observe; the Lesbians to Pittacus, and the Athenians to Pisistratus; all nearly contemporaries.

· for

for elegance and refinement. That taste was encouraged and improved by the ambitious, liberal, and accomplished Pisistratus, and his two aspiring sons and successors. They first decorated the Athenian capital with splendid buildings, and polished the manners of its inhabitants[18]. Under the government of Pisistratus was laid the foundation of the magnificent temple of Jupiter at Athens[19]; and Thespis, under his patronage, gave a beginning to the theatrical entertainments of the Greeks[20].

The Elians, happy in a fertile soil, which they cultivated with much care; and enriched as well as polished by the periodical celebration of the Olympic games and festival, made early advances in civility, and in all the arts connected with religious pomp[21]. A striking proof of that early proficiency appeared in the superb temple of Jupiter at Olympia, erected about six hundred years before the Christian æra, by Libon, a native of Elis[22]. This famous temple, of the Doric order in architecture, was wholly built of a beautiful marble, resembling that of Paros, found in the neighbouring

18. See Lett. VI. and the authors cited.

19. This temple was afterward enlarged by the Athenians during the administration of Pericles, and finished by the bounty of Antiochus Epiphanes, king of Syria, who charged himself with the expense of the nave, and the columns of the portico. It was of the Corinthian order, and considered as a model of perfection in that style of architecture. Vitruv. lib. vii.

20. Plut. et. Diogen. Laert. *Vit. Solon.* Perceiving the abuse that might be made of theatrical exhibitions, Solon called Thespis to him, after being present at the performance of one of his compositions, and asked him, if he was not ashamed of telling so many lies before so great an assembly. Thespis excused himself by saying, that there could be no harm in so doing, as his fictions were not intended to be considered as truths. Solon, striking the ground with his staff, sternly replied, "If we encourage such fictions, we shall find them influ-
"ence our most serious transactions" (Plut. *Vit. Solon.*). Of this truth, the Athenians had fatal experience.

21. Strabo, lib. viii. Pausan. lib. v.   22. Pausan. lib. v.

PART I. country, and surrounded with a colonnade of the
same materials. Its height, from the area to the
dome, or vaulted roof, was sixty-eight feet; its breadth
ninety-five, and its length two hundred and thirty. It
was covered with marble, brought from mount Pente-
licon in Attica, and cut into the form of tiles[23]. Its
decorations I shall afterward have occasion to describe,
in tracing the progress of the Greeks in sculpture and
painting.

Thus have I endeavoured to assign the causes, and
to point out the gradual advances of improvement in
Greece. But it was in the islands of the Ægean sea,
and among the Grecian colonies in Asia Minor, that
the liberal arts first began to disclose themselves to advantage. And there architecture first displayed those
just proportions, and that unity of design, which have
continued to command the approbation, and attract the
admiration of enlightened mankind, in all succeeding
ages[24]. The Dorians and Ionians, on the Asiatic
coast,

23. Id. ibid.

24. This more early proficiency of the Asiatic Greeks in the liberal
arts, and in all the works depending upon imagination and sentiment,
may be ascribed partly to moral, and partly to physical causes; to the
long period of peace and prosperity which they had enjoyed, first in
a state of independency, and afterward under the protection of the
Lydian monarchs; and to a country and climate calculated to awaken,
and to foster all the powers of genius. "The Ionian cities," where
the elegant arts were most successfully cultivated, "are more com-
modiously and happily situated," says the venerable father of history,
" than any other we know among men; for they are neither chilled
with cold, rendered damp by rain, nor exposed to the excesses of heat
and drought" (Herodot. lib. i.). In this fine climate, and in a country beautifully diversified with hills and vallies, intersected by rivers,
broken by bays, and constantly refreshed with gales from the numerous isles that crown the Ægean see, the Asiatic Greeks were favoured
with the gayest, and the grandest views of nature; with every circumstance that can excite or cherish the human faculties. Genius, however, is said to be the produce of every climate; and, in some degree, it
is.

coast, invented those elegant orders that still bear their names; and during the latter part of the present period was laid the foundation of the magnificent temple of Diana at Ephesus[25]. This temple, which was of the Ionic order, became the boast of Grecian architecture, and the wonder of the ancient world; though less on account of its size, than because of the majestic beauty of its structure, the choice materials of which it was composed, and the richness of its ornaments. It was about two hundred feet wide, and four hundred feet long; and it contained, when completely finished, one hundred and twenty-seven columns of the finest marble, sixty feet high, and ingeniously sculptured[26].

Manners kept pace, as they always will, with the progress of the human mind, and the conveniencies and elegancies of life. The manners of the Greeks during the heroic age, so finely pourtrayed (as we have seen) in the poems of Homer, and so frequently offered to unreserved admiration, by modern writers, were accordingly deeply shaded with barbarism.

This, my lord, is an unpleasant truth. But, in historical matters, the least engaging facts are of infinitely more value, than the most captivating illusions of fiction. We must therefore beware, while we take for our guide Homer, the most ancient painter of manners, we must beware of being deceived by the magic of his poetic fancy. Objects seen through the medium of imagination are always magnified to the eye of the observer; and when admiration is the predomi-

---

is. " But the richest growths, and fairest shoots of genius," to use the words of a learned and ingenious author, "spring, like other plants, from the happiest exposition, and most friendly soil." Blackwell's *Inquiry into the life and Writings of Homer*, sect. i.

25. Pausan. lib. v.   26. Vitruv. lib. iii. vij.   Plin. lib. xxxvi.

ment mode of the mind, they will be viewed, invested, and consequently delineated, with many adventitious beauties and extrinsic good qualities. Such we find to be the case, even when truth is the end proposed ; how much greater then must have been the heightenings in the writings of Homer? who wished to hold up to the imitation of his countrymen the reputed wisdom, the virtues, and valiant exploits of a band of heroes, already almost deified in the ardent imaginations of the superstitious Greeks.

Marriage, as I have had occasion to observe, is a law of nature, and its rites are recognized and understood even among savages[27]. The people of Greece in the heroic age, had made several removes from the savage state ; and they had been favoured with instructors from Egypt, where the union of one man with one woman was strictly enjoined by law, and adultery severely punished[28]. The marriage tie was accordingly held sacred among the Greeks, during those gallant times ; nor was a plurality of wives indulged[29]. The latter circumstance is rather remarkable, as they may be said to have purchased their brides[30], and were little delicate in regard to what prior connections they might have formed[31]. The fact, however, is incontrovertible;

27. See Lett. I. and the authors there cited.

28. Id. ibid.   29. Pausan. lib. ii.

30. This matter I know has been disputed (Gillies, *Hist. Greece*, chap. ii.) ; but there is no overturning established facts. Agamemnon tells Achilles as an inducement to an alliance, that he will give him one of his daughters in marriage, without requiring any price (Hom. Iliad. lib. ix.). And Danaus finding nobody disposed to marry his daughters, on account of the atrocity of their character, made a public declaration, that he would not demand any presents from the bridegrooms (Pausan. lib. iii.). The dower given with the bride, in return for such presents, seems not to have been common till latter ages.

31. The proofs of this indelicacy, or indulgence to female weakness, are numberless in ancient Grecian writers. A modern historian

has

trovertible; and so indissoluble were the bands of wedlock supposed to be, on the side of the wife, that it was long considered as disgraceful, and even unlawful, for a widow to marry a second husband[32].

As in every country where the sanctity of the marriage bed is preserved inviolate, the affection between husband and wife, and of parents to their children, was warm during the uncorrupted times of ancient Greece. The respect of children to their parents, an effect proceeding from the same cause, love between the sons and daughters of one family, and all the ties of blood, were also strong in the heroic age[33]. Agreeable to natural justice, an equal division of property took place among the brothers, on the death of their father, or common head[34]. But a portion of respect descended to the eldest son, as his birth-right, with a degree of submission to his authority[35].

This submission, however, seems to have ceased, when the younger brothers became themselves heads of families. To them their sons resorted for commands, and new subdivisions were formed[36]. Yet the heads of all the younger branches of every illustrious family, appear long to have looked up with veneration, though without any sense of inferiority, to the head of the eldest branch of that family, as their chief or centre of consanguinity; as they originally had to his predecessors, as the centre of their political union[37]. For

has given that weakness a very gentle name: "The crime of having too tender a heart!" Gillies, *Hist. Greece*. chap. ii.

32. Pausan. lib. ii. Tradition has even preserved the name of *Gorgaphona*, the first widow that ventured to violate the rule. Id. ibid.

33. Homer, passim.   34. *Arist. Polit.* lib. vi. Homer, *Odyss.* xiv.   35. Hom. *Iliad.* lib. xv.

36. Shuckford's *Connec.* book vi. and the authors cited.

37. Id. ibid. See also Mitford's *Hist. of Greece*, chap. III. sect. iv.

blood

blood procured authority before wisdom or valour, and in conjunction with those still best maintains it.

In the heroic age, wisdom and valour were become essential to the acquisition, as well as to the support of kingship or chief magistracy; and even to entitle a son to succeed his father in that high office, whatever might be the claims of blood to pre-eminence. It was necessary that worth should recommend his hereditary title to the approbation of the elders, or heads of reputable families, and that it should be confirmed by the body of the people[39].

Having thus discovered the claims and the qualities requisite for the attianment and support of royalty in Greece, during the heroic times, let us next consider the nature and privileges of the office itself. The king, as head of the community, enjoyed the important functions of high priest, supreme judge, and commander in chief; as he was supposed to be the most pious, wise, and valiant member of the state[40]. But religious supremacy appears to have been his only exclusive privilege[41]. The elders or senators shared with him the command of the army: they also participated with him in the administration of justice: while the voice of the people confirmed, or reversed, both his and their decisions[42].

Nor was the acknowledged majesty of the people less conspicuous in political affairs. They claimed a

38. See Lett. I. of this work. 39. Hom. Odyss. lib. i. v. vii. 2I.
40. Hom. Iliad. lib. ii. Aristot. Ethic. lib. III. cap. v. Strabo, lib. I.
41. So intimately connected, in the minds of the Greeks and Romans, was the idea of king or head of the state, with that of chief sacrificer or head of the established religion, that they both gave the name to their high priest, after the abolition of royalty. Demosth. in Neær. Cicero, de Divinat. lib. I. Dion. Halicarnass. lib. v.
42. Hom. Iliad. lib. xvi. xviii. Aristot. Polit. lib. iii. cap. xiv. xv.

right

right to be consulted, in regard to all matters of importance; and as the majority of the senate, or council of state, controuled the will of the king, the resolutions of that venerable body were governed by the
popular assembly[43], in the early kingdoms of Greece,
as fully as in the most democratical of the subsequent
republics[44].

The same distribution of power, that happy mixture
of monarchical, aristocratical, and democratical rule,
which characterised the civil government of the early
Grecian kingdoms or states, and which almost every
where prevails among nations in a similar stage of their
social progress, was also found in each particular
town[45], and in the greatest military confederacies.
Agamemnon, though appointed, during the Trojan
war, commander in chief of the combined forces of
Greece, by the voice of its united princes, was not
invested with absolute authority. On the day of
battle, when the whole army was in some measure
under his immediate command, he had the power of
life and death[46]; but, on all other occasions, his
power was very limited. He could adopt no measure
without assembling a council; and in every such coun-

43. Hom. *Iliad.* lib. ii. *Odyss.* lib. iii. viii. Aristot. *Ethic.* lib. iii.
cap. v. Dion. Halicarnass. lib. ii.

44. It would be an insult, however, upon the wisdom of Lycurgus, to say nothing of that of Solon, to suppose " his famous laws
" were almost exact copies of the customs and institutions that uni-
" versally prevailed in Greece during the heroic ages" (Gillies, *Hist.*
Greece, chap. ii.). Lycurgus, indeed, lived too near to the ages of
barbarism, to have a distinct idea of the perfection of the human
character. He accordingly paid too much attention, as I have had
occasion to observe (Lett. V.), to the physical, and too little to the
moral qualities of man. But pedants, secluded from the world, or
men who have viewed it with an undiscerning eye, and never tasted
the pleasures of polished life, only will give the state of society, in
the heroic times, a preference over that of the present enlightened
and civilized age, in modern Europe.

45. Plut. *Vit. Thes.*   46. Hom. *Iliad.* lib. ii.

cil,

cil, whether general or select, the utmost freedom of
speech was allowed, and all resolutions were ultimately
determined by the plurality of voices[47].

The same bold freedom that distinguished the public
deliberations of the Greeks, during the heroic age,
also characterised their manners in private life[48].
Among such a people, little politeness or mutual de-
ference could be expected:—and it was not found; nor
much delicacy in the intercourse of the sexes[49]. Humanity was then even little regarded. Most of the
early Grecian heroes had been guilty of murder[50];
and many of them had fled their country, without satisfying the demands of justice[51]. Yet the satisfaction
required was only a pecuniary mulct[52]. In vain,
therefore, should we attempt to apologise for such
outrages, by ascribing them to the want of legal redress[53]; and still less should we impute them merely

47. Ibid. lib. i. ii. ix.   48. Hom. *Odyss.* passim, et Apollod.
lib. i. ii. iii.

49. Hom. *Iliad.* et *Odyss.* passim. "No language," says Mr. Mitford, "can give a more elegant, or a more highly-coloured picture of
"conjugal affection, than is displayed in the conversation between
"Hector and Andromache in the sixth book of the Iliad" (*Hist. of
Greece*, chap. iii. sect. iv.). Yet Hector had the indelicacy to tell
her, after enumerating the future woes of Troy, of Hecuba, of royal
Priam, and of his brothers many and brave, that not all so much
affected his soul as the griefs which she had to bear; "when some
"rude Greek, in his pride, should come and lead her away, a mourn-
"ful captive of freedom bereft; when far from her native land, she
"should weave the web for some haughty dame, or bear water from
"the spring (Hom. *Iliad.* lib. vi.). Unwilling," adds he, "thou the
"burden bearest; but hard necessity commands" (Id. ibid.). A man
who should so talk, in modern times, would be accounted a brute.

50. Hom. *Iliad.* passim. et Apollod. lib. i. ii. iii.   51. Id. ibid.

52. Hom. *Iliad.* lib. ix. The venerable bard is very precise on this
subject. "A brother," says he, in the person of Ajax, "receives
"the price of a brother's blood: fathers for their slain sons are ap-
"peased. The murderer pays the high fine of his crime, and in his
"city unmolested remains." Id ibid.

53. To this cause those violences have been ascribed by some late
writers. See Mitford's *Hist. of Greece*, chap. iii. sect. iv.

to the want of that refinement, which has been thought subversive of the nobler virtues[54]. They were the natural consequences of that ferocity of disposition, which too frequently tyrannises over men not sufficiently subdued to the restraints of law, or acquainted with the advantages of social union; and which ought to teach us to value the milder virtues, connected with the culture of the heart; without which the prohibitions of the legislature, and the vigilance of the magistrate, will ever be found ineffectual to civilize mankind, or to form them to the habits of polished society.

But if the resentments of the Greeks, in those rude times, were keen, their friendships were proportionably warm. Men, who had shared mutual dangers and toils, were knit in the closest bands of friendship and hospitality[55]. From friendship the transition was easy to love.

54. Dr. Gillies is not singular, in entertaining this opinion (*Hist. of Greece*, chap. ii.): but it requires very little knowledge of human nature to discover, That the crimes resulting from barbarism are more pernicious to society, than the vices allied to refinement.

55. The hospitality of the early Greeks has been a subject of speculation, for both ancient and modern authors. It has been ascribed to the circumstances of the times, and to the want of inns (see Mitford's *Hist. of Greece*, chap. ii. and chap. iii. sect. iv.): but I should ascribe it to the friendly disposition of the people. For all people, in such circumstances, are not equally disposed to hospitality. Homer has shewed us (*Odyss.* passim.), and Thucydides has observed (*Hist.* lib. i. cap. v.), that no inquiry was made concerning the character of the persons, who came to claim the sacred rights of hospitality, until they had shared the repast (Hom. ubi sup.). This indulgence may justly be ascribed to the circumstances of the times; for, in that rude age, if particular inquiry had been made concerning the character and condition of all persons who claimed hospitality, many worthy men, whose pride would not submit to such explanation, or whose modesty could not furnish it, must have been denied hospitable reception. Hence the extension of the virtue of hospitality to men of doubtful character.

As

As rapes, and the capture of women, were commonly practised among the early Greeks, by adventurers of brutal dispositions, or of ungovernable passions, warriors of a more generous nature became the champions of the softer sex[56]; and were deservedly repaid with their favour[57]. Yet must it be admitted, that although the Greeks were enthusiastic admirers of female beauty, and freely hazarded their lives in its defence, or for its possession, the latter was ever their chief object[58]. Nor do they seem to have discovered, in any stage of their social progress, that respectful attachment to women that distinguished the ancient Germans[59], and which was carried to a romantic height by the heroes of modern chivalry; that attachment, which finds its gratification in honouring the beloved fair one with esteem and confidence, and which considers the return of affection as essential to conjugal happiness[60].

From a view of the arts, government, and manners of the early Greeks, we are naturally led to consider their religion; which being, in some measure, formed by the genius of the people, had a reciprocal influence upon their national character, and gave its complexion to their literature. As the Greeks were indebted for their science and civility to the Egyptians and Phœnicians, they also received the rudiments of their religion from the same nations[61]; but chiefly from the Egyptians[62].

In what manner that refined species of superstition, which, under the name of *Zabiism*, had become general over the east in the patriarchal ages, passed from Syria and Egypt into Greece, whence it spread itself

56. Hom. *Iliad* et Apollod. lib. i. ii. iii. passim. .57. Id. ibid.
58. Hom. *Iliad*. et. Apollod. ubi sup. 59. Tacit. de *Morib.*
German. 60. See. *Hist. Mod. Europe,* Part I. Lett. LV.
61. Herodotus, lib. ii. passim. 62. Id. ibid.

among

among the western nations, I have formerly had occasion to notice, in tracing the *progress of idolatry*[63].
I have also had occasion to observe, That the religion
of the zabians, in making these removes, was grossly
corrupted by ignorance and priestcraft. The sensuality
of the Syrian worship I have endeavoured to display;
and I have remarked, That the gloomy minds of the
superstitious and speculative Egyptians, by blending
the worship of the heavenly bodies with dark and
mystical allegories, and veiling their religion in symbols expressive of the attributes of the Deity, and of
the qualities of the elementary principles, deified *in
appearance* every thing around them[64]. In Greece
superstition assumed a new form.

Instead of pure spiritual intelligences, by whom
the zabians believed the planets to be wheeled, and
the universe governed, in subordination to the most
high, the adventurous and barbarous, but grateful
Greeks, peopled heaven with gods and goddesses
partaking of the human nature and form, and subject
to all the excesses of human passions[65].

The Grecian gods, in a word, differed in nothing
from corrupted human beings, but in the possession of
superior power, wisdom, and immortality. They had
all been guilty of violence, cruelty, fraud, or debauchery. Even the chastest of the goddesses was
supposed to have had her amours[66]. The *worship* of
such divinities could not be favourable to morals.—
That it had a contrary effect, we have the assurances
of two of the most respectable Grecian historians[67];
who impute the corruptions of the Greeks to the impurity of their theological system, which might be said

63. Lett. I. of this work.   64. Id. ibid.
65. Hom. *Iliad.* passim.   66. Bannier's *Mythol.* passim.
67. Polyb. lib. vi. cap. liv. Dion. Halicarnass. lib. ii. cap. xx.

to teach, or tolerate every vice.   And the philosophic
and politic Plato, enacts it as a law, for the regulation of his commonwealth, " That the current tradi-
" tions concerning the gods should neither be talked of
" in private, nor mentioned in public[68]."

But if the religion of Greece was hurtful to morals[69], it was by no means so to the human faculties.

68. *Repub.* lib. iii.   From this law it appears, That the allegories
concerning the wars, rebellion, and adulteries of the gods, were believed literally by the vulgar; who were accordingly infected by divine
example (Dion. Halicarnass. lib. ii. cap. xx.).   That these allegories
had all a physical or moral meaning, is admitted (Id. ibid.); but that
meaning was beyond vulgar ken (Dion. Halicarnass. ubi sup.).   " The
ancients," says Aristotle, " have made the principles of being *gods*"
(Aristot. *Metaphys.* lib. ii.).   And, after a sublime description of *God*,
the living, everlasting, best of beings; and of the motion of the heavens, and the disposition of the orbits of the planets, he concludes
the universe to be·one, as its eternal mover is but *one*.   " But," adds
he, " there has been handed down to posterity, from the first ages, a
doctrine in the form of a fable, that these celestial bodies are gods."
Metaphys. lib. xi.

69. It contained no tenet that could counteract the dangerous example of the gods, but the doctrine of a future state of rewards and
punishments.   That this doctrine was universal in the heathen world,
I have endeavoured to shew (Lett. I.).   And Dr. Warburton has in-
contestably proved not only its universality, but that civil government could not have been maintained without it (*Divine Legation*,
book. i. ii. iii. passim.).   Its influence, however, was much weakened
among the early Greeks, by the facility with which absolution, from
the greatest crimes, might be obtained (Hom. *Iliad.* et *Odyss.* passim.).
In speaking of a future state of rewards and punishments, I have formerly had occasion to observe, that this belief, unknown to savages,
was every where received among mankind, as soon as the forms of civil
justice were established.   Consequently, it took its rise from human
institutions.   But we ought to remember, that the *human intellect*, if
not a portion of the divine, was infused by the *first mind;* and, therefore, all its acts may be said to flow from the Deity.   Hence we are
logically led to conclude, that the establishment of rewards and punishments among men, is only a type of that more perfect retribution,
which will take place in a future state; and which, although last, in
the mind of men, was first in that of *God*.

There

There was nothing abject in Grecian superstition.—
Believing the gods to partake of the nature of men,
the Greeks approached their altars with a noble boldness; addressed them in an erect posture, and almost
with the same freedom that they approached their civil
superiors[70]. Nor need this excite our wonder. It
was the natural consequence of the popular creed of
Greece; according to which Jupiter was invested with
sovereign authority, but not despotic rule. His conduct was freely arraigned by the inferior divinities;
his measures were disputed in the assembly of the
gods: and he was perpetually under the controul of
fate, or the political necessity of heaven[71].

Such a religion was highly favourable to the active
and also to the intellectual or cogitative powers of man.
Jupiter was ever ready to support supreme sway law-
fully acquired, and justly administered; Minerva was
the constant guardian of valour directed by prudence,
and aided by skill; Mars gave victory to daring courage; Ceres assisted, and rewarded the labours of the
husbandman; Mercury presided over eloquence, mercantile transactions, and all the ingenious arts; while
Apollo and the muses inspired the song of the poet,
and raised his imagination to the height of divine enthusiasm[72].

Other

---

70. Hom. *Iliad*. passim.   71. Id. ibid. See also Hesiod's
Theog. and Plato's *Timæus*.

72. The rewards held up to merit, in the Grecian Elysium, served
also to stimulate valour and genius, and to animate virtue. "There,
in the number of the blest enrolled," says Pindar, "live Cadmus,
Peleus," &c. (*Olymp*. ii.) And Homer makes Proteus say to Menelaus, "Elysium shall be thine" (*Odys*. lib. iv.)! But these are not
among the number of deified heroes. This observation leads me to
remark, that heroes were not deified in Greece at the time of the
Trojan war. Homer's gods, as I have had occasion to notice (Lett.
III.), were merely allegorical personages; the parts and powers of the
universe mythically shadowed forth; or, to use the words of Aristotle

PART I.   Other circumstances, connected with the religion
            of the Hellenians, conspired to embellish Grecian po-
etry, and awaken genius.   Beside Neptune, the god
of the watery element, to whom the mariner offered
his vows, the sea was peopled with tritons and ne-
reids.   Every river had its god, every fountain its
nymph, or naiad; and every mountain and wood,
their oreades and dryades.   Venus and the graces attended upon female beauty; Juno was the patroness of
marriage; Diana the guardian of virgin innocence;
Hebè gave fresh bloom to the cheek of youth; and
Cupid, ever frolicking in the path of youths and maids,
inspired the amorous passion[73].

                                          Furnished

tle, "the primary substances of things" (*Metaphys.* lib. ii.).   They
were said to be of human shape, in order to procure popular belief
(Id. ibid.).   I shall, therefore, conclude with expressing a hope that,
in future, no christian divine will waste his learning in attempting to
prove, that the *greater gods* of gentile antiquity were deified mortals.

   The charnal-house served the purpose of the early teachers of chris-
tianity: but the supposed tombs of the gods, were only the abandoned
altars or temples of heathen deities, who successively gave place to
one another, as policy or priestcraft directed, in order to enchain the
multitude to the shrine of superstition (See Bryant's *Mythol.* vol. i. ii.
passim.).   And as the knowledge of one *God*, the creator and governor of the universe, is now manifested to the whole christian world,
the acrimony against paganism may cease, without injury to the religion of Jesus.

   73. " Love," says the moral and chaste Euripides, " is the greatest
school of wisdom and virtue.   And of all the powers that preside over
human affairs, Cupid's sway is the sweetest to mortals; for, pouring
joy unmixed into enamoured hearts, he fills them with mutual hope.
Even his toils are pleasures, and his wounds relieving.   May never
friend of mine be exempt from the soothing smart! nor I be condemned to live among men devoid of love.—Attend, ye young! and listen,
ye fair! fly not from the proffered bliss; but welcome the propitious
god, and wisely use his heart-easing bounty"(Euripid. apud Stobeum.).
The practice of this lesson is happily exemplified by Chaeremon, in a
comparison of the influence of love to the effects of wine. " The juice
of the grape," says he, " when mixed with water, produceth health
and mirth; but wine, when drank pure to excess, occasions madness
and mischief.   In the same manner love, when moderate and gentle,

                                                              is

Furnished with such a profusion of imagery, the
Grecian poets had little occasion for invention: they
had only to make use of the popular creed, and the
popular legends, in order to form the finest system of
fable, and the most beautiful assemblage of metaphor
and allegory, that ever adorned the literature of any
people.

The rise and progress of poetry in Greece, forms
one of the most curious subjects of speculation that
can possibly occupy the human mind, and is highly
worthy of your lordship's attention.

The most early Grecian poets, whose names or compositions have reached our times, were enlightened
sages; who delivered their doctrines in mythological
language, in order to inspire their auditors with veneration, and to instruct them by means of allegorical
imagery; scientific reasoning, and philosophic truth,
being as little suited to their rude apprehensions, and
untutored minds, as mild virtue was to their barbarous
manners. Such were Orpheus, Linus, and others;
who taught, in verse, the most sublime tenets, which
they had acquired in Egypt or Phœnicia, concerning
the nature of the Deity, the creation of the world, and
that Providence by which it is governed[74].

The

is the source of pleasure and soft delight; but, when intensely hot,
proves the most horrid and ungovernable passion in the human breast.
Cupid, therefore, is armed with two bows: one he bends, with the
aid of the *graces*, for an happy smiling lot; and the other, with his
bandage on his eyes, to the confusion and misery of the amorous pair."
Chaeremon, ap. Theophrast.

74. I have formerly (Lett. I.) had occasion to quote the beginning
of the Orphic hymn to *Pan;* and shall here add another passage, no
less worthy of being addressed to the creator and governor of the
universe:

" By thee earth's endless plain was firmly fix'd:

" To thee the sea's deep-heaving surge gives way,

" And

PART I. The compositions of these poetical sages, which
perhaps were not committed to writing, as letters were
then little known in Greece, are now lost[75]. But a
Phœnician fragment, preserved by Eusebius, seems
to contain the Orphic account of the creation of the
world.

" The beginning of all things was a dark-breathing
air; or gale of darksome breath, and turbid chaos, obscure as night. These were infinite, and without end
of duration. But when this spirit, or breath, fell in love
with its own principles, and a mixture ensued, that
mixture was called desire, the source of all creation.
It did not know its own creation; but from its conjunction with that spirit sprang moot, slime; and from
moot sprang the seed of creation, and the generation
of the universe. It was framed in the form of an egg;
and matter issued forth, and the sun, and the moon,
and the stars, both small and great. Of the air;
illumined by the fiery gleams from earth and sea,
were generated winds and clouds; whence issued
vast effusions of water from above. These, when
separated, and drawn from their place by the sun's heat,

" And ancient Ocean's waves obey thy voice;
" Ocean, who in his bosom laps the globe.
" Nor less the fleeting air, the vital draught
" That fans the food of every living thing;
" Or e'en the high-enthron'd all-sparkling eye
" Of ever-mounting fire. These all divine,
" Though various, run the course which thou ordain'st;
" And by thy wondrous providence exchange
" Their several jarring natures, to provide
" Food for mankind o'er all the boundless earth."

Ορφ. Υμν. εις ΠΑΝΑ.

75. I say lost; for the hymns that bear the name of Orpheus, and
which are allowed to contain his doctrines, though very ancient, are
not believed to be the genuine productions of that savage-taming poet.
And his Theogonia is certainly lost.

.met

met with in the air mutual shock, and begot lightning
and thunder[76].

To the mythical poets, succeeded the military
bards, who attended the Grecian chieftains, during
the Theban and Trojan wars, and in other hostile
expeditions; who sung their exploits in their halls,
after their return; and, travelling over Greece, and the
islands of the Ægean sea, widely spread their renown.
From the songs of those bards, as I have formerly had
occasion to observe, Homer collected the materials of
his incomparable Iliad[77]; which, as it was not the work
of fancy, but a collection of historical facts, heightened
by the charms of poetry, and blended with allegorical
imagery, suited to popular belief, contains a greater
variety of characters, nicely discriminated, and pourtrayed with the pencil of truth, than any other ancient
or modern composition.

As the object of the Iliad was to teach the necessity
of union among military commanders, in displaying
the distresses occasioned by the quarrel between Achilles and Agamemnon, at the siege of Troy; the Odyssey
had for its moral, the encouragement of wisdom and
virtue under misfortunes, in the happy termination of
the travels and sufferings of Ulysses. And in these
two poems, Homer has comprehended the popular
creed, and the legendary history of Greece to the
Trojan war.

Hesiod, the cotemporary of Homer, being a man
of a sedate and contemplative turn of mind, has furnished us, in his poem of works and days, with the first
didactic composition. It has, for its object, Agricul-

76. Sanchuniathon, ap. Euseb. *Preperat. Evangil.*
77. See on this subject Warburton's *Divine Legation,* book iv. sect. v.

ture ;

ture: with references to the times and seasons best
fitted for the labours of husbandry, according to the
various soils and cultures, and adapted to the superstitious 'notions of the early Greeks. He has also followed the mythical poets; in giving an account of
the creation of the world, or the rise of the universe,
under the name of a Theogonia, or generation of the
gods[78]; all the parts and powers of nature, as I have
frequently had occasion to remark, being deified by
heathen superstition.

" To Homer and Hesiod, succeeded the elegiac and
lyric poets. The first elegiac poets bewailed the
miseries of the sorrowful times that followed the Trojan war; and sought consolation in shortening, by
sensuality, the period of human life[79]. As these, if
their compositions had been preserved, could present
only pictures of local distress, or dissolute manners, I

78. Hesiod's account of the rise of the universe is nearly the same
with that of Sanchuniathon, but less philosophical. He gives the
whole a legendary air; calculated to impose on vulgar credulity, and
foster superstition. " First of all," he makes the Muses say, " existed
" *Chaos:* next in order the broad-bosomed *Earth*," or matter con-
densed; " and then appeared *Love*," or attraction, " the most beautiful
" of the immortals. From CHAOS sprung EREBUS and dusky NIGHT;
" and, from Night and Erebus, sprung ETHER and smiling DAY.
" But first the Earth produced the starry HEAVEN, commensurate to
" herself; and the barren sea, without mutual love; then, conjoined
" with COELUS," the *heaven*, " she bore the tremendous TITANS,"
jarring principles of matter. " The CYCLOPS were afterward engen-
dered; BRONTES," *thunder*," STEROPES," *lightning*, " and ARGES,"
the *flaming bolt.* " Beside these, three other rueful sons were born to
" Heaven and Earth, COTUS, BRIARIUS, and GYGES;" *eruption, hur-*
ricane, and *earthquake.* Hesiod, *Theog.* init.

79. See *Discour. sur l'Elagie* et *Discour. sur les Poets Eligiaques*, par
M. l'Abbe Souchay, et auct. cit. The elegant Minermus cannot be
excepted from this general charge. He was the author of the LOVE
ELEGY (Id. ibid.); consisting of alternate *hexameter* and *hentameter*
verses, afterward used by all Greek and Latin elegiac poets; and the
flow of which has been happily imitated in English elegy, by the
quatern of ten syllables in *alternate rhyme.*

shall

shall not offer them to your lordship's attention. The lyric poets are more worthy of regard, for many reasons. They present us with effusions of the human mind, under the influence of various passions; and naturally lead us to inquire after the origin of poetry and music.

Some critics have ascribed the origin of poetry to love, some to religion, and some to war; but men were surely lovers, before they were warriors or devotees. I shall, therefore, assign it to love. The intercourse of the sexes, gradually ripening sensibility, calls forth the first strong emotions of the youthful breast. Fancy, in that season of life, is warm; and bestows on the beloved object a thousand adventitious charms. As the tongue wants power to express the feelings of the enamoured heart, common language wants force to declare its raptures, or paint its agitations. Fancy catches fire from the torch of admiration; and breathes, in disjointed phrases, the lover's flame. Hence love songs, as they are the first emanations of an ardent mind, have been the first poetical productions in most countries.

But love, though the most early, is not the only strong passion in the human breast. After the formation of political society, other passions take the lead. As soon as religion was called in to the aid of legislation, that devotion which, in simple times, had been paid to woman, was transferred to the gods, and poured out in hymns or sacred songs. Nor did priestcraft, in seeking to inspire veneration for pious ceremonies, alone take advantage of poetry: the early legislators also called it in to their aid, and promulgated their institutions in verse[80]; for better securing the operation of their laws, through the influence of the Muses,

80. Aristot. *Problem.* sect. xix. prob. xxviii. Ælian. *Var. Hist.* lib. ii. cap. xxxix.

the

the daughters of Memory[81].   And the Muses were
ever ready to sound the charge to battle, to sing the
triumphal song[82], or record the actions of heroes.

Music had the same origin with poetry[83].   The
shepherd or herdsman sung the praise of his mistress;
celebrated their happy loves, or bewailed his unreci-
procated passion, in melody suited to the sentiment
which his verses conveyed.   To the voice succeeded
the pipe or reed, through which the lover breathed
his tender emotions; not expressed in language, but by
the mute eloquence of the eye, unless when the beloved fair accompanied the sound of the reed with
her voice; and either declared their mutual bliss, or
lamented their unhappy lot[84].

Musical

81. Hesiod. *Theog.*

82. The most ancient triumphal song is that of Moses, after the
miraculous passage of the Arabian gulf. " Thus sang Moses, and the
children of Israel, this song unto the Lord:—" For he hath triumphed
" gloriously; the horse and his rider hath he thrown into the sea.
" The Lord is my strength and song, and he has become my salvation:
" he is my God, and I will prepare him an habitation; my father's
" God, and I will exalt him.· The Lord is a man of war, the LORD
" is his *name*. Pharaoh's chariots and his host hath he cast into the
" sea: his chosen captains also are drowned in the Red Sea. The
" depths have covered them, they sank to the bottom as a stone. Thy
" right hand, O Lord! is become glorious in power; thy right hand,
" O Lord! hath dashed in pieces the enemy. And in the greatness of
" thine excellency thou hast overthrown them that rose up against
" thee: thou sentest forth thy wrath, which consumed them as stub-
" ble.   And with the blast of thy nostrils, the waters were gathered
" together: the floods stood upright, as an heap, and the depths were
" congealed in the heart of the sea. The enemy said, I will pursue;
" I will overtake, I will divide the spoil: my lust shall be satisfied
" upon them. I will draw my sword; my hand shall destroy them.
" Thou didst blow with thy wind, the sea covered them: they sank
" as lead in the mighty waters. Who is like unto thee, O Lord!
" amongst the gods?" *Exodus*, chap. xv. ver. 1—11.

83. See *Premier Mem. sur les Chansons de l'Ancienne Greece*, par M.
de la Nauze.

84. Here we find, by a natural progression, the *separation* and *reunion*
of poetry and music. The enamoured swain first sung his own
verses; to unburden his mind, or to please his mistress. He next
breathed

Musical instruments, but especially wind instruments, were soon employed in the service of religion. And the harp or lyre, a stringed instrument, was very early in use among the Grecian cheiftains and military bards[85]. The compositions of those bards, rapid, sublime, and wild, were naturally adapted to the lyre[86]; though they had not the perfect form of the higher ode, the merit of constructing which is due to the genius of Pindar[87].

But before Pindar, who does not fall within the period under review, the Greeks had many cele-brated lyric poets. Among those Archilocus, Ter-pander, Stecichorus, and Alcæus, are eminently distinguished by ancient critics: but as their writings, except a few fragments, are now lost, I shall not enter into a dissertation on their reputed merit[88]. Two odes

breathed through his reed the air to which they were attuned; and when his mistress sung his verses, while he played the tune, poetry and music were reunited, though not in the person of the composer. The same things happened in a more advanced stage of poetry and music. The military bards originally sung their verses, and afterward accompanied the song with the sound of the lyre (Blackwell's *Life of Homer*, passim). But as it was found that a good poet might have a bad voice, and be little skilled in touching the lyre or harp, the professions of poetry and music were separated, as we have seen (Lett VI.), on the re-establishment of the pythian games. But although the congenial professions were separated, for the pleasure of the admirers of the *sister-arts*, poetry and music were generally associated at all the Grecian festivals. The ode was sung and accompanied with instrumental music; though that music was not always composed by the poet, or executed either by his voice or instrument.

85. Hom. *Iliad. et Odyss.* passim.

86. Blackwell's *Life of Homer*.

87. See *Discour. sur Pindare, et sur la Poesic Lyrique*, par M. de Char-bahon, et auct. cit.

88. Several of those poets excelled no less in elegiac, than in lyric composition. But as all their elegies, as well as their odes, have perished in the flux of time, or sunk a prey to barbarism, I shall transcribe an elegy of a more early age; by David, king of Israel, the immortal Hebrew lyric poet. "And David lamented with this
" lamentation

odes of Sappho, the Lesbian poetess, and seventy of
Anacreon, the Teian bard, furnish better room for
critical examination.

Sappho appears to have possessed a soul highly
susceptible of love, and her verses convey the soft sentiment in voluptuous excess[89].   But Sappho's love
took an unaccountable direction: it turned upon her
own sex.   And the ardour of this Sapphic passion, is
strikingly described in the celebrated little ode, preserved and applauded by Longinus.   It may thus be
paraphrased, for it cannot admit of translation:

> " Blest as the gods the favour'd swain,
> " Who, sitting by thee, tells his pain;

" lamentation over Saul, and over Jonathan his son. " The beauty
" of Israel is slain upon thy *high places:* how are the mighty fallen!
" —Tell it not in Gath, publish it not in the streets of Askelon, lest
" the daughters of the Philistines rejoice; lest the daughters of the
" uncircumcised triumph. Ye mountains of Gilboa, let there be no
" dew, neither let there be rain upon you, nor fields of offerings; for
" there the shield of the mighty is vilely cast away, the shield of Saul,
" as though he had not been anointed with oil. From the blood of the
" slain, from the fat of the mighty, the bow of Jonathan turned not
" back, and the sword of Saul returned not empty. Saul and Jona-
" than were lovely and pleasant in their lives, and in their deaths they
" were not divided. They were swifter than eagles, they were
" stronger than lions. Ye daughters of Israel, weep over Saul who
" cloathed you in scarlet, with other delights; who put on ornaments
" of gold upon your apparel. How are the mighty fallen in the
" midst of the battle!—O Jonathan, thou wast slain in thine *high*
" *places.* I am distressed for thee, my brother! *very pleasant hast thou*
" *been unto me.* Thy love for me was wonderful, *passing the love of*
" *women.* How are the mighty fallen, and the weapons of war
" perished!"—2. Sam. chap. i. ver. 17—27.

89. A fragment of one of her pieces, seemingly written in early
life, exhibits strong marks of her amorous character.

> ————" Cease, dear mother! cease to chide,
> " I can no more the golden shuttle guide;
> " While Venus thus, through every glowing vein,
> " Asserts the charming youth's resistless reign."

Frag. Sappho.

" Who

" Who hears thee speak, who sees thee smile,
" And sips thy ruby lip the while.
" When I behold thy blooming charms,
" My bosom beats with soft alarms :
" From vein to vein, a subtle flame,
" I feel, run thrilling through my frame ;
" My soul is in love's transports toss'd,
" My speech is gone, my voice is lost ;
" Moist languors all my body seize,
" And all my blood cold tremors freeze ;
" A dim suffusion veils my eyes,
" Unwonted sounds my ears surprise ;
" My throbbing heart beats thick and high ;
" I faint, I sink, and seem to die."

But Sappho's talent for lyric poetry is best displayed
in her Ode to Venus ; one of the most beautiful poems
that antiquity has left us, and which has been translated
into English verse with all the fire, spirit, and flow of
the original[90].

" O Venus ! beauty of the skies,
" To whom a thousand temples rise :
" Gaily false in gentle smiles,
" Full of love-perplexing wiles ;
" O Goddess ! from my heart remove,
" The wasting cares and pains of love.

" If ever thou hast kindly heard
" A song in soft distress preferr'd,
" Propitious to my tuneful vow,
" O gentle Goddess ! hear me now :
" Descend, thou bright immortal guest !
" In all thy radiant charms confest.

90. This translation bears the name of Ambrose Philips, but is
supposed to have been executed by Joseph Addison. See Warton's
Essay on the Genius of Pope, vol. i.

" Thou

" Thou once did'st leave almighty JOVE,
" And all the golden roofs above :
" The car thy wanton sparrows drew ;
" Hovering in air, they lightly flew,
" As to my bower they wing'd their way,
" I saw their quivering pinions play.

" The birds dismiss'd, while you remain,
" Bore back their empty car again ;
" Then you, with looks divinely mild,
" In every heavenly feature smil'd,
" And ask'd what new complaints I made,
" And why I call'd you to my aid ?

" What frenzy in my bosom raged,
" And by what cure to be assuaged ?
" What gentle youth I would allure,
" Whom in my artful toils secure ?—
" Who does thy tender heart subdue ?
" Tell me, my Sappho ! tell me who ?

" Though now he shuns thy longing arms,
" He soon shall court thy slighted charms ;
" Though now thy offerings he despise,
" He soon to thee shall sacrifice ;
" Though now he freeze, he soon shall burn,
" And be thy victim in his turn.

" Celestial visitant ! once more,
" Thy needful presence I implore :
" In pity come and ease my grief,
" Bring my distemper'd soul relief ;
" Favour thy suppliant's *hidden fires*,
" And give me all my soul desires."

Anacreon, though not devoid of feeling, diverted
the anxieties of love by mirth and wine. And he has
given us more perfect examples of gaily amorous and
                                        jovial

jovial songs, than any author in ancient or modern times. His allegorical imagery is altogether magical. Venus and Cupid, the Graces and the Muses, are perpetually at his command. And he has employed them in a manner that must forever excite admiration, and communicate pleasure. He was the poet of taste and of conviviality; and although he lived in an age, when politeness was little understood in Greece, no poet ever had the talent of turning a compliment with more elegance, or of more powerfully awakening social joy. His jovial songs, however, it must be owned, have often a tendency to immerse the soul in sensuality. But those of the complimentary cast are generally free from such blame. I shall, therefore, attempt to imitate his Ode to Woman, as a specimen of his manner of writing:

> " To all creatures of the earth
> " Bounteous Nature, at their birth,
> " Gave the aids, or gave the arms,
> " To secure their lives from harms :
> " To the bull the front of steel,
> " To the horse the horned heel;
> " Swiftness to the timorous hare,
> " Fur and fury to the bear;
> " To the pard the deathful paw,
> " The lion the devouring jaw;
> " MAN the unconquerable mind;
> " What for WOMAN was behind?
> " *Lovely Woman!* Yet in store
> " Nature had one present more;
> " Thee she gave *the power to charm:*
> " Beauty all things can disarm."

I shall afterward have occasion to trace the farther progress of lyric poetry, and to estimate the merit of Pindar. In the mean time, I shall transcribe one of his Olympic odes, as translated by Gilbert West, for the value of the sentiments it conveys.

STROPHE.

STROPHE.

" To wind-bound mariners, most welcome blow
  " The breezy zephyrs through the whistling shrouds:
" Most welcome to the thirsty mountains flow
  " Soft showers, the pearly daughters of the clouds ;
" And when on virtuous toils the gods bestow
  " Success, most welcome sound mellifluous odes ;
" Whose numbers ratify the voice of fame,
" And to illustrious worth insure a lasting name.

ANTISTROPHE.

" Such fame, superior to the hostile dart
  " Of canker'd envy, Pisa's chief attends :
" Fain would my muse th' immortal boon impart,
  " Th'immortal boon which from high heaven descends.
" And now, inspir'd by heaven, thy valiant heart,
  " Agesidamus ! she to fame commends ;
" Now adds the ornament of tuneful praise,
  " And decks thy *olive crown* with sweetly sounding lays.

EPODE.

" But while thy bold achievements I rehearse,
  " Thy youthful victory in Pisa's sand,
" With thee partaking in thy friendly verse,
  " Not unregarded shall thy Locris stand.
  " Then haste, ye muses ! join the choral band
" Of festive youths upon the Locrian plain :
  " To an unciviliz'd, and savage land,
" Think not I now invite your virgin train ;
" Where *barbarous ignorance* and *foul disdain*
  " Of *social virtue's hospitable lore,*
" Prompts the *unmanner'd* and *inhuman swain*
  " To *drive the stranger from his churlish door*[91].

91. I have already had occasion to remark, in opposition to Mr.
Mitford, and his coadjutor Mr. Wood, that although the early Greeks,
while barbarous, were hospitable, *all barbarians are not so kindly disposed.* And I have the satisfaction to find Pindar, an enlightened
Greek, of the same opinion.

A nation

" A nation ye shall find, renowned of yore
" For martial valour, and for worthy deeds ;
" Rich in a vast and unexhausted store
" Of innate wisdom, whose prolific seeds
" Spring in each age : so Nature's laws require,
" And the great laws of Nature ne'er expire.
" Unchang'd the lion's valiant race remains,
" And all his father's wiles the youthful fox retains[92].

92. This ode was sung after the celebration of the games in the
seventy-fourth Olympiad; when Agesidamus, chief of the Epizephy-
rian Locrians, seated near the promontory Zephyrium in Italy, was
victor in the exercise of the cæstus.

LETTER VIII.

ITALY FROM THE MOST EARLY TIMES TO THE BANISH-
MENT OF THE TARQUINS FROM ROME, AND THE ABO-
LITION OF REGAL POWER AMONG THE ROMANS.

PART I. THAT central peninsula of Europe, which extends, in the shape of a boot, from the thirty-
eighth to the forty-seventh degree of latitude, and
is bounded on the north by the Alps, on the south by
the Sicilian strait, and on the east and west by the
Hadriatic and Tuscan seas, was very anciently known
by the name of Italia or Italy[1], and considered as the
most fertile, desirable, and self-supported country in
our division of the world[2]; as producing not only
corn, cattle, wine, and oil in abundance, but fruits of
all kinds, and metals, minerals, stone, and timber, for
all uses; whatever, in a word, can contribute to supply the necessities, or minister to the comforts of life, in
a climate moderately hot, and a territory beautifully
diversified with bays, promontories, rivers, lakes,
mountains, hills, and plains[3].

Ancient Italy is commonly divided by geographers
into three parts; Italia Subalpina, or Italy, under the

1. This name, we are told by Aristotle, it received from Italus, one
of its kings, who reigned before the days of Minos, and changed the
manner of life of the inhabitants from pasturage to agriculture.
(Arist. *Polit.* lib. vii.). It had formerly been known by the names of
Saturnia, Hesperia, Ausonia, and Oenatoria. Dionys. Halicarnass.
Antiq. Rom. lib. i.
2. Dion. Halicarnass. ubi sup. Plin. lib. iii. Strabo, lib. v.
3. Id. ibid.

Alps;

Alps; Italy, properly so called, which was the middle division; and Magna Græcia, or Great Greece, toward the point of the peninsula; where the Greeks, as we have seen, had early planted many colonies. The Romans, when they had made themselves masters of the whole peninsula, divided it first into seven, and afterwards into eleven provinces.

Before the rise of the Roman power, Italy was occupied by a number of independent nations or tribes, who enjoyed, in their several cantons, the blessings of liberty and equality, under a government similar to that of the Greeks during the heroic age[4]. The most considerable of those nations were the Aborigines, who appear to have been of Celtic blood, and whose name became early extinct in that of Latines[5]; the Umbrians, who seem to have been a warlike tribe of the Aborigines, and who, in very ancient times, widely extended their dominion in Italy[6]; the Tyrrhenians or Etruscans, sprung from a Lydian colony, blended with a body of Pelasgian adventurers, that had emigrated from Thessaly; who stript the Umbrians of all their conquests, and confined them to their proper district[7]: the Sabines, a tribe of the Umbrians, who had fled from the victorious arms of the Etruscans, and were reinforced by a colony of Lacedæmonians, whose hardy valour they imbibed, and whose austere

4. Dion. Halicarnass. *Antiq. Rom.* passim.
5. Dion. Halicarnass. lib. i.   6. Plin. *Hist. Nat.* lib. iii. Strabo, *Geog.* lib. v. Dion. Halicarnass. ubi sup.
7. Id. ibid. et Herodot. lib. i. cap. xciv. The Lydian colony was conducted into Italy by Tyrrhenus, the son of Atys (Herodot. ubi sup.), who appears to have reigned in that part of Asia Minor long known by the name of Lydia, about five generations before the appearance of Hercules and Theseus, or the beginning of the heroic age in Greece. The Pelasgian adventurers had found their way into Italy in a still more early period. Dion. Halicarnass. lib. i.

manners

manners they adopted[8]. All the other ancient Italian nations were branches from those, except the Venetes and Ligurians; who seem to have been Gallic or German emigrants, and consequently Celts[9].

The Etruscans, and the Latines or Aborigines of Latium, are the only Italian nations concerning whom history or tradition has furnished us with any particulars worthy of mentioning, till after the building of Rome. The Etruscans appear to have been in possession of the greater part of Italy, and lords of the neighbouring seas, as early as the time of the Argonautic expedition[10]. How long their empire remained unbroken, is uncertain. We only know, that during several centuries subsequent to the Trojan war, they continued to be the most powerful and civilized nation in the Italian peninsula, and successfully cultivated the arts of design before they could be said to have taken root in Greece[11]. Yet a celebrated antiquarian, who admits this more early proficiency, conjectures, from the remains of their sculpture and painting, that the Etruscans must have been indebted for the principles of these arts, and also for those of their literature, to Grecian emigrants[12]. It seems, however, no less probable, that the elements of both were imported with the Lydian colony immediately from Asia Minor,

8. Dion. Halicarnass. lib. ii.   Plut. *Vit. Numa.*

9. See on this intricate subject (the peopling of Italy), the ancient part of the English *Universal History*, vol. ix. and xviii. where the opinions of a multitude of authors, both ancient and modern, are diligently compared and examined. The lovers of such inquiries may also consult *Recherches sur l'Orig. et l'Ancienne Hist. des different Peuple de Italie*, par M. Freret, in the second volume of *Choix des Mémoires de l'Academie Royale des Inscript. et Belles Lettres.*

10. Diod. Sicul. lib. v. Athenæus, lib. vii. Aristid. *Orat. in Bacch.*

11. Append. *Ancient Univ. Hist.* vol. xviii. Art *Etrus.* sec. ii. iii. et auct. cit.

12. Winkelmann, *Hist. de l'Antiquite*, liv. iii.

as the religion of the Etruscans certainly was; the
worship of the *dii cabiri*, or mighty gods, and the
gloomy mysteries of Samothracia[13].

Whence the Latines derived their knowledge of
arts and of letters, we are not left to conjecture. The
Romans, their illustrious descendants, whose virtue
and valour made them sovereigns of Italy, and whose
ambition prompted them to aspire at the empire of the
ancient world, have furnished us with sufficient information on that subject. And in tracing the history
of this great people, we shall gradually become acquainted with every thing necessary to be known concerning the political state of the old Italian nations;
and with all their transactions, civil and military, that
can contribute to your lordship's entertainment, or
which are properly authenticated.

About threescore years before the Trojan war, and
during the reign of Faunus, king of the Aborigines, a
band of Grecian adventurers from Arcadia, under
Evander, their leader, arrived in that part of Italy, afterward known by the name of Latium. Faunus received the strangers, who landed from two ships, with
marks of friendship, and allowed them to settle in his
dominions[14]. They chose for their habitation the foot
of a hill, not far from the river Tiber. There they
built a town; which, from their parent city in Arcadia, they called Pallantium, a name that was in succeeding times corrupted into Palatium[15].

Evander and his followers having thus seated
themselves at the foot of that hill, which was one day

---

13. Dion. Halicarnass. *Antiq. Rom.* lib. i. To these gods, we are
told by the same author, the Etruscans vowed the *Tenths*. Id. ibid.
14. Dion. Halicarnass. lib. i.   15. Id. ibid.

PART I. to become the centre of the city of Rome, and the seat
of the court of the Roman kings and emperors, built
temples, and instituted sacrifices and festivals, after
the manner of their country[16]. They first introduced
into Latium the use of letters, and the practice of instrumental music performed on the lyre[17]; the Aborigines, before the arrival of this colony, being only acquainted with wind-instruments[18].

The Arcadian emigrants, if we may credit tradition, carried their improvements yet farther. They
are said to have framed laws, to have infused into the
barbarous natives a sense of humanity, and to have
taught them many necessary arts[19]. Hence they were
cherished by the Aborigines, and became in a manner
one people with them[20].

In the reign of Latinus, the son and successor of
Ant. Ch. Faunus, Æneas and a body of Trojans, who had
1184. escaped in the general slaughter of their countrymen,
on the subversion of the kingdom of Priam, and the
destruction of Troy by the Greeks, landed at Laurentium on the coast of the Aborigines[21]. And having
obtained permission to form a settlement, they built a
Ant. Ch. city on a hill near the mouth of the Tiber. To that
1180. city the Trojan prince gave the name of Lavinium, in
grateful expression of his affection for Lavinia, the
king's daughter, and only child, who had been granted to him in marriage[22].

The good fortune of Æneas attended his followers.
The Trojans were generally able to form marriages

16. Dion. Halicarnass. lib. i. The Arcadians instituted, in particular, the festival of the Lupercalia, in honour of the god Pan (Id.
ibid.), celebrated with so much licentiousness among the Romans in
latter times.   17. Id. ibid.   18. Dion. Halicarnass. lib. i.
      19. Id. ibid.   20. Dion. Halicarnass. lib. i.
      21. Id. ibid.   22. Tit. Liv. lib. i. Dion. Halicarnass. ubi sup.
                                                              with

with the women of Latium; and soon became so perfectly incorporated with the principal families, that
both they and the Aborigines took the common name
of *Latines*, in honour of Latinus, who had showed
the example of alliance, and formed, with his daughter's hand, the great bond of their union[23].

Alarmed at this coalition, the Rutuli, a fierce
neighbouring nation, and apparently a tribe of the
Aborigines, had recourse to arms. After some ineffectual efforts, they applied for assistance to the
Etruscans; whose name, we are told, was then famous
in Italy, from the Alps to the Sicilian strait, and by
sea as well as by land[24]. The events of the war were
many, and its success various. But, at length, it was
happily terminated by a treaty, which made the Tiber
the boundaries between the Latin and Etruscan territories[25].

During the continuance of hostilities, Latinus was
slain; and Æneas, who succeeded him in the government of Latium, was drowned in the river Numi-
cus, on the banks of which he had fought an unsuccessful battle with the Etruscans[26]. His son, Asca-
nius, however, was able to defend Lavinium; and
having gained, in a vigorous sally, an advantage over
the enemy, he obtained the treaty of peace already
mentioned[27].

About thirty years after the founding of Lavinium, the Latines built a large city, which they surrounded with a wall, and denominated Alba[28]. And
in the neighbouring country they built many other

Ant. Ch.
1152.

23. Id. ibid.   24. Liv. lib. i. cap. ii.
25. Id. ibid.   Dion. Halicarnass. lib. i.
26. Liv. et Dion. Halicarnass. ubi sup.   27. Id. ibid.
28. Dion. Halicarnass. lib. i.

towns,

towns, called in later times the *cities of the ancient Latines*[29]. The building of Alba was attended with circumstances sufficiently memorable to merit particular notice.

A temple and sanctuary having been erected in this city, for the images or emblems of the Gods which Æneas had brought with him from Troy, and placed in a temple at Lavinium, they were removed accordingly to their new habitation. But the following night, to the astonishment of every one, the images changed their situation (by the interposition of priestcraft, as may be presumed), and were found in the morning upon their former pedestals; although the doors of the temple at Alva remained firmly shut; and the walls and roof were entire[30]. Replaced, with expiatory and propitiatory sacrifices, the images again found their way to the old temple[31].

Unwilling to return to their former habitation, or to live in utter separation from the gods of their fathers, the Trojans of Alba, after much deliberation and trouble of mind, came to a resolution, to send back some of their own people to Lavinium, in order to take care of the images[32]. These Trojan gods were called Penates by the Latines, and supposed to preside over domestic affairs[33]. With Æneas also was supposed to have been brought the famous Palladium, afterward said to be kept by the holy virgins, along with the perpetual fire, in the temple of Vesta; and the conservation of which was considered by the Romans, as essential to the safety of the state, or to public security[34].

29. Id. ibid. 30. Dion. Halicarnass. lib. i. cap. lxvii.
31. Id. ibid. 32. Dion. Halicarnass. ubi sup.
33. Dion. Halicarnass. lib. i. passim. 34. Id. ibid.

Four

LETTER
VIII.

Ant. Chr.
752.
Olymp.
vi. 4.

Four hundred years after the building of Alba (during which long period we are left altogether in the dark in regard to the affairs of Italy), the Latines sent out a colony to Pallantium; where the Arcadians under Evander had settled, and where some of their descendants still remained[35]. The first care of the adventurers was to give to Pallantium the form of a city, and to surround it with a wall[36]. That city they called Rome, from Romulus, the head of the colony; who was the seventeenth lineal descendant from Eneas by Lavinia, and grandson of Numitor king of Alba[37].

Every circumstance relative to the building of Rome, or concerning the birth and education of its founder, has been carefully preserved by the ancient Greek and Roman writers. And the leading particulars connected with those events, how significant soever in themselves, derive importance from the æra which they serve to introduce; and thence become too interesting to mankind, to be omitted by a modern historian.

Amulius, the son of Procas, king of Alba, having seized the reins of government on the death of his father, in prejudice of the right of Numitor, his elder brother, sought also to deprive that injured prince of posterity; in order to secure his own usurped power, and transmit the succession to his descendants. With this view, he got Numitor's only son secretly assassinated, being little jealous of the unwarlike and unambitious father, and constituted his only daughter, Ilia or Rhea, a priestess of Vesta; an office, though honour-

35. Id. ibid.   36. Dion. Halicarnass. lib. i.
37. Id. ibid.

able in itself, which condemned her to a life of perpetual virginity[38].

But the vestal state, it should seem, accorded as ill with Rhea's complexion, as it would with the great events in the womb of time, for the future exaltation of her family and nation. She soon proved with child : and insinuated, in extenuation of her crime, that she had been ravished by the god Mars, in a grove sacred to that masculine divinity, adjoining to the temple of Vesta[39]. And which was surely a convenient place for an amour.

In consequence of this violent, or at least vigorous embrace, Rhea was, in due time, delivered of two male children; to one of whom was afterward given the name of Romulus, and to the other that of Remus[40]. What became of their mother, we are not certainly informed. She was either committed to close confinement by Amulius, or put to death, according to the law against incontinent vestals ; and her two

38. Liv. lib. i. Dion. Halicarnass. lib. i. The character of no heathen deity is less understood than that of Vesta. " Among the contemplative priests of the east," says the learned Blackwell, " she passed for the latent power of fire; or that internal texture and disposition of some sorts of matter that renders it combustible, while others are little affected with heat. As such, she was the wife of Cœlus, and mother of Saturn; the sacred *eternal fire*, worshipped with the greatest reverence, and most pious ceremonies, by all the eastern nations. But among the less speculative Europeans, who received the knowledge of this goddess at second hand, she was considered as Saturn's daughter; a national, tutelary divinity, and protectress of the family seat. This hoary recluse goddess," proceeds he, " the pure eternal Vesta, therefore, appears in a double capacity : either as the grand enlivening *genius* of the terrestrial globe, or as the permanent immoveable seat of gods and men, the *earth* itself; and, by an easy transition, the native soil of a nation, or the fixed habitation of a family." *Letters concerning Mythol.* p. 58—62.

39. Id. ibid.   40. Liv. et Dion. Halicarnass. ubi sup.

infants

infants were ordered, in conformity with the same law, to be thrown into the Tiber[41].

Fortunately for the twin brothers, the Tiber had at that time overflowed its banks; so that the cradle, in which they were deposited, was not committed to the bed of that river, but to the super-abounding waters that washed the foot of the Palatine hill[42]. Those waters suddenly retired; and the cradle, which had floated for a time, without entering the main stream of the Tiber, striking against a stone, was overturned, and the children of Rhea were left sprawling in the mud[43].

In that situation the reputed sons of Mars are said to have been recognized by a she wolf, whose dugs were painfully distended with milk, by reason of the loss of her whelps[44]. She offered the infants her teats, which they greedily seized; and, finding relief, she continued with them, and licked off the mud with which they were besmeared[45].

Meanwhile, according to the same traditionary tale, the neighbouring shepherds, driving their flocks to pasture, were filled with astonishment and admiration at the docility of the wolf, and the affection of the children, who hung upon her, as if she had been their mother[46]. These simple people thought they saw something supernatural in the wonderful preservation of the infants, though ignorant of their high birth. And Faustulus, the keeper of the king's herds and flocks, who happened to be among the number, and who had been in Alba at the time of the de-

41. Id. ibid.
Halicarnass. lib. i.
44. Justin, lib. xlili.
46. Id. ibid.

42. Quinct. Fabius Pict. ap. Dion.
43. Id. ibid.
45. Q. Fabius Pict. ubi sup.

livery

livery of Rhea, took home with him the twin brothers, whose parentage he guessed, and made his own
wife nurse them[47].

Thus miraculously saved and reared, Romulus and
Remus, in the cottage of Faustulus, began early to
display an elevation of mind, and a dignity of look,
little suited to the condition of herdsmen, but perfectly consonant to their royal ancestry, and strongly
indicative of the justice of their maternal claim to a
divine sire. Disdaining the tranquil life of shepherds
or neatherds, they devoted themselves to the toils of
the chace, and became famous as hunters. From the
pursuit of wild beasts, they turned their activity to
military sports, and their ambition to skill in arms[48].
This skill they had frequent opportunity of displaying;
not only at their rural festivals, along with their rude
companions, whom they had formed into bands, but
in combating the robbers of the neighbouring mountains, whose booty they frequently seized; and, after
carrying it home with exultation, divided it among
their associates[49]. Hence, perhaps, the remote origin
of the Roman triumph.

On one of those occasions of public rejoicing,
Remus fell into the hands of the banditti, who had
been deprived of their booty; was carried before his
grand uncle Amulius, king of Alba, and accused of
having committed the robberies he had helped to repress[50]. This incident brought matters to a crisis.

Faustulus made Romulus acquainted with his
birth; in order to prevent him from inconsiderately
rushing, at the head of his rustic followers, to the

47. Liv. lib. i. Q. Fabius Pict. ubi sup.
48. Liv. ubi sup. Plut. *Vit. Romul.*   49. Id. ibid.
50. Liv. lib. i. Justin, lib. xliii.

rescue of his brother[51]. Romulus revealed himself to
his grandfather, Numitor; to whose custody Remus
had been committed for punishment, and who had been
struck with his stately person, and majestic mein[52].
A party in Alba, under the conduct of Remus, was
secretly formed in favour of the excluded king; and
Romulus háving assembled the hardy mountaineers,
whom he had trained to arms, entered the capital at
their head; killed the usurper Amulius, and placed
Numitor upon the throne[53].

But the twin brothers, although now restored to
their family, their kindred, and their rank in society,
did not find in their new situation all the satisfaction
it might seem to afford. Two young princes of an
enterprising genius, who had led so active a life, and
accomplished such a memorable revolution before the
years of manhood, were by no means calculated to enjoy that peaceful repose it appeared necessary for them
to maintain, under the government of an aged and
unwarlike king. Romulus and Remus, therefore,
cráved leave of their grandfather to lead a colony
from Alba, and establish an independent state[54]. Their
request was readily granted by Numitor; and so popular was their character, that fifteen hundred adventurers, beside a large body of their former associates,
chose to follow their fortunes[55].

These determined adventurers, the bold and ambitious youths conducted, as already related, to Pallantium; in the neighbourhood of which they had
passed their early days, and where they proposed to
build a city[56]. But a quarrel broke out between the

51. Dion. Halicarnass. lib. i.   52. Plut. Vit. Romul.
53. Id. ibid. Liv. lib. i. Dion. Halicarnass. ubi sup.
54. Dion. Halicarnass. et Liv. lib.   55. Id. ibid.
56. Dion. Halicarnass. lib. i.

haughty

haughty brothers, relative to the founding of that city. Romulus insisted it should be built on the Palatine, and Remus contended for the Aventine hill.   Each was abetted in his opinion by his particular adherents. Recourse was had, in vain, to augury, in order to settle the dispute.   The two parties went to blows, and Remus was killed in the fray[57].

Henceforth Romulus remained undisputed head of the colony.   And he took the most effectual measures, as well for securing his authority, as for promoting the future grandeur of Rome; which was built, according to his destination, on the Palatine hill[58].   The success of these measures, and the measures themselves, now demand your lordship's attention.

As soon as Romulus had founded that city which still bears his name, and which at first was no better than a military station, surrounded with a wall and a ditch[59], he resolved, with the advice of his grandfather, to establish some plan of government, by which the infant community might be held together.   He accordingly assembled his followers, who now amounted to three thousand foot, and three hundred horsemen[60], and asked them, under what form of policy they would chuse to live?—or, if they should make choice of regal government, whom they would wish to rule over them ?—They chose that moderate kingly government, to which they had formerly been accustomed to submit ; and which then, as already observed, prevailed over Italy : and they named, with one voice, their gallant leader as their king[61].

57. Id. ibid.   58. Dion. Halicarnass. Liv. et Plut. ubi sup.
59. Id. ibid.   60. Dion. Halicarnass. lib. ii.
61. Id. ibid.

But

But Romulus was too well acquainted with the factious spirit and restless disposition of his followers, to acquiesce in this choice without the sanction of higher authority. He, therefore, made a solemn appeal to the gods, for their approbation and confirmation; and the omen being in his favour, he proceeded to the exercise of his regal function[62].

The manner of appeal to heaven, on that occasion, was this: Romulus having sacrificed, by break of day, to Jupiter, the king of the gods, and to all the inferior deities, whom he had chosen as the patrons of his new city and state, walked out of his tent, with his face toward the east; when " a flash of lightning ran from the *left* to the *right*," which was interpreted by the augurs as a happy omen[63]. A similar appeal was made, in all succeeding times, by the Roman kings and magistrates, after their election; though latterly it came to be considered as mere form[64].

The measures taken by Romulus, immediately after he was invested with royal authority, shew him to have been worthy of the high office of king; and they, at the same time, tend to establish the authority of an ancient tradition, That he had been sent, while a stripling, to Gabii, a town in the neighbourhood of Pallantium, and there instructed in Greek learning and the use of arms[65]. Romulus began his administration with

---

62. Dion. Halicarnass. ubi sup.   63. Id. ibid.
64. Dion. Halicarnass. lib. ii.
65. Dion. Halicarnass. lib. i. cap. lxxxiv. This attempt to reconcile to credibility the framing of the admirable institutions ascribed to Romulus, will appear absurd to the converts of those modern critics and historians, who affect to consider the early part of the Roman history as altogether fictious. But as I can see no reason for rejecting the ancient traditions of a people proud of their ancestry; who interwove those traditions with their most solemn religious

with dividing the citizens of Rome into three equal portions, to which he gave the name of *tribes;* assigned to each tribe a particular district, or ward of the city to inhabit, and appointed a person of distinction, a tribune or præfect, to preside over it. He next subdivided the tribes into *curiæ* or companies; each tribe consisting of ten, and the whole of thirty *curiæ;* and each of these, he again split into ten *decuriæ;* all under their proper officers, their *curiones* and *decuriones;* who, in peace, presided over them, in their several stations, and could assemble them for war on the shortest notice[66].

Having thus given to his three thousand three hundred followers the form of an army, in a state of encampment, Romulus proceeded to establish, with the consent of the assembled body, such civil institutions as seemed necessary for good government, and the prosperity of a rising community. Actuated by these views, he divided the territory of Rome into thirty equal shares, and gave one to each of the thirty curiæ;

gious ceremonies, and preserved the memory of the things they contain in various monuments, both civil and sacred, I shall treat the Roman history, from the building of the city, with all the gravity of Livy, and the attention of Dionysius Halicarnassensis; two historians of great discernment, who lived in an enlightened age, and had full access to information; who wrote nearly at the same time, and who, without any participation, have related the same events, and with nearly the same leading circumstances. If they have not told always incontrovertible facts, they have at least told us what the Romans in the height of their powers, and when they were neither ignorant nor credulous, believed concerning their early transactions: nor is greater historical certainty necessary. In a word, it may be questioned, whether modern scepticism, by its impertinent cavillings, has not done more hurt to the cause of truth, and to all the fruits to be naturally reaped from historical knowledge, by involving the mind of the inquirer in perpetual doubt, than the credulity of former, and darker ages.

66. Dion. Halicarnass. lib. ii. cap. vii. xiv.

after

after reserving to himself a certain portion for the support of his royal dignity, and appropriating another to the use of religion. And, in order to preserve due subordination among a society of men equal in landed property, and who could have little other wealth to create disparity, he distinguished, by the name of *patricians*, those fathers of families who were eminent for their birth or merit; and comprehended the inferior members of the state, or the common people, under the general name of *plebeians*[67].

To the patricians Romulus confined the higher civil offices and principal military employments, with the superintendence of religious ceremonies: they only could be priests, magistrates, generals, or judges. But while he thus excluded the plebeians from these important and honourable functions, for which he thought them unfit, he was by no means inattentive to their ease or happiness. He recommended to them the exercise of healthful trades; the labours of agriculture, and the grazing of cattle: and, in order to soften that envy which must be excited by the distinction of ranks, as well as to prevent those seditions which it might otherwise occasion, he placed the plebeians as a trust in the hands of the patricians; and united the honour and interest of the two classes, by allowing every plebeian, under the name of *client*, to chuse any patrician he thought proper, for his *patron* or protector[68].

This connexion of *patron* and *client*, though seemingly of a private nature, was a public institution, and regulated by laws. It was the duty of a patron to

67. Id. *Rome. Antiq.* lib. ii. cap. viii.
68. Dion. Halicarnass. lib. ii. cap. ix.

explain

explain to his clients, those statutes of which they were ignorant; to conduct their suits, and defend them when sued; to protect them from injury, whether absent or present; and, in a word, to do every thing for them that a parent owes to his children, either in regard to money, credit, domestic felicity, or public support. On the other side, it was the duty of clients to supply their patron, when necessary, with money for portioning his daughters; to pay his ransom, or that of his children, if taken by an enemy; to bear his losses in private suits, and discharge, out of their own pockets, his fine, when assessed for any public offence; to assist him in supporting the charge of magistracies and other public offices, in the same manner as might have been expected, if they had been closely con_nected with him by the ties of blood[69]. And it was accounted impious and illegal, for either patrons or clients, to accuse one another in courts of justice; to bear witness, or to give their votes against each other[70].

Romulus, having thus harmonized and bound to-gether the two orders of the state, resolved to consti-tute a great council or senate, to assist him in the ad-ministration of government. For this purpose he named from among the patricians, one person, whom he esteemed the most eminent of that body for politi-cal wisdom; then ordered each of the tribes to name three, and each of the curiæ also three; in this man-ner completing the number of one hundred senators[71]. These senators were originally called *fathers*, because of their age and venerable character[72]; and afterward *conscript fathers;* on their number being augmented, by the enrolment of new members, at the establish-ment of the commonwealth[73]. The patrician named

69. Dion. Halicarnass. lib. ii. cap. x.   70. Id ibid.
71. Dion. Halicarnass. lib. ii. cap. xii.
72. Id. ibid. et Plut. *Vit. Romul.*   73. Liv. lib. ii. cap. i. Plut. ubi sup.

by Romulus was appointed by him president, or *prince* of the *senate*, and entrusted with the government of the city during the absence of the king[74].

After he had provided for the wise administration of public affairs, by the election of a council of elders, Romulus saw the need of a body of young men; always armed for sudden service, and as the royal guard. He accordingly formed a troop of three hundred horsemen, the most active and robust in the community, and of the most illustrious families, ordering each curiæ to chuse ten; and he himself named the commander, called *tribunus celerum*, who had three centurions under him[75]. They were distinguished by the general name of *celeres*, from the quickness, as supposed, with which they performed their evolutions, and executed orders[76]. They constantly attended the king in the city, armed with pikes; and, on a day of battle, they charged before him, and defended his person[77]. They fought on horseback where the ground would permit them to act; and on foot, where it was rough, and unfit for the use of cavarly[78].

The next measure adopted by Romulus was no less important than any of the former, and necessary to give the whole effect; namely the ascertaining of the honours and prerogatives, which each of the orders in the state should enjoy. To himself, as king, or head of the community, he reserved the absolute and undivided command of the army in the field, with supremacy in religious ceremonies, sacrifices, and every thing relative to the worship of the gods. His was the guardianship of the laws, and the administration of justice, both civil and criminal, in all cases whatever; though he took cognizance, in person, only of

74. Dion. Halicarnass. lib. ii. cap. xii.   75. Id. ibid. cap. xiii.
76. Dion. Halicarnass. lib. ii. cap. xiii.   77. Id. ibid.
78. Id. *Rom. Antiq.* ♦ bi sup.

the greater causes, leaving the inferior to the senate. He possessed the sole prerogative of convoking the senate and the assembly of the people, and he had the right of delivering his opinion first in both[79]. To the members of the senate, legally convened, beside their juridical capacity, belonged the power of deliberating and voting on all public measures; every question being decided by the majority of voices[80].

The people, in their assemblies, comprehending not only the *plebeians* but the whole body of the Roman citizens, had the privilege of chusing magistrates, enacting laws, and of determining on peace and war[81]. They did not vote promiscuously, but were called in their several *curiæ*[82]; and whatever matter was resolved upon by the majority of the *curiæ* was carried up to the senate, which had originally a power of putting a negative upon any popular resolution[83]. But this order of proceeding was afterwards inverted under the commonwealth. Then the senate did not deliberate on the resolutions of the people, but the people had a power of confirming or reversing the decrees of the senate, and of determining finally in regard to war and peace[84].

No sooner had Romulus completed these civil and military institutions, necessary for the preservation and prosperity of the Roman state, than he proceeded to establish those of religion; yet farther to restrain the licentious humours, and unite the hearts of his fol-

79. Dion. Halicarnass. lib. ii. cap. xiv.   80. Id. ibid.

81. Dion. Halicarnass. ubi sup.

82. This mode of voting by *curiæ*, the most popular of any, as it had no respect to property, was changed by Servius Tullius, as we shall have occasion to see, for that of voting by *centuries*.

83. Dion. Halicarnass. *Rom. Antiq.* lib. ii. cap. xiv.

84. Dion. Halicarnass. lib. ii. cap. xiv. and lib. iv. cap. xx. See also Polb. lib. vi.

lowers and fellow citizens. He accordingly instituted
priests, 'consecrated temples, dedicated altars, and
appointed sacrifices to the gods of his ancestors ; with
festivals, holidays, days of rest, or cessation from
labour, and every thing requisite for the solemn and
devote worship of those divinities, whose power and
beneficence to mankind he publicly declared[85]. But
he rejected, as blasphemies on calumnies, all traditional fables of an indecent kind, relative to the gods,
with all enthusiastic transports, and bacchanalian rites;
accustoming his people to think and speak of their
deities with the greatest reverence, and to attribute to
them no passions unworthy of their exalted nature[86].

This veneration for the gods (whether inspired by
Romulus, or his successor Numa), which long continued to characterize the Romans, and which may be considered as the main spring of their virtue, has been
ascribed to the purity of their theological tenets. " I
" am not insensible," says the learned and enlightened
historian, whose writings I have had occasion so often
to quote in regard to Roman affairs, " that some of
the Greek fables are of use to mankind ; being designed to explain the works of nature by allegories, and
others for various moral purposes. Though not ignorant of these things," adds he, " yet I am much more
inclined to the theology of the Romans ; when I consider that the advantages flowing from the Greek fables
are small and confined to such as have philosophically
examined their mystic meaning, and that the number
of such inquirers are few ; while the great body of the
people, utterly unacquainted with the physical or moral purpose of those fables, generally take them in the
literal and grossest sense, and fall into one of these two
errors—they either utterly disregard religion, because
of its seeming absurdities, or abandon themselves to

85. Dion Halicarnass. lib. ii. cap. xviii.   86. Id. ibid.

the

the most shameful excesses, which they see are ascribed to the gods[87]."

Romulus paid no less regard to the natural rights of man, and to the independent spirit of his new citizens, in establishing his sacred than his civil institutions. Himself the chief minister of religion, the pontifex maximus, and king of sacrifices, he directed each of the three tribes to chuse one aruspex or soothsayer, to inspect the victims; and each of the thirty curiæ to elect two priests, men of distinguished virtue, and above fifty years of age, from the order of patricians, in the same manner they elected their magistrates[88].

Under these priests, the curiæ performed their appointed sacrifices, in a temple common to the whole; and, on holidays, the members of each curiæ feasted together in a public hall, adjoining to the temple[89]. Of such halls every curiæ had one; and beside the civil influence of those religious meals, they were attended with the greatest effects in war; by inspiring every man with shame, and repugnance, to forsake the companions with whom he had lived in a communion of libations, sacrifices, and holy rites, and for whom he came habitually to entertain a brotherly affection[90].

From political and religious institutions, Romulus was naturally induced to turn his eyes to those domestic connexions which are strengthened by religion, and which form the basis of society; the relations of husband and wife, parents and children. And the natural rights which he allowed to remain in the hands of the heads of families, shew in a strong light

87. Dion. Halicarnass. lib. ii. cap. xx.   88. Ibid. Rom. Antiq. lib. ii. cap. xxi.   89. Id. ibid.
90. Plut. Vit. Romul. Dion. Halicarnass. lib. ii. cap. xxiii.

the

the weakness of his authority, or the rudeness of his
ideas respecting the duties of civil life; perhaps both.
A Roman father had the power of putting his son to
death, in case of disobedience or displeasure; and of
selling him as a slave, even three times, if he should so
often regain his freedom[91]. Nor did the laws fix any
age at which this patriarchal power should cease.

A Roman husband, in like manner, was the supreme judge of his wife's indiscretions, and the absolute avenger of his own injured honour; and, having
convened her relations, could put her to death, if she
had proved unfaithful to his bed, or so much as intoxicated herself with liquor[92]. But the Roman wives
had many motives to virtue, beside the fear of punishment. For every woman, " married according to the
holy laws," was as much mistress of the house as her
husband was master of it, " while she continued virtuous, and obedient to him in all things[93]." She was
considered by the civil law, as his inseparable companion, and the joint partaker in all his fortunes and
sacrifices[94]. After his death, if he had died intestate,
and without children, she was his sole heir; and if he
had left children, she had an equal share in his inheritance with them[95].

Romulus, however, very justly regarded terror as a
great restraint upon vice. He therefore assumed to
himself, as head of the state, the same rigour which he
permitted heads of families to exercise. As soon as any
public offence was committed, the criminal was brought
to trial, either before the king or the senate. When
Romulus gave judgment in person, he was seated on
a tribunal erected in the most conspicuous part of the

91. Dion. Halicarnass. lib. ii. cap. xxvi.
92. Id. *Rom. Antiq.* lib. ii. cap. xxv.
93. Id. ibid.   94. Dion. Halicarnass. lib. ii. cap. xxv.
95. Id. ibid.

forum

forum, or market-place, attended by his three hundred guards, armed with pikes, and by twelve lictors or ushers, carrying axes and rods. With the rods, the lictors whipped, in the forum, such criminals as deserved that punishment; and, with the axes, they publicly beheaded others, whose crimes were of greater enormity[96].

Nothing now remained for Romulus, but to provide for the population and power of the Roman state. And the measures which he took for these purposes, though seemingly suggested by circumstances, were worthy of the most profound politician. He opened, by public proclamation, and consecrated with the solemnities of religion, an asylum or sanctuary for outlaws, and fugitives of all descriptions, from the neighbouring nations[97]; and as the government of many of those nations was in great disorder, a number of warlike adventurers, and refugees of various kinds, crowded to Rome, where they were all made welcome[98]. To such as chose to remain with him, and seemed fit for his service, Romulus communicated the rights of Roman citizens, and promised them a share in the lands he should conquer[99]. This encouragement attracted new adventurers, eager to enlist under a young and gallant commander: and Rome rapidly increased in power.

But the Romans were still in want of the natural means of augmenting population and supporting power: they were almost utterly destitute of women[100]. Romulus therefore sent ambassadors, in the name of his people, to the heads of the neighbouring states, soliciting their daughters in marriage[101]. Jealous of the

96. Dion. Halicarnass. lib. ii. cap. xxix.
97. Liv. lib. i. cap. viii.　Dion. Halicarnass. lib. ii. cap. xv.
98. Dion. Halicarnass. ubi sup.　　　　99. Id. ibid.
100. Liv. lib. i. cap. ix.　Strabo, lib. v.　　101. Id. ibid.

growth

growth of Rome, or disdaining affinity with such a motley band, all those states denied his request; and the rulers of some of them scornfully asked, why he did not open, as he had for men, an asylum also for strolling women?—for with such only his followers could form a matrimonial alliance on equal terms[102].

Irritated at this contemptuous refusal, and disappointed in his favourite views, Romulus resolved to employ stratagem, in order to accomplish his purpose. He accordingly made known his design to the senate; and, with the consent of that venerable body, proclaimed the celebration of a solemn festival, accompanied with games, in honour of equestrian Neptune[103].

To these games the Sabines, and other neighbouring nations, crowded with their wives and daughters, as Romulus had foreseen. And they were treated with great kindness and respect at Rome, which they had much curiosity to see[104]. But on the last day of the festival, several bands of young Romans (at a signal given by their king according to concert) drew their swords; and, rushing in amid the gazing multitude, seized all the young women, to the number of six hundred and eighty three[105]. The men made the best of their way home, for fear of worse consequences, being utterly unprepared for defence; and their wives were permitted to follow them: but their daughters were detained, by order of Romulus. No insult, however, was offered to their virtue. They were only told, when brought before the king, that they must submit to the husbands whom fortune and the obstinacy of their fathers had decreed them, and he appointed.

102. Liv. ubi sup. Romul. lib. ii. cap. xxx.
103. Liv. et Strabo, ubi sup. Plut. *Vit.*
104. Liv. lib. i. cap. ix. Dion. Halicarnass.
105. Dion. Halicarnass. ubi sup.

And

PART I. And they were married to those young men who had
seized them, according to the custom of their several
countries, and also agreeable to the Roman manners;
before their embraces were solicited [106].

This amorous ambuscade, commonly known by the
name of the *rape of the Sabine virgins*, proved the
cause of much bloodshed, and had almost occasioned
the ruin of infant Rome. But the Sabines, although
the greatest sufferers, were not the first people that
resented the injury they had sustained. They were
slow in preparing for hostilities [107]; while the Cæninenses and the Antemnates, two tribes of the Aborigines; and the Crustuminians, an ancient colony from
Alba [108], having formed a triple league, instantly took
up arms [109].

The Cæninenses, thinking themselves sufficiently
strong, entered the Roman territory without waiting
for their confederates. But they had reason to repent
their audacity. Romulus suddenly assembled his
army, and fell upon them as they were ravaging the
country; defeated them; forced their camp, which was
but imperfectly fortified; pursued them into their own
territory; killed their king in battle, with his own
hand; stripped him of his accoutrements, and took
Cænina, their capital, by storm [110].

Elated with his success, and willing to inflame the
Romans with ardour for military glory, Romulus returned to Rome in all the pomp and the pride of conquest; carrying the spoils of the king he had slain, exalted on an oaken pole supported by his right shoulder,

106. Id. ibid.   107. Liv. lib. i. cap. x.   Dion. Halicarnass.
lib. ii. cap. xxxiii.   108. Dion. Halicarnass. lib. ii. cap. xxxv. xxxvi.
109. Liv. ubi sup.   Dion. Halicarnass. lib. ii. cap. xxxiii.
110. Id. ibid.

and

and singing the song of victory; his brows encircled
with a laurel crown, and his hair flowing gracefully
over his purple robe[111]. Before him was carried the most
valuable part of the booty taken from the enemy,
and behind him marched his troops, both horse and
foot, completely armed, and ranged in their several divisions, hymning the gods in the songs of their country[112].

Thus attended, Romulus entered his conquering
city amid the acclamations of the Roman people, who
came out to congratulate him on his successful expedition; and who had furnished tables with all kinds of
victuals, and with bowls full of wine, for the refresh-
ment of his army. He ascended, in victorious procession, the Saturnian, named afterward the Capitoline
Hill; and offered to Jupiter Feretrius, or the *trophy-
bearer*, the spoils of the king of the Cæninenses, which
he had seized, as already observed, with his own
hand[113]. Such, my lord, was the first example of the
celebration of the magnificent solemnity, which the
Romans called a *triumph;* which was claimed, after
victory, by the Roman kings and generals, and proved a strong incentive to valour and conduct in war.

But the institution of the Roman triumph was not
the only consequence of Romulus's victory over the
Cæninensis. His conquest of that people and their
territory gave his policy room to display itself. And
it was worthy of a prince, who aspired at extensive dominion, and of a mind formed in more liberal times.
He neither, like the Asiatics, put to death the enemies

111. Dion. Halicarnass. lib. ii. cap. xxxiv. Plut. *Vit. Romul.*
112. Id. ibid.
113. Liv. lib. i. cap. x. Plut. et Dion. Halicarnass. ubi sup. These
spoils, taken by a Roman commander from the king or general of an
enemy, were called *opima spolia,* and were esteemed more honourable than any other. Id. ibid.

he

he had forcibly subdued, whose capital he had violently entered, nor made slaves of them, like the
Greeks; but, after obtaining the consent of the senate,
he admitted them to all the privileges of Roman citizens, and gave them the liberty of removing to Rome,
or of remaining in their own country, as they should
think best[114].

Three thousand of the Cæninensis chose to remove
to the Roman capital, with their wives, children, and
effects; the produce of a portion of their lands being
secured to them. And Romulus sent into their country a colony of three hundred Romans, among whom
he divided, by lot, the third part of the Cæninean territory; in order that they might incorporate with the
remaining natives, and preserve their obedience[115]. The
Cæninenses, who had removed to Rome, he immediately incorporated with the Roman tribes and curiæ[116]. And the same wise policy, as we shall have
occasion to see, was regularly pursued by the Romans,
until they had made themselves masters of the finest
part of Italy.

The valiant and politic king of Rome had soon need
of all his accession of strength. The Antemnates
had passed the Roman frontier, while he was engaged in celebrating his victory; and the Crustuminians also were still in arms. Romulus, with a chosen
body of men, marched first against the Antemnates;
defeated them in the field, and took their city[117].
He next attacked the Crustuminians, whom he likewise routed and conquered, though better prepared
for resistance[118]. And he treated both with the same
humanity and generosity, which he had extended

114. Dion. Halicarnass. lib. ii. cap. xxxv.   115. Id. ibid.
116. Dion. Halicarnass. ubi sup.   117. Liv. lib. i. cap. xi.
118. Dion. Halicarnass. lib. ii. cap. xxxvi.

toward

toward the Cæninensis; transplanting part of his vanquished enemies to Rome, and settling Roman colonies in their territories[119].

This clemency allayed the fears, and conciliated the
affections of many of the smaller Italian states, which
gladly came under the protection of Romulus[120]. But it
had a different effect upon the brave and more powerful Sabines. They blamed their rulers for the opportunity they had lost of crushing the Roman ambition in
the bud, by joining in the general confederacy; and
having leagued themselves, as one people, under the
conduct of Titus Tatius, king of Cures or Quires,
the most considerable city of the Sabine nation, the
inhabitants of the several cantons made vigorous preparations for war[121].

Romulus, aware of his danger, solicited the assistance of his allies; called forth the whole force of the
Roman state, and took every precaution that human
foresight could suggest for the safety of Rome; by
raising higher the wall of the city, and fortifying the
neighbouring hills[122]. But all his precautions proved
ineffectual. The enemy, in consequence of a nocturnal march, arrived unobserved at the foot of the Saturnian hill; and the fortress upon it, the citadel of
Rome, was betrayed to them by Tarpeiu, the governor's daughter; who had been attracted by the ornaments of gold, which the Sabines wore on their left
arm, and corrupted by the presents or promises, perhaps by the blandishments, of Tatius their leader[123].

Amazed at this act of treachery, but not intimidat-
ed by the progress of the enemy, the Romans flew to

119. Id. ibid. Liv. et ubi sup. 120. Dion. Halicarnass. ubi sup.
121. Id. ibid. 122. Dion. Halicarnass. lib. ii. cap. xxxvii.
123. Compare, Liv. lib. i. cap. xi. with Dion. Halicarnass. lib. ii.
cap. xxxviii. xxxix. xl. et Plut. Vit. Romul.

PART I.

arms; and the Sabines having now a place of refuge, in case of disaster, were not afraid to meet them in the field. The two armies accordingly encamped in sight of each other, and several sharp encounters took place, without any decided advantage on either side[124]. These brought on a general engagement, in which both parties exhibited astonishing feats of valour and prowess. The contest for superiority long remained doubtful; but the Romans, though nearly equal in number, were at last forced to give ground[125]. The heroic efforts of Romulus, however, restored the battle, and the combat was renewed with fresh vigour[126]. The Sabines, in their turn, had been compelled to retreat; and victory seemed ready to declare for the Romans[127], when a moving spectacle suspended hostilities.

The Sabine women, who had been seized by order of Romulus, and who were become Roman wives and mothers, losing the natural timidity of their sex in the passions by which they were agitated, rushed in between the two armies, with their locks disheveled and their garments rent; while the spears were uplifted and the darts flying, and begged their fathers and their husbands, if neither tears nor entreaties could soften their obdurate hearts, to pour all their rage upon *them*, as they only were the cause of the war. "Far better," cried they, "would it be for us to pe-"rish, than to live fatherless or widows[128]." Hostile animosity was melted into pity at such an affecting embassy. Every feeling of humanity was awakened, and every nerve of action unstrung. The contending soldiers rested their arms, yet dropping with blood, and thirsting for mutual slaughter. The rival kings

124. Dion. Halicarnass. lib. ii. cap. xli.
125. Liv. lib. i. cap. xii. Dion. Halicarnass. lib. ii. cap. xxxvii—xliii.
126. Id. ibid.   127. Liv. ubi sup.
128. Liv. lib. i. cap. xiii.

consented

sonsented to a truce, which was followed by a conference; and political deliberation cemented an alliance
that sympathy had begun[129].

The fathers of the Roman senate, who had given
their sanction to the interposition of the Sabine women[130], moderated the ambition, and the youthful ardour of Romulus. The Sabines, a brave and powerful people, were still at the gates of Rome ; and if
their present army should be cut off, they could assemble another. The Sabine chiefs likewise saw their
danger. They had to contend, for victory, with the
Romans ; a community of soldiers, who seemed determined, to a man, to conquer or die.

These were strong arguments in favour of an accommodation. But peace, it was foreseen by both
parties, could not be lasting between two warlike nations, circumstanced as the Romans and Sabines were;
near neighbours, and rivals in power as well as in glory. It was therefore resolved, to negociate between
them a treaty of union. And such a treaty was concluded, and ratified, on the following honourable
terms: That the Romans and Sabines should thenceforth be considered as one people ; that Romulus and
Tatius should both reside at Rome, and be joint kings
of the united nation; invested with equal authority,
and equal honours ; that the city of Rome should preserve the name of its founder, and that each individual
citizen should be called a *Roman*, and the whole people *Romans ;* but that the assembled body of the citizens in their civil capacity, should be called *Quirites*,
from Cures, the former capital of Tatius[131] ; that

129. Id. ibid. Plut. *Vit. Romul.* Dion. Halicarnass. lib. ii. cap. xlvi
130. Dion. Halicarnass. lib. ii. cap. xlv.
131. Ibid. *Rom. Antiq.* lib. ii. cap. xlv. Liv. lib. i. cap. xiii. Plut.
Vit. Romul.

such

such of the Sabines, as were willing to settle at Rome, might remove thither, and bring with them the images of their gods; and that they should be incorporated with the Roman tribes and curiæ[132].

The first step taken by Romulus and Tatius, as joint kings of Rome, after disbanding their troops, was to augment the number of patricians, from the most illustrious Sabine families, as the state had received a great accession of people; and to order the curiæ to chuse, out of these new patricians, one hundred new senators, to be incorporated with the former body[133]. The two kings next enrolled, from the class of plebeians, three centuries of horse, or bodies of Roman knights[134]; the first of which was called *romanenses*, from Romulus; the second *tatienses*, from Tatius[135]; and the third *lucerenses*, from the lucus or grove, where the asylum stood for the reception of refugees[136]. Thus was formed a third rank in the state, as well as three bodies of cavalry for its defence.

As soon as Romulus and Tatius had completed their civil and military constitutions, they enlarged the city of Rome[137]; built several temples to the gods they had invoked during the war[138]; instituted the festival called matronalia, in commemoration of the affectionate interposition of the married women, who had

---

132. Dion. Halicarnass. lib. ii. cap. xlvi.   133. Id. cap. xlvii.
134. Liv. lib. i. cap. xiii. I am sensible an attempt has been made by the learned and ingenious Mr. Spelman, (*Translat.* Dion. Halicarnass. *Rom. Antiq.* lib. ii. note 28.) to give a different account of the origin of the equestrian order, or knights among the Romans. But I can see no reason for contradicting general opinion, or rejecting the authority of Livy.
. 135. Id. ibid.   136. Plut. *Vit. Romul.*
137. Dion. Halicarnass. lib. ii. cap. l.
138. Id. ibid.

procured

procured peace and union[139]; and reigned with such harmony and vigour, for five years, that they kept most of the neighbouring nations in awe[140]. The only people who ventured to molest them, were the Camerians, whom they defeated and conquered; and because of a rebellion, stripped of all their lands; transplanted the greater part of the inhabitants to Rome, and sent a Roman colony to inhabit the city of Cameria and its territory[141]. Cameria was a Latin city; and the Camerians, like the Romans, were a colony from Alba.

Tatius, in the sixth year of his reign, at Rome, was assassinated by certain citizens of Laurentium; in resentment of a robbery committed by some of his friends, whom he refused to punish or deliver up[142]. Thenceforth Romulus reigned alone, and had full scope for the exercise of his warlike genius. He forgave the Laurentes, however, for the death of Tatius, which he thought justly merited[143]. But he suffered no other injury to pass unpunished. He chastised a revolt of the Camerians, conquered the Fidenates, and compelled the Veientes to submit to the most humiliating conditions; to deliver up part of their territory, and give hostages in assurance of their future good behaviour[144]. Fidenæ was a Latin, and Veii an Etruscan city of great note[145].

Rendered arrogant by prosperity, like most military leaders who have successfully prosecuted conquest, Romulus disgusted his subjects, both new and old, by his arbitrary administration, after his victory over

---

139. Ovid. *Fastor.* lib. lii. Plut. *Vit. Romul.*
140. Dion. Halicarnass. ubi sup.   141. Id. ibid.
142. Liv. lib. i. cap. xiv. Dion. Halicarnass. lib. ii. cap. li.
143. Id. ibid.   144. Dion. Halicarnass. lib. ii. cap. li—lv.
145. Id. ibid.

PART I. the Veientes. Regardless of the privileges, which circumstances had constrained him to grant to the Sabines, as well as to the Romans, he regulated all things by his own despotic will[146]. The senate, and assembly of the people were convened, as usual, but only to ratify his absolute commands[147]. He divided the ceded lands among his soldiers, without consulting the senate; and restored the hostages of the Veientes, contrary to the advice of that venerable body, and supreme council[148]: assuming, on all occasions, the air of a master, and governing more like a tyrant than a limited monarch[149].

But the Romans were not to be so governed. The free and independent spirits of the patricians revolted against such domination. And the fathers of the senate seeing no probability of being able to moderate the king's authority, or to punish him, by legal means, for his abuse of power, secretly formed, it is said, a conspiracy against his life[150]. Great circumspection, however, was necessary for the execution of their violent purpose; Romulus being in full possession of the hearts of the soldiers, or younger citizens, the companions of his victories, and whom he had trained to danger[151]. But accident, or interposing heaven, furnished the occasion, when little expected.

Ant. Chr. 715. Ann. Romæ, 37.

While Romulus was holding a general assembly of the people, in the neighbourhood of Rome, and mustering the men fit to bear arms, which now amounted to forty-six thousand foot, and near a thousand horse, the sky was suddenly darkened, in consequence of an eclipse of the sun, and a furious tempest arose, accom-

146. Dion. Halicarnass. lib. ii. cap. lvi. Plut. *Vit. Romul.*
147. Id. ibid.   148. Plut. et Dion. Halicarnass. ubi sup.
149. Id. ibid.   150. Dion. Halicarnass. lib. ii. cap. lvi.
151. Plut. *Vit. Romul.* et *Numa.*

. panied

panied with thunder, lightning, and rain[152]. The affrighted multitude was quickly dispersed. But the body of senators closed about the king, and instantly dispatched him, as is supposed, and threw his body into a pit, or conveyed it to a distance; for he was never more seen[153].

When the tempest subsided, the people returned to the ground on which they had formerly stood, and anxiously inquired after Romulus. The patricians told them mysteriously, that he had disappeared in the storm; ascended on a flake of lightning, to take his place among the gods: and, as he had been a gracious prince to them, he would prove a propitious deity[154]. The people retired in silence, and seemingly satisfied.

But some of the king's favourites having inquired more particularly into the matter, began to start doubts in regard to the reality of his ascension[155]. On this occasion, Julius Proculus, a senator of great eminence, famed for his piety and probity, went into the forum, and declared solemnly upon oath, in order to quiet the people, that Romulus had appeared to him, clad in armour of celestial brightness, and desired him to inform the Romans, that it had pleased the gods he should dwell with men, for a time, upon earth; and, having founded a city, which would prove the most powerful and glorious in the world, they had recalled him to heaven, whence he came[156]. " Go, therefore, and tell the Roman people," added the new divinity, according to the testimony of the venerable Proculus, " that, by the exercise of piety, temperance, and for-

---

152. Liv. lib. i. cap. xvi. Plut. et. Dion. Halicarnass. ubi sup.
153. Id. ibid.   154. Plut. *Vit. Romul.*   155. Id. ibid.
156. Plut. ubi sup. Liv. lib. i. cap. xvi. Dion. Halicarnass. lib. ii.
cap. lxiv.

" titude,

" titude, they shall attain to the highest pitch of hu-
" man greatness ; and that I, the god Quirinus, will
" ever be propitious to them[157]."

This tale was readily believed by an ignorant, and
consequently a superstitious herd, united by their common necessities and crimes ; trained in rapine, and
polluted with blood. And taken in conjunction with
the story of the divine generation of Romulus, it might
have imposed on the credulity of a more enlightened,
as well as a more innocent people, who stood less in
need of a friend in heaven ; especially if we consider
his commanding mien, his transcendent abilities, and
heroic actions. For no leader, perhaps, in any age or
country, ever raised a state from so low a beginning,
to such a height of solid power, or maintained, in similar circumstances, such firm authority over so multifarious and licentious a body of men.

As Romulus left no son to claim his sceptre, the
Romans were now without a head. The senate, therefore, assumed the administration of government : but
not as a body. The two hundred senators, of Alban
and Sabine extraction, were divided into twenty decuriæ ; each of which held in succession, by lot, the
supreme authority for fifty days[158]. The whole decuriæ, however, did not reign together ; but each of the
ten members, of which it was composed, being invested
in his turn, with the ensigns of royalty, governed for
five days[159].

Ant. Chr.
714.
Ann.
Romæ, 38. This new government, which lasted about a year,
did not please the people. They looked back with re-
gret, to the victories and the triumphs of Romulus, and
longed for a royal leader, to conduct them again to

---

157. Id. ibid.   158. Dion. Halicarnass. lib. ii. cap. lvii. Liv.
lib. i. cap. xvii.   159. Id. ibid.

conquest. The senate seeing their uneasiness, and
the impossibility of holding any longer the supreme
power, desired them to elect a king [160]. Pleased with
this condescension, the people remitted the right of
election to the senate [161]: and that venerable body chose
for their future sovereign, Numa Pompilius; a Sabine
by birth, distinguished by his sanctity of manners,
and renowned for his wisdom and piety [162]. He was
about forty years of age [163]; of an unambitious character, and philosophic turn of mind, deeply skilled in
divine and human laws [164]; and although married to
the daughter of Tatius, the late king, had never thought
of removing to Rome, but lived on his own estate, in
the neighbourhood of Cures [165]. Nor could he be
persuaded, without difficulty, to quit his retirement,
and engage in public affairs, though invited by regal
honours [166].

The moderation of Numa exalted his character in
the eyes of the Romans. They considered his reluct-
ance to accept the kingly office, as a proof that he was
truly worthy of it [167]. And it must be owned, all
things weighed, whether we regard circumstances or
the event, that he seems to have been the most proper
person for succeeding to the supreme power, at the
time he received the Roman sceptre (by the delegated
authority of the people to the senate, and the approbation of the popular assembly), that human wisdom can
conceive. Being a Sabine, he attached his countrymen more closely to the state of which they were become subjects; while his elevation to the sovereignty,
from a private station, quieted that jealousy and envy
which would have been excited in the breasts of the
senators, as well Sabines as Romans, on the appoint-
ment of one of their own body to rule over them.

Ant. Chr.
713.
Ann. Rom.
39.

160. Liv. et Dion. Halicarnass. ubi sup.   161. Id. ibid.
162. Plut. *Vit. Numa.*   163. Dion. Halicarnass. lib. ii. cap. lviii.
164. Plut. ubi sup. Liv. lib. i. cap. xviii.   165. Id. ibid.
166. Dion. Halicarnass. et Plut. ubi sup.   167. Id. ibid.

If the new king had possessed the military talents of his predecessor, the Romans might have risen more rapidly to grandeur; but their power would have been less durable. The fabric of the state, composed of discordant materials, would soon have fallen to pieces, because too hastily combined; and the different people, that had been incorporated as Roman citizens, would again have formed independent cantons, under various leaders. The structure raised by Romulus required time to settle and cement, before it could bear more weight. Aware of this, or conscious that he wanted the conquering, and all-governing spirit of Romulus, Numa employed himself in strengthening and beautifying, without enlarging the political edifice: —and a long reign of perpetual peace allowed it to gather stability.

Numa began his pacific administration with giving a regular form to the public religion, or ecclesiastical polity of the Romans; blending it with the policy of the state, and connecting it closely with morals. The substance of his creed or theological system was, That the gods, an immortal race inhabiting the sky, the creators and preservers of all things, are intimately acquainted with human affairs, and take cognizance of the actions of men and of states; rewarding the good, and punishing the bad; and that no important action, either public or private, ought to be undertaken without their approbation, declared by their ministers upon earth [168]. He accordingly instituted a venerable society, or college of augurs [169]; who interpreted to the people the will of the gods, by signs in the heavens, the air, the earth [170]: by the

168. Cicero, *de Legib.* lib. ii. Dion. Halicarnass. lib. ii. cap. lxii. Plut. *Vit Numa.*

169. Dion. Halicarnass. lib. ii. cap. lxiv.

170. Id. ibid. et Plut. Vit. Paul. Æmil.

flying,

flying, the chirping, and the feeding of birds[171]; and who, in consequence of their heavenly authority, could put a negative upon the most momentous resolutions of the senate or assembly of the people[172].

For this, and all his other pious constitutions, Numa claimed the positive command of the gods; who communed with him in solitude, he affirmed, by means of a celestial nymph, named Ægeria[173]. Thus instructed and authorised, the sage king erected a temple to Romulus, under the name of the god *Quirinus*, the guardian of the Roman state; and another to his reputed father, Mars[174]; to whom the Romans were to owe their future fame, and by whose favour, through the mediation of his divine and deified son, they were to attain the height of empire.

For the worship of Mars, Numa instituted an order of salant priests, called *Salii*[175]; the exercise of whose function shewed, that although he did not prosecute war himself, he had views of distant ambition, and wished, while he moderated the martial ardour of the Romans, to keep it alive for necessary occasions. The salii, consisting of twelve young men of the most graceful appearance, chosen from the patrician order, danced through the streets of Rome during their solemn festivals, richly dressed and completely armed[176]; striking their swords upon their shields, as if inspired with hostile fury[177]. These shields were called *ancilia*; and the model from which they were formed was supposed to have fallen from heaven[178]; being a buckler, which, no doubt, the pious but politic legisla-

171. Cicero, *de Divinat*. lib. ii.

172. Id. ibid. et Cicero in *Cato Major*.

173. Liv. lib. i. cap. xix. Plut. *Vit. Romul*.

174. Dion. Halicarnass. lib. ii. cap lxiii. lxx. Plut. *Vit. Numa*. Liv. lib. i. cap. xx.   175. Liv. ubi sup.

176. Id. ibid. et Dion. Halicarnass. lib. ii. cap. lxx.

177. Plut. et Dion. Halicarnass. ubi sup.   178. Id. ibid.

tor had secretly procured, because better fitted for defence in war, than any formerly in use among the Romans. And the fashion of which he took care should
not be lost, by rendering it sacred, and getting many
others made, by an ingenious workman, exactly to resemble it [179].

In order to bridle the warlike spirit, which might be
awakened by such an institution, and to prevent the
Romans from rashly engaging in hostilities, Numa
built a temple to Janus [180], or Political Prudence, represented with two faces, looking different ways [181];
examining, at the same time, the past, and probable
future, and weighing the consequences to be hoped or
feared from any public measure. This temple was
shut in peace, and left open during war [182].

Yet farther to curb the predatory disposition of his
people, and make them respect the laws of equity, in
entering into war with their neighbours, Numa instituted the sacred college of *Feciales* [183]; whose peculiar province it was, to take care that the Romans did
not unjustly commit hostilities against any nation or
state; and if any other people with whom the Romans

179. Dion. Halicarnass. lib. ii. cap. lxxi. Plut. *Vit. Numa.*

180. Liv. lib. i. cap. xix.

181. Plut. *Vit. Numa.* But Janus, like Vesta and other Roman
deities, had a mythycal as well as a political character (Ovid. *Fastor.*
lib. i.). The most learned Romans, however, if we may not except
the priesthood, seem to have known only the political part of their
religion; until their empire had attained that height to which it was
calculated to raise them. In proof of this, see the declaration of
Tarentius Varro, ap Augustin. de *Civ. Dei*, lib. vi. cap. v. et lib. vii.
cap. vi. There are, observes he, three methods of treating of the nature of the gods; one *mythical*, another *natural*, and a third *political.*
That called *mythical* is chiefly made use of by the poets; the *natural*
belongs to philosophers, and the *political* to the state.

182. Liv. ubi sup.

183. Dion. Halicarnass. lib. ii. cap. lxxii.

were

were in alliance, had violated engagements, to go as ambassadors, and demand satisfaction, in the first place; then, if such satisfaction was refused, to give their sanction to the commencement of war, and boldly declare it in the name of the Roman senate and people[184]. The mode of denouncing hostilities by the feciales, and the whole proceedings on such occasions, I shall afterward have occasion to describe.

All the other institutions of Numa were dictated by the same mild and honourable principles, and directed to the same wise ends; the good of his subjects, and the happiness of the human race. Conscious that the secure possession of private property, is essential to the encouragement of industry among the people of any state, and contributes greatly to inspire a love of justice, the guardian of concord, he made an accurate division of the lands of the Romans; and ordered every man to surround his own portion with a ditch or furrow, and to set up stones to mark the boundaries[185].

These stones he consecrated to *Jupiter Terminalis*, and instituted a solemn festival, to be observed annually, by the whole body of the Roman people, in honour of the god supposed to preside over those boundaries or marches[186]. And he at the same time enacted a law, which made it sacrilege to demolish or displace any of the *termini*, or boundary stones; and every person guilty of such crime, might be killed with impunity, by any one, and without the imputation of blood, as a sacrifice to the vengeance of the offended deity[187]. This law did not relate only to private possessions, it comprehended also those of the

184. Id. ibid.   185. Dion. Halicarnass. lib. ii. cap. lxxiv.
186. Id. ibid.   187. Dion. Halicarnass. ubi sup.

state; which were likewise circumscribed within obvious boundaries, and placed under the guardianship of the terminal god; that the territory of the Romans, thus protected, might be distinctly separated from that of the neighbouring nations, and the public lands, from such as belonged to individuals[188].

But Numa was not satisfied with teaching his subjects to respect the property of other men, by securing each in his own: he wished to make them not only just in their actions, but true to their word. He therefore erected a temple, and instituted sacrifices, to be performed at the public expense, to Faith[189]; or truth in the performance of engagements, and honesty in trust.

The influence of this institution upon the character of the Romans, both in their public and private capacity, was eminently conspicuous, and continued to distinguish them above all other nations to a very advanced stage of their political progress[190]; insomuch, that the faith of the state was preserved inviolate, and a Roman citizen paid as much regard to his word, or solemn engagement in private, as to a written contract attested by witnesses[191]. Hence the memorable observations of a philosophical historian : That, whereas, amongst the Greeks, a man in office was rarely to be found, whose hands were clean from public robbery; it was no less rare, among the Romans, to discover one who was stained with the crime. And that, in the course of their magistracies and embassies, they disbursed the greatest sums with inviolable honesty, on the single obligation of an oath[192]. And the most

188. Id. ibid.
189. Liv. lib. i. cap. xxi. Dion. Halicarnass. lib. ii. cap. lxxv.
190. Polyb. lib. vi. cap. liv.
191. Id. ibid. et Dion. Halicarnass. ubi sup.
192. Polyb. ubi sup.

sacred

sacred oath a Roman could take was, " By his
faith[193]."

After having taken such effectual measures for making the Romans observant of justice and good faith,
it became incumbent on Numa to free the common
people, as far as possible, from the temptation to violate either, by furnishing them with employment, or
placing them above want. With this view, he divided the public territory of the state, or the unappropriated lands, which had been taken from the enemies of Rome, among the indigent citizens[194]. Those
he planted in a certain number of *pagi* or villages;
over each of which he appointed a magistrate, whose
peculiar province it was to inspect the cultivation of
the lands in his own district; and by reprimanding
and punishing the slothful husbandmen, to stimulate
them to greater industry : while the labours of the di-
ligent were rewarded by the king, with distinguished
marks of his favour and approbation[195].

These agrarian regulations were attended with the
most beneficial effects. The Romans became as fru-
gal and industrious, as they were faithful and just;
and many of them learned to prefer the sober plenty
acquired by agriculture, to the precarious affluence
of a military life[196]. Instead of being the terror, they
grew the admiration of their neighbours ; who often
employed them as mediators of their differences, during this peaceful period. And all the adjacent states
frequently put an. end to their most important disputes, by submitting them to the arbitration of Numa[197]. The good old king, who was worthy of such
confidence, died in the forty-third year of his reign,

193. Dion. Halicarnass. lib. ii. cap. lxxv.
194. Plut. *Vit. Numa.*
195. Id. ibid. et Dion. Halicarnass. lib. ii. cap. lxxvi.
196. Dion. Halicarnass. ubi sup.   197. Id. ibid.

and

and the eighty-second of his age, with the same tranquillity in which he had lived; and universally respected and regretted over Italy [198].

But great as the veneration was which the Romans had for the memory of Numa, they chose, as his successor, a person of a very different description. Tullus Hostilius, an opulent patrician, of a bold and enterprising character, the grandson of one of the first Roman heroes, was elected king by the people; confirmed by the senate, and declared by the augurs to be worthy of the supreme dignity in the eye of heaven [199]. And it must be admitted, that the choice was worthy of approbation in the eye of human policy. The Romans now stood in need of a warlike king.

If the pacific reign, and mild administration of Numa, had softened the manners of his subjects, and given stability to the Roman state, by promoting agriculture and the arts of civil life, the neighbouring states had also gathered strength; and if their hostile animosity was abated, their jealousy was not extinguished. Alba was even become jealous of the growth of her own colony [200]. And Alba, though inferior to Rome in power, was still considered as the capital of the Latin nation, of which the Romans were a branch.

198. Plut. *Vit. Numa.* Dion. Halicarnass. ubi sup. Plutarch bestows great praise upon an institution, by which Numa divided the Roman citizens into companies, according to their several arts or trades; as these smaller divisions, he supposes, more readily mixing, tended finally to abolish the distinction of Romans and Sabines (*Vit. Num.*). But after the Sabines, who removed to Rome, had been incorporated with the Roman tribes and curiæ, I cannot see the necessity of such subdivision, considered in a political light, though it might be a very good civil arrangement. Accordingly, no notice is taken of it by Dionysius or Livy. Numa deserves more praise for his reformation of the Roman calendar, in which he appears to have been not a little successful. Plut. ubi sup.

199. Dion. Halicarnass. lib. iii. cap. i. Liv. lib. i. cap. xxii.
200. Id. ibid.

For

For the elucidation of these matters, some retrospect will be necessary.

Romulus, on the death of his grandfather Numitor, did not claim the Alban sceptre, though lineal heir to the kingdom; but in order to conciliate the favour of the parent-state, he left the administration of government in the hands of the citizens[201]. And they are said to have chosen an annual chief magistrate, vested with regal powers[202].

In consequence of this indulgence (for as such it seems to have been regarded by Romulus, as head of the more potent and warlike state) a treaty of friendship was entered into between the Romans and Albans; by which it was stipulated, that, in case of any injury, neither party should seek redress by arms, but apply to the other for justice. And if that was denied, that the treaty should thenceforth be considered as void, and war a necessary evil[203].

During the subsequent part of the reign of Romulus, and the whole reign of Numa, no complaint or injury appears to have been made by the people of either state. But no sooner was the Roman sceptre bestowed upon Tullus Hostilius, than mutual injuries took place, arising from mutual jealousy; the Albans, who were the agressors, founding their claim to the sovereignty of Latium on their greater antiquity, and unmingled blood; the Romans, on their superior power[204]. And all attempts to accommodate those differences proving ineffectual, both parties took the field[205]. The Albans, however, diffident of their strength, studiously avoided an engagement; and at

201. Plut. *Vit. Numa.*   202. Dion. Halicarnass. lib. v. cap. lxxiv.
203. Dion. Halicarnass. lib. iii. cap. iii.
204. Dion. Halicarnass. lib. iii. cap. iv—liii.   205. Id. ibid.

length,

length, in order to save the effusion of blood, it was agreed, that three champions, on each side, should decide the contest for empire [206].

This agreement was no sooner made known to the two armies, and ratified by them, than a violent emulation arose among the young warriors, in each, for the honour of contending in the important combat. And the pretensions of rank, of valour, and of strength, were so many, that it seemed both difficult and dangerous, for either the Romans or Albans, to give a preference, by naming any three competitors for glory [207]. From the dilemma occasioned by those pretensions, however, they were happily relieved by Mutius Fufetius, the Alban general. He recollected that two sisters, Albans by birth, one married to Curatius, an Alban citizen, the other to Horatius, a citizen of Rome, had each brought forth, at one labour, three male children, now arrived at manhood, and distinguished by their mental and personal accomplishments [208].

These young men Fufetius thought destined by the gods to determine the dispute between Rome and Alba. He, therefore, demanded a conference on the subject with Tullus Hostilius, the Roman king and commander, who readily adopted the same idea [209]. The Roman senate and the two fathers gave their consent; and the Horatii and Curatii, proud of the hostile distinction conferred upon them, though closely united by the ties of friendship as well as of kindred, bravely joined battle in sight of the two armies, in a plain between the two camps [210].

---

206. Dion. Halicarnass. ubi sup. Liv. lib. i. cap. xxiv.
207. Dion. Halicarnass. lib. iii. cap. xiii.   208. Id. ibid.
209. Dion. Halicarnass. lib. iii. cap. xiv. xvii.
210. Id. ibid. Liv. lib. i. cap. xxv.

The

The combat long remained doubtful, and was distinguished by various turns of fortune. At length
victory seemed to declare in favour of Alba; two of
the Horatii being slain, and only one of the Curatii.
But the surviving Horatius, having received no wound,
slew his two antagonists, one after another, by retreating as they advanced, and gained a complete triumph
to Rome [211].

In consequence of this event, and a solemn treaty,
by which the combat had been preceded, Fufetius
saluted Tullus Hostilius as his sovereign, on the field
of victory; and asked, what commands he thought
proper to impose upon him, as the leader of the vanquished?—"I command you," answered the king of
Rome, "to keep the Alban youth in readiness to march
at my orders, in case I should find occasion to make
war upon the Veientes [212]." After that acknowledgment, and this act of sovereignty, the two armies separated, and each returned home; the Albans to mourn
their humiliation, the Romans to celebrate their triumph [213]. But the public joy of the victors was dashed
with private sorrow, and their triumph stained with
guiltless blood.

When young Horatius, named Marcus, approached
the gates of Rome, loaded with the spoils of his vanquished antagonists, he was met by his sister, who had
been promised in marriage to one of the Curatii; and
who, forgetting the delicacy of her sex, and her condition as a bride, had anxiously mingled with the crowd of
applauding spectators. On seeing her brother cloathed
in an embroidered robe, which she had wrought for
her lover, and in which he was to have been dressed
on their nuptial day, she burst into tears; she wildly

211. Liv. ubi sup. Dion. Halicarnass. lib. iii. cap. viii—xx.
212. Liv. lib. i. cap. xxvi.   213. Id. ibid.

tore

tore her hair; and in the anguish of her heart, keenly reproached the exulting conqueror with the murder of his near kinsman, and her bridegroom[214].

"Thy bridegroom!" exclaimed Marcus Horatius; "O sister, lost at once to virtue and to shame! hast "thou no regard for the blood of thy brothers, or "the glory of thy country?—Go then," said he, in the heat of his patriotic indignation, "go to thy bride-"groom!" drawing his sword, and sheathing it in her breast; "Go! and carry with thee a degenerate passion, "which has led thee to disgrace thy family, and sully "the splendour of this illustrious day. Begone! and "so perish all, who weep at the death of an enemy of "Rome[215]."

Old Horatius, their venerable father, though deeply stung with grief, entered into the feelings of his heroic son; and was so far from resenting the death of his daughter, that he would not permit her body to be buried in the sepulchre of her ancestors, or her funeral to be honoured with the usual solemnities[216]. Tullus Hostilius, however, found himself under the necessity of bringing the victorious champion to trial, for the violence he had committed. Marcus Horatius was accordingly cited before the tribunal of the Duumviri, the proper judges of such crimes; and they condemned him to lose his life, and ordered the lictors to bind his hands[217]. But he, by the advice of the king, appealed to the assembly of the Roman people. And they repealed the sentence of the Duumviri, in consideration of the circumstances of the criminal, rather than out of lenity to his crime[218];

214. Dion. Halicarnass. lib. iii. cap. xxi. Liv. lib. i. cap. vi.
215. Id. ibid.   216. Dion. Halicarnass. ubi sup.
217. Liv. lib. i. cap. xxvi.   218. Id. ibid.

establishing

establishing, by that precedent, their right of judging
ultimately in capital cases.

The subsequent part of the reign of Tullus Hostilius was spent in perpetual warfare. During the contest between Rome and Alba, the Fidinates had been
encouraged to throw off the Roman yoke; and they
took the field soon after in conjunction with their
allies, the Veientes, in order to assert their independency.[219]. The king of Rome, determined to reduce
them again to submission, assembled his army; and
being joined by his friends and confederates, marched
against the enemy; gave them battle near Fidenæ, and
gained a complete victory over them, notwithstanding
the treachery of Mutius Fufetius, the Alban general;
who took no share in the engagement, and intended to
have joined the Fidenates, if they had been successful,
or if he had found an opportunity, while the fortune
of the day remained doubtful[220]. This treachery
proved fatal to Alba.

Tullus Hostilius, who had discovered the purpose
of the Alban general in the beginning of the action,
and prevented its operation by keeping a watchful eye
upon him, at the same time that he encouraged the
Romans to maintain the struggle for victory, by assur-
ing them he had directed the Albans to take their station at a distance, with a view of surrounding the
enemy[221]; Tullus did not fail to concert measures for
punishing the traitor and his accomplices. As a mark
of seeming confidence, he commanded Fufetius to
pursue the flying enemy, and to ravage their country[222]. Meanwhile he, in person, made known to

219. Dion. Halicarnass. lib. iii. cap. xxiii. Liv. lib. i. cap. xxvii.
220. Liv. ubi sup. Dion. Halicarnass. lib. iii. cap. xxiii—xxvi.
221. Id. ibid.   222. Dion. Halicarnass. ubi sup.

the Roman senate, the treachery of the Albans; and took, with the sage fathers, a resolution how to act[223].

In consequence of that resolution, Tullus Hostilius, on his return to the camp, reproached Fufetius with his baseness, in presence of the two armies; ordered the lictors to seize him, and bind his legs and arms to two chariots; which, being each drawn by two horses, and driven in opposite directions, tore him in pieces[224]. His principal accomplices were also put to death. The city of Alba was utterly destroyed, but without injury to the property of the inhabitants; and the Albans were transplanted to Rome, and incorporated with the Roman tribes and curiæ[225]. The Julii, the Servilii, the Curatii, the Quinctii, the Cloelii, and some other families of distinction, were even raised to the rank of patricians, and admitted into the senate[226].

Ant. Chr.
662.
Ann. Rom.
90.

This great accession of people, in consequence of the dissolution of the Alban state, enabled Tullus Hostilius to carry on war successfully against all his hostile neighbours. As soon as he had provided his new subjects with accommodation, by enlarging the city of Rome, he reduced the capital of the Fidenates, and obliged them to submit to such conditions as he chose to impose upon them[227]. He humbled the Sabines, who were still a powerful nation[228]; though the kingdom of Cures, as formerly related, had become part of the Roman territory, and its people Roman citizens. He asserted his sovereignty over the Latin cities, which had been subject to Alba; and

---

223. Id. ibid.   224. Liv. lib. i. cap. xxviii xxix. Dion.
Halicarnass. lib. iii. cap. xxxi.   225. Dion. Halicarnass.
lib. iii. cap. xxx—xxxii. Liv. lib. i. cap. xxx.   226. Id. ibid.
227. Dion. Halicarnass. ubi sup.
228. Liv. lib. i. cap. xxx. Dion. Halicarnass. lib. iii. cap. xxxiii.

compelled

compelled them, after a long war, to acknowledge their dependence on Rome[229]. But he did not live long to enjoy the fruits of his victories. When he had thus exalted the Roman power by his conquering arms, and given stability to it by his vigorous administration, he perished, with all his children and domestics, in a fire that consumed his palace[230]; leaving behind him the reputation of a politic and warlike prince, equally resolute in the execution, and cautious in engaging in any enterprise.

LETTER VIII.

Tullus Hostilius was succeeded in the government of Rome by Ancus Martius, the grandson of Numa by a daughter. He was invested with the ensigns of royalty by the unanimous voice of the senate and people, and approved himself worthy of their choice. Like his grandfather, he was a prince of a mild and moderate disposition, and a lover of the arts of peace. He accordingly endeavoured to revive among his subjects a profound respect for the worship of the gods, and a taste for agriculture, which had declined during the late hostile reign[231]. But although naturally disposed to peace, and desirous of cultivating its advantages, he was not afraid of war. And fortunately for his people, he did not want abilities to conduct it with success. His first war was with the Latines.

Ant. Chr. 638. Ann. Rom. 114.

Ascribing the moderation of this pacific prince to want of courage, the Latin cities entered into a confederacy, and refused to acknowledge the authority of Rome; pretending they had submitted to the arms of Tullus Hostilius, but not to the sovereignty of the Roman state[232]. They even ventured to make incur-

---

229. Dion. Halicarnass. lib. iii. cap. xxxv.
230. Id. *Rom. Antiq.* lib. iii. cap. xxxvi.
231. Dion. Halicarnass. lib. iii. cap. xxxvii.
232. Id. *Rom. Antiq.* lib. iii. cap. xxxviii.

sions

sions into the Roman territory[233]. They found them-selves, however, deceived in the character of Ancus Martius. No sooner did he see that war was become necessary, than he took the most judicious and vigorous measures, for carrying it on with effect. But he did not commence hostilities until he had convinced his subjects, his allies, and even his enemies, of the just-ness of his cause.

For this purpose, he assembled the college of Feci-ales, according to the religious forms prescribed by his pious ancestor, Numa; and they having given their sanction to the war, in case satisfaction was denied, de-puted one of their body, clad in his official robes, and bearing the ensigns of his holy dignity, to demand such satisfaction, in the name of the Roman senate and people[234]. That sacred messenger, called Pater Patratus, declared the object of his mission on the frontiers of the Latin territory; at the gates, and in the market-place, of the first city that he entered; conjuring the people, in the name of Jupiter, to give ear to his just demands[235]. On those demands being refused, after he had waited the legal number of days, about thirty, he took his departure with a solemn pro-testation in these awful words: "Hear, O Jupiter! " and thou, Juno! Quirinus, and all ye gods of " heaven, earth, and hell, hear! I call ye to witness, " that the Latin nation is unjust, and void of faith. " We will, therefore, hold deliberations at Rome, on " the means of procuring redress for such breach of " treaty[236]."

In consequence of those deliberations, which were conducted with great formality, the pater patratus was again sent to the Latin frontier, but vested with a

233. Id. ibid.   234. Liv. lib. i. çap. xxxii.
235. Id. ibid.   236. Liv. ubi sup.

very

very different character.   He carried in his hand a
spear tinged with blood ; and uttered, in presence of
witnesses, the following denunciation of vengeance :—
" Because of the wrongs committed by the Latin na-
" tion against the Roman state, the Roman senate and
" people have resolved to declare war against the
" Latines ; and I and the Roman people," cried he,
" declare and begin it!"—And he threw his spear into
the hostile territory[237].

Having thus vindicated himself, in the sight of
gods and men, from the imputation of wanton violence or ambitious views, Ancus Martius led his army
into the field ; reduced successively many of the Latin
cities, and transplanted the inhabitants to Rome, which
he greatly enlarged for their accommodation : and
after a vigorous struggle for dominion, maintained for
several years, he gained a complete victory over the
whole Latin nation[238].   He next humbled the Fidenates, who had revolted along with the other Latin
cantons ; and he compelled their old confederates, the
Veientes, to relinquish a valuable territory, containing
salt pits, near the mouth of the Tiber, where he built
the city of Ostia, which became the seaport of Rome[239].
Nor did the hostile Sabines escape his just resentment ; or the predatory Volsci, an independent and
fierce tribe of the Aborigines, who had never felt the
force of the Roman arms[240].

In the prosecution of these wars, Ancus Martius
had been much indebted for his success to the valour
and conduct of Lucius Tarquinius, his general of
horse, who succeeded him in the government of
Rome[241].   This king, commonly known by the name

Ant. Chr.
614.
Ann. Rom.
138.

---

237. Id. ibid.   238. Liv. lib. i. cap. xxxiii. Dion. Halicarnass.
lib. iii. cap. xxxviii—xliii.   239. Dion. Halicarnass. ubi sup.
240. Id. ibid.   241. Dion. Halicarnass. lib. iii. cap. xlii—xlix.

of

of Tarquin the elder, was an Etruscan by birth, but of Grecian extraction; his father having been a rich Corinthian merchant, who had settled in Etruria, and there married a woman of an illustrious family [242]. The wealth and talents of the son, who removed to Rome in early manhood, procured him among the Romans, that rank and those honours which he had despaired of attaining in his native country, and at last raised him to the supreme power [243]. and his conduct during his whole reign, both in civil and military affairs, was such as shed lustre upon his exalted station.

As Tarquin I. had owed his elevation to the people, he began his administration with a popular act. He created an hundred new senators, chosen from the body of plebeians [244]; having first raised them to the rank of patricians, in order to obviate all objections against the legality of such a measure [245]: so that the Roman senate now consisted of three hundred members; a number at which it continued for several ages.

When the new king had thus strengthened his civil authority, he proceeded to the exercise of those military talents, which had first lifted him to distinction among the Romans. His predecessor had left the war with the Latines unfinished. They had been vanquished but not subdued. Tarquin resolved to reduce them under the dominion of Rome; and he accomplished his purpose by vigour and perseverance, in spite of their bravest efforts, though powerfully seconded by the Sabines and Etruscans [246]. The Latines

---

242. Id. ibid. et. Liv. lib. i. cap. xxxiv.
243. Dion. Halicarnass. et. Liv. ubi. sup.
244. Dion. Halicarnass. lib. iii. cap. lxviii.   245. Id. ibid.
246. Dion. Halicarnass. lib. iii. cap. li—lv.

agreed

agreed to yield obedience to all the commands of the
Romans[247].

But the Romans had other enemies to contend with
for dominion. The Sabines and Etruscans were still
in arms. Tarquin, by a stratagem, divided their forces ; took both camps, by cutting off all communication between them, and routed both armies with great
slaughter[248]. The Sabines, discouraged by their loss,
perhaps jealous of their allies, sued for peace; and
a truce of six years was granted them[249]. The pride
of the Etruscans with-held them from submission, and
their power inspired them with confidence. Their
martial spirit was rather rouzed than humbled, by the
defeat they had suffered.

If the Veientes, one of the twelve tribes into which
the Etruscans were divided, had been able alone to
dispute the field with the Romans, it was presumable
that the whole united nation could not fail to resist the
arms, and set bounds to the ambition of that aspiring
people. A hostile confederacy was accordingly formed among the twelve lucumonies or cantons of
Etruria, at a general assembly or national council ; in
which it was decreed, That they should make war
upon the Romans with their combined forces; and
that, if any canton did not take part in the war, it
should receive no assistance from the army of the confederates[250].

In consequence of this confederacy, the Etruscans
assembled their forces, and passed the Tiber ; took
Fidenæ, invaded the territory of Rome, and returned
home loaded with plunder[251]. But this insult did not

247. Id. ibid.   248. Dion. Halicarnass. lib. iii. cap. lvi. lvii.
249. Id. *Rom. Antiq* lib. iii. cap. lviii.   250. Id. ibid.
251. Dion. Halicarnass. ubi sup.

pass

pass unrevenged. Tarquin entered Etruria early next campaign, at the head of a Roman army; vanquished the enemy in a great battle; ravaged their country, and retook Fidenæ[252].

. The Etruscans again assembled their forces, after the lapse of some years, and were again defeated by the Romans in another great battle, when preparing to pass the Roman frontier[253]. Now convinced of their inability to contend for empire with Rome, while governed by so warlike a king, they sent deputies from their several cantons to treat of peace[254]. Tarquin met their advances with generous magnanimity. He told them, That he wished neither to deprive them of their possessions, to fetter them with garrisons, oppress them with tributes, nor to change the form of their government. But he expected they would voluntarily grant, what the fortune of war had enabled him to force them to yield, the sovereignty of their cities[255].

Having received this answer, the deputies retired; and, after a few days, returned with the ensigns of sovereignty with which the Etruscans were wont to invest their own kings, who had the controul over all the twelve lucumonies of Etruria; namely, a crown of gold, an ivory throne, a sceptre, on the head of which was the figure of an eagle, a purple vest wrought with gold, and a purple robe richly embroidered[256]. These regal ornaments Tarquin wore, with the consent of the Roman senate and people:—and they were retained by all his successors[257].

252. Dion. Halicarnass. lib. iii. cap. lix.
253. Id. *Rom. Antiq.* lib. iii. cap. lx.　　254. Id. ibid.
255. Dion. Halicarnass. lib. iii. cap. lxi.
256. Id. *Rom. Antiq.* lib. iii. cap. lxii. lxiii.
257. Id. ibid.

The

The only Italian nation now able to dispute the field of glory with the Romans, was that of the Sabines. And the truce with this warlike people being now expired, Tarquin was desirous of reducing them under his dominion, while the spirits of his troops were elated with conquest, and before they had tasted the sweets of peace. Nor had he occasion, with that view, to force a pretence for commencing hostilities, or to provoke a quarrel. The Sabines, conscious they had encouraged and aided the Etruscans, in their last struggle for independency, were no sooner made acquainted with Tarquin's intentions, than they invaded the Roman territory[258]. The ambitious and valiant king marched against them with a chosen body of forces; defeated them, as they were dispersed in plundering the country; took from them all their booty, and drove them to their camp[259].

The Sabines, however, were not disheartened by that severe check. Confiding in their strength, they remained firm within their entrenchments, until their broken troops had recovered from their consternation. Meantime the Roman army, having been greatly augmented, advanced against the invaders in order of battle. The Sabines did not decline the challenge. They boldly led out an army not inferior to Tarquin's either in numbers or in valour. But that prince far surpassed their general in military skill. While both armies were fighting with desperate resolution, and the event of the day seemed doubtful, a Roman body of reserve, which had been posted in a concealed place, appeared behind the Sabines, and struck them with terror. Thinking it a fresh army, they fled in all directions; and being pursued, and surrounded by the Romans, were almost utterly cut off[260]. Their camp was forced;

258. Dion. Halicarnass. lib. iii. cap. lxiv.   259. Id. ibid.
260. Dion. Halicarnass. lib. iii. cap. lxv.

and the troops left to guard it surrendered themselves prisoners, without striking a blow [261].

Though mortified at this disaster, the Sabine cantons were not dismayed. Considering their defeat as the effect of stratagem, rather than a proof of the superior power or valour of the enemy, they raised a new army, and sent it into the field under a more experienced general [262]. Tarquin marched against the Sabines, and offered them battle, before they were prepared to receive him. They were therefore obliged to act on the defensive, and permit their country to be ravaged; yet by their vigour and perseverance, they protracted the war to the length of five years. At last, collecting the whole force of their nation, they resolved upon a final trial of strength [263].

Tarquin, who had long sought for such an opportunity, embraced it with ardour. He met the enemy at the head of the Roman troops; the Etruscan auxiliaries he intrusted to the command of his nephew Aruns; and those of the Latines to the conduct of Servius Tullius, who became afterward his son-in-law, and who was a man of tried courage and consummate prudence [264]. The Sabines also divided their forces into three bodies. And the battle that ensued was fierce, obstinate, and bloody. The Sabines maintained their ground, with great firmness, from morning until the approach of night. But they were at length broken by the Romans, who occupied the left wing of the royal army, and routed with incredible slaughter [265]. Despairing of being able any longer to support their independency, they now sent deputies to the conqueror with proposals of peace; and Tarquin granted

261. Id. ibid.   262. Dion. Halicarnass. ubi sup.
263. Id. Rom. Antiq. lib. iii. cap. lxvi.   264. Dion. Halicarnass,
lib. iii. cap. lxvii.   265. Id. ibid.

them,

them, on their submission, the same favourable conditions, which his generosity had extended to the Etruscans[266].

Having thus brought under the dominion of the
Romans all the neighbouring nations, this victorious
king devoted himself, during the latter part of his
reign, to the arts of peace; and executed such magnificent public works, as have made his memory immortal. He built the great circus at Rome; adorned the
forum with porticoes; surrounded the city with a
superb wall of hewn stone, and began the sinking and
building of the capacious common-sewers[267]; which
were finished by Tarquin II. and have been ranked,
by all succeeding ages, among the most extraordinary
monuments of human labour[268].

But all these civil and military services could not
save the first Tarquin from the vengeance of private
enemies. He was murdered, in the thirty-eighth year
of his reign, by assassins hired by the sons of Ancus
Martius[269]. Envious of his greatness, they seemed to
think he had robbed them of their paternal inheritance;
though they could not fail to know, that the regal
office in Rome was elective, not hereditary.

The Romans, however, who detested such an atrocious action, as much as they valued their constitu-

---

266. Dion. Halicarnass. ubi sup.   267. Id. lib. iii. cap. lxviii.
268. These sewers, through which the water and filth collected
from every street in Rome were conveyed into the Tiber, Dionysius of
Halicarnassus calls "a wonderful work, exceeding all description."
(Rom. Antiq. lib. iii. cap. lxviii.). And Pliny tells us, that they were
of sufficient height and breadth to admit a waggon loaded with hay
(Nat. Hist. lib. xxxvi. cap. xv.). The walls of Rome were scarcely
less wonderful; each of the square stones, with which they were
built, being of a ton weight, if we may credit the accurate Dionysius.
Rome. Antiq. ubi sup.
269. Dion. Halicarnass. lib. iii. cap. lxxiii. lxxiv.

tional rights, raised to the supreme power Servius Tullius; the son of a famous Latin captive, and son-in-law of the late king[270]. This man owed his elevation partly to his own high character; to his distinguished civil and military talents, and partly to the interest which he took in prosecuting the conspirators, while he acted as guardian to the two grandsons of his illustrious predecessor[271]. Of these young princes I shall afterward have occasion to speak.

Servius Tullius was no sooner seated on the throne of Rome, than he found himself involved in hostilities with the Etruscans; who, hoping to profit by the disorders, that followed the murder of Lucius Tarquinius, had refused to acknowledge the sovereignty of the new king[272]. The war occasioned by this revolt lasted twenty years; in which period both parties made frequent incursions into each other's territories, and many battles were fought between them with great armies. But Tullius, having been victorious in all those battles, for which he was honoured with three splendid triumphs, forced not only particular cantons, but the whole Etruscan nation, at last, to supplicate his clemency, and again submit to the Roman yoke[273]. He upbraided the deputies of the several cities with folly and breach of faith, in wantonly violating their engagements, and drawing upon their country so many calamities. Yet he politically granted peace to nine of the twelve lucumonies of Etruria, on the same conditions prescribed by his predecessor. But the Caeretani, the Tarquinienses, and the Veientes, who had been the authors of the revolt, he punished, by seizing their lands[274].

270. Id. lib. iv. cap. i.—xii.   271. Id ibid.
272. Dion. Halicarnass. lib. iv. cap. xxvii.
273. Id. ibid.   274. Dion. Halicarnass. ubi sup.

During

During this tedious war, Servius Tullius established many civil institutions for the better government of the city of Rome, which he had adorned and enlarged, as well as for the general good of the state. And a long reign of forty-four years enabled him to perfect the plan of Roman polity. He began his administration with dividing the lately conquered lands, or the unappropriated part of the public territory, among such of the Roman citizens, as, having no lands of their own, were employed in cultivating the possessions of others[275]. And he enacted, among many statutes for the benefit of the poorer plebeians, a law which provided, Th t no man should lend money on the *liberty* of the *persons* of freemen, as a *security;* but that the property of the debtor should be deemed sufficient security to the creditor[276].

After Tullius had taken these measures for the benefit of the commonalty, he made a new division of the free inhabitants, or citizens of Rome, of all ranks, into four tribes or wards, instead of three[277]. He, at the same time, divided the Roman citizens, or free inhabitants of the country, into twenty-six tribes[278]; and built places of strength upon such eminences as could most easily be made defensible, for the security of the husbandmen[279]. In these strong holds, which might be considered as the citadels of the pagi or villages, the people of the neighbourhood took shelter, on the appearance of an enemy[280].

It was the business of the governors of such fortified places to take cognizance of the industry, as well as of the morals of the inhabitants, conformable to the

275. Id. lib. iv. cap. ix —xiii.   276. Id. ibid.
277. Dion. Halicarnass. lib. iv. cap. xiv.
278. Fabius Pictor ap. Dion. Halicarnass. lib. iv. cap. xv.
279. Dion. Halicarnass. ubi sup.   280. Id. ibid.

laws

laws of Numa[281]. Tullius ordered them also to collect the taxes, and keep a register of the number of
people, of all descriptions, in their several districts.
And he appointed, for each pagi, an annual festival of
great solemnity, called the *paganalia*[282]. So high can
we trace the appellation *pagan*, which was afterwards
employed, as we shall have occasion to see, by the first
christians, to denominate the whole unconverted world,
except the Jews.

The next institution of Servius Tullius was of yet
more importance : namely, the *census*, which made
the government of the Roman state as simple and regular as that of a private family, and which was equally
well calculated for peace and war. He wished to
lighten the taxes upon the poor citizens, and give the
rich an interest in public affairs in proportion to
their property[283]; a regulation which was become
highly necessary, and could not fail to be acceptable to
both parties. For the possessions of the Romans, having been originally almost equal, every citizen was
assessed alike for the support of the state, and had an
equal power of influencing its measures, as we have
seen, by his equal vote in the assembly of the people ;
though the poorer sort, by reason of their indigence,
were now in danger of being corrupted by the rich,
and wanted the means of fulfilling their constitutional engagements, either in a civil or military capacity[284].

As a prelude to such regulation, the wise and politic
king ordered all the Roman citizens, arrived at the
military age, to insert their names in a public register,
opened in the forum : and to give in, upon oath, a va-

281. Dion. Halicarnass. lib. iv. cap. xv.   282. Id. ibid.
283. Dion. Halicarnass. iv. cap. xix.   284. Id. ibid.

luation of their property[285]. They were also required
to give in their own age, with the names of their wives
and children; and to specify in what ward of the city,
or district of the country, they resided[286].

Having completed this register, or census of persons and possessions, Tullius proceeded to the execution of that great political plan, for which chiefly the
census had been taken; the proportioning of taxes to
property, and connecting the interests of the state with
the opulence of its members. Actuated with these
views, he divided the whole body of Roman citizens
able to bear arms, amounting to about eighty thousand men, into six classes, according to the value of
their property. The first class consisted of citizens,
whose lands and effects exceeded the value of one
hundred thousand *asses* or pounds of copper. This
class was subdivided into ninety-eight centuries or
companies; fourscore centuries of foot, and eighteen
of horsemen[287].

The second class was composed of citizens, whose
property was valued at seventy-five thousand asses,
and divided into twenty-two centuries; the third
class, consisting of citizens whose property was valued
at fifty thousand asses, was divided into twenty centuries; the fourth class, consisting of citizens whose
property was valued at twenty-five thousand asses, was
divided into twenty-two centuries; the fifth class, consisting of citizens whose property was valued at eleven
thousand asses, was divided into thirty centuries;
and the sixth and lowest class, which consisted of citizens, whose property was below the value of eleven

285. Dion. Halicarnass. ubi sup.   286. Id. ibid.
287. Dion. Halicarnass. lib. iv. cap. xvi.—xviii.   Liv. lib. i.
cap. xliii.

PART I. thousand asses formed only one century though it concluded a multitude of people[288].

The citizens of all these classes, except the last, paid taxes in proportion to their property[289], and occupied their station in the army, according to their priority of class : those of the first class, between the age of seventeen and forty-five ; being posted in the front line ; while those, above forty-five, were entrusted with the defence of the city[290]. The younger citizens of the second and third classes held their stations, in like manner, in the second and third lines, and the elder on the walls of Rome[291]. The citizens of the fourth class, within the military age, formed a body of reserve ; and those of the fifth class acted as light troops, out of the line of battle[292]. But the citizens of the sixth class were exempted from all taxes, and excused from all military service ; Tullius considering it as unreasonable, that men, who were in want of the common necessaries of life, or but slenderly provided, should be loaded with any assessment. And he was not willing that men, who had nothing to lose, should be intrusted with the defence of the state ; especially as they must, in such case, be maintained, like

288. Id ibid. The value of the pound of copper among the Romans, in those early times, and its proportion to that of silver or gold, are so doubtful, that it cannot, with certainty, be reduced to English money. I shall, therefore, only observe, that by the *As* is here to be understood the *pound weight* (Pliny. *Nat. Hist.* lib. xxxiii. cap. iii), and not the Roman coin of the same name afterward in use, and which was reduced so low as half an ounce (Id. ibid). Consequently the estates of the Roman citizens of the highest class, computed by the present value of copper, were worth about *five thousand pounds* sterling, and those of the lowest class about *five hundred and fifty pounds*.

289. Dion. Halicarnass. lib. iv. cap. xix.

290. Id. *Rom. Antiq.* lib. iv. cap. xvi. Liv. lib. i. cap. xliii.

291. Id. ibid. 292. Liv. ubi sup. Dion. Halicarnass. lib. iv. cap. xvii.

common

common mercenaries, at the expence of the community[293].

The Roman citizens of the superior classes enjoyed, by the institutions of this sage king, the same priority in the public assembly, as in the army; in voting for the enacting of laws, or on the resolutions concerning peace and war[294]. In that assembly, or *comitia*, the Romans no longer voted as individuals, in their several curiæ, but by centuries[295]; and as the first class consisted of ninety-eight centuries, which formed a majority of the whole one hundred and ninety-three, it had the power, as its centuries were first called, of deciding ultimately upon every question, if unanimous[296].

If the centuries of the first class disagreed, those of the second, the third, and of other inferior classes, were called in to vote. But there was seldom occasion to go below the centuries of the third class[297]:—so that, by this politic regulation, all public measures came to be determined by the more considerable citizens; who understood the interests of the state better, and were less liable to corruption, or subject to undue influence, than the lower populace. That mode of voting, however, was afterward changed for one more popular[298]; the centuries no longer being called to give suffrage in the order of their classes, but by the drawing of lots[299].

When Servius Tullius had thus established the census, and the several institutions connected with it,

293. Dion. Halicarnass. lib. iv. cap. xviii. xix. Liv. lib. i. cap. xliii.
294. Dion. Halicarnass. lib. iv. cap. xx.   295. Id. ibid.
296. Dion. Halicarnass. ubi sup.   297. Id. ibid.
298. Dion. Halicarnass. lib. iv. cap. xxi.
299. Liv. lib. xxvi. cap. xxii. At what time this change took place is not known, no historian having made particular mention of it.

THE HISTORY OF

he ordered all the Roman citizens to assemble in arms, in the Campius Martius; a large field in the neighbourhood of Rome, and on the banks of the Tiber, which Romulus had dedicated to Mars, and there perform an expiatory sacrifice to the god of war[300]. This sacrifice, called lustrum, continued to be regularly repeated after the census, which was taken at the end of every five years[301]. Hence the Romans came to compute time by lustrations, as the Greeks did by olympiads. And by repeating the census, after such short intervals, they were at all times acquainted with the strength and resources of the state.

Another institution was still necessary to perfect the system of Roman polity. And it was not overlooked by this truly sagacious and beneficent prince. The Romans, from maxims of sound policy, had originally admitted into the number, and communicated the privileges of Roman citizens, as we have seen, to refugees from the neighbouring states, and to the prisoners made in war, as well as to the people of several cantons which they had conquered. But when any of the vanquished people rebelled, they were generally deprived of their lands, on being again subdued, and the captives taken in war were subjected to the condition of slaves[302] Numbers of those captives, however, had now obtained their freedom; some by purchase, some as the recompense of long and faithful service[303].

Among the slaves thus manumitted, were many men of high birth, tried courage, and distinguished talents, who could have contributed to the advancement of any state; but who, having no share in the government

300. Dion. Halicarnass. lib. iv. cap. xxii. Liv. lib. i. cap. xliv.
301. Id. ibid. et *Plin, Nat. Hist.* lib. vii. cap. xlviii.
302. Dion. Halicarnass. lib. iv. cap. xxii—xxv. 303. Id. ibid.

of

of Rome, might be considered as its concealed enemies. Tullius, therefore, with the consent of the
senate, and the approbation of the people, passed a
law, which gave those freedmen the choice of returning to their several countries, or becoming Roman
citizens[304]. And such as embraced the latter alternative, were distributed among the four city-tribes[305].
This law continued ever after in force, and was frequently abused by the Romans; especially in latter
times, when freedom and citizenship were often the
reward of the vilest services, and most abominable
prostitution.

The last institution of Servius Tullius was no less
worthy of praise than any of the former; and it gives
us a very high idea of the extent of his capacity. Desirous of forming a grand confederacy of the Latin
nation, resembling that of the Amphictyons in Greece,
he invited deputies from the several cities to meet at
Rome; and there explained to them his purpose, in
presence of the Roman senate[306]. Having obtained
their concurrence, and acknowledgment of Rome
as head of the confederacy, he built a temple to
Diana on mount Aventine, the highest of the seven
hills, then inclosed within the walls of the city; and
instituted an annual festival, and communion of sacrifices for the whole people of the Latin name, with
a general council or assembly; in which measures
should be taken for mutual defence, and where all
differences might be amicably adjusted[307]. He at the
same time composed laws for regulating those matters,
and ordered them to be engraved on a pillar of brass,

304. Dion. Halicarnass. ubi sup.   305. Id. ibid.
306. Dion. Halicarnass. lib. iv. cap. xxvi.
307. Id. ibid. Livy (lib. i. cap. xlv.) has included the Sabines in
this confederacy; but I have chosen to follow probability, and the
authority of Dionysius, who confines it to the Latin nation.

which

which were to be seen in the temple of Diana, as late as the reign of Augustus[308].

While this politic and moderate king was employed in taking these, and other wise measures, for the security and happiness of his people, and had relinquished to them every privilege not utterly inconsistent with royalty; when he was ready to resign even royalty itself, he was assassinated at the instigation of Lucius Tarquinius II. his ambitious son-in-law, commonly known by the name of *Tarquin the Proud,* who usurped the government of Rome, and reigned with absolute authority[309]. That usurpation was preceded by circumstances sufficiently interesting to merit notice.

· Servius Tullius, who had acted the part of a faithful guardian to the two grandsons of Tarquin I, married them, when they came of age, to his two daughters; Lucius, the eldest, to his eldest daughter, and Aruns to Tullia, the youngest. But unfortunately they happened to be ill-matched. Tullia, a woman of bold and insatiable ambition, therefore contrived, by poison, to get rid of her husband, who was a man of a mild and unaspiring disposition. Lucius Tarquinius, at her solicitation, also poisoned his wife, whose gentle virtues did not suit his haughty character[310]. Thus disengaged, the two fierce spirits, who had before indulged in a criminal commerce, were united in wedlock; and to crown their atrocious guilt, made their way to the throne by the murder of the good old king[311].

308. Dion. Halicarnass. ubi sup.

309. Liv. lib. i. cap. xlviii. xlix.

310. Dion. Halicarnass. lib. iv. cap xviii—xxx. Liv. lib. i. cap. xlvi.

311. Liv. ubi sup. Dion. Halicarnass. lib. iv. cap. xxxix. The particulars of this horrid transaction, as related by ancient historians, are too shocking for modern ears.

LETTER
VIII.

Ant. Chr.
532.
Ann. Rom.
220.

As Tarquin II. founded his title to the supreme power on his being the grandson of Tarquin I. and pleaded his hereditary right, as an apology for seeking to depose, if not for assassinating Servius Tullius, he no sooner saw himself possessed of the Roman sceptre, than he acted as if he had been born master of the lives and fortunes of his subjects. Equally regardless of the privileges of the patricians, who had abetted his ambitious claim, and of those of the plebeians, who had opposed it, he directed all things by his own arbitrary will, without either consulting the senate or the assembly of the people[312].

Conscious that a dominion so absolute, over a brave and high spirited race of men, jealous of their natural and constitutional rights, could only be maintained by force and fear, Tarquin paid peculiar attention to the army, and to all the enslaving arts of despotism. For the security of his person, he supported a strong body of guards; composed of the most resolute and daring soldiers, both natives and foreigners, that he could bribe into his service; and who continually surrounded his palace, or attended him when he went abroad[313]. He seldom appeared in public, until he had firmly established his authority; and when he did, he assumed an imperious air, more calculated to inspire terror than love, which procured him the surname of *Superbus*[314]. He brought before his own arbitrary tribunal causes of all kinds; and such of the patricians as had opposed his elevation, or were otherwise obnoxious to him, saw themselves, by means of false accusations, condemned to death or banishment[315].

312. Liv. lib. i. cap. xlix. Dion. Halicarnass. lib. iv. cap. xli.
313 Id. ibid.   314. Dion. Halicarnass. et Liv. ubi sup.
315. Liv. lib. i. cap. xlix. Dion. Halicarnass. lib. iv. cap. xlii.

The

The plebians, at first, beheld with indifference these attainders and executions, from which they were exempted; and seemed even to rejoice in the sufferings of their haughty superiors, as if they had hoped to share in the forfeitures and confiscations, while they considered them as just judgments, for the countenance the patricians had shewn to the tyrant[316]. But they soon found, that they also were become the objects of his jealousy. He prohibited all those assemblies, both in the city and country, to which they used to resort, for the performance of their religious ceremonies; being afraid lest a multitude of people, thus collected together, and connected by the common tie of religion, might hatch some conspiracy against his life or throne[317]. Nor was this all. Having selected from among the body of plebeians, fit for military service, such as seemed attached to his interest, and ingrafted them into his army, he employed the greater part of the rest in laborious public works; in finishing the common sewers begun, as we have seen, by his grandfather; in surrounding the circus with porticoes, and in building a magnificent temple to the three great gods; Jupiter, Juno, and Minerva; under one roof[318].

The building of that temple is said to have been attended with a singular circumstance. As the workmen were sinking the foundations, on the Saturnian or Tarpeian-hill, they found, deep in the ground, we are told, the head of a man, as if newly killed, from which the blood flowed warm and fresh[319]. Alarmed at this prodigy, Tarquin ordered the workmen to leave off digging, and consulted the sooth-sayers concerning its meaning. The interpretation artfully given was,

316. Dion. Halicarnass. lib. iv. cap. xliii   317. Id. ibid.
318. Dion. Halicarnass. lib. iv. cap. xliv. xlv. lxii.
319. Id. *Rom. Antiq.* lib. iv. cap. lix. Liv. lib. i. cap. lv.

                                   That

That the place where the head was found should become the head of all Italy, and *Rome* the metropolis
of the universe[320]. Hence the Tarpeian was called.
the Capitoline-hill, from the Latin word for a head;
and the temple built upon it, the *capitol*[321].

While these public works were carrying on, Tarquin was not inactive. Aware that a prince, who
has usurped authority over his fellow-citizens, and
who exercises it with a high hand, stands in need
of foreign support, he began his reign with courting
the friendship of the Latines. And through his pliant
and insidious policy, in gaining Mamilius, the most
powerful man of the Latin nation, by giving him his
daughter in marriage; at the same time that he brought
to ruin and disgrace, by his treacherous arts, Turnus,
the only person of distinction who opposed an alliance
with him, he got all the Latin cities to acknowledge
him sovereign of the nation; upon the same conditions, which they had yielded that dignity, first to his
grandfather, Tarquin I. and afterward to Servius Tullius [322].

This supple and aspiring tyrant, next solicited and
obtained the friendship of the Hernici, an independent tribe of the Aborigines. He also secured an alliance with two cities belonging to the Volsci; but
the great body of the nation set him at defiance[323].
Tarquin, who eagerly longed for an opportunity of
displaying his military talents, and of leading the
Romans against some of their old enemies, marched
an army into the hostile territory; defeated the Volsci
in the field; took Suessa, their most opulent city, by
storm, after an obstinate siege, and collected an im-

320. Liv. ubi sup. Dion. Halicarnass. lib. iv. cap. lx.
321. Id. ibid.   322. Dion. Halicarnass. lib. iv. cap. xlv—xlviii.
323. Id. *Rom. Antiq.* lib. iv. cap. xlix.

mense

mense booty; which he liberally distributed among his soldiers, after setting aside the tenth part for the building of the capitol [324].

Before Tarquin left Suessa, he received intelligence, that the Sabines had invaded the Roman territory, in two bodies, and were laying waste the country. Leaving his baggage and the booty under a guard, he instantly marched against the enemy; defeated their most advanced body, and obliged the other to surrender at discretion [325]. And the Sabines, having thus lost their whole army, and seeing their country defenceless, sent deputies to the conqueror, and submitted to such terms as he was pleased to impose upon them [326].

Now victorious on all sides, Tarquin returned in triumph to Rome, loaded with the spoils of his vanquished enemies [327]. But he had soon occasion again to take the field.

The people of Gabii, a Latin city, encouraged by the Volsci, and strengthened by a band of Roman refugees, threw off the tyrant's yoke; defeated a body of his troops, and pursued them to the gates of Rome [328]. Tarquin assembled his forces; advanced against the invaders; and obliged them, after various encounters, to shut themselves up within the walls of their city [329]. But they again grew formidable; repeatedly ravaged the Roman terri·ory; and being constantly reinforced with dissatisfied Romans, protracted the war to the length of seven years, in defiance of all the

---

324. Liv. lib. i. cap. liii. Dion. Halicarnass. lib. iv. cap. l.

325. Dion. Halicarnass. lib. iv. cap. li. lii.　　326. Id. ibid.

327. Dion. Halicarnass. ubi sup.　　328. Id. lib. iv. cap. liii.

329. Dion. Halicarnass. ubi sup.

most

most vigorous efforts of the tyrant to reduce them to
obedience[330].

Tarquin, however, at last got possession of Gabii;
though not by the superiority of his arms, or his
distinguished military skill, but by treachery. Sextus,
his eldest son, pretending to desert to the enemy, was
admitted into their confidence ; and, being invested
with the command of their forces, delivered up the city to his father by night[331]. But the politic tyrant
took no advantage of this circumstance to the .preju-
dice of the Gabini. On the contrary he treated them
with the greatest lenity; restored to them their city,
without plundering it ; secured them in the possession
of their lands, and admitted them to all the rights of
Roman citizens[332].

Having now fully established his authority, as well
over the Romans as the neighbouring nations, Tarquin allowed his subjects some respite from the toils
of war. But he still continued to harrass them with
the execution of his great public works[333]. And the
people of Ardea, a city of Latium, soon excited his
jealousy ; by affording an asylum to Roman fugitives,
whose resentment he feared ; and they his avidity, by
their riches, which he longed to possess[334]. That
. city he invested[335]. But before he could make himself

330. Dion. Halicarnass. lib. iv. cap. liv.
331. Liv. lib. i. cap. liv. Dion. Halicarnass. lib. iv. cap. lv—lviii.
332. Dion. Halicarnass. ubi sup.   333. Id. lib. iv. cap. lix.
334. Dion. Halicarnass. lib. iv. cap. lxiv. Liv. lib. i. cap. lvii.
335. Id. ibid. Ardea, we are told by Strabo, was built by a colony
of the Rutuli (Geog. lib. v. p. 332. edit. Lutet. Paris. Typ. Reg. 1620.).
But Dionysius numbers it among the cities of the Latines (Rom. Antiq.
lib. v. cap. lxi.). And as a Latin city it seems to have been considered in the reign of Tarquin II. by the Roman fugitives taking refuge in it, as they had formerly in Gabii. Yet Livy speaks of it as
then belonging to the Rutuli, Rom. Hist. lib. i. cap. lvii.; who were
still an independent nation, and had no part in the Latin confederacy.
Dion. Halicarnass. lib. v. cap. lxii.

master of the place, the intemperate lust of his son, Sextus, threw all his affairs into confusion, and roused the depressed spirits of the Romans to sentiments of liberty and vengeance.

Sextus Tarquinius, the eldest son of the tyrant, whose treachery to the Gabini shewed that he was capable of any baseness, had lately become enamoured of Lucretia; a Roman lady of high birth, equally distinguished by her beauty and virtue, and the wife of his relation, Colatinus[336]. Taking occasion to visit the city of Colatia, where she lived, while Colatinus was in the camp before Ardea, Sextus was received, and entertained as her husband's kinsman. After supper he went to bed, and kept himself quiet great part of the night. But when he thought the family asleep, he rose; and drawing his sword, entered the room in which Lucretia lay, without being discovered by any of her domestics[337]. On approaching her bedside, he laid his left hand upon her breast, and made her acquainted with his wishes, and the weapon with which he was armed; threatening, at the same time, to kill her, if she attempted to escape, or offered to cry out[338]. " I am Sextus Tarquinius" said he :—" be still, or you die !"

Lucretia, though much alarmed, remained firm in her resistance; so that Sextus had recourse to entreaties and menaces in vain. Determined, however, to accomplish his purpose, he sternly desired her to take choice of two conditions; of death, with dishonour, or life, with happiness. " For if you agree " to gratify my passion," whispered he, " I will make " you my wife; and with me you shall enjoy all the

336. Liv. lib. i. cap. lviii. Dion. Halicarnass. lib. iv. cap. lxv.
337. Dion. Halicarnass. ubi sup. Liv. lib. i. cap. lviii.
338. Id. ibid.

" power

LETTER
VIII.

Ant. Chr.
508.
Ann. Rom.
244.

" power and honours, which I possess, or have in
" prospect; the kingdom of Rome, and the sovereign-
" ty of Italy. But if you refuse to yield, I will first
" kill you, and then stab one of your male slaves; and,
" laying your bodies together, declare that I caught
" you in his embrace, and slew you to revenge the
" injured honour of Colatinus[339]." Subdued by the
fear of shame, Lucretia, who had set at defiance the
fear of death, submitted to the desire of her ravisher;
and Sextus Tarquinius having satiated his lust, returned next morning to the camp, with the exulting
air of a conqueror[340].

The feelings of a beautiful and virtuous lady, thus
dishonoured and abandoned, may easier, my lord, be
conceived than described. Lucretia, however, be-
haved with composure and dignity. Having dressed
herself in black, she ordered her chariot, and drove
from Colatia to Rome. On entering the house of her
father, Lucretius, she threw herself at his feet; and
embracing his knees remained for some time bathed in
tears, without uttering a word. He raised her affec-
tionately, and asked what misfortune had befallen her.
" To you, O father!" cried she, " I fly for refuge,
" under a dreadful and irreparable injury. In her ca-
" lamities, forsake not your daughter, who has suffer-
" ed worse than death[341].

Struck with wonder and astonishment, at what he
heard and saw, her father desired her to explain the
nature of the injury she had sustained. " That,"
said Lucretia, " you will know too soon for your peace.
" In the meantime, assemble your friends and rela-
" tions, that they may learn, from my lips, the shame-
" ful and severe necessity to which I have been com-

339. Dion. Halicarnass. lib. iv. cap. lxv. lxvi. Liv. ubi sup.
340. Id. ibid.   341. Dion. Halicarnass. lib. iv. cap. lvi.

" pelled

" pelled to submit; and that they may concert with
" you the means of revenge[342]."

Lucretius, according to the desire of his daughter, invited to his house, by a hasty message, the most
considerable of his kindred and connections in Rome,
both male and female.   When they were assembled,
Lucretia unfolded to them her melancholy tale, with
all its cruel circumstances; then embracing her father,
and recommending herself to him, to all present, and
to the gods, the just avengers of guilt, she drew a
dagger, which she had concealed beneath her robes;
and plunging it into her breast, at one stroke pierced
her heart[343].   The women, distracted with grief, beat
their bosoms, and filled the house with shrieks and lamentations; while Lucretius embraced the bleeding
body of his daughter, who expired in his agonizing
arms[344].

This awful spectacle filled all the Romans, who
were present, with so much horror, blended with compassion, that they unanimously exclaimed, they would
rather die ten thousand deaths, in defence of their
liberties, than suffer such abuses to be committed by
the Tarquins[345].   Among the persons of distinction,
thus affected, was included Publius Valerius, afterward surnamed *Publicola*, a man of great prudence and
patriotism.   He was chosen to go to the camp before
Ardea, in order to acquaint Colatinus, the husband of
Lucretia, with her fate; and to endeavour, in conjunction with him, to engage the army to revolt[346].

But Valerius had hardly begun his journey, when
he met Colatinus coming to Rome, yet ignorant of the

342. Id. ibid.
343. Liv. lib. i. cap. lviii. Dion. Halicarnass. lib. iv. cap. lxvii.
344. Dion. Halicarnass. ubi sup.   345. Id. ibid.
346. Dion. Halicarnass. lib. iv. cap. lxvii.

misfortunes

LETTER
VIII.

Ant. Chr.
508.
Ann. Rom.
244.

misfortunes of his family; and with him came Lucius Junius, surnamed *Brutus*, or *the fool*, from the air of stupidity which had hitherto marked his character[347]. That stupid appearance, however, was only assumed by Junius as a mask, to conceal his superior talents from the jealous eye of Tarquin II. who had put to death his father, and his eldest brother, as too powerful and high-minded men, to submit to his tyrannical government[348].

Thus hid in the disguise of folly, Brutus excited neither envy nor jealousy, while he only waited for a proper opportunity of recovering the lost liberties of his country. And no sooner did he hear Valerius relate the unhappy story of Lucretia, than he lifted his hands and eyes to heaven, and said, " O Jupiter! and " all ye gods, who superintend human affairs, is the time " now come, in expectation of which I have so long " worn this humiliating disguise ?—Has heaven or- " dained, That the Romans shall by me, and through " my exertions, be delivered from the accursed tyran- " ny under which they groan[349]?"—Having uttered that ejaculation, he hastened to the house of mourning : where, finding the father and husband of Lucretia sunk in the deepest sorrow, he told them they would afterward have leisure to bewail her fate : they ought now to think of revenging it[350].

In consequence of this advice a consultation was instantly held ; at which Brutus explained the cause of the degrading character he had assumed, and prevailed upon Lucretius, Colatinus, Valerius, and their common friends, to join in a resolution of expelling Tar-

347. Id. lib. iv. cap. lxviii. Liv. lib. i. cap. lvi.   348. Id. ibid.
349. Dion. Halicarnass. lib. iv. cap. lxx.   350. Id. ibid.

quin

quin II. and his usurping family. "But neither
"words nor promises," exclaimed he, "can accom-
"plish this: actions must!—And I myself will be the
"first actor[351]." In so saying, he snatched up the
dagger with which Lucretia had stabbed herself; and
standing by the body, which was still exposed to view;
"I swear," cried he, "by that blood which was once
"so pure, and which nothing but the atrocious vil-
"lainy of Sextus Tarquinius could have stained—by
"that once spotless blood I swear, and I call the gods
"to witness this my oath, That I will pursue Lucius
"Tarquinius Superbus, his wicked wife, and all their
"hated offspring, with fire and sword. Nor will I
"ever suffer any person of that family, while I live, to
"reign at Rome; but will persecute, with unrelenting
"vengeance, till death, both the tyrants and their
"abettors[352]." He next delivered the dagger to Colatinus, then to Lucretius, Valerius, and their other
friends, who all took the same oath[353].

After having entered into this solemn engagement, the sacred band of patriots deliberated in what
manner they should accomplish their purpose, and what
form of government they should establish, if their generous efforts should be crowned with success. These
points also being settled to their mutual satisfaction,
they prayed to the gods to assist them in the prosecution of their pious and just designs; then went in a
body to the forum[354]. Thither they were followed
by their domestics, who carried on a bier, covered
with black cloth, the body of Lucretia; and having
placed it on a high and conspicuous place, before the
assembled senate, they sent heralds to summon the peo-

351. Dion. Halicarnass. ubi sup.
352. Id. ibid. et Liv. lib. i. cap. lix.
353. Liv. ubi sup. Dion. Halicarnass. lib. iv. cap. lxxi.
354. Liv. ibid. et Dion. Halicarnass. lib. iv. cap. lxxi—lxxvi.

ple.

LETTER
VIII.

Ant. Chr.
508.
Ann. Rom.
244.

ple[355]. When the assembly was full, Brutus mounted the rostra; and placing the patricians near him, explained, in a long and animated speech, the reasons for calling the citizens together, and the views of the confederates[356].

He began his address with claiming the attention of the people, and by laying open his motives for counterfeiting folly. He next recapitulated, and painted in all their horror, the crimes of Lucius Tarquinius II. before he attained the sovereignty. " And how did " he attain it ?"—cried the patriotic orator. " Did " he follow, in this matter, the example of former " kings?—By no means. They were all advanced to " that dignity by us, their fellow-citizens ! according to " the laws and customs of the Roman nation; but he ac- " quired the sovereignty by arms, by violence, and the " conspiracies of wicked men, according to the custom " of tyrants. And after he had possessed himself of " the supreme power, did he use it in a manner be- " coming a king? No man in his senses will say so; " who sees the miserable condition to which we are " reduced, or who knows the cruelties to which we " have been exposed.

" I shall say nothing," continued he, " of the " calamities which we, who are patricians, suffer; " calamities, which even our enemies could not hear " described without tears, and which have reduced us " from a numerous body to a few; from splendour, " to obscurity; from prosperity and affluence, to po- " verty and want. But what is your condition ple- " beians ?—for that I cannot pass over in silence. Has " not Tarquinius Superbus robbed you of your na-

355. Id. ibid.
356. Dion. Halicarnass. lib. iv. cap. lxxvii—lxxxiii. Liv. lib. i. cap. lix.

" tional

" tional rights?—Has he not abolished your meetings
" on account of religion?—Your solemn festivals and
" sacrifices! Has he not put an end to your election of
" magistrates?—to your right of voting, and your
" assemblies for the concerns of the state?—Does he
" not force you, like slaves, purchased with money, to
" labour in a degrading manner?—to cut stones, saw
" timber, carry burdens, and waste your strength in
" deep pits and subterraneous caverns, without allow-
" ing you the least respite from servile toils?—What
" then will be the issue of your calamities?—Where
" will your miseries terminate?—How long shall we
" submit to these indignities, or when shall we recover
" our native liberty?—When Tarquin dies, do you
" say?—And shall we then be in a better condition?—
" No! but in a worse; for instead of one Tarquin, we
" shall have three, and each more detestable than the
" present tyrant."

Here Brutus gave an account of the horrid triumph
of Sextus Tarquinius over the virtue of Lucretia, with
a description of her intrepid death. " O admirable
" woman!" exclaimed he, " great are the praises you
" merit, for your heroic resolution. To you, after
" being robbed of your unsullied chastity, by the vio-
" lence of one night, death appeared more eligible
" than life; and shall not we adopt the same noble
" sentiment?—we whom Tarquin has robbed of all
" the pleasures of life, in robbing us of our liberty;
" and who have yet suffered his haughty domination,
" and oppressive tyranny for twenty-five years!—
" We cannot live any longer, fellow-citizens! under
" these grievances. If we would prove ourselves the
" descendants of those illustrious Romans, who thought
" themselves worthy to give laws to the neighbouring
" nations, we have now no other choice left, but life
" with liberty, or death with glory[357]."

357. Dion. Halicarnass. *Rom. Antiq.* lib. iv. cap. lxxx—lxxxiii.

At

LETTER
VIII.

Ant. Chr.
508.
Ann. Rom.
244.

At these words, the whole body of the people, as if with one voice, called, out for arms. "Hear first," subjoined Brutus, charmed with such alacrity, "hear "the resolution of our associates. We have deter- "mined, that the Tarquins, and all their posterity, "shall be banished from the city of Rome and the ter- "ritories of the Roman state; and that, if any person "shall act contrary to our determination, in abetting, "either by words or deeds, the cause of the tyrants, "he shall be put to death. If you are willing this "resolution be confirmed, divide yourselves into your "curiæ, and give your votes. And let the exercise "of that right be considered as the beginning of your "restored liberty [358]."

Those forms were complied with; and all the curiæ having given their votes for the banishment of the Tarquins, Brutus again stood up, and said, "Citi- "zens, since you have confirmed the first resolution, "in a manner worthy of the Roman people, hear "what we have resolved concerning the plan of our "future government. After we had considered," observed he "what order of magistracy should be "invested with sovereign authority, we came to a re- "solution to chuse no more kings; but to elect two "annual magistrates, under the name of CONSULS, to "be chosen by yourselves in the *comitia centuriata*, "and invested with regal power. If it is your plea- "sure, that this resolution also do pass, give your "votes [359]." They were unanimous in their approba- tion of it.

Having thus collected the sense of the people, and obtained their sanction to the proceedings of the confederates, Brutus appointed Spurius Lucretius to

---

358. Dion. Halicarnass. lib. iv. cap. lxxxiv.   359. Id. ibid.

preside, as *inter-rex*, at the election of chief magistrates, according to the laws in that case established. And he, having dismissed the assembly, ordered all the people to appear in arms, in the Campus Martius, the usual place for such elections. When they were there mustered, Lucretius nominated two persons to discharge the functions which had belonged to the Roman kings; namely, Brutus the head of the confederacy, and Colatinus the husband of Lucretia. And the people being called to give their votes, in their centuries, confirmed, by their election, the magistracy of the first consuls [360].

Meanwhile Tarquin having received intelligence, by certain messengers, who had left the city before the gates were shut, that Brutus was haranguing the people, and exciting them to attempt the recovery of their freedom, took with him his three sons, and a chosen body of troops, in which he could confide, and advanced to Rome, in hopes of suppressing the insurrection. But finding the gates fast, and the battlements planted with armed men, he returned to the camp with all speed; bewailing his misfortune, and boiling with resentment against the insurgents [361].

Tarquin, however, on his arrival at Ardea, found new cause to complain of fortune; and, instead of harbouring revenge, to blame himself for that despotic government which had made him obnoxious to his subjects of all descriptions. For the consuls, foreseeing that he would present himself before the walls of Rome, had sent letters, by secret roads, to their friends in the camp; exhorting them to revolt from the tyrant, and informing them of the votes passed in the assembly of the people. And Titus Herminius, and Marcus Ho-

360. Dion. Halicarnass. ubi sup. Liv. lib. i. cap. lx.
361. Id. ibid.

ratius,

LETTER
VIII.

Ant. Chr.
508.
Ann. Rom.
254.

ratius, who had been appointed by Tarquin to command in his absence, having received these letters, and read them to the army, refused to admit the king into the camp on his return; as the soldiers had unanimously declared, that they considered the votes passed in the city, for his exclusion, to be valid [362].

Tarquin II, who had reigned twenty-five years, and was now grown grey with age, finding himself thus disappointed in his last hope, by the desertion of his army, fled with a small retinue to the city of Gabii, into which he had thrown a strong garrison. And Herminius and Horatius, having made a truce with the Ardeates, returned home with the troops under their command [363].—In this manner, my lord, was monarchy abolished at Rome, after it had continued two hundred and forty-four years; because, under the last king, it had degenerated into tyranny, rather than because of the violent and illegal means by which he had obtained the Roman sceptre.

While liberty, in consequence of the abuse of kingly power, was thus advancing toward its full establishment in Europe, despotism, in the train of conquest, was making giant strides in Asia.

362. Dion. Halicarnass. lib. iv. cap. lxxxv.   363. Id. ibid.